'What a wonderful read ... certainly knows
the China scene and the ways of the Chinese in their "haggling
society". There is a vividness to her writing and the use of case
studies is detailed and insightful. This is going to be a very valuable work.'

'Mos
nese
book
day
signp
prose

'The
tually
cultu
estee
show
negot

'Card
dealir
ing ir
comn
Kingc
theme

'Read
Great
good
guarai

    DAF

'This
ness ii
in whi
tive ai
withou

BILL

# NEGOTIATING CHINA

## Case studies and strategies

*Carolyn Blackman*

ALLEN & UNWIN

*To Jean and Alex Christison*

In order to protect confidentiality, in some cases names and some other details have been changed.

First published in 1997 by
Allen & Unwin Pty Ltd
83 Alexander Street
Crows Nest, NSW 2065
Australia
Phone: (61 2) 8425 0100
Fax:    (61 2) 9906 2218
E-mail: info@allenandunwin.com
Web:    www.allenandunwin.com

National Library of Australia
Cataloguing-in-Publication entry:

Blackman, Carolyn.
  Negotiating China: case studies and strategies.

  Bibliography.
  Includes index.
  ISBN 1 86448 070  X.

  1. Negotiation in business—China. 2. Negotiation in business—China—Case studies. 3. Corporate culture—China. I. Title.

302.30951

Set in 10.5/12.5 pt New Plantin by DOCUPRO, Sydney
Printed by KHL Printing Co Pte Limited, Singapore

10 9 8 7 6 5

1002666900

# Contents

# Preface

Negotiating in any environment is a fascinating undertaking, but it is even more so across cultures where there are different expectations and different perspectives. To most western business people, negotiating in China is *terra incognita*. This book aims to provide a ground map.

As I wrote the book I was engaged in daily negotiations of my own with my Chinese colleagues about a range of issues from finance to friendship. I was always conscious that I had to think more about what I said and did, and how I said and did it, than would be normal in my dealings with western colleagues. No doubt my Chinese colleagues were similarly charting their course around the obstacles they perceived in dealing with me.

There are many people I would like to thank, too many to name individually, but first and foremost the business people who spoke to me so frankly and colourfully of their negotiation experiences in China. I found them, almost without exception, deeply interested in those experiences and challenged by how to negotiate effectively there. In particular I would like to single out George Preston, negotiator for Pacific Dunlop, who spent many hours discussing with me the negotiation process in China. I also owe a debt of gratitude to Paul Goode, general manager corporate projects, TNT Australia, Michael Pointer, Leo Hawkins and Michael Hudson, co-founders of Effective Negotiation Services, and my friends on the Executive of the Australia–China Chamber of Commerce and Industry, especially Tony Kosky and Bill O'Shea. I would especially like to thank Toni Feddersen at CEDA for her encouragement over many years.

There are many Chinese friends and colleagues I wish to thank for taking me into the heart of Chinese culture and for many hours of pleasure spent in their company: Fang Fei, Zhu Shiguo, Cao Yamin, Zhang Min, Shen Gensheng, Jiang Xiaoli and Hu Chengyi, as well as many more whom I am unable to name here.

Comments on the manuscript were given by Shelley Warner of Asia Pacific Access in Beijing, Thomas KP Leung of Hong Kong Polytechnic University, Kevin Livingston and Jim Quinn of the University of Ballarat. I would like to thank Joshua Dowse for his advice and encouragement. Support during the writing of the book was provided by the University of Ballarat.

My thanks to my husband, Wilson, who helped me in many ways with the manuscript; to my sons, Merric and Jeremy, for their support; to my uncle, Don Longfield, for his negotiation coaching; and to my mother and father, Jean and Alex Christison, who always encouraged and supported my interest in China.

Although I have drawn on the experiences of many people, the final synthesis is my own and I therefore take responsibility for any mistakes or misinterpretations.

# Introduction

Soon after the Communist Party came to power in 1949, western business withdrew from China and remained absent for the next 30 years. During most of that time only commodity sellers and traders did business there. It was not until the Sino-Foreign Equity Joint Venture Law of 1979 that western businesses in any numbers started to negotiate with the Chinese.

Some companies, particularly European ones, still had employees who had worked in China before the Communist Liberation, and therefore had some understanding of China, its business practices and its industrial capacity. But the majority of western companies went into China largely uninformed. They nevertheless had plans for industrial cooperation on a grand scale.

When negotiations did not go smoothly, or failed to realise western dreams, foreign executives blamed the Chinese. The American Motor Corporation story, which began in 1979 and is told in *Beijing Jeep* (1989), documents the profound ignorance of American executives in their pursuit of business in China. They assumed that the Chinese operated in an environment like the one they were used to, and that the aims of the Chinese negotiators would match their own. This was not the case, and it was a hard lesson the American executives had to learn.

At this early stage in the rapprochement of China and the west, negotiations were dominated by Communist Party cadres, many of whom viewed western capitalists with deep suspicion and dislike. China was coming out of a period of isolation from the west that had been imposed by Mao Zedong. In this period management, industrial and commercial expertise had effectively been demolished. These two factors, affecting attitude and expertise, made negotiations with foreigners difficult. If an agreement was reached, implementation usually presented as many difficulties as the initial negotiation.

As the right wing of the Communist Party has gradually gained control and sought western investment, technology and markets, the business environment has changed. Whereas once the central government corporations dominated business with westerners and guaranteed payments, this is no longer the case. In many places in China there is now a 'wild west' feel about doing business, with very little apparent control from the centre. Local authorities exercise their right to draw up their own economic plans and their own regulations, which often clash with central government regulations. The role of the central authorities is unclear but is still there. China is a complex environment in which to do business. It is unwise to go uninformed to negotiate there, as the examples and case studies in this book make abundantly clear.

A wealth of Chinese sayings capture the current obsession with making money: 'It's bad luck not to have a business' (*wushang bu fu*), and 'One billion Chinese people, 900 million shopkeepers, and another 100 million waiting on the sidelines to see how it goes' (*shiyi renmin, jiuyi shang, haiyou baiyi zai guanshang*).

Since making money involves international trade and investment, the Chinese are producing more and more handbooks on how to negotiate with foreigners. A recent book produced in Fujian province made the following observations about different national negotiating characteristics:

> The way the Japanese get along with people is very polite and modest, but they are also very astute and patient. They often try to put things off so they can find out your real intention. Americans prefer to be quick, so we should not take too long when we negotiate with them.
> The British are very careful and very hard to get close to. We should call them British, not English. English means they come only from England.
> Germans pay attention to the contract, they require every detail to be negotiated, and afterwards everything has to be followed strictly by the contract.
> Australians normally have the power to make decisions, and they expect it to be the same with us. They are very efficient, prefer

to invite tenders, and do not like to set the price high at the
start and then reduce it by haggling. (Zhang 1993)

These judgments demonstrate that the Chinese have noted
differences in national negotiation styles and expectations, and
are making an effort to adjust their negotiation behaviour to be
more effective with foreigners.

From a foreign perspective, negotiating in China is rarely an
easy matter. The Chinese stick very firmly to their own agenda
and stonewall in many different ways to divert the foreigner from
pursuing his own goals. The Chinese side is, almost without
exception, represented by large teams who take extensive notes
throughout the discussions and compare ideas afterwards. Every
day they are able to begin with a new attack built on the input
of a large number of people who have either taken part in the
discussions or been behind the scenes. The time a negotiation
takes is usually not of great importance to them, unlike western
negotiators, to whom time means money.

Western business people departing for China are commonly
advised that the Chinese value harmony, good relationships and
politeness. Yet when they get to China and enter a negotiation,
they are confronted with fierce adversarial bargaining that appears
to lack the politeness and consideration they expected. The high
pressure of such bargaining, which is often backed with threats
and pep talks about the way things are done in China, takes
them completely by surprise.

The following comments sum up the feelings of many foreign
business people who negotiate in China. The speakers represent
both experienced and inexperienced people, and industries as
diverse as petroleum exploration and shoe buying.

'It was a character-building experience. There were times
when it would have been very easy to say, "I'll get on the plane
and I won't return."'

'We negotiated regularly over five years. Each time, by the
second day I'd be thinking, "God! We've got another three weeks
of this! Is the Kraft cheese going to last out?"'

'Trying to deal with the bureaucracy there! Man! You sit
round and have cups of tea until it is coming out of your gills.
Their head man tells you the history of the world as he sees it,
and you tell him the history of the world as you see it. You'd
get to the end of the meeting before they'd tell you they weren't
really the people to speak to.'

'You're in Beijing in a hotel costing $150 a day, and they

are spending only $4 a month to rent their apartment, so they can negotiate forever to get what they want. It gives them total comparative advantage.'

'I was quite surprised to find that three people supplying the same equipment and commodities arrived in Beijing at about the same time as I did to talk about an identical contract.'

'I came out of the meeting really fuming. The Chinese director had varied the financial estimates 50 per cent and tried to make out my analysis was wrong.'

'It was absolute blackmail! It was clearly in breach of contract!'

In my experience, foreigners negotiating in China have some or all of these feelings and experiences at some stage. It is said that foreigners involved in negotiations in China fall into two categories: those who get burned out and never want to go back, and those who take on Chinese approaches to negotiating, who become the 'Taoists' of the Chinese negotiating scene, bending with the wind and flowing with the water.

There are three main reasons why negotiating in China carries such a charge among western business people. The first is the method and manner by which the Chinese conduct the negotiations. The second is the influence of the surrounding environment, which includes business norms and the role of the bureaucracy. The third is the complications of culture. This includes differences in what behaviour means and how translation from one language to another does not necessarily lead to mutual understanding.

These features can be summarised as follows:

*Method and manner*

negotiating norms
underlying motivations and attitudes
expectations and assumptions

*Surrounding environment*

stage of economic development
power and influence centres
levels of bureaucracy
government policy

*Cross-cultural complications*

interpreting behaviour

language
cultural expectations

It has been estimated that 450 000 westerners are currently doing business in China, and that this number will increase as China's massive industrial juggernaut comes to dominate the world economy in the 21st century. This dominance is not likely to make negotiating with the Chinese any easier, as it will give Chinese negotiators great strength and reinforce Chinese negotiation norms.

In the interests of clarity and simplicity, I have used the term 'the west' throughout the book to indicate 'English-speaking countries'. The characteristics I attribute to a 'western' style of negotiation may also be shared by people from non-English-speaking countries to a greater or lesser degree. I also use the word 'China' to stand for the 'Chineseness' of the Chinese negotiating style. China is a vast country with many regional differences, and it is not uncommon to have different regional groups pointed out as differing in their approach to business. The Shanghainese are usually said to be more astute than other groups, the Cantonese are supposed to be faster and less principled than northerners, and so on. These judgments depend upon who is making them. However, regional differences are but minor variations in an overall Chinese approach to negotiating. There is a consensus among western business people about the major elements of a shared 'Chinese negotiating style'.

Part I of the book focuses on the Chinese side of negotiations. Chapter 1 introduces the way the Chinese negotiate with one another in Chinese political, commercial and social life. Many of the points in this chapter are relevant to negotiating with Chinese people wherever you find them—in China, within the Chinese diaspora (Southeast Asia, Taiwan and Hong Kong), or in the west.

Chapter 2 deals with the impact of recent history on the way Chinese negotiators see business and political dealings with foreigners. It describes the constraints placed on Chinese individuals by their society, and the way in which power and influence are exercised in business culture. It also discusses the extent to which Chinese government policy impinges on negotiations and how the current stage of business development in China affects negotiations.

Part II proposes an overall framework and approach for dealing with Chinese negotiations. Chapter 3 concentrates on the pre-negotiation period and its importance to the success of the formal negotiation. Chapter 4 follows the formal negotiation through its different stages, and Chapter 5 details Chinese tactics and a number of difficulties that present themselves in Chinese–western negotiations. In each chapter, I suggest effective strategies and give examples of their use by western negotiators.

Part III presents case studies of westerners negotiating in China in the constantly changing environment of real-life negotiations. The aim of these case studies and the analysis which follows each one is to highlight the features described in Part II as they occur in different negotiations. The case studies have been chosen to show both success and failure, and to cover a wide range of industries and different stages in the development of a business relationship with China.

This part of the book includes many lessons for people whose job takes them to China to negotiate. These include not only strategy, tactics, and ways to influence the Chinese side, but insights into how China affects individuals. This needs to be accounted for just as much as the strategy of negotiation.

Inevitably the actual people on both sides, their negotiation skills and their ability to deal with the cultural differences, play a large part in the character and level of success of each negotiation. It is noticeable that for foreigners, an ability to negotiate successfully in the west does not necessarily transfer to China.

The final chapter distils much of the wisdom of the case studies, international research on negotiation, and my own experience from a lifetime of business and social interactions with the Chinese in China, Singapore and Taiwan.

A negotiator in a hurry could read the first five chapters and the final chapter and at least have a framework for negotiating effectively. However, the case studies drive the lessons home and provide an opportunity to experience some of the flavour (and stresses) of a China negotiation that can be invaluable preparation for the real thing.

Finally, the bibliography provides a wide range of references for the reader's further study according to his interests and perspective, whether he is a business or government negotiator, an academic, or an armchair traveller with an interest in China.

# Quick reference chart to Chinese negotiating characteristics

| Chinese characteristic | Cultural background | Response | Case study number |
|---|---|---|---|
| Set guiding principles—general-ised position without consultation | • Traditional preference for generalities before specifics<br>• Paternalistic: high power distance. Powerful set the agenda for lower level staff or the less powerful (westerners)<br>• Show of public harmony important, divisions hidden<br>• Need to meet government policy | • Exchange views before formal negotiation<br>• Negotiate the negotiation procedures<br>• Take guiding principles seriously, but realise they are tradable | 5 (p. 156)<br>6 (p. 171) |
| Begin with ambit claim: step-by-step trade-offs | • Haggling tradition: fear of cheating/insider–outsider ethics<br>• Preservation of 'face': everyone must look to be a winner<br>• Only settle at the very end: always keep door open to withdraw | • Pad your offers<br>• Start with a reasonable position, move from it only slowly<br>• Structure trade-offs<br>• Meet personal needs to maintain 'face'<br>• Leave price until last | 3 (p. 123)<br>5 (p. 156)<br>6 (p. 171) |
| Adversarial atmosphere | • Anti-foreign attitudes: colonial and communist legacy<br>• Traditional individualist bargaining style | • Personal goodwill<br>• Take control: guide the process<br>• Work on the relationship in informal settings<br>• Don't take the attack personally: maintain civility<br>• Look for underlying needs: do not respond directly | 3 (p. 123)<br>4 (p. 139)<br>6 (p. 171) |
| Repetitive questioning | • Tradition of meticulous, detailed note-taking<br>• Need to learn about western technology and business practices<br>• Risk-averse bureaucratic culture<br>• Team strategy: everyone has input<br>• Have a hidden agenda | • Allow time to explain<br>• Provide written and visual information<br>• Be consistent<br>• Know when to close/recess<br>• Watch where the questions are coming from: reveals their goals and concerns | 2 (p. 107)<br>3 (p. 123)<br>4 (p. 139) |

© Carolyn Blackman, *Negotiating China*, Allen & Unwin, 1997

| Chinese characteristic | Cultural background | Response | Case study number |
|---|---|---|---|
| Using false authority: 'This is what the tax authorities say.' 'This is the way it is done by other westerners.' 'This is the local custom/the way it is done in China.' | • Tradition of pressured persuasion<br>• Outsider 'ethics'<br>• China-centredness: unfamiliar with international practice<br>• Hidden agenda that cannot be disclosed: need to gain agreement | • Never accept anything as a fact<br>• Verify with the authorities or other companies<br>• Go back to first principles | 4 (p. 139) |
| Psychological pressure: exaggerating Chinese concession, minimizing yours; patronising, blaming, criticising | • Paternalistic stance<br>• Competitive, individualistic bargaining tradition<br>• Dislike of foreigners: colonial and communist legacy<br>• Know westerners have decision-making power<br>• Need to meet demands/restraints of higher authorities | • Remind them of what you have to offer<br>• Patience and control: model civility<br>• Go behind the scenes<br>• Spell out the consequences | 2 (p. 107)<br>4 (p. 139)<br>6 (p. 171) |
| Lack of sympathy/taking advantage of weakness | • Strong adherence to group goals<br>• Outsider 'ethics'<br>• Hidden agenda<br>• Lack of experience with western business processes | • Use appeals to fairness and loyalty to China<br>• Focus on your goal: be firm<br>• Argue interests of the joint venture<br>• Do not undermine yourself | 2 (p. 107)<br>3 (p. 123)<br>5 (p. 156)<br>6 (p. 171) |
| Left-field, illogical or ridiculous demands | • Concern with 'face': indirectness in communication style<br>• 'Muddy the water to catch the fish': trickery tactic<br>• Team planning: input of many individuals, pressure to meet group goals and those of higher authorities: win at any price | • Go behind the scenes<br>• Do not respond directly: look to satisfy hidden need, not the expressed need/demand<br>• Keep focused on your goal—don't be led astray<br>• Get reciprocal trade-offs for any yielded | 5 (p. 156) |
| Time pressure | • Know westerners have decision-making power/are in a hurry<br>• Need to meet demands/restraints of higher authorities | • Do not accept: use the excuse of referring to your own 'higher authority'<br>• Alert HO to time-line and vulnerability | 4 (p. 139)<br>6 (p. 171) |
| Use of competitor offers to pressure for concessions | • Marketplace haggling tradition: to undermine opposition's confidence, create artificial competition<br>• Focus on price: want to get most for least cost<br>• To gain technical knowledge<br>• Checking from fear of exploitation | • Know you bottom line and do not go below it<br>• Don't believe all they say<br>• Be prepared to go home/recess<br>• Beware of giving away alll your advantages | 2 (p. 107)<br>6 (p. 171) |
| Change of negotiators, change of location | • Group strategy<br>• Responsible to goals of higher authorities | • Avoid getting upset<br>• Keep good documents on the negotiations | 4 (p. 139)<br>5 (p. 156) |

| Chinese characteristic | Cultural background | Response | Case study number |
|---|---|---|---|
| Pushing to find the bottom line | • Marketplace haggling<br>• Distrust of foreigners<br>• Team strategy and responsibility to higher authorities<br>• Tradition of agreement only at the end | • Broaden the scope of the discussion<br>• Watch your bottom line: use limited responsibility/regulations<br>• Disclose bottom line if necessary to force them to make a counter-proposal | 2 (p. 107)<br>4 (p. 139)<br>6 (p. 171) |
| Reopening previously closed/settled issues | • Team strategy<br>• Hidden agenda: goals differ from western goals<br>• Perceptions of westerners as wealthy | • Give lesser value concessions<br>• Go behind the scenes<br>• Use ultimate consequences | 2 (p. 107)<br>5 (p. 156) |
| Lack of coordination | • Multiple parties with internal tensions<br>• Insider–outsider orientation of each party<br>• Inheritance of communist era: weak management control and lack of managerial skills | • Negotiate the negotiation procedure first: insist on a steering committee, clear responsibilities and time-line<br>• Show your organising strength | 2 (p. 107)<br>4 (p. 139) |
| Uncooperative in giving information | • Hidden agendas<br>• Inter-party disputes and jealousy<br>• Suspicion of foreigners | • Take the initiative: model goodwill, explain your role<br>• Go cautiously and discreetly<br>• Negotiate the negotiation process | 2 (p. 107) |
| Stalling, slowness, lack of progress | • Problematic information-gathering<br>• Money more important than time<br>• Approval required from higher authorities: risk-averse, unsure about changing policies<br>• 'Face': hiding unpleasant facts such as no authority/money and other problems | • Use fake time-line<br>• Recess/go home<br>• Go behind the scenes<br>• Spell out ultimate consequences<br>• Make time available | 2 (p. 107)<br>4 (p. 139)<br>6 (p. 171) |
| Changing levels/specialist negotiators | • Different bureaus involved: compartmentalisation<br>• Tradition of narrow specialism<br>• Separation of financial and technical decision-making<br>• Training for new negotiators | • Pre-negotiation: establish you status<br>• Provide documentation<br>• Move only slowly from starting position<br>• Prepare trade-offs and non-negotiable items<br>• Bring support team | 5 (p. 156) |
| Fixed position | • Strategy devised by group/higher authorities<br>• Tradition of negotiator having limited authority<br>• Lack of technical/international business knowledge<br>• Hidden agenda | • Go back to first principles<br>• Use documentary evidence<br>• Recess/go behind the scenes<br>• Get their assistance to bypass or fudge the technical sticking point<br>• Listen for their genuine concerns | 2 (p. 107)<br>4 (p. 139)<br>5 (p. 156)<br>6 (p. 171) |

| Chinese characteristic | Cultural background | Response | Case study number |
|---|---|---|---|
| Concentration on price | • Strong memories of recent poverty<br>• National goal to gain foreign currency<br>• Short-term focus on benefit to group<br>• Separation of financial and technical decision-making<br>• Lack of business experience<br>• Haggling tradition | • Signal you understand but broaden the discussion<br>• Explain ultimate consequences<br>• Prepare 'add-ons'/concessions | 2 (p. 107)<br>6 (p. 171) |
| Deadlock | • Incompatible goals<br>• Misunderstandings on both sides<br>• China-centredness vs international business practice | • Go behind the scenes: use a go-between<br>• Recess<br>• Question understanding<br>• Put troublesome issues to one side but keep on agenda<br>• Broaden the scope: create alternatives from a broad range of issues | 2 (p. 107)<br>4 (p. 139)<br>5 (p. 156)<br>6 (p. 171) |
| Renegotiating the contract, contract breaking | • Unrealisable expectations: lack of quality management or infrastructure support<br>• Tradition of ongoing renegotiation<br>• Outsider 'ethics': expectation of short-term relationship<br>• Traditional lack of legal enforcement for commercial contracts | • Check the background: are your goals realisable?<br>• Long-term focus: compromise/negotiate some degree of compensation<br>• Always prepare to renegotiate after contract signing | 1 (p. 98)<br>6 (p. 171) |
| Banquets, sightseeing, karaoke | • Traditional hospitality<br>• Testing method<br>• Informal forum<br>• Perk to compensate for low pay<br>• Group focus of Chinese life: manager-to-clerk social groups | • Show acceptance of Chinese ways<br>• Use to increase trust<br>• Use to gather information and to put forward a point of view<br>• Beware of hidden agendas | 1 (p. 98)<br>3 (p. 123)<br>4 (p. 139)<br>5 (p. 156) |
| Language use | • Dialects used to establish insider–outsider status<br>• Area of ambiguity left in interpretation<br>• A tool to establish power | • Use appropriate go-betweens: not all overseas Chinese are acceptable<br>• Check interpreter competence and loyalties<br>• Double-check understanding through multiple questions | 2 (p. 107)<br>4 (p. 139)<br>5 (p. 156) |
| Body language/facial expression | • Private opinions/emotions controlled through childhood training<br>• Haggling: never show enthusiasm or give away one's real thinking | • Do not take things at face value<br>• Watch hands, sitting position<br>• Listen and watch<br>• Watch people other than the speaker | 2 (p. 107)<br>5 (p. 156) |

© Carolyn Blackman, *Negotiating China*, Allen & Unwin, 1997

# Part I

# THE CHINESE BACKGROUND

# 1    The haggling society

A high-ranking government official from a western ministry of education went to China to tackle the problem of thousands of Chinese using private English colleges in his own country as an illegal immigration route out of China. Before he went in to the negotiations, members of the embassy staff tried to give him advice on how to negotiate with the Chinese, but he refused it. He assured them he would be able to handle it in his own way.

The Chinese negotiator, an official from the Chinese ministry of education, was most gracious and spoke about fostering goodwill between the two countries. On the first day, the foreign official gave everything the Chinese asked for, expecting that when they met on the following day, his own government's requests would be granted. The following day, the Chinese negotiator, as gracious as ever, refused those requests. The foreign official had effectively given away $50 million of his government's money, with very little in return, because he expected that the Chinese negotiator would be, like him, an accommodating person, and also interested in fostering goodwill between the two countries, as he had declared at the beginning of the negotiation.

This story contrasts with another one, told by a longtime western trader well used to the reality of negotiating in China. On one of his regular buying trips to China, Tony Kosky saw exactly the rabbit jacket he wanted to buy in the hotel shop. So he bought one and took it to the negotiations. The Chinese agreed to supply him with jackets of the same style and colour, and asked him to get another jacket from the shop so that both sides would have the same jacket and there would be no mistake. All the details were written into the contract. When the jackets arrived, by air instead of by sea (because they were late sending them), and at his expense, he discovered that they were a different colour from the one they had agreed on. He wrote letters and sent faxes, but the Chinese did not reply.

At the next trade show he took the samples back, but the Chinese showed no interest. He wrote to the Trade Commission at the Chinese Embassy, and to the trading corporation's head office in Beijing, but still got nowhere. For two years he took the jackets back and forth to China. Finally, after a lot of pressure, the Chinese agreed to take them back. Even so, Kosky had to pay for the freight. Then he had to wait another three or four months for the cheque. By the time he got it, two and a half years had passed. Needless to say, he did not make a profit on that deal.

What he did win was a reputation. The Chinese in all departments knew that Kosky had hung on and been the first person ever to send garments back to that corporation. The Chinese now knew he could play according to Chinese rules. From then on his negotiations became a lot easier.

Why should negotiations in China have this fabled reputation for toughness? One reason is that Chinese society is based on inequalities and on fierce competition between different groups. In Chinese law courts, you will not find any images of blind Justice weighing the scales, impartially offering equal justice to all.

In its place is imperial fiat, personal power to override rules and regulations, and a long tradition of negotiation as the only way to win advantages for oneself and one's group. A Chinese saying captures the spirit of the 'negotiability' of Chinese society: 'Above are government policies, below are the people's counter-policies.'

Most western countries have a legal and administrative environment that minimises risk and thus makes it easier for strangers to do business with one another. In China, where there is no widely respected commercial legal code and no certainty about getting legal redress, negotiation is the commonest way to insure oneself against being caught in a bad deal.

## MARKETPLACE HAGGLING: STEP BY STEP

Expecting to be cheated, the Chinese cover themselves by following a certain procedure in negotiating. There is no shortcut from A to Z. One can only get there by going through A, B, C, D and E, with an excursion back to B, C, and D, then on to E, F, G, and so on, right through the alphabet until you finally get to Z. There is uncertainty about everything, so one never accepts anything as given.

Haggling is so common in Chinese life that when the last Emperor of China, Pu Yi, was forced to leave the Imperial Palace after the Qing dynasty fell in 1911, his minders singled out 'how to bargain' as a key survival skill he would have to be taught. Along with 'how to bargain', he was taught how to handle money and how to speak without using emperor-to-subordinate language. Having grown up behind the walls of the Forbidden City, he had never been taught these three 'keys' to ordinary Chinese life (FitzGerald 1985).

When I lived as a Chinese person in a Chinese household, I watched the bargaining that went on around me every day. My landlady, Mrs Zhou, bought her fruit from the fruit seller who pedalled his bike and tray past our place about 10 a.m. every day. They started by exchanging a few words of banter, then she began to pick up the fruit and have a good look at it. To my way of thinking, Mrs Zhou was unbelievably thorough. She would examine just about every piece of fruit on the tray.

She would accuse the fruit seller of charging too much. She would say the bananas were too thin or the apples were not red enough. She did it with good humour, expecting the fruit seller to defend his produce, which he did.

Wanting to make a sale, the seller put time and thought into answering her criticisms. He kept the bargaining going and I could see that there was a strong relationship between the two of them, despite the parrying. Mrs Zhou, as the buyer, expected to have the upper hand. The fruit seller would always give enough to make Mrs Zhou feel she had got the better part of the deal, but not enough to make the bargaining too easy. She always seemed to come back from this exercise proud of her ability to push the price down or to get more than she had originally been offered for the same amount of money.

There is no doubt that this way of going about a transaction takes time, because both sides, but particularly the buyer, have to test how far the other person is prepared to go. Mrs Zhou needed to know how much was being charged for different pieces of fruit and what would make the seller vary his initial price. She also needed time to inject into the conversation some piece of information that would disorient the seller and induce him to give her more for her money than he originally offered. Quite often such information was blatantly fabricated—about the good deals his competitors were offering, or how inferior his fruit was. I remember that she always compared the bananas with those of her girlhood spent on a farm in South China. These northern city ones were 'all skin and no flesh'. She used information the seller could not argue with.

Mrs Zhou also tried humour to lead him off the track, thus giving her more information, and shamelessly flattered his ego. If she did not get what she wanted, she would wait until the next day. In any case it was a bit of fun, and the two of them always parted with some good-humoured badinage.

## MARKETPLACE HAGGLING: PERSISTENCE

Down the road at the free market I used to see the same kind of thing going on. A plump grandmother shopping for her extended family went to the pork stall and chose a piece of pork with skin on it and five layers of fat, perfect for making that mouth-watering dish Su Dongpo pork, named after the famous poet. When the pork butcher told her the price, she disputed it hotly. She offered him much less, grabbed the pork and went to put it into her basket. The butcher, having less than its cash value in his hand, grabbed the other end of the pork. A tug-of-war began, the lady pulling on one end of the piece of meat, the butcher on the other, neither willing to let go, and each shouting prices and evidence to defend his own point of view. The battle only ended when they noticed that the other shoppers were helping themselves to the pieces of pork lying under the counter—and to some of the items in the woman's shopping basket.

This kind of persistence is a cardinal virtue in China, taught to children through old and new folklore. 'The Old Man who Moved the Mountains' is an old tale about persistence through generations that has been reinvigorated by the Communist government. An old man wanted to move two mountains that were obstructing the view from his front door. He and his sons started to move the mountains bucket by bucket. People laughed at them, but the old man replied, 'When I am gone, my children and my grandchildren and their children and grandchildren will carry on until the mountains are levelled.'

This is the model the Chinese use for negotiating: persistence (generally through superior numbers) and 'bucket by bucket'. Chinese persistence in negotiations is summed up in one of Mao Zedong's maxims for guerrilla warfare, 'When the enemy tires, we harass' which he learnt from reading Sunzi's great classic of strategy, *The Art of War*, and the dynastic histories dating back to the first century BC. This kind of approach clearly has a long lineage in China. It offers a point of comparison with the following scenario.

A foreign girl walks into the market. All the stall owners know her. Although she speaks Chinese and comes into the market just about every day, they know she does not know much about bargaining. They all call out to her, 'Foreign girl! Come over here and buy! Beautiful fresh chickens today!' 'Foreign girl, do you want some shrimps? Really cheap today! Cook some for your dinner!'

She smiles at their obvious selling spiels and at their keenness to make money out of her. She goes up to the chicken seller, who looks after her well and flatters her by saying how clever she is to be studying at the university. He serves her first. He knows that it will be quick, he just has to tell her the price. She pays without argument, and he guts the chicken and puts it in a bag. All the Chinese shoppers have to wait. He knows that with them he will have to put in a lot of time to make a sale. He is friendly and helpful to the foreign girl, and wishes her well as he hands her the change. Some of the other stall keepers are disappointed that she did not buy from them, and tell her to come to their stalls next time.

That foreign girl was me; a sitting duck for the Chinese stall holders. At the time I found their system completely alien to my way of shopping. As far as I was concerned, you saw what you wanted, asked the price and handed over the money if you wanted to buy the item. Since that time I have seen many foreign business people go into a Chinese negotiation much as I went into that market: slightly disoriented by the strange surroundings, unfamiliar with the habits of Chinese traders, glad when some were helpful and reassuring, and pleased to get what I wanted without too much hassle. Unfortunately, not knowing the Chinese bargaining method, I paid double or triple (maybe I underestimate!) what I needed to. Many foreign companies have paid a comparable premium.

## MARKETPLACE HAGGLING: 'ETHICS'

In a Chinese bargaining situation, it is quite ethical to multiply prices several times and to offer faulty merchandise and not disclose this to the customer, all the while being charming and supportive. Of course, this kind of ethics is not exclusive to mainland China, but is encountered in other Chinese societies, including those of Taiwan and Southeast Asia.

In a business negotiation in China, it is equally ethical to distort any item to your advantage and to call on any regulation, real or imagined, to bring the other negotiator around to your way of doing something. This practice can be traced back to the lack of strong administrative and legal controls. The upside is that since there are no hard and fast rules, Chinese negotiators are always open to influence through the force of argument.

Practice at bargaining makes the Chinese quick to identify business people who do not know how to bargain in the Chinese way and who want the deal to be done quickly, close to the asking price. Just as the chicken seller did, they take advantage of the opportunity this presents without any scruples whatsoever, thankful that they do not have to engage in a long battle to get a reasonable outcome.

The popular American 'win–win' negotiation model is not strong in China. A popular saying in Shanghai is 'Behead the customer.' Another common saying is 'All businessmen cheat.' Two recent Chinese textbooks on negotiating joint ventures with foreigners advised Chinese negotiators that 'economic negotiation is not just simple marketplace haggling' (Zhang 1993) and urged them not to 'use lies to cheat the opposite negotiator' (Li 1988). That such instructions have to be given indicates that marketplace haggling and its 'ethics' are still well entrenched among Chinese negotiators.

## BUREAUCRATIC HAGGLING

The tradition of haggling extends far beyond the marketplace. Because there are few administrative or legal rules to guide the way policy is decided and implemented in Chinese political, educational and industrial spheres, the main players—the bureaucracies at national, provincial, county, prefectural and city level—rely on person-to-person negotiation to decide matters.

David Lampton (1992) studied the way groups in China bargain and build consensus about policy matters. He calls it 'protracted guerrilla warfare' and gives the 'iron law of bargaining' which underpins it. Each group will 'exaggerate the costs that another unit's proposal will inflict, minimise the benefits received . . . exaggerate the benefits others receive, overstate the resources of others, and generate one-sided data supportive of its case'. One of Lampton's Chinese interviewees told him the National Planning Conference resembled a Chinese market.

Bargaining takes place at every step of the process because the normal method is to agree first on the broad principles and leave the details to be worked out later. The details must be resolved through further bargaining, with the added difficulty that these details often conflict with the general principles. Implementing agreements made by the central authorities is particularly problematic, because each organisation or locality responsible for implementing the decision tries to distort the implementation to benefit itself. This process is complicated because many agencies are involved, and their responsibilities overlap.

Corruption enters the scene because decisions are guided not by well-established administrative frameworks but by personal influence. Powerful individuals are brought in to support the competing parties. Bargaining between different regional areas and interest groups has accelerated as the economy has been liberalised, and with this, powerful people have acquired great wealth. Lampton notes that during the first ten years of liberalisation following the death of Mao, 'bargaining behavior (legal, illegal and quasi-legal) . . . the pursuit of individual, local, and organizational interest was legitimate in a way which it never was under Mao'.

Industrial enterprises negotiate for changes to the government regulations that control their operations. If enterprise managers can present a persuasive case to their superiors, they can have the central plan altered to suit their needs (Naughton 1992).

Before the Communists came to power, most companies considered the tax laws as no more than the authorities' opening bargaining position (Lieberthal 1980). Since then, even under

Communist rule, traditional attitudes appear to have survived. Enterprise managers still negotiate with the local bureaucracy to lower the tax on their enterprise. In 1986, as a result of enterprise managers' bargaining with the authorities in Jiangsu, taxes equal to 12 per cent of total budgetary revenue were cancelled. The local government officials in turn are engaged in negotiating favourable treatment from higher authorities.

Every stage of the business chain is decided by negotiation through the 'spider's web': the network of people who give and receive favours to ensure favourable outcomes for their own group. Enterprise personnel negotiate prices for buying materials and selling products that have little to do with any 'market price'. A product price might be raised 10 per cent to cover 'handling charges', and this amount is shared by various buyers and sellers in the chain to facilitate later purchases of inputs for the enterprise. Given the extent of bargaining in China, it is not surprising that the Chinese are so practised at it.

## THE IN GROUP AND THE OUT GROUP

Social organisation in China and in the diaspora is characterised by membership of exclusive groups. The use of dialects is fundamental to this membership, because a person's dialect is identified with his home town or county. No matter where you go there is a multiplicity of mutually incomprehensible dialects. In the Yangtse valley region, a flat area with no natural geographical divisions as in the mountainous south, where dialect differences can be easily explained by the terrain, every town still has its own dialect. Within a few hundred square kilometres there are the dialects of Suzhou, Wuxi, Yangzhou and Shanghai. Apart from dialect groups, there are many other exclusive 'clubs', such as 'lao tongxue' (alumni associations) and kinship groups.

Home town and county groups form the basis of business networks. In the overseas Chinese communities in western countries, businesses will often recruit only Chinese from the same home town or dialect groups. The Shanghai business empires before the Communist period showed the same preference for the home town group and exclusion of outsiders. The banking industry was dominated by people from Ningpo, the cotton and cigarette industries by Cantonese and Jiangsu people. (Bergère 1989)

In the Chinese world it is relationships, not law, that provide the security necessary to do business. Relationships are also treasured because the interpretation of what laws there are is flexible. This comes through very clearly in the case studies in this book. In every area there are 'fixers' who can 'smooth the way'. These are usually the most senior people, who have built up the necessary connections over a lifetime. They may have started off in the accounting section, where they got to know the tax people. As they moved up through the organisation they cemented those relationships, deliberately keeping them up, so they could call on them some day. Now, when they do business, they are in a position to say, 'Let *me* talk to him . . .' Thanks to the relationships they have built, they know who to contact, what their background is, who they work with, who they admire, who has the power and which faction he is associated with. Chinese people consciously use the network. If an enquiry goes one way, another enquiry will come back.

A famous example of the overriding Chinese concern with knowing your business associates by more than reputation is the account of the first meeting between the two shipping giants Aristotle Onassis and Sir YK Pao. After exchanging pleasantries, Onassis proposed a joint venture. Pao was appalled. How, he asked, could two ship owners who had never met before have a joint venture? (Hutcheon 1990)

Family relationships are also profoundly important in Chinese business. Indeed, the term for an individual company in Chinese is *jia*, or 'family'. Family members in private enterprise control the crucial management roles and, as a further insurance of loyalty, usually do not keep individual bank accounts—everything is pooled.

Research on different national groups supports the view that there are distinct differences between Chinese and western attitudes to society. Hofstede's monumental work *Culture's Consequences* (1980) identified two important social organisational principles: 'individualism' and 'collectivism'. China and most Asian cultures tend to the collectivist end of the scale, while English-speaking cultures gravitate to the individualistic end.

On a scale of 0 to 100, the US rated 91 for individualism, Australia 90, Great Britain 89 and Canada 80. China rated 36. (Lai and Lam 1986).

Collectivists, such as the Chinese, spend more time in groups than individualists. They believe that group decisions are superior to decisions made by individuals, and follow the attitudes, beliefs and norms of their own group more closely than individualists do. They have a fatalistic view of life, because the welfare of the group is valued more highly than the welfare of the individual. And, of most relevance to foreigners negotiating with the Chinese, collectivists treat people differently according to whether they are in their own group or outside it.

The Chinese banquet is a prime example of a collectivist society in action. Rather than an individual executive inviting a business associate to his home as in the west, the whole office, from the managing director to the clerk, entertains the visitor at a restaurant banquet. That provides lots of fun for everyone and bonds all members of the group together.

## INSIDERS–OUTSIDERS: 'ETHICS'

One researcher has described collectivists as 'extremely hospitable, cooperative and helpful to the in group, but rude, exploitative and even hostile to out groups'. He also noted that because different treatment is given to out group members, it is acceptable in collectivist societies to cheat strangers in business transactions (Triandis 1990).

Triandis happened to be talking about Greece, and interestingly, Greece and China rate very similarly on measures of collectivism and support for a strong hierarchy. The saying 'beware of Greeks bearing gifts' would do good service with the Chinese, too. It points to a degree of trickery both peoples employ in their dealings with outsiders. Both also share the need to give expensive gifts and banquets to bond people to their group and its goals. They display fierce loyalty to people in their own group, and openness to arguments that are based on loyalty and commitment.

Much of Chinese populist history tells of the deception of one group by another, and the use of clever tricks to gain the advantage. Sunzi's *Art of War* is full of such stratagems, and is a popular book in China. A present-day Chinese negotiator described his strategies with foreigners as 'strong and tough'. In a typical case he offered $US90 000 on a product quoted at $US150 000 and stuck to his position, *mixing truth and falsehood* to confuse the opposition about his intention to buy, and to find out the opposition's intentions. His settling price on this occasion was $US91 500.

Suspicion, a cold attitude, an attacking style, the use of

spurious 'regulations' and secret internal 'regulations', delay and renegotiation of what has apparently already been agreed on, are signs of the stonewalling and trickery which typify a society where strong distinctions are made between insiders and outsiders. Any negotiator will recognise these as common practices in China.

'The great unity', or *da tong*, has long been a central ideal in Chinese society. It represents a glorious future where all divisions cease to exist. It is a favourite name for a business. The Taiwanese national anthem, brought from China by the exiled Nationalist government, has 'unity' as a major theme. It is arguable that the Chinese place so much stress on unity as an ideal precisely because there is so much disunity in Chinese society. Factional disagreements and gossip are endemic in Chinese workplaces and in society at large (Silin 1976; Yang 1989, 1994).

The Chinese have a saying, 'Each person sweeps the snow on his own path, but ignores the frost on his neighbour's roof.' This strong identification with one's own group and coldness towards outsiders was dramatically illustrated during the Cultural Revolution. Those out of favour were branded 'capitalist roaders', 'fiends', 'monsters' and 'the stinking ninth' (intellectuals) and paraded through the streets wearing dunce's caps and placards listing their 'crimes'. Even the President of China, Liu Shaoqi, was not immune from the treatment meted out to outsiders when he fell foul of Mao. He was imprisoned by Red Guards and died, naked and alone, in a bitterly cold concrete cell in 1969. Immediately after the Cultural Revolution, children in kindergartens were throwing balls at targets pasted with pictures of the disgraced Gang of Four as part of their sports practice. In China one is in, or unequivocally out.

## INSIDERS–OUTSIDERS: TRADE

In this system, westerners are outsiders. The early western traders to China were commonly referred to as 'barbarians' and 'red-haired devils'. Cantonese authorities allegedly translated the name of Lord Napier, the chief superintendent of British trade in Canton in 1834, as 'laboriously vile'. He was in the post for a mere three months. He died soon after leaving China as a result, his doctors said, of 'the severe labour and anxiety which devolved upon him while in Canton' and the 'cruel, needless and vexatious detention' imposed upon him by the Chinese authorities (Morse I 1910).

Part of the stress of negotiating in China is that westerners mistakenly feel they have been singled out for especially unsympathetic treatment. In fact, what they face is no worse than the treatment the Chinese give to fellow Chinese who are not members of their own group.

Practical obstacles to business are thrown up by the focus on the benefit to one's own group. Rather than China being one united economic entity, each province imposes its own trade tariffs and transit dues on goods from other provinces. When westerners first exported goods from inland China in the nineteenth century, they frequently encountered problems moving their purchases through different provinces to the coast, although the goods were meant to be covered by one transit tax only, mandated by Beijing. In 1878 a complaint was made that the Hankou authorities refused to issue transit passes to goods coming from Sichuan. The Beijing authorities ordered that passes be issued, but the Sichuan authorities refused to recognise the passes until they were disciplined by Beijing. When the goods reached Guizhou, they were seized by the local authorities on the ground that the passes had freed them from tax in Sichuan and Hubei, but not in Guizhou. Once again, Beijing had to intervene for the goods to be released (Morse II 1917).

Negotiating a contract in China today involves similar competitiveness between different groups. The central government puts out its regulations, but the local authorities insist that the contract conform to their rules. This involves foreigners in many rounds of negotiations with each party. Land use fees, building costs, water and infrastructure costs may all be varied at the whim of local officials, depending upon your degree of familiarity with them.

## INSIDERS–OUTSIDERS: LOYALTY

Lucian Pye, who wrote the seminal *Chinese Commercial Negotiating Style* (1982), believes deep commitment is necessary in doing business with the Chinese, and that western companies are afraid to make this commitment. The Chinese show a strong preference for shared and mutual benefits in business dealings, which stems from their fear of being cheated by an outside group. The negotiators quoted in this book, who have been successful over the long term, stress commitment to China as an essential part of their negotiation and business strategy. As one of them said, 'China isn't a short-term play.'

Valuing commitment, the Chinese are acutely sensitive to disloyalty. The US, in China's eyes, fell badly short on this score in the early days of the People's Republic. Arthur Lall (1968), a former ambassador to the UN, quotes the Chinese negotiator, Qiao Guanhua, as saying, 'Mr Lall, I know you mean well. You think you can persuade the Americans to accept your proposal. We know them better than you. We dealt with them for a long time after the war. They went back on all the promises they made to us through General Marshall.'

American and Chinese business behaviour rests on diametrically opposed traditions: one constantly in flux and ready to respond to the best opportunities as they appear, the other deeply wary of disloyalty and reliant on demonstrated and sworn commitment.

Confucius emphasised the importance of loyalty to a dependable in group. He said, 'Hold loyalty and faithfulness to be fundamental. Have no friends who are not as good as yourself' (Analects 1:8). And again, 'The superior man . . . associates with men of moral principle and thereby realizes himself' (Analects 1:14). Clearly, he did not recommend treating everyone alike.

## INSIDERS–OUTSIDERS: 'OLD FRIENDS'

Another facet of the insider–outsider mentality is that very soon after meeting you, the Chinese will call you 'an old friend of China'. This strikes westerners as odd and charming. It underlines the way the Chinese divide the world into insiders and outsiders, friends and foes. It is a first step towards requests for favours and understanding that would otherwise not be expected from an outsider. If you fail to respond, the Chinese will attempt to shame you because your behaviour is not what is expected of an 'old friend', that is, it does not demonstrate unconditional loyalty and support.

Western and Chinese expectations about friendship differ. Western friendships are generally more arms-length and based on feelings. Chinese friendships are more about doing favours. You can only prove genuine friendship in China by action. For example, if a Chinese official comes to buy wool, the way to establish yourself as his business friend is to present him with a superb, high-quality suit made from the wool you wish to sell him. Every time he wears the suit he will think favourably of you, his business friend. What is bribery in western thinking is a sign of dependable friendship to the Chinese. At a personal level it might mean lending money without any assurance that it will be repaid, welcoming telephone calls at any hour of the night or day, and arranging for your friend's son to get a job in your company, even though you know he is entirely unsuited to it. In fact, Chinese friendship can be very burdensome.

It involves give and take, favours for favours, and always giving precedence to the personal over the objective and institutional. The Chinese often accuse westerners of having no *renqingwei* or 'human feeling' when they refuse to bend the rules to help. Friendship is about insider connections. It also involves maintaining face, because if you refuse a request from a friend you will lose face, or respect within the in group.

What effect will being an 'old friend' have on your business success in China? It is possible to use the notion to influence Chinese partners to act in your interests, to lobby associates to speed up approvals, or to strike a more favourable land-use fee. It should cut through the Chinese suspicion of foreigners and make relationships easier and new contracts less time consuming. On the evidence I collected during my study, a three-year negotiation can be cut to six months if the two parties are well known to one another. In negotiating prices, the Chinese will tell you the best that your competitor is offering and allow you to meet it, rather than going immediately with the competitor's offer.

## JOINING THE IN GROUP

Because the Chinese use different rules for out groups, it is important for westerners, the ultimate outsiders, to move the ground inside the Chinese camp. The more an outsider makes himself sympathetic to the Chinese, or calls their bluff by demanding that they use the same rules of fairness for him as for their own group, the greater is his chance of swaying the argument in his favour. Tony Kosky used both Chinese rules and his status as an 'old friend of China' in the following incident.

He was in Canton for the annual Canton Trade Fair. At that

time Maoism was in full swing, and the Little Red Book of Mao's sayings was given to everyone when they arrived at the Canton railway station. Kosky's company bought furs and sold skins through the one Chinese trading corporation. So he knew people reasonably well on both the buying and the selling sides, and they always knew whether he had bought or sold. He had bought Chinese furs but had not been able to sell his sheepskins. Since he had been trading with the Chinese for some years, he was, in the popular Chinese terminology, 'a very old friend'. Although this might sound trite to westerners, Kosky knew that in a business context it could open doors.

He was frustrated because his time was running out and nothing was happening on the sheepskin front. One lunchtime, he sat next to an old English fellow who had been a China trader for many, many years. When Kosky explained his troubles, the Englishman said to him, 'Tony, you should look at the Little Red Book of Mao's sayings. That's got everything in it.' Kosky replied, 'What do you mean?' The Englishman took the Little Red Book from his pocket. He knew it back to front. He flicked through it, found a certain page and handed it to Kosky to read. The next day, prepared, Kosky went into the negotiations. Of the five Chinese negotiators, only one supposedly spoke English. Kosky said, 'You know, in the Little Red Book, the great Chairman Mao said that trading between countries should be equal, and no one country should take advantage of another. It really means the same for corporations. Here we are trading, and I've done my buying, but I haven't done my selling. This is one company taking advantage of another.'

He could see that three of them obviously did not understand anything. But one of the Chinese, who said he did not speak English, had a little twitch in his mouth. Kosky knew he had understood. The next day he got his contract.

## FRANKNESS VS FACE

Face is the other crucial factor in Chinese negotiating style. Face refers to a person's reputation, the respect in which he is held by others. Most English-speaking societies value frankness, freedom of expression, independence and personal rights. From childhood we are told to speak our mind. Our legal systems protect our right to express our ideas, and our traditions of debate foster this expression. We are encouraged to say our piece and not to worry what others think.

Chinese tradition is very different. The Chinese are taught to be cautious in expressing personal opinions, particularly if those opinions are critical of others. Children are told not to dispute the instructions of their parents. The Chinese are particularly sensitive to what is said in public, valuing comments which bolster others' reputation, prestige and status.

Deng Xiaoping's daughter used the typical Chinese face-giving approach when she addressed a group of reporters in the US. She said, 'In China we have a saying that journalists are the uncrowned kings. Therefore I should change places with you. You should be up here on the podium, and I should be down there where you are sitting.' Her own high position was an essential ingredient. She was graciously lifting the journalists to her level, giving them face. But what would have received polite acknowledgment in China made no impression on the American journalists. All they wanted was for her to get down to business and answer their questions. They did not need to have their face lifted.

A strong respect for hierarchy underlies face. One must follow the proper form in speaking to people at different levels, and show respect to one's seniors and those in positions of authority. This emphasis on a person's position in society is a fundamental of Chinese social life, going back to the time of Confucius. Western officials in the nineteenth century were outraged when they learned that to discuss any commercial issue, they had to approach the local Chinese officials as supplicants. Their requests would only be heard if they used subservient language appropriate to their lowly position vis-à-vis the officials, and humbly asked the officials to act benevolently towards them.

The official who signed the first Chinese treaties with the west, Imperial Commissioner Qiying, considered western traders as 'from outside the bounds of civilisation' because they had no idea about 'styles of address and forms of ceremony'. He urged his fellow officials to indulge the westerners somewhat, because although he and his fellow Chinese might instruct them in the proper way until 'our tongues were dry and our throats parched', there was no hope that they would ever understand (Hsu 1986).

In 1840 the Chinese Commissioner, Keshan, advised the British that they should approach the Emperor and his representatives with 'dutiful reverence' and 'humbly' request permission to trade. He reminded the British that 'under the whole Heaven, there lives none who are not the Children and People of the Great Emperor'. As Lord Palmerston wrote to his ambassadors in China at the time, 'it is well known that in China, matters which apparently relate merely to forms are considered of substantial importance' (Morse I 1910).

We now know that such matters are not 'merely' related to form, but express a fundamental aspect of Chinese life. In China, the age, status, position, style and manner of a foreign negotiator will all have a bearing on the negotiation because these things count. It means something to have the foreign company chairman and the managing director personally negotiate on behalf of their company. Maintaining high-level person-to-person contact, even while negotiators at a lower level carry out substantive negotiations, gives the Chinese officials face.

## LOSS OF FACE

If you attack a person's reputation or good name, he will take revenge sooner or later. He may show no reaction at the time, since to do so would itself cause him to lose face and show him to be an uncivilised person who does not know how to behave in public. There is a Chinese saying that 'jade is not valuable until it is cut'. This expresses the Chinese admiration for cultivating self-control rather than letting one's hair down. But the slight will still be deeply felt, and is unlikely to be forgotten. A common cause of violence in the Chinese countryside is vengeance wreaked on one kinship group by another on which it has inflicted a loss of face. Until recent times, if a person was treated so badly by his boss that he committed suicide, his family and friends, who had lost face, had the right to demolish the business premises. This was called 'beating a man's life'.

To offend against Chinese face can be disastrous. In my early days in China, I once lost my temper after two days trying to get someone to put the first 'chop' of approval on a permit that needed ten chops. In absolute desperation, I broke down and lashed out against the Chinese system and all the people who ran it. The people in the office at the time showed me no mercy. I was taken in to face the boss, who demanded a full public apology, delivered abjectly and with sincerity, to all members of the department in which I had lashed out. After that I had to go away until time had eased the memory. When I started afresh on my quest for the chops, I went about it in a very humble and contrite manner. I got them in the end.

There is a temptation in China for western business people to take a superior attitude. Those who do so quickly learn that they have offended against Chinese face, when the discussions stop or the workers down tools. Instead of criticising the way things are done in China, they should say, 'We do things differently in the west.' This is a face-saving way of discussing divergent approaches, and far more effective than forthright criticism. Sir Robert Hart, who ran the Chinese customs service from 1863 to 1911, offered westerners this wise advice: 'Introduce remedies without causing the irritation that attends the exposure of defects.' More than irritation is at stake. Because Chinese people live in close personal networks, one person's loss of face quickly becomes known to all. And the pain this public humiliation brings can be so severe as to drive the person to suicide.

The bureaucratic system is another network in which sensitivity is needed when dealing with individuals' mistakes. A Chinese factory sent defective goods to a buyer in Australia. Although the factory representative privately acknowledged that the goods were not what had been agreed to in the contract, his superiors did not accept the buyer's request for compensation. They were afraid of losing face with the local Foreign Trade Office officials, because the Foreign Trade Office had asked each factory to take responsibility for quality and packaging, and obviously they had not attended to this directive.

The Australian buyer chose to go through a third person, a Hong Kong agent, rather than tackle the problem himself. The factory representative gave the agent a special price on the next lot of goods the Australian bought through him. The special price, to be carried over two years, met the compensation claim. Because the Australian buyer did not personally handle the case, or make public mention of the error, this solution saved the factory from losing face with the local Foreign Trade Office—and also preserved the buyer's relations with the factory.

## FACE: INDIRECTNESS

Face may also become an issue in negotiations when the Chinese avoid speaking openly about a sensitive problem. They deflect the burning issue onto something else. This creates opportunities for serious misunderstanding between westerners and the Chinese. The following incident clearly illustrates how this happens.

A group of Chinese geologists and government officials were visiting an Australian university for a training course. Suddenly, without warning, they started to express dissatisfaction about the program and its arrangements. They wanted changes to the program that made no sense to the Australians. They complained about their accommodation, criticised the lecturers, insisted that the Australians provide a new interpreter, and asked for more detailed written material.

The Australians in charge of the course had been doing their utmost to provide the very best of everything and were completely bemused by the flood of demands which seemed to come out of nowhere. They were particularly upset by the criticism of the interpreter, whom they had chosen because of her fluency in both Chinese and English, and her knowledge of geology. The Australians began to feel that no matter what they did, they could not please the Chinese. They were on the point of cancelling the whole course and telling the Chinese to go back home and forget any future programs. In a last desperate bid, the program leader telephoned me late one night.

I discussed the case with a Chinese friend, who hit on the problem immediately. It was breathtakingly simple. The Chinese were allowed by their government to keep the daily living allowance for their own use. Any money they saved they could take back home to their families. The money being spent on them in Australia would probably keep their families for years in China and buy them the goods they longed to have, like washing machines and refrigerators. The arrangements made for them by the Australians—the upmarket accommodation, planned flights to remote mining sites, dinners and entertainment—were, in their terms, a waste of money.

After I passed this advice on to the program leader, he discussed the matter with the Chinese, but did not reveal that he had 'inside information' about what was really driving them. Together, he and the visitors agreed that they would move into more modest accommodation, forgo some of the plane trips and visits to the theatre, cook for themselves, and keep the money thus saved. Their complaints about the interpreter miraculously ceased, and the course proceeded without further problems.

The real reason behind the visitors' attacks and demands—the desperate need for money to take back to China—was far too embarrassing for them to discuss frankly with strangers. If the program leader had not managed to discover it indirectly, what has since proven to be a fruitful, ongoing training relationship would probably have been wrecked.

Another example of the way a fear of losing face stops people discussing problems openly was given to me by a group of foreign engineers working on a contract in Shanghai during the democracy protests leading up to the Tiananmen Square incident in 1989. The engineers' Chinese colleagues told them they could not go to the office because the regular blue bus which took them had broken down. Then they said, 'We suggest you work in your hotel. We also suggest that you limit your travel to the vicinity of the hotel.' There was no mention of the political unrest.

The next day, the engineers were still not able to go to the office. The Chinese said, 'There is a problem with the road system.' They bicycled all the files from the office to the hotel, and everyone involved in the contract meetings turned up at the hotel. None of the Chinese mentioned a word about what was going on outside.

Embarrassment about admitting internal company problems, too, can seriously affect business success. One Chinese group proceeded with negotiations for two years without informing the western side that it had no authority to contract for the project in question. In such cases western business people become reluctant to pursue further Chinese business, believing that it takes too long and involves them in fruitless expense. In this particular case, quite by chance, another Chinese group at a much higher level in the hierarchy told the western team what was happening and later helped the Chinese team get permission to negotiate the contract (Nixon 1994). It never occurred to the Americans that the Chinese were too embarrassed to disclose the real reason they were dragging out the negotiations. You can always expect that you too will need to go looking for the reason when there are problems or hold-ups in negotiations.

When foreign managers in China tell their Chinese staff what to do, the latter's fear of losing face can once again cause misunderstandings. The manager explains what is to be done, and the staff assure him they have understood. But the task is done wrongly or not at all. The reason is that the Chinese were too embarrassed (or afraid) to admit that in fact they did not understand the manager's instructions.

In China, vague phrases such as 'in principle it is OK' and 'I will do my best' are used to avoid that too-confronting word 'no'. Western business people will only discover that 'no' is in fact the answer, and learn why, by careful and sympathetic—and above all discreet—discussion of the problem. Never take any situation at face value. When you are confronted with unreasonable demands or puzzling circumstances, Roderick Macleod (1988) suggests you 'poke around with a stick to find what is under the stone'. There is a reason for everything, but it takes time to find it in China. Asking straight out just does not work.

This concern with maintaining appearances influences the Chinese negotiating style. A western negotiator never knows whose 'face' is vulnerable, who has proposed a certain strategy, what parties' interests are being served by different issues that are raised. A negotiator with 30 years experience describes his approach as avoiding head-on clashes that could put someone's reputation on the line. He tests his assumptions about the situation as he goes: 'When I negotiate, I negotiate as it goes. I never allocate myself half an hour, or an hour. The Chinese get involved in one small point and until you solve that point you cannot go further to more important questions. To move the point along, I negotiate back and forth, back and forth. They compromise a little bit here, compromise a little bit there, that's how it goes. You cannot do it in one hit. It doesn't work that way.' This is the ABCDEF pattern. Examples of what happens when negotiators try to operate in a typically western way, straight to the point, and with an emphasis on efficiency, will be given later in this book.

# 2    The world of the Chinese negotiator

When Chinese negotiate with westerners, they act in ways that can be difficult to understand. We have already discussed the effects of the division between in group and out group, and the concern with maintaining face. At a more fundamental level, westerners ask, Why do the Chinese reject western suggestions which seem efficient and sensible? Why do they always refer decisions to a higher authority? Why are they so slow? Why do they always draw a distinction between 'the way things are done in China' and what they imply is the inferior western way?

Every Chinese negotiator is embedded in his own group, which has its own goals. Although he does not necessarily see the negotiation in the same way as his foreign counterpart, there are usually quite straightforward, logical explanations for the way he behaves.

## CHINESE SUSPICION OF WESTERNERS

For the last 150 years, westerners have had a very bad press in China. Britain attacked China in the Opium Wars of 1841 and 1857. In 1860, to force the Chinese government to come to heel, Lord Elgin burnt down the Summer Palace in Beijing while French and British soldiers smashed its priceless treasures. Anti-foreign feeling was so strong during the last dynasty of China that Li Hongzhang, a high official, declined to recommend competent men to serve as members of the Foreign Affairs Office for fear of offending them (Smith *et al.* 1991).

After the Communists came to power in 1949, they used

anti-foreign propaganda to unite the people behind them and to wipe out their right-wing opponents. Mao wrote, 'The imperialists will never lay down their butcher knives, and they will never become Buddhas till their doom.' Many people who were educated in the west or otherwise had contact with foreigners were purged, or punished as spies. Their outside contacts were labelled *litong waiguo* (collaborating with foreign countries). They were regularly targeted in anti-rightist campaigns and rectification movements. American and Western European books and publications were banned, and Russian was taught in place of English. This isolated the population, and particularly the young people, from developments in the west (Liao 1984).

During the Cultural Revolution in the 1960s and '70s, xenophobia reached new heights. Western economics and technology were vehemently rejected. Anyone even remotely associated with foreign influences was publicly criticised and physically attacked; many were hounded to suicide. Chinese textbooks commonly portray the nineteenth and twentieth-century experience with foreigners emotionally and negatively. The following extract is from a current English-studies text.

> The imperialist partition of China occurred at the time when the chief capitalist countries (Britain, Russia, the United States, Japan, France and Germany) reached the stage of imperialism.
>
> In addition to *dumping* merchandise and *seizing* raw materials, the powers were also in competition in investing capital in China. They also lent money to the Qing government and opened more banks . . . They opened up factories, built railways and operated mines, *monopolizing* and *controlling* Chinese finance and economy.
>
> The imperialist powers also *grabbed* 'leased land' and *divided* China into spheres of influence. (*emphasis added*)

Chinese feelings about their experience with the west are being captured in a film about the Opium Wars which will be shown throughout China on 1 July 1997, the day China regains sovereignty over Hong Kong.

Although current policies welcome foreign investment, many Chinese still see the west as exploitative and are afraid to work for foreign–Chinese joint ventures, despite the significantly higher pay. Their families may also exhort them to remember the dangers of associating with foreigners.

China adopts different negotiating attitudes for different countries. Paul Kreisberg (1994) found that when the Chinese government negotiates with countries which are lower in the hierarchy of nations than China and which have never been colonial powers, its stance is benevolent. Zambians reported that 'Chinese negotiators . . . were unconcerned about bargaining, simply agreeing to remedy any problems that arose in negotiations.' In negotiations with Thailand, once a tributary nation to China, 'the Chinese expect deferential respect from Thailand and reciprocate once this is extended by Thai leaders'. When Thailand wanted China to purchase Thai rice as a favour, Deng Xiaoping or Li Peng invariably agreed, although they left the details to be discussed at lower levels. A Thai negotiator commented that 'in our tradition the less powerful party is not expected to be as generous as the more powerful one.'

This concept influences Chinese expectations in negotiations with western and Japanese companies that are obviously affluent. Large-scale strategic negotiations with the US, European countries and Japan, all of which are wealthy and have a history of colonial domination in China, are likely to be strongly influenced by the belief that the richer party owes benevolence to the poorer party. Many Australians report that the Chinese tell them they prefer to do business with them than with other westerners because their country is not threatening and has never been a colonial power. This contrasts with the troubled relationship with the United States. Antiforeign demonstrations in the Communist period were directed mainly against the US.

## CHINESE EXPERIENCES OF WESTERN ARROGANCE

During the 1930s and '40s Chinese—many of whom are still alive today—suffered the contempt of western business people living in the major port cities. Etched in their memories is the story of the sign on the best park in Shanghai, which allegedly read: 'Dogs and Chinese Not Allowed'. The sinologist CP FitzGerald (1985) described his experience of the attitudes of western expatriates to the Chinese in Shanghai in 1930, at the height of foreign domination. Soon after his arrival in Shanghai, an English lady, Mrs Ward, took him shopping. As they walked along the narrow footpath, a coolie carrying a huge load came from the other direction. Fitzgerald moved onto the road to let him pass. Mrs Ward gripped him by the arm and hissed, 'Never do that!' Stunned, FitzGerald asked her what it was that he should not do. She replied, 'No one gives way to any Chinese!'

Western arrogance and superiority are alive and well today, but the Chinese do not have to put up with them. A buyer for a major German retail company bought a shipment of goods for Christmas, but they arrived two months late. (This is not unusual in trading with China, and happens because of poor management control, difficulties with production—the power might go off for two days in every week—and insufficient transport. Also, the people in the factory often have no appreciation of western time lines, have been operating for many years under central control, and have little idea of western market economics.)

The following year, the buyer berated the Chinese trade representative at the Canton Trade Fair. He pointed out that what had occurred was contrary to the terms of the contract. He said, very loudly and aggressively, 'It is no good. At least try and do better next time. If you don't do better I am going somewhere else to buy.' Having finished with that subject, he turned to his order book and said, 'Now we'll look at the new orders. Here are all the numbers I want to order.'

The representative looked at the list and said, 'I'm sorry. I've got no stock. Nothing. All gone, sold.'

'It can't be,' replied the German, 'Today is only the second day of the Fair! How can it all be sold?' The Chinese just repeated, 'It's all sold, I'm sorry.' Next in line was an overseas Chinese trader. As he sat down he asked the representative if everything had been sold. 'No! No!' was the answer, 'We've got everything in stock. What do you want?'

The German's insensitive approach was partly a product of the colonial inheritance and partly just western plain-spokenness. But even though he was a big customer, it did not matter to the Chinese representative, who was probably on a low salary, stood to gain nothing from the transaction, and would be able to sell his quota of goods to another customer. What is more, the representative had no control over the factory making the goods, its efficiency or its delivery schedule. What mattered to him was his loss of face.

A better way for the German to have approached this problem would have been to say, 'Look, you should have shipped the goods on time, because now we've got all these holding charges until next year.' And with a half-joking, pleasant manner, to add, 'I know you've got a problem with the factory, but the goods came late. We're out of pocket, what can you do for me? How about you reduce the price on my next order by . . . ?' This would have been far better than having an argument and ending up with nothing.

Condescending attitudes are only too easy for westerners to adopt in a developing country where telephones do not work efficiently, planes do not necessarily run on time, and many aspects of life are unlike home. The Chinese are proud of their culture, which is much richer and more sophisticated than many foreigners realise. Showing appreciation for things Chinese can help foreigners overcome negative stereotypes branding them as barbaric, short-tempered and rapacious.

## THE LINK BETWEEN POLITICS AND BUSINESS

Internal politics and China's experiences with the west shape its economic behaviour. In early 1996, when China and the US were embroiled in diplomatic conflict over the private visit of the President of Taiwan to the US, China awarded a major truck manufacturing contract to the German Mercedes-Benz corporation rather than to the American Chrysler. The constant American criticism of human-rights abuses in China probably also influenced official thinking against the American company. It is true that there were hard-headed economic reasons for the decision, but the political climate was also a significant factor.

(Changes in Chinese government policy can also have a huge impact on business agreements) An outstanding example of this was the cancellation in 1980 of the Japanese-funded, $US5 billion Baoshan Iron and Steel Plant after the first stage had been built. The reason was that China no longer needed a large amount of steel, and had neither the foreign exchange to pay for the plant nor the energy and transportation network to support it. The minister responsible said, 'I am aware that this may make us lose international credibility . . . but China's priority is to improve its people's standard of living.' About-turns of policy such as this are undertaken even when the Chinese know they will face international censure (Lampton 1986).

I should point out that the Chinese later made good their promises to many of the companies originally involved in the Baoshan project. This incident highlights the importance of negotiating with the Chinese to overcome problems rather than throwing one's hands in the air and resigning oneself to the situation.

The Chinese government deserves a certain sympathy for its sudden imposition of restraints on development, as frustrating as this may be for western companies. As the economy has been liberalised, the central government has lost control over developments. Many work units have teamed up with foreigners (including overseas Chinese) and funnelled capital into projects which return no income because of oversupply, such as the office buildings in Hainan which sit in darkness because they are totally empty, and the extravagent condominiums which cannot find buyers and so return no dividends on significant investments of government capital. Guangdong recently revoked the licences of seven golf-course projects under a resolution passed by the provincial legislature to curb encroachments on farming land. Central authorities had seen a fall of 12 million tonnes of grain and a loss of 400 000 ha of the best farmland to development in 1994, and had issued instructions to the provinces to freeze new luxury constructions. This type of economics is called in China 'bird cage economics', that is, containing growth by central policies.

## CHINESE GOALS

The most influential factor in China's negotiations with western countries is its desire to become strong, wealthy and respected. Chinese visitors to the west note the high standard of living, the personal affluence and the consumer goods. Quite naturally they want the same for China, for their families and for themselves. The force of this desire should not be underestimated. Most Chinese have had to do without those conveniences that are taken for granted in most western households: gas or electric stoves, washing machines, refrigerators, VCRs, telephones, instant hot water and heating, not to mention family cars. In the cities families live in incredibly cramped conditions. Middle managers may still pedal to and from work on a bicycle, even—in Beijing and further north—through winter snow and sleet. Alternatively, they have to fight for a standing space on a dilapidated bus.

These are strong personal motivators for negotiators, which reinforce their group and national motivations when they negotiate benefits from wealthy westerners. But for some they have a downside. One Chinese negotiator lamented foreign companies' exploitation of Chinese desires for consumer goods:

> To gain profit for their companies, capitalists utilise all approaches to draw in and buy over our traders. They send them gifts of colour TVs, refrigerators and other high level consumer goods, and offer them commissions on sales. If I were a little selfish and accepted such gifts, I could not stick to my position and protect our country's benefit. (Huang 1985)

It is quite common for Chinese negotiators to believe that the foreigners are there to take advantage of them. If western negotiators are to be successful in China they need to understand the tensions created by such attitudes, their impact on the negotiation and how to handle them.

## FITTING IN WITH THE GROUP

The large number of people in China is the first thing that strikes western visitors. It is the main reason for the communal lives most Chinese lead. There is very little privacy, though it is probably not wanted anyway. The Chinese live and work in stable communities. In most parts of China, everyone is registered as belonging to one employment group or another. The majority of workers belong to a work unit, a *danwei*, which they stay with their entire lives. It provides their medical benefits, retirement pensions, employment and social life. Most Chinese workers live in the work unit's housing compound with other workers from their own department. For example, negotiators in an import–export corporation all live in a particular area. Members of factories, from the boss down to the message boy, live within the factory compound. Within this compound they are observed and gossiped about day after day for their whole lives.

It is possible to argue that gossip and envy are more prevalent in China because of the group living, control by powerful people and constraints on personal independence. This makes Chinese people very cautious about putting forward opinions that will invite the criticism of their fellow workers. There is a common saying that 'It is better to make friends in a distant place than to make them with one's close neighbours.' But the close contact with other people is not seen as a bad thing. It provides a sense of security and is the natural style of Chinese society. You can see it in the rural villages, where the houses are clustered together rather than standing singly in the middle of huge farms as in the US, Canada and Australia. Chinese who travel overseas can very quickly feel threatened in a foreign environment, even if it is Hong Kong.

The importance of fitting in with the group was demonstrated in a study which looked at the motivations of Chinese and Canadian managers as they solved conflict situations. The Chinese negotiators were driven by a concern to maintain face within their own group, irrespective of the type of conflict, or whether the members of the opposing group were Chinese or Canadian (Tse *et al.* 1994). On an aggregate of scores showing how much the negotiator valued being well regarded by the others in his group, the Chinese scored 12.5 out of 15, and the Canadians 7.4.

## GOVERNMENT CONTROL OVER THE INDIVIDUAL

Until very recently the free labour market in China was very small. Even now, since the liberalisation of business, most school and university graduates are allocated jobs by the relevant labour bureau, unless they have powerful relatives who can organise special appointments for them. Most people cannot change jobs at will. They are moved around by the authorities. A German language specialist may be assigned as an agricultural research worker, and a science graduate as an auditor. The assignments often seem random and show the control individuals are subject to. Every time Chinese friends of mine were offered a better job than their current one, they were prevented from taking it because their work unit refused to release their personnel files.

A personnel file is kept on each employee. Cadres, who make up the majority of the negotiators westerners deal with, have the most comprehensive files of all. These contain a political history of the employee and his immediate family members, including information on family allegiances before the Communist Revolution in 1949. Work evaluations, criticisms, punishments, ideology, professional career and, most interestingly, assessments of people who have studied overseas, are all documented. Workers are not entitled to see the contents of their personnel file, but it is scrutinized by government and party leaders in the work unit as well as personnel department workers (Dutton 1992).

If workers change jobs without official approval, they lose

their entitlement to all the social benefits of the state—housing, medical care, schooling and retirement benefits. The personnel files are used in reviewing candidates for promotions and raises, and for determining who gets priority in housing (an area of critical shortage) and other social services. In the past they were also used to select targets for political campaigns (Walder 1986).

As the free labour market in the cities has expanded, a new department has been formed which looks after the personnel files of graduates seeking employment in joint ventures. After a certain time their personnel files are cancelled, and with that goes their entitlement to welfare benefits. From then on they must pay for these themselves. Whatever system operates, the state exerts strong control over people. Some western negotiators with long experience negotiating in the central bureaucracy have said that they try to protect young Chinese negotiators from being too enthusiastic, friendly and entrepreneurial for fear that their behaviour will lay them open to criticism from their own group.

The Chinese often just shrug their shoulders at government control over their lives. Before the Asian Games in Beijing in 1990, the government appropriated a certain number of weeks' wages from government employees to fund the Games. People complained, but their main response was to say that that is just the way life is.

## SOURCES OF CENSURE AND PUNISHMENT

If western business people make a wrong decision, they can resign and move to another job, another town, even another country. The Chinese do not have that freedom. If they make a mistake it will be common knowledge not only in their work environment but in the compound they live in. It will be recorded in their personnel file. And because they cannot move house or job without permission, they are likely to face the consequences of their decision for the rest of their lives.

During the Mao era, Chinese workers came under close surveillance in Chinese factories. Regular group meetings were presided over by a party member and notes taken on what each person said at the meetings. It was impossible for people not to participate in the discussions. The notes were submitted to the party branch. Because rewards were based on how much and how often a worker took part in discussion, workers tended to conform outwardly to the party line whether they privately agreed with it or not (Walder 1986).

Since many negotiators dealing with westerners are employed in the bureaucracy, they are used to this background of close scrutiny. It is not surprising, therefore, that Chinese negotiators look very carefully at proposals put forward by western companies. They minimise the possibility of failure by preferring to work with well-known, internationally recognised companies or ones with which they have had a long relationship.

The Swedish telecommunications company Ericsson installed telephones in Shanghai 100 years ago, and has contacts with former employees dating back to before the establishment of the People's Republic of China in 1949. These people still act as referees for the company. When the Chinese wanted to start producing cars in 1971, they favoured Toyota because after the Japanese surrender at the end of World War II, the Communists took over the Toyota trucks that had been left behind and used them in fighting the Nationalist Chinese in the Civil War (Harwitt 1992). Pacific Dunlop, an Australian company with a long track record in China and whose negotiation experience there is described in Chapter 11, has been approached again and again by the Chinese to develop new joint ventures with them.

Chinese negotiators protect themselves from criticism by staying very close to the detailed specifications. In approving foreign consultants, they favour those whose résumés show they are perfect matches for the project in question. In product purchase they explore every aspect of the product, not only with the sellers but with their competitors.

This meticulousness is also a natural development from their education. Mastering the characters of written Chinese demands attention to detail, precision and constant repetition. The same approach is evident in the way mathematics is taught in China. Every step to a solution will be painstakingly written down. A solution that takes up five lines in a western maths exercise will consume three pages in China. Copying from models is another widespread learning strategy. The fact that academic courses and exams are centrally set and controlled reinforces the Chinese habit of following guidelines very closely.

In his article 'The China trade: Making the deal', Lucian Pye contrasts Chinese attention to 'effort and skills' with the American emphasis on 'enthusiasm'. Arthur Lall (1968) also noted this characteristic in the negotiations he attended. He wrote:

> the importance of a detailed analysis of issues—a tactic that greatly influences negotiations— . . . is strongly stressed by Mao . . . This meticulous attention to concrete details has been adopted by the Chinese in the conduct of international negotiations . . . this helps them to gain an impressive mastery of the issues and situations that are under negotiation.

Another reason for the close scrutiny of proposals is that the Chinese are aware how open to exploitation they are in many areas new to them, and that there are foreign business people who will deliberately take advantage of their ignorance of foreign business and technology to sell them outdated or inappropriate equipment. A Chinese negotiator gave this assessment of the problem:

> The normal approach of foreign traders is to exaggerate the quality of their products and to raise the price very high. If the buyer is a layman, the seller will make big money . . . because we have closed our door and locked our country away for so long, we do not have experience in international trade. Thus we have had to pay some 'tuition fees'. (Huang 1985)

## HARSH PENALTIES

Chinese officials in earlier times were exiled to remote provinces for criticising the ruling elite, and whole families were executed when an official fell foul of the emperor and his supporters. Under the imperial criminal justice system, a criminal's family would share the punishment. One of the negotiators who concluded a treaty favourable to the British last century was sent a silk cord by the emperor to indicate that he had failed in his task and should take his own life. Nowadays penalties are still harsh, and they may still affect a person's whole family.

Fear of punishment for failure pushes individuals within the bureaucracy to cover themselves, in dealings with westerners, by demanding guarantees that go way beyond what is considered normal in the west—for example, guarantees as to the exact amount and quality of output of the equipment, regardless of the quality of materials fed into it, or the skill of those operating and repairing it (Breth and Jin, n.d.). They must be able to place the blame for failure anywhere but on themselves.

It is almost impossible for us to imagine how much power the group and powerful people have over the lives of Chinese people. The extremes of such power are related by Mao Zedong's doctor, Li Zhisui, in his book *The Private Life of Chairman Mao*. Kang Sheng was a Politburo member and security chief during the Mao Zedong era. His sister-in-law, Su Mei, committed suicide in 1967. While still alive she was admitted to Beijing hospital where the emergency-room doctor tried to save her life. After she died, he and 50 other workers at the hospital were arrested. The doctor was accused of putting poison in the stomach pump, and the others were accused of conspiring with the doctor. The doctor was sentenced to prison. Thirteen years later he was adjudged innocent and released.

How severe Chinese punishments can be is illustrated in a recent case at a joint-venture factory in northern China. A young girl whose father was the assistant general manager of the factory won a scholarship to America. Because her boyfriend wanted to go with her, but had no money and no exit permit, he secretly broke some high-tech machinery he worked with in the expectation that he would accompany the machinery to the US, where it would have to be repaired.

Meanwhile, the girl's brother embezzled $US130 000 for his sister to use in America. They were found out. The brother was sentenced to death. To avoid the disgrace he swallowed a smashed beer bottle. He survived and his death sentence was commuted to sixteen years' gaol. The boyfriend was sent to a reform camp for twelve years and her father was demoted. The girl proceeded to America on her scholarship.

With such draconian punishments, it is easy to understand why the Chinese typically ask, 'Why stick your head up? You'll probably only get it chopped off!' Caution would seem to be the best survival tool. It is unreasonable, given this background, to expect individual Chinese negotiators to promote foreign interests within their side. On the contrary, it is of utmost importance for them to conform to group goals. The consequences of failure explain, I believe, why the Chinese form a united front in negotiations and are hard to influence, and why they insist on going over and over every aspect of a proposal.

## RESPECT FOR PEOPLE IN POWER

Because individuals depend on the group for their welfare, they are bound in a dependent relationship to their leader. Because of this the Chinese are more respectful of authority than westerners (Pye 1985). People in power are always surrounded by a large, attentive group that goes out of its way to meet their needs.

Research confirms the Chinese respect for authority. Using data collected in a major survey, Hofstede (1980) ranked countries on a 100-point scale according to the degree to which subordinates accept authority. The US scored 40, Canada 39, Australia 36 and the UK 35. The small sample of Chinese managers in a similar survey scored 56 on the same scale (Lai and Lam 1986). In China and other high 'power-distance' societies, leaders make their decisions autocratically or paternalistically, and employees fear to disagree with them. They are used to taking orders and prefer it that way.

Many negotiators in China have noted that when high-level officials are involved, lower-level workers are deeply afraid of inconveniencing them in any way. It is very obvious that they have a strong need to comply with the wishes of those in authority. If the leader of the group or a high-ranking person has put his personal imprimatur on a decision, lower-level negotiators find it impossible to respond to western demands for changes because to do so would damage the more powerful person's reputation.

What happens when the Chinese, with their respect for their superiors, come face to face with the western respect for the law, regardless of the people involved? A group of international consultants were to work with the Chinese at a high level of the bureaucracy. The Chinese team came to the initial meeting in Washington with the terms of reference already decided. When the consultants looked at the document, they saw that in western terms it was a lawyer's nightmare, because the wording was open to many different interpretations. But because it had been devised and agreed to by the State Council, the Chinese negotiators refused to change anything. To agree would amount to an open criticism of the senior officials who had prepared the brief (and were not present at the negotiations), and a consequent loss of face for them. The Chinese negotiators saw the consultants' objections to the wording as a western cultural problem, not a Chinese one. When the western team insisted on a limited-liability clause, the Chinese said, 'We do not talk about the divorce before the marriage.' And when they wanted to introduce 'what if' clauses, the Chinese replied, 'We do not talk about the dowry before the son is born.'

For the first three days of discussion the consultants had trouble with their own lawyers and their accountant, who refused to accommodate the Chinese arguments about the terms of reference and insisted they be rewritten. The team leader called a break, and his team had 'a flaming row internally'. He consigned the hard-liners to the back room and forbade them to attend the meetings. Within two days the problem had been resolved in a way that was satisfactory to both sides.

The way out was to adopt letters of understanding which redefined the original terms of reference and provided for the situation to be reassessed a year later. This preserved the reputation of the Chinese officials. The western team also tried very hard to show the Chinese that they were not capitalist bogeymen trying to renege on commitments contained in the terms of reference.

They selected a certain issue and discussed it in open forum, keeping notes which they printed up and gave to the Chinese team for internal discussion over two days. After this they addressed another issue in open forum and so on. They made speeches in Chinese, invited the Chinese into their work group and spent time explaining things thoroughly so the Chinese understood the implications of everything. They emphasised trust and confidentiality. They were thus able to overcome two serious impediments to the project: the problem of the terms of reference which were identified with the high-ranking officials, and Chinese distrust. Negotiators who make the effort to understand the Chinese point of view do better than those who blunder in like barbarians.

## THE CONSTRAINTS OF BUREAUCRATIC LIFE

The majority of westerners in China represent private business. As a result they are generally used to a fairly direct relationship between action and profit. Few have had experience of working in a bureaucracy, and therefore cannot appreciate the constraints imposed on Chinese negotiators by the bureaucratic environment, where power is more commonly related to action (or non-action), than profit is.

Much western criticism of Chinese stalling in negotiations is simply a problem with the approval process. An individual manager has to negotiate with many different constituencies and gain official ratification before he is allowed to conclude an agreement with the western side.

An added complication is that these different agencies cannot cooperate easily, because they are integrated vertically rather than horizontally. As in most bureaucracies worldwide, the emphasis is on making action conform to the rules rather than on expediting it. The problem in China is that the bureaucracy plays a much greater part in business than in the west.

The Chinese themselves complain about bureaucrats, who commonly hold back decisions until the deadline. Chen and Faure (1995) report on a case where some Chinese managers had been negotiating with government bureaus for four months on their enterprise's profit target for the following year. They complained about the bureaus' representatives, saying, 'They don't need to manage a real business, so they can spend three days a week in meetings, but we can't.'

Chinese managers negotiating with westerners usually have to go through an enormously complicated network of bureaus for approvals. A classic case concerned the manager of a vegetable canning factory in Liaoning province who wanted to go into partnership with a US vegetable canning company. He had to convince at least sixteen different constituents, some of whom favoured other foreign partners, before he could give a clear answer to the American company. There were the suppliers of electricity, water, roads and other infrastructure; the local county officials and magistrate, who were more powerful people in the county than he; and three divisions of the controlling bureaucracy, the Cereals Oils and Foodstuffs Import Export Corporation (CEROF): one division in Shenyang, the provincial capital; one in Dalian, the nearby special development city; and the national CEROF in Beijing. In addition, the manager had to overcome jealousy between the Shenyang and Dalian CEROF divisions, which were vying for development funds, and which each supported an alternative foreign partner.

Most unfortunately for the manager, a year after he succeeded in getting the agreement signed and in securing a big investment by the Chinese side in new infrastructure and the vegetable planting scheme, the American company cancelled the agreement for reasons that had nothing to do with the success of the Chinese enterprise (Grow 1989).

This case offers a salutary lesson for western business people who complain about the slowness of their Chinese counterparts in concluding agreements.

In China, central and provincial government departments each demand compliance with their own regulations, and these, more often than not, are at odds with one another. Chinese bureaucracies pass responsibilities up the line. Departments which might be required to work together horizontally have no mutual relationship or loyalty. They are like fiefdoms, responsible to their own leaders.

Sometimes only a top leader can resolve bureaucratic wrangling. It is said that Deng Xiaoping had to be brought in to negotiate between the Ministry of Coal and the Ministry of Railways over getting coal from the Antaibao mines to the port for shipment (Shapiro *et al.* 1991). Respect for those at the top of the hierarchy at least means that when things get intractably bogged down, the mayor or some other powerful person generally has the power to get them going again. But such is the power of individual bureaucracies that they can stymie even the highest-ranking officials from other bureaucracies. In a case involving the Bank of China, western consultants had ordered, with official approval, special computer equipment, which was sitting in Hong Kong waiting for approval from the Chinese Customs. The bank's top officials could not move the Customs department in any reasonable time frame. In the end they were forced to buy computer equipment already in Beijing that was less efficient and more expensive.

## CONTRACTS AND THE LEGAL SYSTEM

China has a long tradition of rule by moral principles and of the interpretation of those principles by people in authority. It has never adopted the concept that individuals have a right to due process under law. Although the Economic Contract Law was enacted in 1982, there is considerable evidence that Chinese society at large is unconvinced by the legal principles and processes that this law enshrines (Zweig *et al.* 1987).

People with power override contracts if it suits them because they are used to exercising power without any legal restraints. People bringing contract disputes to the courts face strong social pressure to settle by mediation rather than to insist on their legal entitlements. In an investigation of cases brought to court under the rural contract system in Jiangpu county, in Jiangsu province, one of the most progressive and commercialised provinces in China, 73 per cent of cases were settled by mediation.

The legal system does not operate in a separate sphere from normal social life. Personal relationships and insider–outsider distinctions affect legal judgments just as much as those in any other area. This is demonstrated in the commentary on a judgment made by the People's Court which said, 'The parties concerned should be treated without discrimination regardless of *whether they are from another province or another county.*' The judgment underlines the particular strength of personal loyalties and the weakness of the legal system in the face of them.

There is also a different emphasis on the role of lawyers. Lawyers are employees of the state and are expected to serve party policy rather than to provide individuals with a fair hearing under the law.

Since the enactment of the first Sino-Foreign Equity Joint Venture Law in 1979, every year has seen a string of new laws and regulations as China attempts to bring its business environment into line with international practice. The lack of a well-understood, respected and integrated commercial legal framework places a burden on negotiators to solve many issues by negotiation rather than by reference to legislation.

One of the commonest complaints from western business people is the Chinese failure to fulfil the conditions agreed to and signed on in contracts. Stephen FitzGerald, a business consultant and former Australian ambassador to China, complained to the Chinese officials attending the 1986 Australia–China Senior Executive Forum that they tended to use rulings and approvals to induce foreigners to accept certain views and to sign agreements, then change them if they 'no longer suit the interests of the ruling or approving authority or the Chinese partner' (1986).

Many western companies have discovered that getting legal redress for failure to comply with a contract is just about impossible. This leaves only one way out if the company is to continue in China: negotiation.

In ordinary Chinese life one cannot help but notice the way people get around rules and regulations and do not see them as binding. They have a different view of what constitutes honesty and cheating from the western one. Some examples:

- 'My taxi left the Urumchi airport by a back way, over rutted paths and fields, so that it would avoid paying the parking fee' (Kristof and Wudunn 1994).

- A storekeeper in Shanghai explained in 1989 how the local business tax system worked: 'You have a room that faces onto the street. You manage to get some goods. Then you open a store. Period.' It appears that not much had changed since 1932, when the Shanghai city government could collect no more than one-sixth of the anticipated shopkeeper tax (Lu 1995).

- In 1949, when the Communists took over Tianjin, one of China's largest ports and manufacturing centres, most, if not all, Chinese businesses routinely evaded tax. They would keep two separate account books, an official one which declared only half of their profits, and a private one which documented the true picture. Believing that this was common business practice, the Communists imposed excessive taxes on foreign firms because they refused to believe foreign managers when they said they only had one book of accounts (Lieberthal 1980).

- The ultimate example of the flexibility of the Chinese in the way they handle rules and regulations is the traffic. Red lights do not bring cars to a halt as they do in the west.

The Chinese also commonly make up their own rules and regulations. A foreigner in a recent negotiation was told foreigners were required by law to pay $US5000 on every $US20 000 of a contract for 'contract approval procedures'. The Chinese negotiators were as pleased as the chicken seller in Chapter 1 when the foreigner paid up without argument. It is unwise ever to forget that this is a 'haggling society', in which it is legitimate to cheat outsiders.

# Part II

# CHINESE–WESTERN NEGOTIATIONS

# 3 Preparing to negotiate in China

The vast size of China, its particular social fabric, and its long history as an Asian power reinforce its people's preferred styles of negotiating. These are not temporary aberrations that will disappear once the west has waved a magic wand of law and commerce over China. This is shown in the analysis of the historical examples and case studies in this book.

Western negotiators who do not take account of the way the Chinese negotiate and the reasons behind it can find themselves in situations where the relationship between the two sides breaks down. The negotiators feel anxiety, frustration and anger, and their company loses money as well as opportunities. It therefore behoves western business people setting out for China to know what they will encounter.

This chapter, and the two that follow, provide the framework for negotiating in China, and give examples of successful strategies. Such knowledge will assist western negotiators to keep what is most necessary in China—a cool head—and provide an array of methods to help move the negotiation towards a mutually satisfactory outcome.

## BEFORE THE FORMAL NEGOTIATION

Inexperienced negotiators focus on the formal negotiation period itself and underestimate the period preceding it (Hawkins & Hudson 1991). The pre-negotiation period in fact has enormous influence on the attitude of the opposite negotiators and on the outcome.

The pre-negotiation relationship is a key issue in cross-cultural negotiations. In going to a foreign country to achieve a business goal, it is natural to focus on what you want the outcome to be, without paying attention to the fact that you may be entirely unknown to the locals, and have neither credibility nor a history of helping them which would have put them in your debt. In China, you are foreign-looking with your blond, red or brown hair, blue-green or grey eyes, large frame and unpredictable behaviour.

Under these circumstances, what obligation do the Chinese have to treat you favourably? What they owe to you is negligible in comparison with what they owe to the people they work with, their bosses and other business associates. Whatever they do with you is short-term compared with what they have done and will do within the Chinese business environment over a lifetime.

These are formidable hurdles, and generally are not even perceived by many negotiators. When the negotiation turns out to be difficult, they blame the Chinese instead of looking at the shortcomings of their own pre-negotiation preparation.

It is far better to allow time to get to know your Chinese associates, and give them time to get to know you, than to rush straight into the formal negotiation. You need to build up some degree of credibility by giving the Chinese time to relate to you as a person rather than as a foreign stereotype. The same goes for yourself. You must take time to find out about them. In the informal exchanges, you can learn about their attitude to the negotiation and, depending upon the time you devote to it, how possible it will be to achieve your own goals. It is an opportunity to influence their thinking about you and your business.

You can create this change in their perceptions in many different ways. Being able to solve some problems the Chinese have, and to do so without charge, is an advantage. You might help sort out computer problems or advise about international marketing. If you are seeking your opponents' recommendation to international funding bodies, you will make a better impression by sending a team of people rather than just one person. This shows how seriously you take the matter and that you have access to a wide range of expertise.

The overseas Chinese are, on the whole, accomplished at negotiating in China (particularly in the provinces adjacent to Hong Kong). They give high priority to developing good relations and gift-giving as a way of influencing the Chinese in their favour. Negotiation sessions are preceded and punctuated by banquets, and often by karaoke sessions. These are used to strengthen relationships among the Chinese, to build trust, flatter associates and provide an ambience in which to talk about the negotiation in a relaxed way. A recent study of Hong Kong business people negotiating in China confirmed the role relationships play in a successful negotiation. 'Good personal relationships' was the only factor rated of 'high importance' by the 168 business people who responded to the survey. Seventy-three per cent said they had social meetings in restaurants, and 68 per cent sent gifts to their Chinese counterparts (Leung and Yeung 1995).

Another indicator of the role banquets play in influencing opportunities in Chinese business life is that officials (who control approvals) spent more than 100 billion yuan in 1993 on food and drink, more than the central government spent on health, education, science and welfare combined (Pye 1995).

## RESPECT FOR HIERARCHY

People have power in China to interpret the laws and regulations and to facilitate or obstruct proposals. Nothing is as clear-cut as in the west. All Chinese have their networks and long-standing obligations. The networks are dominated by powerful people. Westerners, as newcomers into this society, need to be associated with people who can exert influence.

Negotiators supported by their governments, and people of influence in Chinese eyes, will find it easier to secure agreements. The managing director of the company should be involved in establishing relations with his opposite number in China. This is related to trust and having a good reputation. Making oneself known to local officials and members of the bureaucracy can put you on your way to building a network of support. Having an advocate for the company who is well respected by the Chinese and has authority will generate a more trusting attitude from the Chinese side and will be useful whenever there are hold-ups and difficulties.

This century, there have been many political and economic changes in China that have affected people's ability to meet western requirements for quality and timely delivery. They appreciate western business people who have stood by them through everything, such as the Pacific Dunlop executives you will meet later in this book. The Chinese will support you if you demonstrate your loyalty and emphasise mutual gains.

Looking after one's contacts is important in any country, but particularly in China, where it is very difficult to get anything done without the right personal connections. If you don't groom these contacts, people will politely nod and appear to agree, but nothing will happen.

Many negotiators going to China overlook the fact that in their home country the reason the pre-negotiation period looks after itself is that they are dealing with people they know, and with whom they have ongoing contact. Even if they are not in a long relationship, they share the same language and culture, and can ask other business associates to support them.

The same problem affects Chinese attempting to do business in the west. They find it very difficult to get western managers to take them seriously because they speak poor English, the name of their business may sound odd ('Sincere Company' or 'Righteous Inc.', for example) and the managers owe them nothing. Such experiences prompt many Chinese to use a multicultural go-between to give them credibility.

Westerners who have lived and worked in China take these things seriously. Many who have not had that experience fail to see that they can have any bearing on business success.

## INFORMATION SCARCITY

A negotiator's strength lies in knowing his own industry and knowing the situation of his counterpart. One of the major difficulties of negotiating in China is that both sides are operating in an information vacuum. There is almost no industry information available in China: few data bases, credit ratings or industry analyses. Because the Chinese have gone from a bicycle culture to high technology in a matter of twenty years, many managers and negotiators have a huge gap in their understanding of the context of foreign industry.

Foreigners also often lack a real appreciation of the difficulties that confront Chinese negotiators and managers. They sign a contract and expect that everything will work out well, without looking to see if the Chinese can actually fulfil the conditions they have agreed to.

By doing your own research on the ground, you will have a better understanding of the capacity of your negotiating partner.

Foreign competitors, your own country's representatives, and the Chinese ministries associated with your industry can all give valuable information. You will then have some idea of what basis your Chinese counterparts are negotiating on.

In this book I have sketched in something of recent political history and how it affects negotiations. I have also emphasised the importance of getting to know the relevant government officials, because the central government and its regulatory bodies have the capacity to restrain or assist business. It is also important to get to know local officials because they control the local area and its regulatory authorities as if they were part of a personal fiefdom. There is a constant struggle between the central government and the provincial and local governments, so the rules for business can be contradictory and, as with most rules in China, can be negotiated around or modified by the influence of powerful people.

## BRINGING DIFFERENT PERCEPTIONS TO THE NEGOTIATION

Chinese perceptions of the negotiation will be quite different from western ones. A westerner may see China as a technologically backward country which will welcome his product or expertise and accept it without question. He may regard China as an undeveloped country that will be easy to sell to because the people know so little about western technology. He probably also sees China as a huge market that will embrace his unique product once it has been introduced.

However, the Chinese see China as a powerful country with a huge market sought by every country in the world. They believe that it is only temporarily poor, largely because of Japanese and western exploitation during the 'century of humiliation'. The Chinese view may be that Japan and the west owe it support. In addition, these foreign corporations are rich and exploitative, and therefore to be distrusted.

When both sides believe that they are negotiating from strength, negotiations will be difficult. If this belief is underlaid with distrust, the negotiation will tend towards conflict. It is not an exaggeration to say that many Chinese–foreign negotiations are marked by a level of distrust similar to that between Arabs and Israelis in recent times.

Logic will not persuade the Chinese of your point of view,

because their history has provided a different frame of reference for them. It is important to check your assumptions about how they see this particular negotiation. Questioning the Chinese in informal situations before the real negotiations start will yield valuable information about their point of view which you will need to address in planning a negotiation strategy. Listening carefully to their principle and position statements once in negotiations will indicate what kind of objectives they have decided on. Once these are known, you should frame your case to meet them. Some objectives will be commercial, some will concern power and prestige.

## BEFORE LEAVING FOR CHINA

Because the Chinese side will rarely know about the qualities of your company and product, you must prepare documentation on your company's track record, and its product or service, in English and in Chinese. Colour photographs and visual material should tell your story just as much as the words do. This information is important, as it will be disseminated to all the people behind the scenes who have input into the conduct of the negotiation and the decision process.

Before leaving for China you should try to establish who you will be negotiating with. You should also inform the Chinese of your position in the company, particularly if you are the managing director, to encourage them to put in a negotiator with as high a position as possible. The reason for this is that the Chinese often use different levels of negotiating teams, and you could find yourself starting with the junior teams, then having to work your way up. Not only does this take a very long time, but it wears down your resolve to stick by your own interests.

You should also let the Chinese know how long you intend to stay. If in your own mind you have five days, you should tell them you have only four days. This will set a time limit, since the Chinese always drag out discussions and only begin to negotiate in earnest close to the deadline.

A clear strategy, worked out on your side before the negotiations, should include the rules of the negotiation, the responsibilities of team members, multiple issues which could be brought in to widen the scope of the negotiation, multiple concessions and their costs, a range of positions between the aspiration point and satisfaction, as well as 'crunch points' which cannot be compromised. You must decide on how much technical information to give without losing control over the intellectual property of your product or process. This is precisely the information the Chinese will push to get so they can copy your product for free.

You should also have some items which can be given to the Chinese when they are insisting on a concession. Making the gesture is often more important than the substance of the item.

## STARTING THE NEGOTIATION

### The room

It is a surprise for westerners to find that most Chinese negotiation rooms have no central table. Instead there are a number of couches down both sides and at the end. In front of each couch is a low table with thermos flasks full of hot water so the Chinese can make tea. While they negotiate, they eat fruit, probably smoke heavily and talk among themselves. If they are representing different groups, the members of each group will cluster around their own couch and table. Many westerners feel a lack of control in these surroundings because there are so many people and they all talk together without any regard for the discussion the western negotiator is having with individuals.

Westerners usually want to identify the decision maker, even though it is not through one decision maker that most decisions are made in China, because decisions are usually group decisions. Even managers with the power to make decisions disguise this fact by working through a committee meeting. Most of the power brokers will not be present at the negotiations. Trying to identify who in the group is important and influential and who is not, is not a useful exercise as it is peripheral to the Chinese decision-making process.

The negotiators dress in a wide variety of styles: they do not all wear a suit. They may have jumpers on, or shirts hanging out over their trousers, and they treat everyone with equal courtesy. People wander in and out of the room without any introduction or explanation of who they are and what they are doing there. Someone might come in, and all the Chinese will stop the negotiations to talk to him. They will treat him as if he is some very important person coming in to see how the negotiation is going. He is just as likely to be the driver wanting to know when they will be stopping for lunch.

The best strategy is not to be fazed by the differences, to realise that everyone has input into the decision, and to focus on the person you are talking to rather than on what is happening in other parts of the room.

Because of the number of parties usually involved in a negotiation in China, it is wise to negotiate how the negotiation itself will proceed before the substantial negotiation begins. This preliminary agreement could cover who will speak for the Chinese side and coordinate its numerous parties. It will also include a time line and sequence of issues. This is easier said than done but worth the effort!

## The haggling process

The most notable feature of a Chinese negotiation is the haggling process. It is impossible to go straight to the bottom line, or to set out your position and expect the Chinese to accept it as it stands. As I showed in the marketplace examples in Chapter 1, the Chinese argue about everything step by step and in immense detail. They always engage in give and take.

Two things make haggling necessary. One is the ethics the Chinese apply to dealing with strangers. Cheating is OK, so the haggling process is based on the assumption that there is an element of dishonesty in the initial proposal. The other is the need to preserve face. Frankness and going straight to the point can endanger the other person's face because you do not know what needs they have lurking in the background. These can only be uncovered bit by bit. Everyone must look as if he is a skilled negotiator because public esteem is very important to the Chinese. So they prefer to cover every concession by gaining a counter-concession.

Issues must be negotiated around step by step, in small increments. A foreign negotiator must start with an ambit claim and create areas for concession making. This requires the foreign side to inflate costs and build in concessions so that there is an area for negotiation. Cost should be the last item discussed. If you talk about money first up, you will lose the cooperative atmosphere. Talk about clauses, products, and benefits one by one.

The Chinese have a tendency to individualistic bargaining.

The dominant motive is to maximise their own gain without considering the results for the other side (Druckman 1973). This contrasts with the 'win-win' cooperative negotiation model presented by Fisher and Ury in their best-seller *Getting to Yes* (1981) and which reflects American preferences for a friendly atmosphere in negotiations. Because the Chinese are very cautious about westerners taking their resources and their money and then going away, you have to show your sincerity and commitment. You need to emphasise your contribution. You cannot say, 'You give everything and I will take everything.'

The demands the Chinese make do not always give a clear indication of what they really want. It is always necessary to look for what will satisfy the need behind a demand, while not necessarily giving what is demanded. If the Chinese objective is to save money and they complain, as the geology officials did in Chapter 1, about the expensive accommodation and want the interpreter sacked, you may be able to satisfy them by providing cheaper accommodation without firing the interpreter. Everything can be negotiated, so it is unwise to take 'no' for an answer, or to accept everything as it is put to you.

## The atmosphere

### Face

There are many ways to overcome the potential for conflict caused by Chinese sensitivity to face. It is vital to show genuine respect. Body language will betray disrespect, as the Chinese say, 'like paper wrapping fire'. Responding sensitively to the hidden agendas, such as by boosting a negotiator's self-esteem, being friendly and listening carefully, going behind the scenes on touchy issues to gather information about the feelings of the other side and the personalities involved, is an essential strategy in China.

The way in which a reply is given is important. If a negotiator, unable to get the price he wants, says, 'Well, it's cheaper in Egypt, we'll go there,' he will hurt the pride of the Chinese and turn them against him. It is better to try to find out why they will not agree to your price, or find out other things that could be traded. Using threats is counterproductive. In China, more than anywhere else in the world, one must beware of arrogance.

Never allow yourself to lose your temper. You need to show self-control and quiet strength. This will eventually bring respect.

Act as if this were the beginning of a long relationship which you are very concerned to start off on a sound footing. Precedents have unusual power in China, not only in the conduct of negotiations but in the management of workers and staff. Whatever precedent you set you will have to follow, because it will be almost impossible to change the initial impression later.

Protocol must be observed. In the working negotiations, you can argue back and forth, let your hair down and generally do what you must to support your own position. However, when the top-level people come for signing or to give their imprimatur, that is the time for restraint and formal polite behaviour, no matter what you might be feeling.

## The adversarial atmosphere

Chinese negotiators see it as quite normal to use a cold, attacking approach with people who are not their intimates. This is a long way from the western preference for formally pleasant exchanges. You should not take this unsympathetic style at face value, as it is not necessarily an attack on you as an individual or an indication of what the Chinese side really thinks about the negotiation.

The Chinese are naturally a noisy and quarrelsome race, who get noisier as you move south. To give you some idea of how their argumentativeness is no more than a style of communication, I draw on an amusing story from CP FitzGerald.

He was travelling by foot in inland China in the 1930s. The whole area was infested by bandits, so the local warlord's army was providing protection for himself and his travelling companions, a group of Chinese merchants. One part of their journey took them through a high, narrow mountain pass. They stopped at the pass to have lunch. After lunch, the colonel and his soldiers placed a table from the gatehouse across the gateway, leaving only a narrow passage. This was guarded by the soldiers. Every person in the convoy had to pay as he passed through the gateway, and they all bargained about the price. It took so long that FitzGerald feared night would fall before they could reach the next walled town and they would be shut out.

They did reach the town in time, and the colonel and his major took the room next to FitzGerald's. Through the flimsy wall he could hear them dividing up the protection money they had squeezed out of the merchants at the pass. They argued, shouted, swore, cursed and banged their fists on the table.

FitzGerald was terrified that at any moment a fight would break out and bullets would come flying through the thin partition. After an hour the arguing suddenly stopped, and the two men exchanged friendly words as they parted for the night. FitzGerald commented, 'They had struck their bargain and all was well. The noise and fury were just part of the discussion process.'

The Chinese have changed very little. In a negotiation, a noisy argument may start up in one of the negotiating groups that makes you think, 'Oh no, a problem in the contract!'. In fact, it will probably turn out to be nothing more than a minor disagreement among members of the group. Everyone wants to express his opinion, and they shout over the top of one another so they can be heard.

In *The Ugly Chinaman*, a most amusing book read widely throughout the Chinese diaspora, the author, Bo Yang, satirises Chinese loudness and argumentativeness. He tells the story of two Chinese men chatting together on a New York pavement. A passing American calls the police to break up what he thinks is an argument. When the policeman intervenes, they tell him they were only whispering. It may be this natural tendency to be disputatious that accounts for a Chinese negotiation handbook's instruction to 'discuss all the key issues but avoid arguing without any reason for it'!

Although the Chinese prefer to maintain harmonious relations, there are certain circumstances in which negotiators may adopt an antagonistic attitude towards foreigners, using invective and insult. There is an increasing trend for negotiators to be young, ambitious and pushy. The other group that tends to be antagonistic is middle-aged managers and Party people, who have been nurtured on the strident anti-foreignism of the Maoist period from 1949 to 1972. They very likely also missed out on an education, so they lack technical skills and knowledge. Their positions are therefore vulnerable to the younger, better-educated technocrats who are pushing up into middle management. They also have had no impartial information about the west because of the blackout on foreign news and publications during most of their lives.

Dealing with this older group requires patience and forbearance. If you respond with an equally aggressive style, you will only reinforce their negative view of westerners. Handle their attacks politely, but without giving in. This group may be particularly anxious about having their faults exposed by westerners. The best approach is to listen to their point of view and build up an atmosphere of trust so they become willing to give you information without fear that it will be used to one-up them or to undermine their authority.

The negotiators on the Chinese side comprise both the groups present in the room and other groups outside it. This reinforces their propensity to be tough and unmoving, as does the attitude that outsiders should be treated differently from insiders—that is, coldly and unsympathetically. Large teams increase this tendency. The larger the teams, the more likely it is that there will be an adversarial atmosphere.

If western negotiators do not take control in such circumstances, feelings between the teams may become bitter and punitive. In very bad cases, punishing or defeating the other side becomes more important than the substantive issues of the negotiation. Time will drag out in unending debate and no agreement will be reached.

Using banquets, travelling to different places, singing in the karaoke bar and other opportunities for informal socialising break down the exclusionary barriers the Chinese erect around their team, and the us-vs.-them mentality. Inviting individuals or a small group of negotiators to eat with you in the hotel also gives both sides the opportunity to talk more frankly, to move beyond the stereotyping that occurs between people from different cultures, and to gather information about attitudes and objectives.

Those negotiators who begin your company's contact with China should always be the ones assigned to further contacts and negotiations. The Chinese put their trust in individuals rather than in institutions, and changing negotiators undermines this trust.

# 4 The formal negotiation

There are all kinds of business negotiations: for setting up joint ventures, licensing technology, developing natural resources, undertaking infrastructure provision, organising educational and governmental exchanges, buying and selling in import–export, and managing contractors and workers. The first section of this chapter relates specifically to contract negotiations. Techniques for general-management and other less structured negotiations will be given later.

Formal contract negotiations with the Chinese follow a set pattern:

- a pleasant, general *opening phase*
- a penetrating and drawn-out *technical discussion*
- a *terms of contract discussion* involving challenges on technicalities
- a *contract signing* immediately preceded by demands for new concessions, followed by
- the ongoing *post-contract negotiation*.

## THE OPENING PHASE

The beginning of any negotiation, anywhere in the world, is a period during which it is possible to influence the other side. Each side is measuring its own goals and expectations against its opponent's position. The Chinese use this opening phase to full advantage.

Sometimes they will insist that the western side put its case first. At other times they will start with their position. This probably depends on how clear they are about what they want. Some western negotiators feel that starting first gives them an advantage in leading the discussion where they want it to go. Others feel that going first disadvantages them, as the Chinese are able to use the information thus gained to their benefit.

In the opening phase, the Chinese insist on principles they claim are not negotiable, such as 'arbitration must be done in Beijing' or 'delivery time must be 20 months and no less'. They do this in an effort to influence the expectations of their opponents. In fact, they will often trade these principles later in the negotiation to get concessions.

Their principles are actually no more than demands which have been agreed upon by the team, and which serve to structure the negotiation so that one side gets its needs met without having to take into account the needs of the other side. The way the Chinese use principles and 'regulations' to force their opponents to fit in with their plans will be discussed in more detail in Chapter 5.

In the opening phase, the Chinese also require agreement to a Letter of Intent which outlines the major provisions of the future contract agreement. The Chinese team has generally worked hard on this well before the first meeting with the foreign team, and will naturally have devised it to meet their own goals. It is an important document because it represents the basis on which the Chinese controlling authorities permit the negotiating party to proceed with contract negotiations.

The wording may be vague, misleading western negotiators into assuming the Letter of Intent is just a high-sounding expression of the general intention of the negotiating parties. But foreign negotiators should think carefully through all its implications, in the process ensuring that it covers items important to their goals, such as tax provisions. It may be difficult, once the Letter of Intent has been signed, to put other items into the final contract, because this will involve extensive negotiations with the controlling authorities.

A notable feature of the opening phase is that the Chinese aim high. This is due in part to the horse-trading or marketplace haggling tradition, in which one starts the bargaining with an ambit claim that is pitched high and from which one expects to be beaten down. It is often very hard to move the Chinese from their opening position. The Chinese tradition is to ask for far more than they expect to get. Westerners new to China may believe that what the Chinese ask for is necessary. This is very far from the truth.

The other reason for the high initial claim is that it has been determined by committee, and a feature of committees is that members vie with one another for higher and higher goals. The committee approach to negotiations stems from the collectivism of Chinese society. And once the committee has determined the goals, the up-front negotiators will stick by them very strongly. To concede would be face-losing for individuals, showing them up before their fellow committee members and the superior who approved the goals.

When I was discussing this feature of Chinese negotiations with a foreign engineering marketer, he told me that as a young engineer he and his fellow recruits were instructed by their boss to go and sell some equipment at no less than a certain price. Being young and very much under the boss's control, they dared not do other than instructed, and generally succeeded in getting a high price for the equipment.

The committee system and the power of superiors in the Chinese system gives Chinese negotiating teams the same kind of strength. A western mining engineer summed up how he and his fellow negotiators felt facing the strength of Chinese negotiating teams: 'Some guys in our team had really had it. They would have agreed to anything just to go home.' You can see the negotiating advantage this kind of feeling gives to the Chinese.

Unnaturally high aspiration points are also a result of Chinese negotiators' not knowing the real costs of what they are buying. They have little experience of the costs of R&D, of achieving high quality or of maintenance. They do not understand that individual items of machinery may be useless without the whole system, or that software is an essential complement to hardware in computer systems. There is a gap between theory and practice. Most Chinese educated in technical institutes are very strong on theory but not necessarily on practice. They will demand a huge number of spare parts because they lack confidence that they can maintain the machinery. Such shortcomings lead them to make demands which are often out of touch with costs.

## THE TECHNICAL DISCUSSION PHASE

This can take days, weeks and months. Negotiating in China is a slow process. The time it takes does not seem to matter at all to the Chinese. World Bank officials have calculated that what takes half a day to be resolved in the west takes three days in China.

It is true that stalling is used to exploit foreign impatience. It is one of the games the Chinese play because they know westerners are in a hurry. Time can be filled with irrelevant questions, visits to tourist sights and banquets. But on closer examination I believe that the main reason for what we consider to be time wasting is not guile but simply the way the Chinese system works.

### Time is not money

Until very recently, time had no money value in China. The economy was centrally planned and capitalist business practices were unknown. So the Chinese are not used to the speed of western business. At times they suffer because of this if the market moves quickly or if they are investing in overseas industry, because the opportunities are snapped up by more flexible investors, such as the overseas Chinese.

### Establishing a precedent

If what you want to do is new to China, regulations regarding it may not exist, and you may encounter disbelief that your method is necessary. If you cannot get a particular bureau to agree with you, you may have to talk to others: MOFTEC, power, coal, textiles, transportation, even the State Council. If yours is really an important project the Chinese may have to put through special legislation, which requires approval from the State Council.

### Bureaucratic delay

The attitude of the bureaucracy is an important factor in delays. Apart from being hampered by an attitude that is often anti-business—as in many bureaucracies worldwide—the approval process in China requires everyone in the department assigned to the negotiation to agree. The internal discussions this necessitates are meticulous and slow.

Most decisions also involve many different sections of the bureaucracy. In each case the decision will be made only after consensus is achieved. Building consensus among so many different groups is time consuming. Each department jealously guards its own turf. After a consensus is reached, the responsible person has to make the final decision. Because the Chinese push decisions upward rather than making them at a middle-managerial level, top decision makers are overburdened with work. This adds to the delays.

The majority of Chinese working in government organisations are risk-averse. They prefer to keep their heads down. They get their pay anyway, and it is generally low. Although under the new changes in management structures, the department director can make a decision, he takes great care to insure himself against a future difficulty or dispute. To him it is well worth taking as much time as he needs to go meticulously through the documentation.

Only if everybody agrees will a decision be made. Very few Chinese managers are prepared to bypass the hierarchy, unlike in the west, where managers have the authority to make decisions based on their own assessment of the situation. A study of managers' attitudes found that in China only 34 per cent were willing to bypass the hierarchy, compared with 65 per cent in the UK and 82 per cent in the US (Lai and Lam 1986).

All these reasons account for the common Chinese response that they will have to refer a sticky issue to 'some other person', or 'the director', or just 'back'. Who the matter is being referred back to is rarely disclosed. At this point, many experienced negotiators try to push the decision making along by setting time limits or by leaving China (but stating when they will return to continue the negotiation).

For the foreign negotiator, getting bureaucratic approval takes many meetings, especially if the Chinese are unfamiliar with him or his product or service. The number and length of these meetings, as well as their repetitiveness, creates a tremendous level of frustration for western business people used to fast, independent and profit-driven decision making.

## Lack of approval to conclude the contract

If the Chinese side is not able to decide on things you can decide on, they may not have approval to conclude the contract. It is possible to deduce this from the way the negotiation is going, but they will not necessarily tell you directly that they have a problem lest they lose face. They may be keen to get your equipment and be trying to find ways to get permission to buy it, but time will be passing without any result because they are too embarrassed to tell you they have no authority to purchase.

You must find out whether or not the Chinese team has approval, otherwise the negotiations will be fruitless. You can check this with the authorities. Since the opening of China to foreign investment, a great deal of wishful thinking has been going on. Many Chinese groups have great plans but no capital to realise them—and no approval either, because their project is not a priority for the authorities. Many western groups have been caught up in this syndrome to their cost.

## Information snags

A common reason for slowness in negotiations is that China has very poor information-gathering systems and communications infrastructure. It is no exaggeration to say that even getting paper to write on is difficult in China. Although communications systems are improving all the time, particularly in the eastern coastal regions, they are almost nonexistent in many areas. It may take time for a Chinese negotiating team to get information relevant to the negotiations.

## Coordination problems

Rarely does a negotiation in China take place with only one entity on the Chinese side. A given Chinese negotiator will represent a number of parties, each with its own agenda which he and his team must satisfy. Negotiations are slowed down while behind the scenes the parties negotiate, both among themselves and internally, on how to make the negotiation serve their respective interests. It is often almost impossible to do anything about such hold-ups. Go-betweens can help by trying to discover what issue or person is causing the problem.

These inter-party relationships complicate negotiations and are hidden from the foreign negotiator. He will believe that there is no hope of agreement, then, quite suddenly, after months or even years of no apparent progress, a decision will be made which accepts his point of view. This may happen when the criteria imposed by one of the parties is finally met by approval from a trusted foreign expert, or by additional information that has only just come to light.

There are times when the Chinese team itself is not unified about a decision. It is not very obviously disunited, but it is clearly not going in a single direction. You can judge this by the team members' language. The chief negotiator may say, 'This is our position, this is what we want in the wording . . .' and his colleague will support him, but not very clearly. He will say something a little bit off the track. You can sense that he is not very happy and does not agree with the chief negotiator, but he expresses his disagreement subtly for fear of offending his superior. Even though Chinese teams always try to present a united front, an experienced negotiator can tell when their members disagree with one another by listening, watching and talking behind the scenes.

## A hidden message

Some delays may occur because the Chinese are reluctant to give a clear 'no', or because they have made a mistake or do not understand the economics of the situation. In a joint-venture negotiation, the people sent to gather information may not comprehend it but may be too embarrassed to say so. The department head may then make a wrong decision based on that information, they will drag out the negotiations with nothing to offer, and so it goes on until the western partner gets tired of it. This kind of scenario is not caused by malice, but just by the fact that the Chinese do not come from a profit-making environment.

## Government priorities

If the project is not a priority for the Chinese government, it can get bogged down. China's stage of development may therefore influence the negotiation, so you must understand which industries are welcome. There are national, provincial and local plans, and projects in line with these plans experience less delay.

## The language issue: interpreters and translations

In a recent survey, 77 per cent of Australian executives in China said a knowledge of the Chinese language was of medium to great importance when operating there (Blackman 1995). The survey also revealed that only 3 per cent of executives could speak Chinese. For the overwhelming majority of western negotiators, everything said by both sides has to go through an interpreter.

Even negotiators who speak the same language can have misunderstandings. When negotiations are taking place in two languages and with large negotiating teams on both sides, the risk is very much greater. It is enormously time-consuming for each side to put its ideas across and make them understood by everyone on the other side. The interpreter becomes the linchpin of the negotiation. He may translate the words one by one but not be able to put them into context. He may translate whole sentences but not grasp their true meanings, their subtext. The discussion may be very technical, and since many interpreters have studied only language, they have problems with specialised language and the ideas behind it.

If the translator has a background in electronic engineering and the negotiation involves chemical engineering, he may not understand the importance of certain issues, why particular points are stressed, or why a particular clause must be in the contract. Nuances of phrasing may also be lost. A proposal may have been carefully phrased to make it softer and more acceptable to the Chinese listener, with expressions such as, 'let us see how it works if we . . .', 'I see what your problem is, but . . .', 'suppose we were to . . .' and 'so you're prepared to . . .' These subtleties are not always conveyed in translation, and so clues to a desire for agreement are missed and the proposal comes across as an aggressive-sounding demand.

A simple case illustrates how fine a line there is between understanding and misunderstanding a speaker's intention. After a week showing a foreign executive around various shopping centres, the Chinese interpreter came to the agent accompanying the executive and, most upset, said, 'I cannot please Mr X. He doubts everything I tell him.' Apparently Mr X's habit was to reply to anything he was told with 'Is that so?' (meaning 'That's interesting.'). The interpreter, not being used to colloquial English, thought Mr X was expressing disbelief and had no interest in pursuing business in China. In fact his real thoughts were just the opposite, and he was saying to himself, 'If only I could get the chance to put a few supermarkets in here!'

The fragile relationship between ideas, language and understanding accounts for many a raging debate on the Chinese side after a western negotiator has said only one sentence in English. Aware of the lack of complete equivalence between two languages, the Chinese have mandated that only the Chinese-language version of a contract is valid in any dispute arbitrated in China.

It takes time, perseverence, observation and sensitivity to know how well an interpreter is representing both you and the Chinese negotiators. To minimise the risk of misunderstanding, it is advisable to speak in short, straightforward sentences, with regular pauses between them. Asking questions will enable you to check on how accurate the interpretation has been and how far the Chinese side has understood what you are trying to convey. A translated negotiation can be like a game of 'Chinese whispers', where the final understanding is quite different from the original message.

Because even English-speaking Chinese are often struggling with the language, they can be slow to put forward their point of view or to give information. Western negotiators can make the fatal mistake of thinking this means they are dull or stupid, when the problem is merely language.

The more written and visual information you have, the easier it will be for the interpreter and the other side to understand what you are talking about. Providing photographs or a video is infinitely better than relying only on words. If you put down some printed information which has English on one side and Chinese on the other, you will note that even English-speaking Chinese turn straight to the Chinese side. This is perfectly natural: one's mother tongue goes deep.

There are many excellent interpreters in China but nowhere near enough to go around. So a foreign negotiator will often be in the hands of a high-school graduate or an interpreter who is studying the language in college and has never had experience of the language as it is really spoken. He may be totally unfamiliar with your product, and he may lean heavily to the Chinese side and fail to pass on vital information to you. He may give the wrong feeling or tone to your words, making you sound aggressive and arrogant. Whatever the case, you need to pay great attention to his competence.

During negotiation sessions you must take control and insist that everything be interpreted. You will also have to brief your interpreter very thoroughly before negotiation sessions and build a rapport based on trust and respect. Face will play a part in how honest the interpreter is with you about his competence in English, so be sympathetic and tread gently.

## A different approach to time

Chinese attitudes are summed up in the comment, 'What's a month in 4000 years of history?'

## An appetite for detail

Another striking feature of negotiations in China is the repetitive questioning and the demand for explanations. Members of the Chinese team may be as exacting as surgeons in probing for information from the western side. They are supported by a lot of people who have the time to check every detail of what is said in the negotiation and compare it with information from competitor companies. Checking and rechecking what has been said, and challenging the authority of the foreign negotiator on what he said previously, is normal procedure. Chinese teams are advised to 'ask questions . . . clear all doubts, take a clear-cut stand. We have to get an answer for every single question in case disputes are caused over trifles later' (Zhang 1993).

Many western business people are bringing new technologies to China. This involves them in a great deal of explanation. The Chinese may ask why the technologies are necessary; what is the point of using them. This can be very frustrating for foreign negotiators.

You have to do more work in negotiating with the Chinese than with people of most other nationalities. They ask not only for explanations and justifications but for many supporting documents, because they have to go back and report to their supervisors.

You must take time to explain the rationale behind costs very clearly. If you can support your explanation with documentary evidence it will be more convincing. Because of China's present technology level, it is often an uphill battle to convince the Chinese that disputed costs or clauses are actually reasonable. The gap is so great that they may expect to buy a 2400 megawatt power station which costs $250 million for $80 million, because their only yardstick is the 6 megawatt power station they have already. Concepts such as quality guarantees, management by objectives, competitive recruitment and performance remuneration have to be explained in great detail and justified. Then time must be allowed for the Chinese to discuss and accept the new ideas.

Rojot (1991) stresses the need for negotiators to allow time for new information to be considered and assimilated. This is particularly true in China. He also emphasises that concrete facts are more persuasive than abstract information and reasoning, because the other party can grasp them more easily.

Another driving force behind Chinese negotiators' endless questioning and demands for documents and explanations is that they want to catch up with the west, and one way to do so is by copying technology. They will ask for printed material they think will help them do this in future, and insist that without it no agreement can be reached. A foreign negotiator has to decide how much information he will give them access to. There are many cases where the Chinese have been totally honourable, but just as many where they have used such information to make their own products and cut out the foreign supplier. In this they are emulating the way the Japanese acquired western technology after the Second World War.

Handling questioning is a very important skill when negotiating in China. It takes good judgment and emotional control. It is important to be consistent. The Chinese can cross-check what you say very quickly. If you are dishonest or inconsistent, it will damage your credibility. If you give them a false bottom line, they will tell you where it is wrong. They will show you a contract with some other company to prove it to you. They will also research your reputation.

How well you handle questioning by the Chinese will influence their judgments about you as a desirable business partner. Michael Pointer paid attention to answering questions correctly. Those he could not answer he told the Chinese he would research when he returned home. He did this, was invited back to China, and thus began a very successful business partnership of more than 20 years. There is a personality type that handles the Chinese questioning and explanation demands well. It has been said of one successful negotiator, George Preston, that he is successful in China because he 'is patient and has a good nature'. The contrast can be draw between the 'good nature' of Preston and the type who gets angry and impatient.

The Chinese test your commitment through their questions and demands. They find out whether you really want the contract. They might give you the contract if they know that you have done a lot of work. They will say, 'I know you have worked very hard . . .' I discussed the Chinese admiration for persistence and hard work in Chapter 1, in the story about the man who moved the mountain. Showing your capacity for sticking with things can influence the Chinese in your favour. But be careful. They may try to get you to do a great deal of unnecessary work to meet some hidden agenda of their own. Such a distinction can, however, only be made at the time.

The more important the negotiation, the more scrutiny the Chinese will give to each point. They will test the limits at every stage until you say, 'No! That is the best I can do! That's it!' Then they will drop the matter and move on. Later they will come back to the issue again. On each item they will ask for more than you are offering, squeezing first on technical features and then on price. This happens over and over again.

In this phase, concessions are exchanged. The Chinese expect returns on any concessions they make. This requires a thorough analysis of concessions and their values by the western side, which should ask for matching concessions when it makes any. At the end of the technical discussion the Chinese will discuss the price. Only if you come to an agreement on price will they start negotiating the terms of the contract.

## THE TERMS OF CONTRACT DISCUSSION PHASE

The Chinese, unlike most other nationalities, take none of the standard international contract terms for granted, so contract discussion is dominated by technicalities. The Chinese often do not understand standard commercial practice because western contract law is fairly new to China.

The principle that arbitration of a contract must be in a third country would be accepted without dispute in the west. The Chinese, however, will insist that arbitration be in Beijing. A recent handbook instructed Chinese negotiators to 'make the arbitration in China, and only if there is no choice, make it in a third country' (Zhang 1993).

Since arbitration is a way of settling a dispute as a last resort, it should be done by a neutral party in a third country. If it is done in Beijing, the foreign company risks being disadvantaged. The Chinese will say, 'China is a big country and we have an arbitration commission in Beijing.' They will make it a political issue, saying, 'It will be an honour to have the arbitration in

Beijing,' and citing the difficulties they will have if they go abroad in terms of the language barrier and the problem of travelling overseas.

This 'China-centredness', insisting everything be done the Chinese way and making you seem unreasonable if you object, shows through at all stages of negotiation, and is clearly the reason for many of the influence strategies that the Chinese use. China has been cut off from international trade for a long time, and it is so big in any case that negotiators are genuinely convinced the Chinese way is the best. Their China-centredness is reinforced by the fear that foreigners will cheat them.

During contract discussions they will look at all the clauses put into the contract by the western side and put in their own counter-clauses, which can lead to a spiral of tit for tat. For example, if the foreign company secures a clause stating that delays in payment to it will incur interest, the Chinese may want a counter-clause saying that if the foreign workers are late for work, the Chinese will deduct money from the total payment.

This tit-for-tat attitude stems from the division between in groups and out groups. Mao used it in his confrontations with the US. Being of peasant origin, he was used to the idea of vendettas between clans, but western negotiators can be taken by surprise when a tit-for-tat spiral begins. This is when they must consider whether to modify their normal legal-centred business thinking and drop the western need to cover for every possible failure in the contract. This does not mean that the contract should be downplayed, only that the really important things must be signalled clearly and the 'what if' clauses downplayed.

## THE CONTRACT SIGNING PHASE

When the final version of the contract is presented for signing, the Chinese may well have changed some terms already agreed to, or added some of their own—without consultation, and without pointing them out. This is common practice among the Chinese themselves. A Chinese negotiator recently advised his own countrymen when negotiating with one another to check the language again and again before signing, particularly if the contract had been drafted by the other side. This would prevent the negotiator from 'falling into the "trap" that the opposition have smartly set up' (Li 1989).

As a long-time foreign trader with China explains, trap-laying is a common occurrence, and foreign negotiators need to be on the look-out for it: 'You talk for five days about a deal and you agree about the specification, shipping terms and price. When you come back the next day to sign the contract, they produce a piece of paper that has something on it that you never, ever discussed. It will be something right out of the blue, such as, "The goods must be wrapped in gold-plated plastic" or "You agree to an extra 20 per cent on the price," something as absurd as that. You've got to start all over again. And that will go on for hours and hours. It happens regularly. I expect it.'

It is wise for westerners to check the contract as diligently as the Chinese are advised to do, and not be lulled or rushed into believing that everything is all right. Otherwise you could be in for a nasty shock when you get home! This is yet another demonstration of the influence of in group–out group thinking, by which the Chinese concentrate on maximising the benefits for their own group, without much regard for the losses to be incurred by the outside group. This is a practical case of the 'in group–out group ethics' we discussed in chapter 1.

It is also usual for them to come back right on the deadline wanting changes. Clearly spelling out the consequences the Chinese side will face if they don't close the deal is an effective way to stop them dragging out their negotiations indefinitely. But the negotiator must mean what he says. Bjorn Andersson, a telecommunications engineer, has used the threat of 'ultimate consequences' many times in such situations. On one occasion he had finished the contract negotiation on supplying telecommunications equipment to a southern province when a woman official from Beijing suddenly joined the team. She demanded changes to the agreed-upon wording that Andersson could see no good reason for. He guessed that she was doing it to impress everybody with her power. The negotiation went on for two hours. Andersson could see that they were getting nowhere, so he started to close up his books and slam one on top of another. He said 'Right. I am going to phone the [European] funding agencies and tell them you are changing the contract, and if they won't sign the loan agreement on Monday, let it be on your head, and it will be your fault if the equipment isn't delivered before Christmas.'

As he said this, he was packing up and getting ready to walk out of the room. He looked around and saw that the eyes of the Chinese he normally worked with were wide-open in amazement. He had just got outside the door when one of them hurried out after him. He said, 'You go and have your lunch and I'll talk to Madame Zhao.' After lunch, Madame Zhao said, 'We think the contract wording is fine.' They obviously had too much to lose and had talked her around.

The critical issue is when and how to use forcing strategies like this, as there is a risk that they will lead to loss of face for the Chinese negotiator and to deadlock. The key is to avoid arrogance and disrespect and to emphasise future consequences.

## THE POST-CONTRACT NEGOTIATION PHASE

Even more neglected by negotiators than the pre-negotiation period is the post-negotiation period. The mere fact that an agreement has been reached and a contract signed amid a flourish of flags and protocol does not mean the contract is now fixed and unalterable and will be implemented in line with the printed document.

In the west, contracts are seen as fixed points, the unalterable conclusions of an agreement. In China, they are seen as stepping stones in an ongoing relationship. A lack of administrative sanctions means that if they want to, people can generally get around them. The problem is acknowledged in a handbook for Chinese negotiators which says, 'Currently, supervising structures for contracts are not perfect in China.' Note the face-saving way in which this is phrased: the emphasis is on the positive rather than on the negative side.

After signing the contract, the Chinese will request 'clarification meetings' at which they will demand more than is stated in the contract and, often, ask for something they had to sacrifice earlier on to secure the contract. There are always additional demands. It might be overseas training for five people for three weeks, or more people for longer. They might say, 'My manager would like to go. Would you give us an invitation and pay for the ticket?'

Such requests obviously reflect the collectivism of Chinese society: the group wants benefits for itself, and since both sides are now in a relationship, it is OK for the poorer side to ask the wealthier one for some favours. They also reflect the committee pressures I discussed earlier in connection with high aspirations and standing firm. The Chinese are not at all embarrassed about asking for more, at any stage, or about coming back to things they wanted originally and had to give up.

Always expect a contract to be open to renegotiation after the formal signing. The contract generally sets the minimum agreement, and the Chinese assume that items will be added or adjustments made to meet changing circumstances. This is another demonstration of the negotiable nature of Chinese business relationships.

This view of contracts arises from the fact that Chinese business relationships are shaped by individuals rather than by impersonal entities. Large businesses in China assign representatives to live permanently in their important supplier and customer organisations, to facilitate preferential treatment, and to intercede in the case of difficulties. A number of overseas Chinese have expressed frustration to me about the 'freeloading' of the Chinese in China, which they claim would never occur among the overseas Chinese. If they invite eight people to a banquet as part of the relationship-building of their business, the Chinese will come to the restaurant with twenty. This has happened over and over again, involving them in considerable expense.

Implementation of the contract usually involves extensive renegotiation in China. Just as a western business person needs to influence the Chinese before the negotiation, he must find a way to influence implementation of the contract after the negotiation. If the negotiator goes home and leaves the Chinese to handle the real action, many things can intervene to his disadvantage. Other Chinese groups may put pressure on the Chinese signatory party to meet their needs by doing things a different way from what was agreed to; the factory machinery may break down and the goods may be faulty; it may be harvest time and there may be no trains available to transport the goods to the port; the local sheriff may want his five sons put into management positions although they have no training in management, finance, or production; or the Chinese may decide to save money by putting up the building their way and not the western way. If the westerner has gone home, and there are no safeguards or penalties ensuring the contract is carried out to the letter, why would the Chinese not adjust it to meet the pressures of those close at hand?

Since there are usually a number of parties on the Chinese side, disputes between them may result in breaches of the contract. If there is no one group taking responsibility for the Chinese parties, such disputes may be difficult to resolve. Once again, this is the in group–out group aspect of Chinese society in action. The high level of competitiveness between different groups can lead to additional expenses that were not envisaged when the original negotiation was taking place and each party temporarily agreed to things as they stood just to get the contract signed. An example of this is the following story from a telecommunications engineer about breaches to the contract during the implementation stage:

Hans Waller had negotiated a series of contracts covering the installation of telephone switching stations in a number of different localities. The contract said that the foreign technicians would initially train a number of Chinese construction and testing teams. After the initial training, these teams would proceed to other localities to do the same job. The foreign technicians would then move around between teams, checking on their work and thus reinforcing their training. In the contract, the man-days of the foreign technicians had been estimated on this basis.

When the trained Chinese teams got ready to move to the next district, the local Chinese authorities would not let them leave. Instead, Waller's expatriate technicians would be given an entirely new team in the next district to be trained from scratch. The high cost of doing this had not been taken into account in the contract.

Waller talked to the Chinese about it. He pointed out that they were not sticking to the contract they had signed. He was trying to work with nine different administrations, and they all wanted their own people trained. The Chinese were totally unsympathetic and did nothing to solve the problem. They said, 'Well maybe it says [what it says] in the contract, but we want our people trained.'

Waller's expatriate technicians were stretched beyond their capacity to supervise the work. Different Chinese work groups started complaining, 'Why isn't there someone down here helping us?' In the end he had to put in extra technicians at considerable cost to his company. He worried that the Chinese teams were only being trained to a superficial level. With considerable bitterness, he said, 'It will never be their fault if something fails because they haven't been trained adequately; it will always be our fault for doing it wrong'.

A solution to a problem like this is to be aware that many parties are usually involved on the Chinese side and to insist very early that a supervising person or committee take responsibility for the Chinese side. Another solution is to build a percentage for unforeseen costs into the total cost or to break the implementation into stages, each successive stage being dependent upon successful completion of the preceding one.

One of the commonest forms of contract-breaking is failure to meet quality standards and delivery schedules. A western negotiator must be realistic about what it is possible for the Chinese to achieve given their poor infrastructure, particularly transport, and an economy and work force in an early stage of development. If what is agreed to in a contract is impossible to produce in reality, of course the contract will be broken.

We saw in Chapter 1 how Tony Kosky handled a broken contract by going back to China again and again with his rabbit jackets. He was setting a precedent with the Chinese, showing them that he expected compensation when they failed to carry out their promises. According to him, this worked, although he did not get full compensation because of the time-lapse.

We also saw what happened to the German buyer at the Canton Trade Fair when he complained about his Christmas goods arriving late. A better approach would have been to discreetly ask for something extra to compensate, which is the way the Chinese normally tackle such problems of contract-breaking. This avoids loss of face, and helps maintain goodwill in the business relationship. But you need to walk the line here between arguing for full compensation and letting the other side get off scot-free. In the Chinese view, failure to demand something back makes you seem stupid, weak, and easy to cheat. It also suggests you have money to throw away, and that gives them another opening!

The other common reason the Chinese break contracts is that they simply cannot deliver what they have undertaken to deliver because their equipment is out of date or because they have inadequate management skills. For about 30 years 'management by expertise' and 'profit first' were condemned by the Communist government. The results of this, poor and inconsistent quality as well as schedule failings, are the western negotiator's problem. Before drawing up the contract you must know the Chinese side's capabilities. Research the situation thoroughly and talk to other westerners who have done similar business in China.

In the case studies, negotiators with experience in China demonstrate different ways to accomplish post-contract negotiation: by immediate face-to-face discussions, by regular visits, by making the second part of their equity investment only after the first stage of the contract has been successfully completed, by having an agent who checks regularly on quality, and so on. But all make post-contract negotiation an integral part of their overall negotiation strategy. Those who do not are not uncommonly amazed and outraged when things do not turn out as they expected.

# 5 Chinese influence tactics

In this section we will look in detail at the 'micro' aspects of negotiating with the Chinese. It is at this level that western negotiators find 'Chineseness' most evident. I will highlight those tactics that typically give trouble and suggest ways to handle them successfully.

## USING FALSE AUTHORITY

The Chinese may appeal to supposed local 'regulations' and central government 'secret regulations' to push the foreign negotiator to give them what they want. What the Chinese negotiation team says is mandated always needs to be checked, for almost nothing in China is fixed and certain. What the Chinese say may be based simply on rumour, or on the desires of their group.

'Regulations' are similarly used in daily life. A policeman might pull a foreigner's car off the road and demand a 'fine' because the foreigner has broken some 'rule'. Both the 'fine' and the 'rule' are arbitrary. It is up to you to negotiate a discount on the 'fine'. On a major highway, the traffic may be halted for 'windscreen washing'. Each driver has to pay the required fee and have his windscreen washed. The operation will be run by an army unit. These two cases illustrate not only the arbitrariness of rules and regulations in China but the respect for (or fear of) people in positions of power. It would be foolish to take on the police or the army. And of course they exploit their power.

A common issue in commercial negotiations that appears to

be subject to 'regulations' is tax. The Chinese will say, 'We can't do that! It's the tax bureau that forces us . . . you have to follow the tax rules.' Their tax rules may just be a rumour, but the Chinese will put them over as a fact. You should talk to the tax bureau about tax issues.

When the Chinese involve foreigners in arguments with the bureaucracy as a result of such claims, they pay no heed to whether their behaviour is illegal or corrupt. Whatever the 'regulation' they bring up, you need to investigate it with the responsible authorities. An overseas Chinese go-between can be very helpful and effective at this task.

As we have seen already, the pressures on Chinese negotiators from their group, from their superiors, and from their own drive to improve their lives mean they are prepared to do almost anything if it will ensure they meet their negotiation goals. It is the same when they negotiate with other Chinese, as in the description of bureaucratic bargaining in Chapter 1. And they are not restrained in their claims by a western ethical system. Their 'ethics' depend mainly on whether you are in the in group or the out group.

## PSYCHOLOGICAL PRESSURE

When the Chinese do not want to agree with your point of view, they commonly use a form of psychological pressure that is aimed at undermining your confidence in your own proposal and building up the legitimacy of theirs. They say, 'This is the way it is done in China,' 'You do not understand the Chinese way,' 'You may do it that way in your country, but here we do it this way' or 'You've got your way, you've got no regard for the way we do it here!' They accuse you of being ignorant about how to do business in China. They claim that 'This is the way it is done by other westerners.' They tell you that you ask for too much, that other companies are not so aggressive and that they give the Chinese very good deals. They may also criticise your country and the capabilities of its people in a very subtle way, implying that the Chinese are superior.

They exaggerate their concessions and minimise yours. They may try to split the foreign team by befriending individuals and being sympathetic. They may suddenly address questions to subordinate members rather than to the chief negotiator, thus gaining information which they can use to unsettle the foreign team.

A Chinese negotiator advised his countrymen to 'utilise a strategy of "twisting and turning" to uncover the goal of the opposition. Then you apply a smart strategy and change accordingly' (Li 1989).

Never allow yourself to lose your temper (unless it is a show of temper that is calculated, controlled and pointed, like that of Bjorn Andersson when the Beijing negotiator demanded changes to the agreed-on contract). You need to show self-control and quiet strength. This will eventually bring respect. Even if you are under intense pressure, be polite but firm. You could say to the interpreter, 'Please tell Mr Li that I do not wish to continue this discussion. If he is not prepared to give the same politeness to me that I give to him, I suggest we close the book.' Another way is to say, 'There is no point in continuing. I think I'll go back to the hotel and maybe we should meet another time or maybe I should make plans for going home.' It is the way you handle the pressure that is important. Some westerners who are unused to dealing with the Chinese are afraid to speak out like this in case they cause offence.

## LEFT-FIELD ISSUES

The Chinese, as they plan their strategy in their committees, often employ 'left-field' tactics. They may bring up false issues, irrelevant clauses or some other red herring. This oblique approach is a legitimate negotiation tactic anywhere, but it seems to be used with great frequency by the Chinese.

They will bring up a small matter or make an unexpected and ridiculous demand, and spend a lot of time arguing about it. This draws the opposite negotiator off the main path, puzzles him, and forces him to spend time and energy trying to deal with the issue. It will then suddenly be resolved quite easily, or dropped. At the end of the bargaining the opposite negotiator is vulnerable to giving away something important just from the sheer relief of having settled the matter.

The Chinese are partial to the 'left-field' tactic for a number of reasons. They use it when they might lose face by coming straight out with what they really want. They use it to test out the position and strength of the other side. They use it to weaken an opponent's resolve. And they use it before they demand a major concession. The left-field tactic supports their need to get as many advantages as possible for their side to prove their commitment to their own group. There are many Chinese sayings that recommend this kind of oblique tactic, such as 'make a feint attack', 'make a false show of strength', 'say you will attack in the east, but launch the attack in the west' and 'muddy the water to catch the fish'.

With experience it is possible to identify such tactics, step back and calculate what could be gained in return for giving in. A western negotiator, after his first experience in China, said of left-field tactics, 'Now I'd know that we are up to paragraph 53 of the negotiation manual, and that if I wait for two or three days that matter will be dropped and another brought in.'

George Preston was negotiating to build a tannery on the outskirts of Shanghai, on farming land. Discussions about the cost of leasing the land, the water and other infrastructure charges had been going on for weeks and the details had been agreed on. The Chinese walked into the next meeting and demanded half a million dollars to compensate the cabbage farmers because they would lose a harvest. Preston is a very experienced negotiator. He told them, 'All right, let them stay and we'll take the land next year.' The Chinese gave in.

If you do make a concession to a left-field demand, you must never forget to get something back. This is a normal expectation in China. I have seen it in workplaces when someone has needed a colleague to cover for them in an emergency: the asking person must return the favour. In schools, if there is a public holiday, teachers have to make up their class hours some other time. If you do not get something back in a negotiation, the Chinese will interpret this as a weakness and push for more and more concessions.

## EXERTING TIME PRESSURE

The Chinese use time pressures to force you into a decision. They say, 'We are running late and we need to get approval on a Letter of Intent.' If you are not experienced in dealing with China you may believe them. If you know about their method of pushing for a quick decision, you can show that you are not in a hurry and that you do not bow to their pressure. They will give a hundred excuses, so you need to be quick and know it is not necessary to make a decision immediately.

Sometimes the Chinese genuinely need a contract to be completed because their higher authorities have imposed a deadline on negotiations or the funding has a cut-off point. This top-down control is often responsible for sudden demands that the contract be concluded or some other matter attended to. These are cases where you have to determine the cause through 'poking under the stone with a stick' as I recommended earlier.

Using Chinese-style excuses such as saying 'I have to consult my boss on that' or alluding to company 'regulations' to resist making a hasty decision is acceptable to the Chinese. Calling for time out can reduce pressure and allow you to regain your composure or consult with others about problematic issues.

When there was a dock strike in the US and some equipment was waiting to be shipped, the Chinese used it to pressure US negotiators. They said, 'Your country has a dock strike and the machinery will be late. You have to put in somebody extra to make the job go faster.' The Americans resisted the pressure by saying, 'Look, if it is going to be late, then we will put someone there to help you. But first we must know it is definitely going to be late.' In the end it arrived on time. By contrast, the Chinese are quite unsympathetic to the factors that concern foreigners, such as the need to forecast their equipment needs for the following year so that components can be ordered in time and not hold the job up. They flatly refuse to discuss what worries the foreigner.

Sometimes this can be put down to their fear of their superiors. The hierarchical power structure and the power held by individuals can make lower-level functionaries anxious if things do not go as ordered.

Another use the Chinese make of weakness is to identify sympathetic members of a western team and try to influence them in their favour. Throughout their long history, Chinese officials have had to deal with aggressive nomadic tribes on their northern and western borders. Their well-developed tactic of divide and conquer comes naturally to them when negotiating with foreign company executives. 'You are our old friend' is an influence strategy that is used to get you on their side, along with other diplomatic methods such as charm and graciousness and references to the grandeur of China. The Chinese have a particular ability to exploit any weakness where they see that further movement is possible.

## USING COMPETITORS

The Chinese usually talk to a minimum of three competitor companies at the same time. They want to make the competition tangible to their negotiating partner. They use the information they gain to demand changes, extra items, greater disclosure of intellectual property and advantageous funding.

The Chinese use information from competitors to force changes to the initial proposal, and to push a company to give more than its competitors are offering. If you have a good (and particularly long) relationship with them, they will ask for a mutually beneficial deal. They do not necessarily want win–lose. If they are friendly they will say, 'That's my bottom line, can you match that?' or, 'Your competitor is offering . . . , can you match that? I can give you their offer, have a look at it. Go back and talk to your senior. Can you match it?'

You can usually find out whether the Chinese have negotiations going on with other foreign companies. You might find you and your competitor have the same problems. You can talk to him and perhaps form an alliance with him.

When the Chinese are pressing very hard with information about what competitors are offering, it is best to step back and wait. It may be advisable to let the opportunity go. You may leave it to the other company and, after it has gone through the gruelling negotiations, contract for a share of its business or look for openings it has created.

Using a 'loss leader' in the expectation that it will lead to future business, or believing the Chinese when they offer a rosy future of ongoing contracts, is dangerous. There is no intention on the Chinese side to ensure that you will be offered further contracts, nor will it be possible to lift prices in such contracts.

The use of competitors is just a tactic, and although it gives the Chinese good intelligence on what they can ask for, it should not be taken at face value. There is a gap between the way the Chinese behave in the negotiation, such as pressing for more concessions because 'a competitor' is prepared to give them, and what they really think as to which company they would prefer to work with. Again, taking control, stepping back, being unprepared to go beyond your resistance point, are the best responses to this tactic. As I've suggested, you could also talk to your competitors and devise a joint strategy.

Before a negotiation, the Chinese look at all the contracts

that have been signed on similar projects, and ask for items from those contracts to be inserted in the current contract whether they are relevant or not. This is a result of competition between different groups. Many scientific laboratories in China have the most up-to-date equipment, sometimes sitting unused and covered with dust. They have acquired it not because it was relevant to what they were doing, but because other units had it and they had to keep up. I am not suggesting that this does not happen in the west. It does, particularly in bureaucracies—and much of Chinese business is done within a bureaucratic structure.

The Chinese industrial intelligence network should not be underestimated. At a seminar in Shanghai led by an Australian waste-water engineer, a member of the audience held up a piece of equipment installed by a competitor company, also Australian. He asked, 'Their equipment didn't work. Why should yours?' At his next seminar, hundreds of kilometres to the south, the Australian engineer was again challenged on the same issue. He commented to his hosts, 'Gee, you don't need to make any mistakes around here!' They replied, 'That's right!'

## CHANGING NEGOTIATORS AND LOCATION

To destabilise the western negotiator when discussions are not going in their favour, the Chinese side will change both negotiators and the location of the negotiation. When a new negotiator is brought in, negotiations start again from the beginning and former understandings are negated.

This tactic shows very clearly how the negotiations are managed by people who are not necessarily in the face-to-face negotiations. It may be used in a small one-on-one negotiation such as buying furs for export, or in a high-level government negotiation where the Chinese stand to gain large sums of foreign exchange.

The western negotiator can use the same tactic, by inviting the Chinese to talk informally with him over lunch or in other venues, by bringing in influential people from his own side to lend weight to what he says, and by inviting members of the Chinese team to his own country where different people can be brought into the discussions, even if the formal negotiation still takes place in China. Experts and officials who are well-regarded by the Chinese side will have influence with them.

## PUSHING TO FIND THE BOTTOM LINE

The Chinese want you to be frank about your bottom line, but they distrust what you tell them. They are prepared to negotiate only when the cost or detail in question is close to your bottom line. When they make you really angry, they usually assume they have hit your bottom line. Any sign that you can still be flexible encourages them to demand more.

The Chinese press for major concessions towards the end of the negotiation. This is a time when foreign negotiators may be vulnerable because of the strain of dealing with the large number of people, changes in negotiators, pressures on costs and technical features, repetitive questioning and long hours.

Many negotiators show the Chinese documentary evidence of their bottom line when they have reached a deadlock, which forces the Chinese to negotiate around that bottom line. Documentary evidence is effective in overcoming the Chinese mistrust of what their negotiating opponent says. This is not to be wondered at, given the uncertainty in marketplace haggling over pre-inflated prices, and their own use of supposed 'regulations' to force agreement.

## RE-OPENING CLOSED ISSUES

The Chinese may agree about an issue early on in a negotiation, but raise it again later. They will say, 'Yours is a good idea, but ours is a good idea too.' They see it as quite legitimate to push for a seemingly endless array of concessions. One western negotiator dubbed this 'the fifteen times principle'. It is also known as the 'salami' tactic. However, the Chinese do recognise that there is a point beyond which it is unwise to go. If confronted, they can quite suddenly drop all demands, as happened in the following negotiation.

After weeks of discussion, everything was agreed about a telecommunications contract. Then suddenly the Chinese wanted changes. They had gone through every contract signed with the company in any part of China over the previous seven years, and wanted all the items ever given in those contracts included in the present one. They said everything was OK, except that the foreign company should provide four service vans.

The western negotiator said, 'At some stage we had to draw the line, so I decided this was it. It was a series of telephone calls over two days. I said "I've talked to the managing director. We can't go any further. We definitely can't supply any service vans." They would go away and think about it for a while, then they would come back and ask us for three service vans, then two service vans, then one service van. I knew that if I gave in then and agreed to one service van, it would have led on to training for the driver, spare parts for three years, and petrol. They wanted to get a little bit extra, but I had decided that they weren't going to get the service vans.'

A lucky mistake saved him. He had forgotten some things that had been in other contracts and so should have been part of the giveaway: tape recorders and a telephone training exchange. They said to him, 'If we give up on the service vans, you will give us magnetic tape recorders and a training exchange.' He agreed. He says, 'You've got to know where to draw the line, and you can't budge from it. If you just give an inch, they will see that as a sign that the negotiations are still on. We figured that there had been so many other contracts signed that didn't have service vans associated with them, there was no reason to give them in this one'.

The Chinese accepted the tape recorders and training exchange and dropped their demand for the service vans. This is a clear example of trying to get more advantages than originally negotiated. What those advantages are is less important than the principle of squeezing extra concessions as the deadline approaches, probably to bolster the negotiators' esteem among their group. Had this negotiator not had the tape recorders and training exchange to meet the last-minute Chinese demands, his company would have had to supply some other concession.

The lesson for foreign negotiators is to plan concessions that can be given at the deadline, even though you do not know what the Chinese may demand. You could plan a financial bonus, such as a 1 per cent discount, or some other bonus. It is wise not to be too generous in the final concession. Precedents take hold in China and can be virtually impossible to alter, so give thought to the future.

## CHANGING LEVELS AND SPECIALISTS

The large number of people in China really tells in large-scale negotiations. These are divided into discrete sections which are conducted by different teams. If they are buying industrial products, the Chinese start with a group of technical specialists. They ask you to make a presentation on the product, then they go through all the specifications in great detail to see the extent to which your product meets their requirements. This part of the discussion is not only for clarification. They are looking for where they can ask for more, where they will be able to squeeze on price. Experts discuss the technical features, demanding large amounts of information as well as asking for details not generally demanded by businesses in the west. In this stage of the negotiation it is unwise to use anyone not fully acquainted with the product, such as a marketer rather than a technical expert, because the Chinese ask questions based on a thorough investigation of the specifications by their own experts.

Following the technical team there may be the financial or regulatory teams from the provincial or central bureaucracies. Because they have less appreciation of the technical aspects and the way these relate to price, or the way service relates to price, it is very difficult to convince them on issues linking cost and value. They will also not take into account any concessions given during the technical negotiation. And the demands of the central bureaucracy can often be at odds with those of the local authorities.

The status of the people on the Chinese side will influence how easy or difficult the negotiations are. If you are dealing with a factory manager or a manager of an organisation in close contact with the object of the negotiation, and who has influence and wants the business to go ahead, the negotiation can be reasonably straightforward. If you are dealing with bureaucrats, it can be very tedious and difficult.

As soon as possible, the western negotiator should bring the Chinese team onto his side, so that in discussions with the bureaucracy and local regulatory authorities the Chinese partners are negotiating in the interests of the joint venture.

## STANDING ON FIXED POSITIONS

The Chinese negotiator may repeat the same position over and over—'black is white', 'day is night'—because he does not have authority to make decisions about issues that affect a number of different constituents. He is simply sticking to the orders he has been given by the group and others behind the scenes. He may therefore have very little room for manoeuvre.

The statement he makes has usually been decided on beforehand. When challenged, he will reiterate the group point of view until there is a break in negotiations and he can discuss the situation with the larger team. He may then come out and turn 180 degrees from his previous position without any explanation or apology. In such cases it is pointless for a foreign negotiator to persist in arguing his point of view. Far better to call a recess.

Quite often deals have been done between Chinese parties which make it impossible for them to change their stand. These are not disclosed to the foreign party. In a negotiation on the rehabilitation of mining areas, it was agreed that three vehicles would be supplied to the Beijing headquarters. One was a Buick, which was only for prestige and had no real role in the project. The other two were work vehicles that would transport ores from the airport to the laboratories for analysis. When the final details were being discussed, the foreign negotiator suddenly found that only the Buick was destined for Beijing. The other two vehicles were to be sent to mines in Jiangsu and Shanxi. This would seriously impair the efficiency of the project, because the research was to be done in Beijing and the provinces had no need for the vehicles.

The foreign negotiator asked the Chinese how they were going to manage the project with only a Buick. Although he discussed the issue in great detail, emphasising the efficiency aspects and the focus of the project, he could not dissuade the Chinese. The two work vehicles were to go elsewhere.

After four weeks of daily discussion on this important matter—because it put in jeopardy the success of the whole project—he finally found out why the Chinese negotiating team were immovable. They had done a deal with the Jiangsu and Shanxi people about the work vehicles long before the negotiations began, in an effort to get the provincial people to cooperate with headquarters. There was no way the foreign negotiator could change this agreement. His only alternative was to get his company to put in an extra work vehicle. As with my suggestion concerning 'the fifteen times principle', one should never go to China without a hidden resource to meet last-minute demands.

This example illustrates a characteristically Chinese approach to negotiation. In the west we would probably explain, fairly early on, that we had made a deal with the provincial people on the work vehicles, and could not renege on it. In China, such a deal will not be discussed openly. The only way to find out why the Chinese will not move on an issue is to go behind the scenes. They may be more willing to talk in an informal setting. Chat with one of them on a trip, or with the chauffeur.

Other reasons Chinese negotiators take a fixed position are that they feel unsure how far they can trust the other side, and that they lack understanding about international business practices and products. Quite high-ranking officials may not know what a limited liability company is, because China has not had any company law. This knowledge is so fundamental for a western business person that it may not occur to him that the Chinese do not understand it. And the Chinese cover up their lack of knowledge because they find it humiliating to have to ask for such notions to be explained to them. As a result, the western negotiator is baffled by the Chinese party's inflexible stand.

The only way to solve such problems is to probe discreetly and gain an understanding of their point of view. The problem may be one of protecting someone's face. This requires a circuitous route to a conclusion.

## CONCENTRATING ON PRICE

Owing to the government's (and individuals') need for foreign currency, price is a common sticking point in negotiations with the Chinese. When they buy products from overseas, they want to buy as much as they can for the money, so they exert tremendous pressure on price, product features and commercial terms. Since the Chinese have not developed state-of-the-art technology, they generally do not understand the costs of R&D. Nor have they had any experience of quality and service issues, because of the basic nature of Chinese industry during the Maoist period. Mao forced China into, and lauded, reliance on its own resources. This led to the disastrous steel-making effort, when people all over China melted down their pots and pans to produce backyard steel.

Most Chinese factories produced (and still produce) according to the government plan, with no concern for quality. A foreign operations manager assigned to train workers in a sock factory in Beijing in 1987 found only five of twenty machines working and most of the factory workers asleep. The factory managers spent most of their time playing cards instead of attending to factory business. When he spoke to the supervisor about it, she retorted, 'You are here to train, not to criticise!'

One of the reasons it takes so long to shop in China is that you have to check out the quality of everything before you buy it. I once bought a shoulder bag in the Friendship Store which supposedly had the best quality goods and found that the zipper only worked from the inside! So price, not quality, becomes a focus for most Chinese negotiators.

Government instructions are that technology is to be evaluated according to the current needs of the country. Purchases of the latest technology must be balanced against price considerations and the need to create maximum employment for Chinese workers. There are serious liquidity problems in China and workers often do not get paid because of this, so foreign currency is a desperate need for the whole country.

The other reason for the emphasis on price is that individual groups often want money for themselves, not necessarily for the interests of the joint venture. Once a joint venture is running, it can be difficult to get the Chinese parties to reinvest to develop it. They want to use the money for their own purposes: consumption or other investments.

Once again, a foreign negotiator needs to control the direction of the negotiations. This requires the strength to persist with your point of view and to widen the scope of the discussion to take in more than just price. If they are selling, the Chinese will say, in effect, 'the price is not enough.' You say, 'Well what about this and what about that?'—bringing in other relevant items such as quality, shipping or marketing. The Chinese will not be interested. They will persist with 'The price is not enough.' You may have to say, 'Well, look, we understand what you're saying about price. Let's agree to differ for the moment on the price and talk about these other things. We will come back to your point in a minute.'

If the negotiation is about matching the investment equity of both sides, the western negotiator must make sure that the Chinese investment, usually in kind, is valued by some objective measure, and not just on what the Chinese side says it is worth. Using concepts of 'fairness' and auditing the trail of Chinese investment in the joint venture are effective strategies here.

## NEEDING GUARANTEES OR CONFORMITY TO BUREAUCRATIC CODES

A problem created by the bureaucracy is its demand for projects to conform to certain guidelines before approval can be given. In many technical areas, such as mining and engineering, Chinese technical expertise is based on Russian standards of 30 or more years ago, and the bureaucratic regulations are devised according to these standards. With modern western technology, such standards are out of date, but the Chinese still demand that they be met.

The most recent international experience and research was presented to Chinese engineers in Shanghai who were building a sewerage system, but they replied that they could not follow it because their design had to agree with the national code. The western engineers told them the national code was wrong and explained from first principles where the new approach came from.

The Chinese engineers understood and appreciated the superiority of the western way but still said they had to use the old code. They said, 'We agree with you, but you have to understand our point that we can't put anything in our calculations and not use the national code. It won't get through the hierarchy.'

Eventually they came up with fudge factors to get around the bureaucratic requirements. Say the western factor was .017. They put in a factor which was .017 divided by .014 and said they were designing the system according to the national code with this factor. Final approval would be given by bureaucrats, not engineers, so unless the scheme appeared to conform to the official regulations it would not be passed. Many such problems confront western negotiators, particularly those bringing new technologies to China. They must work with the Chinese to find ways around them.

For anyone who works in a bureaucracy, feigning conformity to the rules is a matter of daily survival. I do not think there is anything particularly Chinese about the insistence that western products and processes conform to bureaucratic guidelines.

## SOME PROBLEMS IN NEGOTIATIONS

### Lack of cooperation

Several parties on the Chinese side may negotiate independently and without coordination. It is not unusual for there to be four or five partners on the Chinese side. Each will say, 'Why do I have to agree with the others? I want to speak when I need to.'

If you allow them to do this, you will lose control over the negotiation process. Each group will have its own translator, each chief negotiator will talk as he pleases with his own translator sitting beside him. This can lead to many arguments. Sometimes no one is prepared to speak at all because of inter-party rivalry and antagonism to the foreigner. In such cases the silence can go on for as long as the meeting lasts.

## Lack of coordination

It is particularly important to take control. If you do not begin with a structure, it is very hard to impose one later. In China control is very loose. All through the Maoist period, and particularly during the Cultural Revolution, managers were criticised and replaced by party faithful with no management skills. The Chinese lost their best managers and management systems.

Conflicting interests which arise because of loyalty to the in group also override the interests of efficiency.

Westerners therefore need to take control of who they will negotiate with, the agenda and the time line. Because there are so many parties involved, because many lower-level officials are afraid of those in power, because Chinese negotiators concentrate on certain aspects such as cost while neglecting other elements, because they have a different attitude towards time and because of the legacy of the command economy, taking a lead in the negotiations can have a decisive effect on the outcome.

Talk through the timetable and procedures for the negotiations before any negotiation starts. You might argue for one week on, one week off. You might say that in Week 1 the discussion will be exploratory, in Week 2 it will focus on content, in Week 3 it will go clause by clause and in Week 4 it will centre on cost.

You also need to agree about who will be the chief negotiator, who will be the speaker. Otherwise you will have too many speakers at once. If the staff want to speak up they should ask for permission and follow the rule of only one person speaking at a time. Much depends on the Chinese chief negotiator. If he wants to maintain discipline he will work out a system. You must determine it with him.

At the implementation stage, if the Chinese corporation does not have plans to jointly steer the project, you should convince them that it is necessary. You may need to find someone who can influence them. Contractors involved in the implementation stage create many problems because they serve different masters. You need to establish some administrative means to control them. Form a steering committee which meets once or twice a month to guide the project, agree on everything, and document it.

## Deadlock

Deadlocks are an ever-present danger in negotiations in China. They can happen very suddenly. Both sides lose patience. Both think the other side does not understand what they are saying and that what it wants is wrong. The prevalence of deadlock is made worse by the lack of a common language, culture and background between negotiators. Actions and words may easily be misinterpreted and misunderstood.

When things do not go your way, it is very easy, in a cross-cultural negotiation, to base judgments on racial stereotypes, rather than on reason. Whatever one's own side does is good, whatever the other side does is bad. Each party then throws up his hands because the other is 'impossible' or 'unreasonable'. In fact, each has good reasons, in his own eyes, for the stand he takes.

Another reason for deadlock is that Chinese officials are used to dictating to people below them in the hierarchy or under their control. Certain Chinese officials place western business people in this lowly category. They think westerners should do as they are told. Western business people take offence at this attitude. They also object to accepting dictates that are out of touch with modern technology and procedure.

Issues which seem straightforward to the western side may appear to the Chinese to threaten China's sovereignty or undermine Chinese principles. These create numerous intangible issues, particularly in large negotiations involving strategic industries such as petroleum exploration. The Chinese are very wary about giving westerners control of key resources and industries. The lessons of imperialist domination before 1949 have been well learnt.

Deadlock also comes about because of the attitude of some western lawyers. If they are sticklers for the letter of their law books or instructions, and have no interest in China, they may just want to complete the negotiation quickly and not make an effort to find an area of agreement or a culturally appropriate solution.

A frequent cause of deadlock is technology transfer. The Chinese side will be asked to guarantee that the contract will not be infringed for so many years. They will say, 'We just fulfil the contract. We cannot guarantee that nobody will break the contract. It is out of our control. Anyone who wants to can take the joint venture product and produce something similar.' In such cases the licensors should register their patent with the patent office, which will give them protection if there is an infringement.

Deadlock can be avoided or diffused by a go-between. Overseas Chinese can be very effective in this role. With their language skills and cultural understanding, they are able to probe the rationale underlying the Chinese position and see what alternatives they would accept, as well as helping put the western side's views. This sort of facilitation is vital when two large negotiating teams are facing one another in the formal negotiation setting.

The go-between must understand the context of each side's arguments. He may have to take different people aside and find out about trade-offs or compromises they could make. They may not compromise on cost but on legislation, on a principle, or on tax. The go-between must be someone who is very positive, does not easily give up, and who is skilled at investigating all avenues to a solution. There is always a way out of deadlock.

The Chinese side may have been quibbling over a single word for an hour, saying, 'No, we cannot put it in our contract.' You need to know why. Perhaps they have trouble understanding what the word means, especially if it is in English. They may need time to go away and digest it. If you ask them, 'Do you agree on that point?' or 'Do you agree on using that word?' they will hesitate. When this tense moment comes, ask them, on the side, why they disagree. They will tell you frankly, 'You know we are not asking for something unreasonable. This is the problem we have. You have to understand our position.'

Finding an acceptable way out of such an impasse often requires the foreign negotiator to frame the problem in a way that helps the Chinese negotiator maintain his reputation in his own group. He may settle for a temporary or partial solution which can be reconsidered later, as in the case of the terms of reference in Chapter 2.

Emphasising how far the negotiation has already gone, and pointing out the items already agreed to, encourages a cooperative attitude and brings into focus the investment of time and effort that has been made. If the personality of some of the negotiators is harming the negotiation, they should be removed and others given responsibility for finding a way out of the impasse.

Log rolling between separate issues is an important way to open up an acceptable solution. Yet another is to put the difficult issues aside until later, meanwhile moving on to other items that can be agreed upon.

## CROSS-CULTURAL ISSUES

### Body language

From childhood, the Chinese are taught to control the expression of their emotions. This habit has been blamed for the high incidence of stomach ailments in China.

To many westerners, the Chinese seem to have expressionless faces which betray none of the thinking going on underneath. This makes it difficult for negotiators to read how their words are being received. The hands of the Chinese will often be more expressive than their faces, at least betraying hidden tensions.

### First impressions

First impressions can shape expectations. When a negotiator is dealing with a different culture, the degree of hostility or of dissonant values he encounters may lead him to form excessively negative judgments about the other society and people. This may affect the way he interacts with the opposite team members. Sensing antipathy, they may become more hostile, which may further harden his views, and so on in a vicious circle. Excessively positive views of the other team may also jeopardise the outcome, as when interpreters dissociate from their own side and leak information to the opposite side.

# Part III

# EFFECTIVE AND INEFFECTIVE NEGOTIATIONS

# 6 A bridge between east and west: the overseas Chinese

So far we have documented a very fluid and, to western eyes, dishonest business environment. Chinese enterprises not only haggle extensively with the bureaucracy over what appear to be mandated requirements and regulations, but adopt an equally flexible approach to negotiating with westerners. It sometimes seems to western business people that there is no firm place to get a foothold.

The overseas Chinese can provide invaluable guidance on negotiating business agreements in China. Coming as they do from western or western-style business environments and generally having a capitalist or private-enterprise background, they are accustomed to meeting the same targets as western business people: profitability, quality and deadlines. These concerns often do not have the same meaning for managers and bureaucrats in China itself.

The ability of the overseas Chinese to bridge the gap between western and Chinese business cultures is demonstrated in the growing numbers being chosen by western companies as members of their negotiating teams and as managers of their China business activities. For example, 24 per cent of Australian expatriates in China are overseas Chinese (Blackman 1995).

What do the overseas Chinese do in their negotiations that other westerners can learn from? First, they work on breaching the in group–out group divide discussed in Chapter 1. They need no interpreters, because they speak the same language, and this enables them to influence the Chinese directly when they put their point of view across or explain the background. They prefer to work in their ancestral areas, where they may still have family connections. This is very obvious in Fujian province, the ancestral home of the majority of Taiwanese, and in Guangdong province from where most Hong Kong and Southeast Asian Chinese once set out. Overseas Chinese investment in these areas far exceeds that in other parts of China.

Another activity the overseas Chinese stress as a way to forge in-group ties is holding banquets and social events. These are usually lavish affairs with many more dishes than anyone could possibly eat and a great many toasts, at each of which it is a point of honour to drain the glass of *mao tai*, the potent Chinese spirit. This usually leads to a lot of laughter and enjoyment, creating a lively atmosphere. Such events are used to get to know the officials who can facilitate approvals and provide opportunities, give face to these officials and to Chinese business associates, learn how inclined the other team members are to identify with the interests of their group, and generally let both sides see each other as fellow human beings, not scheming enemies.

A very simple way the overseas Chinese keep up the relationship side of their business with other overseas Chinese is by dropping in on their customers without an appointment, just to have a friendly chat, not necessarily to talk business. Overseas Chinese who try this with western customers are often amazed when the latter declare they are too busy, look at their watch, and ask whether the supplier has made an appointment.

Since face is as much a part of overseas Chinese business as it is of business in China, the overseas Chinese know instinctively how to negotiate around it. Let us see how one overseas Chinese businesswoman brings these elements into her business negotiations in China.

## CASE STUDY 1: 'WE ARE FRIENDLY PEOPLE OURSELVES'

Teresa Chung is striking to meet. She is about 40, slim, with dark hair pulled back smoothly from a wide, lively face. She dresses superbly in well-cut, elegant clothes: a purple dress with a white jacket, or a red suit. She is friendly and talks fluently, yet there is a seriousness behind what she says that comes from her experience in business. She was born in Hong Kong but has lived in Australia for twenty years.

Chung owns Chinese Art House, a Chinese furniture

importer specialising in decorated cabinets, carved and painted wooden screens and traditional Chinese-style tables and chairs in mahogany, rosewood and teak. A large mahogany sign with gold lettering hangs on the wall of her office. It confers on her the sole Australian agency for the furniture she imports, which she sells to large department stores, decorator boutiques and the general public.

Chung began in business with a tiny shop selling small collector items—ornaments, pictures and art books from China. Fifteen years ago she decided to go to China to negotiate for an agency to sell Chinese furniture in Australia. Although she had very little capital when she approached the China Arts and Crafts representatives at the Canton Spring Fair, she was known to them because she had bought many small items from them for her shop.

When she proposed that they make her their agent in Australia, she was surprised and amused to be asked how many shops she had in each province and state. She replied, 'I have only a small place in Melbourne.' The Chinese were disappointed that she did not own a chain of large shops all around Australia, but they wrote down all the details and went off to see what they could do to help her. They came back the next day and said they would be quite interested, but would give her a selling agency only in Victoria. They then tried to pin her down on how much stock she could turn over for them in a year. She really had no idea. That night she made up some figures to put into the agreement. Whether the figures were appropriate or not, the Chinese decided to go along with her idea.

Chung returned to Australia with an agreement that said she would have to reach a certain sales target if she were to continue to be the China Arts and Crafts agent. In return, the Chinese agreed to give her a commission to subsidise advertising and promotion. Things went well, so the next year Chung asked for the agency for the whole of Australia. She agreed to promote the goods once a year in every state, and give the Chinese a report on what she had done. She told them this would take a very big capital outlay which she could not afford, and asked them, 'How are we going to make this a mutual thing?' She added, 'You must give us certain stock on a consignment basis.' The Chinese agreed, after some negotiation, to give her the stock on 30 days credit.

As Chung's business grew, so did the Chinese side's confidence in her. After two years she got them to extend the credit period to 60 days. When she asked for 90 days credit, they told her they gave this to only one store, the big Chinese emporium in Hong Kong. She got it in the end.

Chung says of that negotiation: 'We are friendly people ourselves. I find that in the actual negotiations you have to place yourself in their position, meaning that I am no longer the boss, so to speak, we are friends. We are always that, you know, friends. They always say when they have dinner, "a toast to friendship". To them probably friendship is more important than business. So you just open that area first, establish that friendship. Then after a few toasts of *yum xing* and *mao tai* or whatever, you will normally find it's quite easy to do the negotiation.'

But despite her good relations with the Chinese and the help they have given her, at certain times they send goods with immediate payment requests. She always goes back to them and says, 'You cannot do this to us.' Whenever she has not been able to sell the goods quickly enough, and consequently has not had enough money to pay, she explains her difficulties. She has found that negotiating with them under these conditions is not difficult. Every year she goes to China to review her agency agreement and sign a contract for purchases over the next six or twelve months, because the furniture takes a long time to make.

Chung does not deny that there are certain frustrations in dealing with the Chinese. 'Our contract covers maybe 50 screens, 120 tables and maybe 900 chairs. Sometimes, without consulting you, the Chinese will send 50 chairs at once, but no tables. Or you may say you want cabinets and they will send you twenty sets of screens. They start producing things—in the order they choose—once they have a contract in hand. It doesn't matter what you require. If you suggest breaking the contract down into one container a month with, say, ten screens, two tables and four cabinets, they will send you a container a month with only one or two items in it.

'Because the contract is for a whole year, they no longer wait for your letter of credit each month specifying the things you want. They just send you whatever is available or maybe whatever they cannot sell elsewhere! I don't suppose I really have to take that, but to maintain the friendship I don't criticise.

Instead I say, 'You sent me so many of these things I cannot possibly sell them in 90 days,' and ask for 120 days. Maybe they will consent to that!'

Once, in January, when she needed goods early for her Chinese New Year sale, Chung received six months' supply in one go: seven container loads of goods. She says, 'We were absolutely staggered! Normally we have one container a month. We had nowhere to hold the goods, so we had to put them into bond stores at tremendous cost. We went back to the Chinese and said, "What are you doing to us?"' Eventually she found out that because it was Chinese New Year, the Chinese representatives got a bonus for whatever they sold. So they quickly pushed everything on to her. She says: 'This is very unbusinesslike, but it was a new provincial branch of China Arts and Crafts with new young heads of department. Still, this sort of thing can be very damaging. I may have understood, but fancy an Australian businessman being confronted with it! He would scream blue murder and send everything back to them, refuse to accept delivery or sue them! This is why people say it is very hard to deal with the Chinese.

'You need to make certain friendly allowances. Sometimes there are disputes, but you never get compensation in cash. In the next contract they might reduce the price. But who knows, they might also lower the quality of the goods! In any case they will never give you back money for your loss.'

Reflecting on her first agency, Chung says that if she had not already had some small dealings with the Chinese representatives, they would probably have given her a cold shoulder. She has also noticed that they scrutinise people who want to represent them. She says: 'Believe me, they know how to look at a person. They ask themselves, "Is he smart?", "Does he have contacts?", "Will he open up certain areas for us?", "Does he have capital?" They have been exploited by many overseas business people in the last fifteen years, so they have learnt to be cautious.'

It has always been the custom in Chinese society to give gifts to business associates. Chung follows this practice. 'If I go to Shanghai I normally take them a gift like cigarettes, or little things—a lapel pin, say—with an Australian flavour. Or I might just bring chewing gum, or a bottle of cognac when we are having dinner. But I know that a lot of the Hong Kong people have spoilt the people in areas near the border with lavish gifts like videos, TV sets, motor cycles, refrigerators and overseas bank accounts.

'Once, because we were on such friendly terms and they did not have a really good typewriter, I said, "Next time I will bring you a typewriter." So I bought a very nice typewriter in Hong Kong and took it in to them. The people I deal with were quite shocked that I had not had it inscribed with their names, because any gift of that nature goes immediately into the big pool, and they never see it again.'

## DISCUSSION

### 1 Build personal relationships and be friendly

Case study 1 highlights aspects of making relationships in China that may not apply in many western countries. One of these is the sheer friendliness of the relationship—and this is developed by giving face. As Chung says, 'I am no longer the boss . . . we are friends . . . to them probably friendship is more important than business.'

It is notable that she extends friendship to the whole Chinese group. They all come to her banquets and are part of the friendly atmosphere. In the west, on the other hand, formal dinners between business associates tend to be on a one-to-one basis, or involve only executives at a certain level. Chung's extension of friendship and hospitality to everyone who will be involved in the business with her is an acknowledgment of the collectivist nature of Chinese society.

Chung has a wide, ready smile and is easy to talk to. The Chinese are often unsure about western business people. They do not know if they can trust them, if they can be frank with them about their problems. They do not know how to approach them. Many westerners appear brusque, as if they cannot spare enough time to develop a conversation. They stay at posh, expensive hotels and are therefore removed from ordinary Chinese life. There is a language barrier, so it is not very easy to chat with them. So the Chinese do not know if they will be laughed at or their concerns dismissed. They are worried they will make fools of themselves. Because of all these things, they find it easier to relate to overseas Chinese and to talk to them frankly about the real situation as opposed to the one put forward in the negotiations.

Chung emphasises her friendship with the Chinese by giving them gifts, usually small tokens or, in the case of the typewriter, something that expresses her concern for the whole group. Gift-giving is important in China as a way of expressing friendliness and concern. However, as Chung indicates, some overseas Chinese (as well as the Japanese, who share the gift-giving culture) have taken it to a point verging on bribery. Westerners need to learn how to give appropriate gifts without becoming embroiled in what amounts to corruption in the eyes of the government. It is worth noting that a number of overseas Chinese have received long gaol sentences in China for corrupt practices involving so-called gifts.

Chung believes relationships were important to getting her furniture business going in the first place. She believes that it was because the Chinese already knew her that they decided to do the furniture deal with her, even though she was very small fry at the time.

Her advice about relationships and friendliness is worth repeating: 'You just open that area first, establish that friendship. Then after a few toasts of *yum xing* and *mao tai* or whatever, you will normally find it's quite easy to do the negotiation.'

All overseas Chinese emphasise this aspect of negotiating in China. In my experience they speak about it far more frequently than western business people, who tend to stress tactics or the negatives of the negotiation itself.

## 2 Argue in the interests of the joint business

Chung used this technique from the very beginning, when she asked the Chinese to provide a budget for advertising and promotion. She always stresses their moral involvement in the success of her business. When she wants to extend, she asks for their support in giving her stock on a consignment basis and extending her credit from 30 to 60 days, and then to 90 days. Her whole approach is summed up in the words, 'How are we going to make this a mutual thing?' This is a typically Chinese appeal to fairness. Usually the Chinese begin negotiations by stating the principle of mutual benefit.

While we saw in the last chapter that mutual benefit does not necessarily guide Chinese actions in practice, it is useful to remind them of this principle occasionally. This is necessary because of their tendency to identify strongly with the interests of their own group.

Chung knows what is important to the Chinese. She reports to them what she has accomplished, giving them documentary evidence that justifies their decision to support her and protects them from criticism by their superiors. She keeps her promises to them through extending the business. This meets their goal of earning foreign currency.

Many joint ventures have found that the Chinese are quite happy to relinquish day-to-day management involvement and many 'principles', as long as their needs for foreign currency (i.e. profit) are met. As we saw in Chapter 5, you must look behind the position statements of the Chinese to the underlying motivations and goals. This is good negotiation practice in any country. It just happens that for westerners negotiating in China, it is harder to identify the underlying goals because of language difficulties, face and genuine differences in what is considered important.

## 3 Meet hidden needs: preserve face

With the Chinese, things promised in the contract do not always materialise. Every time this happens to Chung, she avoids attacking the Chinese directly. This would cause them to lose face. Instead, she emphasises their moral obligation to their shared business and asks for something in return. When they sent her more furniture than she could possibly sell, she said, 'I cannot possibly sell them in 90 days,' and asked for 120 days credit.

At the New Year sale, when she got seven container loads at once, she did not expect compensation in cash but looked for another way, hoping the Chinese might lower the price on the next contract. She knew it would be more productive to negotiate around the problem rather than demanding compensation. This kind of response indicates to the other side that she expects the business relationship to continue, a point that overseas Chinese business people often stress.

In her own way, Chung overcomes many of the obstacles to doing business in China: their suspicion of outsiders and fear of being cheated, their low pay, limited advancement and openness to criticism, the practice of decision making by consensus, and the limited power of contracts.

## 4 Use the overseas Chinese as go-betweens

Ever since westerners started to do business in China they have used local Chinese as go-betweens. Since 1972, however, it has been more common to use the overseas Chinese or recent Chinese immigrants to the west. Such people are an important resource for westerners wanting to do business in China. However, there are some cautions to be observed in employing them. One is that because of the regionality of China, a Hong Kong Chinese may not be welcome in northern or central China, and in fact may not be able to communicate with the locals any better than a westerner because he does not speak their dialect. Also, recent Chinese immigrants to the west may be distrusted by the locals, who will wonder about their allegiances and whether they are only back in China doing business because they failed in the west.

As with all agents, there is the opportunity for a go-between to be dishonest with both sides, concentrating on making a profit for himself at the expense of his clients (Blackman 1993). However, if go-betweens are carefully chosen and consulted in the right way, they have valuable skills and insights to offer western negotiators.

# 7 Coming out of China crying

Starting from scratch in a negotiation with the Chinese involves some major obstacles: you are unknown, therefore you are placed in the out group, and will be treated with the ethics due to outsiders; your credibility is low, since to the Chinese side you represent the stereotype of the amoral capitalist; you share no moral bonds, those debts and favours which intertwine Chinese businesses in relationships involving family members that can go back generations.

Another potential obstacle resides in your personality: will you be able to build friendly relationships to overcome the obstacle of your foreignness? Will you be able to negotiate through the wall of subtleties thrown up by the Chinese to maintain face in front of their group?

In case study 2, the ignorance and personality of the negotiator led the negotiation into a mire and ultimate failure. One company that consciously seeks to avoid outcomes like this is Shell. Its managers look for a special type of person to operate in China, someone who loves China and the Chinese. Shell considers building genuine relationships so important to the success of its China business that it appoints representatives to China for five years at a time, rather than the three years typical of most other companies.

When you read the case study you will find it easy to understand why Shell handles its China business in this way. The company division in question had not engaged in international business before, and the parent company, although it had sold commodities into North China, had no particular policy about who should negotiate for it in China. So it simply sent the person with the necessary technical expertise. The result is a salutary lesson for companies which think that China can be approached as if it were no different from any western country.

## CASE STUDY 2: 'YOU DON'T KNOW IF THEY ARE THICK, OR JUST PLAYING AT BEING THICK'

Martin Benton is an experienced mining engineer in his early 40s. He is a very 'can-do' sort of person: energetic, committed and straight-talking. In 1983, a Chinese provincial government asked the multinational mining company he worked for to design and build a two-million-tonne cement plant and to advise about mining the limestone which would supply the plant. Benton was assigned the latter task.

The company's main motive for going to China was that an economic slump had severely reduced opportunities for construction work in its own country. The whole company was downsizing and reorganising, and the negotiating team members felt that they were really working for their own survival. A Chinese team had visited the mining sites and cement plants belonging to the company. Benton had accompanied them for two weeks, and had enjoyed showing them the high-tech operations. They had all shared breakfasts, lunches and dinners, and bumpy rides to mining sites. Benton felt that he had made a particular friend of the Chinese interpreter.

On the Chinese side there was one overriding concern which was not communicated to Benton's group. This was to reduce the cost and thus minimise their expenditure of foreign currency. To them the plant represented a large commitment of scarce foreign currency. Oblivious to this, Benton and his team concentrated on the quality and sophistication of their product and technology. They believed they were bringing to China the best technology and expertise the west had to offer.

During the three-and-a-half-year negotiating period, Benton's experiences and attitudes, which we will focus on here, mirrored those of the rest of his team of twenty, which included financial, design and technical experts. For four weeks at a time, they spent every day from 8.30 a.m. until 6 or 10 p.m. negotiating in the same room. Towards the end, some negotiation sessions finished at 3 or 4 a.m. In all, most of the team members spent a total of nine months each in China.

When Benton arrived in China he was amazed at the primitive methods being used to mine the limestone. People were using hand-held jackhammers and shovelling rock by hand. Women carried the rock away in baskets balanced on their heads. He loathed the idea of women working in such dirty, rough conditions.

Benton heard that just to the north, a cement plant built not long before by a European consortium had not operated to design standard because local officials had diverted money from the project into their own pockets. A couple of the provincial officials involved had recently been executed. This made Benton suspicious of the Chinese on his own project. The official in charge of finances was a young fellow who drove around in a brand-new maroon Mercedes-Benz. He drove so fast and carelessly that he sometimes knocked people off their bicycles into the roadside ditches. Benton considered him 'a real head-kicker'.

There were a number of Chinese groups involved in the negotiations, from the provincial government, the local controlling ministry, a mining institute in another province and people from Beijing who had input into the financial aspects. The Chinese side's leader was a mining engineer in his 50s called Zhang who had not been part of the team that visited Benton's company. According to Benton, he was 'a rather old-fashioned type of Chinese'. When they were talking he would spit across Benton to the spittoon alongside the wall. One night, quite early in the negotiations, he started to undress for bed in front of the westerners. The interpreter turned to Benton and said, 'I think the meeting is finished.' From the start, Benton found Zhang uncooperative. When he asked Zhang about the geology of the region, he never got a satisfactory reply.

The local area was karst country, with limestone outcrops rising sheer out of the plain. A hog's-back mountain rose about 800m above the plain, surrounded by villages. During the Cultural Revolution, Chinese mining engineers had started to investigate the potential of the limestone on top of the mountain, but Red Guards had attacked them, forcing them to abandon their work. Benton was frustrated that he could not obtain any of their results. He was given a few documents which showed that the limestone was lying in flat beds with a capping of overburden that needed to be taken off.

Zhang wanted to drive tunnels into the mountain below the

cap, load them with explosive and blow the top off. Benton explained to Zhang and his team of young engineers that there were new technologies for removing the overburden bit by bit, so that the limestone was not contaminated. He thought blowing up the mountain the way Zhang wanted to would be chaotic. The underground explosion would mix all the overburden with the limestone and leave boulders too big to remove. The resulting mix would damage the high-technology equipment in the cement plant.

Whenever Benton tried to get a discussion going on the best way to mine the limestone, Zhang and his group of engineers would say, 'We know how to do it. We've done it before. Our way is the way the book says.' They had handbooks with rules on how to develop a mine: how far apart you should drill the holes to get an understanding of the ore body, what tests to do, and how to mine the ore. Benton pointed out that these rules did not allow for the fact that individual deposits all differ in some way. He tried to tell them how to do things in the most up-to-date way.

As the discussions went on, the Chinese would ask the same question in ten different ways. Benton observes, 'You don't know whether they are thick or just playing at being thick. There's a lot of them, so you repeat yourself. It doesn't matter what angle you come from, you just get nowhere. Some guys in our team had really had it. They would have agreed to anything just to go home.'

The sessions went on long into the night and resumed the next day. The Chinese subjected the team to verbal abuse, accusing the foreign team of deliberately falsifying the cost structure, for example, and pointing out minor inconsistencies in what they had said on different occasions, thus putting their reliability into question. The design engineer had such a bad time of it, and got so angry with the Chinese negotiators' intransigence, that he came out of negotiating sessions wanting to fight them. To release the tension, Benton started to drink with him and sing football songs. They put on some music and all these tall, solid Caucasians started dancing with one another. Then they went on a run through the streets and the government pavilions at 2 a.m.

Benton became extremely frustrated with the endless sessions in which he would explain the best way to mine and the Chinese would disagree and criticise his explanation. After each session he would come out fuming that all the western side was doing was educating the Chinese. There would be 30 people from the mining institute sitting there as if in a lecture. He said, 'It was just a way of using you, getting whatever knowledge they could get out of you, while you ran up your foreign exchange bills.'

Finally, because he could get no information from Zhang about how the limestone was lying on top of the mountain, Benton demanded to go out and see it for himself. The Chinese managed to put him off by saying, 'Yes, but you can't go tomorrow, we're having a banquet. You'll have to wait until after the banquet. You've got to meet the deputy provincial governor.' This happened a number of times. He says, 'There was no sense of urgency.' But by constantly nagging and invoking the governor's name, Benton finally got his way. The Chinese agreed to take him to the mountain. They went by bus, stopping along the way for meetings with district authorities. He was asked the same questions he had already answered numerous times in the provincial capital. When they finally got to the foot of the mountain Benton announced that he wanted to start off early the next morning to walk to the top before it got too hot. Zhang objected, but eventually Benton got agreement.

But the next morning, before they left, there was another meeting which put Benton in such a rage that he charged off to the mountain by himself. On the way he bought a big watermelon and stuffed it into his rucksack. He was so angry by this time that he said to himself, 'A watermelon is the only damned thing the Chinese can't muck up.' He was used to roughing it at mining sites and he had come prepared. He had a rucksack with water bottles, biscuits, baked beans, sardines and peanut butter. He had also brought solid hiking boots. The Chinese group insisted on climbing the mountain with him, although they had only flimsy sandshoes and no food or water.

It was a very hot day, over 30°C, and the climb was hard going. The slope was steep and covered with dense bush. When Benton looked behind he saw all the Chinese, most of them considerably older than himself, toiling after him. They were looking much the worse for wear.

At the top of the mountain, the Chinese group sat down, exhausted. Benton cut up his watermelon and gave them each a slice. They were mopping the sweat off their foreheads and were quite done in. While they were sitting there having a rest, Benton fossicked around and found that there were fluctuations in the content of the overburden, as he had originally told Zhang. He pointed this out with a fair amount of satisfaction, feeling it confirmed his assessment that blowing the top off the mountain would contaminate the limestone.

The Chinese party wanted to go back down the mountain for lunch and a siesta. They had arranged to have lunch in the quarry canteen at the foot of the mountain. Benton told them he was not going back. He wanted to look for the drilling that had been done at the beginning of the Cultural Revolution. The Chinese party did not want to leave him there alone. They said, 'We can't leave you up here, the tigers will get you.'

In all the meetings in the provincial capital, the Chinese had ridiculed Benton's idea that there were caves and cavities at the top of the mountain. So when he found some, he made the young geologists inspect them closely. He also found the old drill holes, and cores with red paint identifying them, lying about under the bushes. He was so incensed that the geologists had not discovered any of this for themselves that he pulled them into the bushes to show them, and asked them what they had been doing for the past seven years, and why they hadn't bothered to even walk over the mountain.

Finally, all but a couple of the Chinese went off down the mountain for a siesta. He asked the geologists who remained what they thought would happen when their explosives went off in the drill holes. He told them it would be like a huge bomb, and that the shock waves would fell trees for miles around and flatten the houses in the little villages. The Chinese laughed. He took this to mean that they didn't know and couldn't care. When he got back down the mountain at about 4 p.m., the Chinese officials were waiting for him, their lunch uneaten.

Benton also wanted to go to the cement plant site to look at the foundations. Zhang said, 'That is nothing to do with you. You're here as the mining expert. What have you got to do with foundations?' Once again they had a very heated exchange, although the Chinese did finally take Benton to the site.

After the visit to the mountain, relations between Benton and Zhang fell apart. Before the final presentation, Benton tried to get the interpreter on side with him in attacking Zhang. He had got on very well with the interpreter and had become totally dependent on him to understand what was being said on the Chinese side and to get his point of view across to them.

The interpreter seemed to go along with Benton, although when he and the Chinese spoke, Benton had no idea what they were saying. They did laugh a lot, which unsettled him. Benton gave his presentation to the group, including the deputy provincial governor. He used the overhead projector his team had brought along, and drew diagrams. He went through the project chapter and verse. Zhang criticised everything he said.

Benton said that one of the sites proposed for mining the clay which would go into the cement was totally inappropriate, and that they would need to find another source of clay. Zhang flatly contradicted this. Benton shot back, 'Well, I've walked all over it. You didn't, so how would you know?' He also said that he had found the information from the drilling before the Cultural Revolution that Zhang had denied was there. Zhang just replied, 'No.' So Benton said, 'Well, I've kept a couple of specimens, so what's this?' And he took the cores out of his bag and held them in front of Zhang. All the other people in Zhang's team supported Zhang's opinion.

After an hour of being contradicted by Zhang at every step, Benton told the deputy governor: 'If you're going to listen to him, I've wasted my time coming here. It's obvious that from when I arrived, nobody wanted to hear my story. You've wasted my company's time and money, and some of your own time, so I'm going. I'm taking all my plans with me. It is a waste of time talking to you people any more.'

He stood up to go, and started to roll up his plans. The deputy governor was horror struck. He jumped up and started patting Benton, trying to calm him down. The interpreter said to Benton, 'Both your company and your country are very wealthy. This is their gift to China.' Benton could not believe it.

After the final presentation, Benton decided he had really had enough. He told the Chinese he wanted to leave. They said, 'There's no air ticket for you. We've got a banquet for you in three days time with the provincial governor. You can't go before that.'

Unbeknown to the Chinese officials, Benton made an arrangement with some of the hotel attendants to buy a train ticket. He got out after a two-day trip, on a hard seat, southward to Hong Kong. On the train he finished off his tins of sardines and baked beans and his packet of biscuits.

He says of his experience, and that of other members of his team, 'The Chinese subjected us to verbal and almost physical bashing. They really do work at getting you angry and wearing you down and getting you to agree to what are pretty unreasonable terms. You get dragged into the thing more, and you get more frustrated. The thing takes on its own momentum, you start to enjoy the challenge, trying to beat these bastards and trying to win the project. All the time you are conscious that firstly, you are away from home and secondly, that the whole thing is being drawn out and you are having your money ripped off you.'

After Benton left, the other members of the team had to stay on. Like Benton, they were suffering from exhaustion because of the gruelling negotiation sessions. Staying alert was difficult. Whatever price they proposed, the Chinese said it was $2 million too high. At one stage, the team flew home for a week to completely redesign the cement plant and recost it. This placed enormous strain on them. Each time they went to China, after three days they would start thinking, 'God, we've got another three weeks of this! Is the Kraft cheese going to last out?'

Over the three years of the negotiations, pressure was put on the western team in many different ways. During the 1984 Olympics, the Chinese boasted about every win. If another country's athletes beat theirs, it was because they had cheated. They mocked the westerners when their athletes did not win medals. The western team felt as if they were being lectured on everything, on how they should live and work, and on how the Chinese had been doing something since the fifteenth century, and how beneficial it was. There seemed to be no let-up either in the negotiations or outside them.

Agreement was eventually reached on the contract for the cement plant, but the Chinese did not follow Benton's advice about how to mine the limestone. They blew the top off the mountain as they had said they would. As Benton predicted, the blast flattened villages for miles around, and resulted in rocky, contaminated limestone. However, the cement plant has continued to function and now exports cement to neighbouring provinces.

No member of the negotiating team has returned to China. Their general feeling is expressed in the comment, 'I can't think of any job that would get me to go back.'

## DISCUSSION

This case demonstrates how badly things can go for two groups of people from different cultural backgrounds who have no basis on which to meet halfway and understand each other. Benton represented a wealthy mining company which had been trading with China for 100 years, yet he and his team were given no information about the country, about how to relate to the Chinese, or about how to negotiate with them. Nor did they have their own interpreter or a go-between who knew something about the Chinese.

Because they had no guide to help them overcome the language and cultural barriers, it took them two years to find out that the guest house they were staying in had a menu. Until that revelation, they just accepted whatever Chinese food was put in front of them—and much of it was not to their liking. This simple incident typifies the lack of control they had over their negotiations in China.

I have introduced this case study because it illustrates the difficulties foreign negotiators can face in China, and how profoundly these difficulties can affect their performance and ultimately the success of the negotiation. Other case studies in this book illustrate how negotiators with more help, more experience or better bargaining talents have handled negotiations which could have been as devastating to them as this one was to the participants and to the company.

The unpleasant memory of this project lingered for years and probably soured the company's attitude to undertaking further investment in China. Only now, thirteen years later, is the company relearning how to operate in China and planning large-scale developments. Reports of its harrowing experience with the cement plant also spread to other companies, discouraging them from initiating ventures with the Chinese.

How might the foreign negotiators in this case have better served their own cause? What did they fail to understand about the Chinese business and cultural environment?

## 1 Keep an emotional distance

From the moment the western negotiators arrived in China, they were fazed by what they saw: by the finance official driving his car without any concern for the bicyclists sharing the road, by the low level of technology, by the rough conditions in which women worked, not to mention Zhang's traditional behaviour with the spittoon. The contrast between what they had expected and what they found made them hostile to the Chinese from the very beginning.

They had expected the Chinese to welcome their technology and to be friendly to them. They found the lack of cooperation and the adversarial atmosphere were shocking. Their experience in the negotiations was compounded by the callousness they experienced in Chinese life generally, such as the apparent indifference to the likelihood that the explosion would knock down people's homes. Their hostility accelerated as time passed, affecting them personally, as reflected in Benton's comment about the watermelon, and also undermined their ability to handle the negotiations rationally and to form any meaningful relationship with the Chinese.

People going from one culture to another tend to judge anything new as bad, rather than just different. The way the finance official drove illustrates the power of official position in China. Ordinary people accept this kind of behaviour. Similarly, the hardships of the women working in the quarry, which Benton found completely unacceptable, were simply a fact of life for the local people. I do not wish to condemn Benton and his fellow negotiators, as they were put into a difficult situation by their company. My purpose is to point out how a person's emotional responses can affect the way he conducts business in a foreign country. I think this aspect of international business is widely overlooked in company headquarters.

This case study also illustrates that the greater the gap between expectations and reality, the greater the disillusionment. Benton set off for China with feelings of benevolence. He and his company were going to help China, bringing it the benefits of the latest western technology. He probably had visions of China as an exotic, storybook land. When he came face to face with the Chinese negotiators and found them so unsympathetic, his illusions were shattered. His first bad experiences coloured everything that followed. In fact, they locked him into a vicious circle of negativism. Benton's was not an unusual response to first experiences in a foreign culture. Good first experiences compound, bad first experiences also compound. By the end, Benton had made the distinction between himself and the Chinese absolute: 'It is a waste of time talking to you people any more.'

## 2 Use the pre-negotiation period to check assumptions

Towards the end of the negotiations, the interpreter told Benton that the Chinese considered his company and his country to be wealthy. This belief gave strength to the Chinese side's accelerating push for more and more concessions, which stunned the foreign side. Underlying the Chinese approach is the cultural expectation that the wealthier party should be more generous than the poorer one, together with the tradition of inflating the price and then negotiating it down.

In this negotiation, the Chinese were making what were to them completely reasonable assumptions: the foreigners are wealthy and should be generous, and they have put their prices up so the Chinese must beat them down. We can see how far this was from the foreign perception of the game.

Another comment gives a clue to the difference between Chinese and foreign views about the negotiation process. Benton said, 'You start to enjoy the challenge, trying to beat these bastards and *trying to win the project*.' The Chinese evidently used the 'competitor tactic' discussed in Chapter 5. They may not have intended to give the contract to a competitor, but because the foreign team took them at their word it was drawn into a cycle of competitive tendering that may well have been unnecessary. Negotiators should be ready for the 'competitor' tactic and respond to it in a controlled manner, as was done in other examples in this book.

It is even possible that the Chinese never intended to use Benton's expertise to mine the limestone. Cost considerations were driving the whole project, and the Chinese probably saw their method as more cost-effective than Benton's. He could probably have found out what Zhang's real agenda was, and why, by some sympathetic listening and diligent face-giving.

## 3 Consider face: meet hidden needs

Zhang's intransigence was one of the things that most bothered the negotiators. There are a number of reasons for it. Given his age, he probably missed out on most of his education during the Cultural Revolution, when all schools and colleges were closed for ten years. He probably had little engineering expertise. This would have made him vulnerable in front of the young, better-educated engineers.

Benton's attacks, delivered explicitly before the whole group, humiliated Zhang in the most excruciating manner. For a stranger to come in and criticise a senior person in front of his younger colleagues is not permissible in any society. In China, it is even less so, given the Chinese respect for older people, the strong hierarchical system, and the requirement of supporting a person's reputation in public.

Zhang would have spent most of his adult life absorbing Communist Party propaganda against western commercial rapacity. This would have made him suspicious of the motives of Benton's company, and led him to see Benton as a capitalist exploiter. Benton and his group were probably the first westerners he had ever met, so he would have had no idea whether he could trust them or not. Some of his habits certainly indicate that he was not familiar with western manners.

Furthermore, as an engineer, and therefore a member of the intellectual class ('the stinking ninth'), he had most likely been criticised during the Communist Party's many campaigns against intellectuals whose expertise derives from abroad, and so would have feared being tainted with western influence.

## 4 Check your assumptions: who holds power?

Benton assumed that Zhang was the key decision maker and directed all his attacks at him. He was probably wrong. Men like Zhang are answerable to many other interested groups who have input into the negotiations. His job was probably an extremely difficult one. The provincial governor and deputy governor were involved, as were all the district authorities between the mine and the cement plant, the local and central representatives of the Ministry of Mines, and a large team from another province's mining institute. Zhang and his team were probably spending as much time negotiating with all the different interest groups on their own side as they were with the western team.

Benton got very impatient with the meetings with local officials along the way to the mountain, and with the final meeting at the foot of the mountain. He did not realise that these meetings were necessary for Zhang to get all the local authorities on side. The local county officials have almost unchallenged control over their area, and Zhang would have to take this into account. Also, Chinese decision making is by consensus *par excellence*. Benton's brash and impatient manner would have transmitted itself clearly to the Chinese officials he met on the way and would have won him no friends.

## 5 Use a go-between and your own interpreter

Benton and his team pressed for Zhang to change his mind publicly. This is completely contrary to normal Chinese negotiating procedure. Because the interpreter was on the Chinese team, the westerners really had no one to act as an intermediary, put their case sympathetically to the Chinese, or convey the nuances of Chinese thinking to them. They assumed the Chinese team was united. It may not have been at all, and they could have tried to influence individual members through an intermediary. They certainly needed someone who could diffuse the confrontations.

The interpreter's English was not very good. When Benton arrived in China, the interpreter showed him around the hotel garden. Pointing to an exotic flower, he said, 'They taste very nice.' When Benton went to put it in his mouth, the interpreter rushed to stop him. He had meant, 'They smell very nice.' Not a firm foundation on which to base a negotiation!

Members of the western team were amazed when a three-minute explanation was conveyed to the Chinese side in a few words. One can only surmise that the interpreter did not understand what was being said, or censored it. But, inexperienced in using interpreters, the western team let these problems pass without realising how damning misinterpretation could be to their case. Here again, out of ignorance, the westerners effectively handed control of communication to the Chinese side. Throughout the negotiations they felt they were being laughed at. At one stage, the interpreter explained that the laughter was a sign of embarrassment. Crossed lines like this drove a wedge of mistrust between the two sides.

There were openings that Benton might have exploited, occasions when the Chinese showed their natural concern for visitors. They worried about the tigers on top of the mountain, refrained from eating lunch until their guest arrived, and insisted that he attend the governor's banquet. Even this last opportunity, to establish a relationship with a high-ranking public figure, went unrecognised.

## 6 Negotiate around 'regulations': define the issue and look for alternatives

Benton accepted the Chinese claim that they could only do things according to the book without looking for a way around them. There are 'regulations' governing most areas of Chinese life, but the Chinese are a pragmatic people and can usually find some way to appear to conform to the 'regulations' while actually getting around them.

## 7 Allow time: do not be pushed by your predetermined time line

Benton's team started off with a certain disadvantage: they looked at the project as a short-term way to save their jobs. They had no alternative project to protect them from Chinese pressures. This gave Benton in particular a desperation which is reflected in many of his statements about the cost of being in China and his frustration at the length and number of meetings.

Although most westerners cannot devote as much time as the Chinese can to negotiations, there are many ways to push things along without reducing your negotiation strength, as we will see in later chapters.

## 8 Use the network and Chinese respect for influential people

Many things have a bearing on the way Chinese business negotiations proceed. Prestige is an important one. This team went into a province where they were unknown. It was far from Beijing and Shanghai, where their company had contacts from its trading activities. To enhance their prestige, they should have organised visits from politicians, eminent persons and foreign friends of the Chinese, diplomatic and commercial representatives in China, or leaders of the sister-state and sister-city organisations. This would have helped foster a more positive attitude from the Chinese side.

Benton's team put no store in cultivating the contacts they had established, fraught as they were, with the provincial governor, deputy governor and other officials throughout the three and a half years of the negotiation. None of the overseas Chinese who have built business empires in China since the 1980s would have been so negligent.

Even non-Chinese with questionable businesses but the right attitude towards relationship building have gained Chinese support. Panda Motors, which started out in 1988, had none of the industrial track record of the mining company in this case study, but it built support in China through astute public relations. Like the mining company, it operated in the provinces far from Beijing. Panda appointed as its chairman Douglas MacArthur II, nephew of General Douglas MacArthur, who led the American occupation of Japan after World War II. Its president was Dr Charles Kim, a Korean American and brother-in-law of former South Korean president Kim Young Sam and its depty chairman was former South Korean general Bo Hi Pak. Panda's management team used Guangdong's governor and deputy governor as well as the mayor and deputy mayor of Huizhou, where it was to be located, to lobby Beijing leaders to support the project.

It also organised for a delegation of twelve former US congressmen to meet Premier Li Peng and Party Secretary Jiang Zemin and lobby on Panda's behalf. This resulted in a promise of a $6.4 million investment of state money to improve infrastructure for the project. Eric Harwit, who tells the story of Panda Motors in his book *China's Automobile Industry*, says, 'Huizhou officials knew Panda was a new company, but were impressed by the presence of Douglas MacArthur II as board chairman. One high-ranking Huizhou official commented in an interview that he believed MacArthur would not work for a bad company.'

Panda eventually collapsed as a result of poor business planning. But its success in winning support from Chinese officials emphasises the importance of influential people to doing business in China.

## 9 The advantage of knowing about Chinese negotiation practices

Because Benton and his team knew nothing about Chinese negotiation practices, they were unable to influence the course of the talks. Issues that they might have put aside and returned to later consumed an enormous amount of their time, energy and patience. Quite often, small issues were used by the Chinese to test them out and wear them down.

In the end the Chinese prevailed. They bought the cement

plant for the minimum price and saved money by blowing up the limestone. It seems very likely that Benton's team's case was lost before they ever got to China, and that their inability to perceive this soured relations between them and the Chinese side. It also gave them many days of anger and unhappiness.

# 8 Working the network

When you study actual negotiations in China, it is impossible to ignore the personality of the negotiator himself. As we saw so graphically illustrated in Chapter 7, a negotiator's ability to perceive what really motivates the other side, and to adjust his behaviour so as not to antagonise and belittle them, is critical to his success.

In this chapter and those that follow, we will meet a number of successful western negotiators. Although their personalities differ, what distinguishes them all from Benton is their ability to understand and control certain aspects of the negotiation: to maintain a good atmosphere, to probe the Chinese point of view, and to identify 'Chinese' characteristics in the negotiation that require adjustment to their normal approach.

Michael Pointer, the negotiator in this case study, uses many of the techniques of Teresa Chung in case study 1, thus demonstrating that westerners are just as capable as the overseas Chinese of negotiating successfully in China over the long term. Like Chung, he makes being known personally to the Chinese the foundation stone of his negotiating approach. This enables him to overcome the outsider label and the ethics that go along with it.

Many overseas Chinese say of doing business in China that 'You just have to stick at it and build up your networks from the bottom.' After demonstrating regular contact and dependability, usually over a period of about three years, you can then ask for business advantages such as price discounts and favourable treatment. Pointer, to advance his business, has not only nurtured his personal relationships with people from the bottom up, but has cut out some of the work by using the Chinese respect for people in positions of power and for officially sanctioned friendship ties.

## CASE STUDY 3: 'I DID MORE BUSINESS OVER BANQUETS THAN I EVER DID IN NEGOTIATING ROOMS'

Michael Pointer is the managing director of his own sheepskin trading company in Australia. He first went to China in 1974, when the London Export Corporation unexpectedly asked him if he would represent them in an arbitration there. The LEC had been trading with China for decades. The arbitration was about skins from a US supplier which the LEC had sold to the Chinese, only to be told they were different from the sample and hit with a demand for a £500 000 refund.

Pointer had never been to China, nor had he ever been in an arbitration. Before leaving, he read books about commercial arbitrations, but nothing about China and the Chinese. With hindsight, he feels that the latter would have been more useful.

As soon as he arrived in Shanghai, the Chinese separated him from the American and told him, in no uncertain terms, that the LEC was their old friend and that, although the arbitration would be conducted totally fairly, they expected the LEC to win. Pointer says, 'I began to see how things worked in China.'

The first part of the arbitration involved inspecting the skins to determine whether or not they were identical with the original sample. Pointer and the American were taken, along with fourteen Chinese, to a large warehouse where the 600 bales were stored. It was midwinter and absolutely freezing. Pointer started to sort the skins. The Chinese all had notebooks and wrote down everything he said. The trouble was that they questioned him about every skin he handled. As a result, at the end of the day, frozen to the bone in that enormous warehouse, Pointer had only managed to grade one bale.

Back at the hotel, Pointer and the American had a strategy meeting on how they could, in Pointer's words, 'conclude the operation in something less than a year'. They decided to mentally grade the skins but say nothing, and then to write out the documentation at the hotel in the evening. That way the

Chinese could not question them on every grading they made. This worked, and they finished in five days. Although, according to Pointer, both sides were in the wrong, the arbitration found in favour of the LEC.

After the arbitration, the Chinese asked Pointer to stay on because they wanted to find out about the Australian sheepskin business. He had been shipping skins to China through European merchants. He was grilled for three days on absolutely everything. He thought to himself, 'How can I deal with this?' There were so many people, all taking copious notes. After a few days they started comparing what he was saying with what he had said days before. They would ask him, 'How does this relate to what you said earlier?' When they asked him a question he did not know the answer to, he simply said, 'I don't know the answer to that. I'll research it and let you know.' When he got back to Australia, he meticulously followed up on every question. He sent the Chinese the information and kept on doing so.

Four months later, he got a letter from the Chinese Animal By-Products Corporation saying it wanted to buy sheepskins from him and asking if he could come to the Canton Trade Fair. 'I sent a cable back, and I shall never forget this,' he says, 'It was a Wednesday. I told them I'd be delighted to come and talk business. When would they like me to come? I got a cable in return saying "Next Monday, and we've advised the Embassy to issue you with a visa." I got my visa and I did, in fact, arrive in China on the Monday.'

For most of the three weeks he spent at the fair, Pointer discussed the price of some sheepskins he was to sell the Chinese. 'That was just good, old-fashioned horse trading,' he says. Recalling this and many subsequent haggling sessions, he says: 'The negotiation starts with a fairly lengthy discussion on what the state of the market is. Then I talk about the specifications and give the Chinese a reference price, which will be 130 if my bottom line is 100. It is expected that the bargaining will start with an ambit claim so that there is something to negotiate.

'The Chinese will tell me that they can buy from my competitor at 85. I play with my calculator for a few minutes, pretending to make some calculations, consult a couple of blank pieces of paper inside a file and give them a firm price of 125. They will offer me 90. We talk about something else for a while, then I will come back to the subject and offer them 115. They might offer me 97 and so on it goes. It might take days. In fact, if they know you are there for days, it *will* take days.'

Pointer never puts 100 on the table first. His experience is that it is impossible to win a round of negotiations with the Chinese. He aims to get them to put 100 on the table. Then he accepts it. If he puts 100 on the table, he knows they will never ever go to more than 95.

Pointer spent three weeks discussing the price of that initial batch of sheepskins. He also sold the Chinese traders some hides, which he had not expected to. They already knew what Pointer had done in the arbitration in Shanghai, and one of the Shanghai people was at the bargaining table.

After his first experience of doing business with the Chinese, Pointer determined that as managing director of his company, he would always be the one to deal with them. It seemed important to him to have continuity of contact and to build on his relationships. From that time, Pointer devoted time and resources to developing the business with China.

He thought this would take two to three years, but after three years he still had a daunting number of problems. The Chinese were short of foreign exchange, so they did not send ships to pick up goods that they had bought FOB. 'This was a good way of not paying for them and still saving face,' Pointer comments with a laugh. 'It wasn't their fault, it was the ship chartering service's!'

Then there was a blue-tongue scare among the sheep in Australia and the Chinese stopped buying. But Pointer still kept going to China, throughout the political turmoil at the end of the Cultural Revolution, as well as natural disasters such as the Tangshan earthquake in 1976, when he was negotiating in Tianjin. He says, 'I just got bloody-minded and decided that there was an opportunity to build the business there, and one way or another I was going to do it!'

Pointer not only sold to the Chinese, but committed himself to buying from them as well. Trading both ways with the Animal By-products Corporation gave him the opportunity to expand dramatically his contacts in the corporation. As part of his diverse efforts to increase two-way trade, he became the largest importer of tea to Australia. 'It was terrible tea,' he laughs. 'The best thing about it was it was cheap!' He sold it to a supermarket chain which sold on the tea under its generic label. Pointer also sold angora and cashmere into Europe. On another occasion, he got caught with Chinese carpets in traditional designs that no one in Australia wanted to buy. He ended up carpeting his office and his house with them.

In the early days the Chinese monitored all incoming and outgoing telex calls. Pointer remembers one day when, having just settled on a price at which to sell hides to the Chinese, he telexed the Swiss producer to order hides from him. In the middle of his call, the line fell out. He telexed again, delaying his return to the negotiations with the Chinese.

He was feeling particularly pleased with himself as he went back to the negotiating room. He had bought the hides from the Swiss at a price that would give him a nice margin when he sold them to the Chinese. He intended to tell the Chinese person he was dealing with that he needed an extra two cents a pound. This would increase his profit even more.

Pointer walked into the discussion room and apologised for being late, explaining that he had been delayed on the telex. The Chinese negotiator replied, 'I know,' and pushed the original contract across the table to him. The negotiator already had a copy of the telex exchange. He knew not only that Pointer had already bought the hides, but also what price he had paid for them. Without saying anything about it, the negotiator let Pointer know he was not going to make any more profit than he was already making.

Pointer just laughed and signed the contract. The Chinese clearly thought it was a great joke, so Pointer felt the only thing to do was to enjoy the joke. He discovered that the Chinese had a marvellous sense of humour, which they used in all sorts of unlikely situations. Once he got to know them, he found there was no need to be terribly serious.

Pointer's policy in negotiating with the Chinese is never to paint himself—or them—into a corner. He always tries to leave room to move. He would never insist, 'It's either yes or no.' He says, 'If you have a major victory over an individual who loses the argument, you might have a nice contract, but it would be the only one you would ever have.' To illustrate his point he tells this story:

Pointer had shipped goods to Tianjin, but the Chinese said that the goods were not what they were supposed to be. Pointer believed they were correct and, moreover, that he had proven this to the Chinese. But he also understood that the Chinese commercial system is carefully compartmentalised and that no individual has responsibility for the whole thing. Just as in any bureaucracy, each department wants to hold on to its power, and it does so by causing problems for other departments that need its approval.

In this case, the Commodity Inspection Bureau said the goods were not right. So the person who had bought them told Pointer that because the bureau said they were not right, then they weren't. The Chinese buyer was in no position to contradict the Commodity Inspection Bureau, so he was not going to agree with Pointer.

What Pointer had to do was give something that would enable the buyer to save face. The buyer could then tell the Commodity Inspection Bureau people, 'You were right,' so *they* could save face. Pointer had to do this at minimal cost to himself. So he took the time to devise a reasonably logical argument for offering them an amount of compensation that Pointer knew he could get back on his next contract.

They argued over the claim all day and, as is the custom in China, at 5 p.m. the Chinese wanted to go home to dinner. Pointer had no intention of leaving the table until they had finished his new contract, which would cover the amount of the compensation. The Chinese could have got up and walked out, but he knew they would stay out of politeness. They tried a number of times to say, 'Well, we'll come back tomorrow.' Pointer replied, 'No, we won't come back tomorrow because I'm going to leave tomorrow and we're going to resolve this problem before I leave.'

He kept them sitting there until 11 p.m., well past the usual Chinese bedtime. In the end they agreed on the new contract and the amount of compensation. They only did so, he claims, because they got tired and hungry.

Pointer uses social occasions to further his business with the Chinese, although not in a straightforward way. He says, 'You've got to give them the opportunity to drop the pearls of wisdom. They will talk about all sorts of things. They'll say, "That was a pretty tough discussion we had yesterday. Our price is 90, yours is 110. Perhaps at 105 we might be able to do something."'

On one occasion, after a morning of sightseeing in the valley of the Ming Tombs north of Beijing, Pointer and his hosts reached an agreement about a piece of business while they were having lunch at a little roadside restaurant. They wrote the contract out on the paper tablecloth, tore it in two, and each party took their part back to Beijing to be typed up that night.

Nothing upsets Pointer more than hearing western business people complain about having to go to a banquet. 'I do more business over banquets than I ever do in negotiating rooms,' he says. 'All we ever do in negotiating rooms is have a long argument to arrive at the point that we reached the evening before over dinner.' Over the meal (which many westerners find a stiff and awkward occasion), Pointer makes sure he develops a nice, friendly, personal relationship with the Chinese. He asks individuals about themselves, their role, their families and where they come from. He also attempts to find out the Chinese position.

In business terms, the most important information Pointer gets from banquet conversation is the market price. If the market is 100, the Chinese expect to buy at 90. Pointer knows there is no point going in at 150. This helps him determine his starting point, from which he can negotiate down to 100.

One of Pointer's biggest strengths is his friendly way of taking the initiative. Although, in his experience, the Chinese like to open meetings by setting out their view of the matter in question, Pointer makes a determined effort to beat them to it. He is experienced in chairing meetings, and does it well. When he meets with the Chinese he tries to maintain de facto chairmanship of the meeting so he can lead it in the direction he wants, rather than in the direction the Chinese want. Many western negotiators resist presenting their position first, believing that this puts them at a disadvantage.

To Pointer, it is as simple as making the first statement. As the visitor he has an advantage. When he comes to a negotiation, he knows he will first speak to one or two people he knows, then be introduced to a couple of extras. He sits down and uses the pause to start: 'Thank you for the opportunity of meeting with you today. I'd like to give you a briefing on the situation as I see it at the moment.' He says, 'You've got to be quick.' He believes doing this gives him a tactical advantage by obliging the Chinese to respond to his initiative. He gives them information to begin with because they will not offer any unless they get some in return.

Although he works to develop his personal relationships with the Chinese, Pointer does not fall for what he calls 'the old line, "You're our old friend and you've got to help us because of the potential and it will be all right in the end."' He says, 'That is a great stunt and a very good way of getting someone to sell them something at a discount.' He is never prepared to sell at a lower price than he can sell to somebody else. Because of this attitude, there have been times when he has gone to China and done no business at all.

What gives the Chinese this bargaining power is that in the overall scheme of things, their business with an individual company is unimportant. If they do not do the business with that company, they will do it with another one. Apart from some particular pieces of equipment, that applies to just about everything. The Chinese understand the commercial clout of their buying power. However, according to Pointer, this does not make them disloyal business partners. If they have an offer from a competitor at a lower price, they will tell him what it is so he can negotiate with them, usually to the same price as the competitor. In his experience this is different from the American approach of going with the lowest bid. In the US he would have to offer a lower price than the competitor to get the business—if the buyers were to tell him about the competitor in the first place, which he doubts.

In the end, Pointer considers that the people one knows are the most important factor in doing business in China. When he began his business he was working through the bureaucracy from the bottom up. Later, as president of the Australia–China Chamber of Commerce and Industry, and as chairman of the China Advisory Committee to the Premier of Victoria, he was able to expand his contacts from the top down. Starting at the top was a lot easier because he got to the right person more quickly.

He says, 'The same thing happens anywhere. If you are introduced at the right level as somebody who is acceptable, you are instantly able to make contact with the decision makers. In dealing with China, 'sister-state' and 'sister-city' relationships facilitate introductions to influential people, and act as bona fide referees.' He has seen the power of these associations on a number of occasions.

In Nanjing, the capital of Jiangsu, which is sister state to Pointer's Victoria, he was known through the work he had done with the chamber of commerce and the Victorian government. He had been trying for several years to buy silk noiles. This is a very valuable product that is spun into other products, and the market was dominated by Japanese buyers. Every time Pointer was in Nanjing he would try to buy, and every time the man in charge of silk noiles would be 'away'.

One evening Pointer was with the Chinese director of Foreign Affairs and the director of the Foreign Trade Bureau, and they had been discussing all the exchanges with Victoria. The director of Foreign Affairs turned the conversation to Pointer's business with Jiangsu. Pointer brought up the problems he had in contacting the man in charge of silk noiles. The director replied, 'We'll see what we can do about that.' At 7.30 the next morning there was a knock on Pointer's bedroom door. Standing there was the man in charge of silk noiles.

Pointer had a similar experience when he was trying to buy angora rabbit hair. Shanghai produced the best quality hair but he was finding it impossible to buy any. Then one day, as leader of a sister-state delegation, he was invited to lunch by Johnson Liu, then chairman of the Shanghai International Trust and Investment Corporation and the son of the 'match king of China'.

The day before, Liu had asked Pointer how his business was going. Pointer replied that it was fine, but that he was having a problem buying angora rabbit hair. Nothing more was said. Pointer and his delegation went to a lunch with a number of leaders of Shanghai commerce as well as the deputy mayor. Among the people at Pointer's table was the deputy manager of the department responsible for angora rabbit hair, although he was quite out of his level among the other guests. They had a pleasant lunch and not a word was said about rabbit hair. That afternoon Pointer signed a contract with the deputy manager.

Chinese slowness frustrates Pointer, as it does most westerners trying to do business in China. He says of it, 'The only time that is important is the time of day. It's important to be punctual. But the time it takes to do something is of no consequence whatsoever. They'll invite you to come and do some negotiation with them on Monday. The responsible person will not turn up until Wednesday. There will be someone there to give you lunch and dinner, show you around and talk to you. They are quite likely to finish Wednesday's discussion and say, "We'll come back to this next Monday."

'If they need you more than you need them, you can do something about it. But again it becomes a negotiating thing. I'll say to them, because I believe that they always wilt under the force of argument, "I've come all this way to see you, and really I have some other things to do. Can we meet tomorrow morning at 11 o'clock instead of next Monday?" Ninety nine times out of 100, you finish up meeting on Saturday.'

Chinese slowness worked both for and against Pointer's business in China. He deals in a commodity with a highly volatile value. When the market was rising, it was difficult to do business with the Chinese because they would have their committee meetings, decide that the market price was 100, and want to buy at 100. But by the time they had made that decision, the price would have gone to 120. When the market was falling, it would take them just as long to find out that the price was not 100, it had gone down to 80.

Pointer has traded through all the enormous changes that have taken place in China during recent years. The people he once dealt with in the import–export corporations now manage the many independent businesses that have formed. It is much closer to a free-enterprise system. Pointer can no longer rely on the government to guarantee payment. Nowadays a contract is only as good as the person on the other end of it. Even so, he still feels that the Chinese are remarkably loyal to those with whom they do business.

Recently the market price on a contract which still had a way to run increased sharply. The Chinese realised that Pointer would suffer a substantial loss. So they contacted him and renegotiated the contract so that both sides lost a little. The Chinese man involved had done many deals over fifteen years with Pointer. He was a long-standing business associate and friend.

Thinking back to his first visit to China in 1974, Pointer says, 'I guess the one thing I left Shanghai with then was the overwhelming impression of this huge mass of humanity, but at the same time of what delightful individual people they were. Just gentle, nice people, and therefore I didn't find it difficult to get to know a lot of them quite well.'

Pointer is very clear about the motives driving each side in a negotiation, and says these have changed over the years. Now the Chinese want to make a profit on everything. In a joint venture they want to get as much for their side as they can. I ask him what he thinks of the idea that the Chinese have a win–lose mentality in negotiations. He laughs and replies, 'No. More like a "win–win" mentality . . . the Chinese have no intention of losing!'

## DISCUSSION

### 1 Value relationships

Pointer's attitude to the people he is dealing with contrasts markedly with that of the mining engineers in case study 2. They put all their emphasis on their technical knowledge, as if that would be enough in itself to persuade the Chinese to accept their proposals. But this approach also made Chinese lack of compliance all the more incomprehensible and destabilising for them. Pointer puts as much time and effort into developing his personal relationships with the Chinese as he puts into the technical aspects of the negotiation itself.

This point is reinforced in several of the case studies in this book. In any country the people involved and their views of one another are important to the outcome of negotiations. In China, the relationship factor probably plays a greater role because of the factors discussed in Chapter 2: the preference for dealing with people who are well known and tied to the group over a lifetime, and the suspicion of westerners.

Very early in his experience in China, Pointer saw the effects of the network: when the Chinese told him the London Export Corporation would win the arbitration, when he learned word about him had passed from Shanghai to the Canton Trade Fair, and when one of the Shanghai people appeared at the fair.

The issue of breaking or honouring contracts is a vexed one for people doing business in China. The depth of the relationship may be the key to the ethics that govern the situation. When Pointer was set to lose money on a contract because of a change in the market, his trading partners volunteered to renegotiate it in a typically Chinese way, so that both sides lost a little, rather than all the loss being on one side.

This incident brings to mind a story about the Co-hong traders, who were appointed to handle trade with westerners in Canton in the mid-nineteenth century. Seeing an American stranded in Canton by his business reverses, Howqua, one of the richest of the Co-hong traders, called him in and tore up an I.O.U. from the American for $72 000. He announced: 'You and I are No. 1 old friends; you are an honest man, only you had some bad luck' (MacNair 1913).

## 2 Get to know influential people

There are a number of examples in this case study of how Chinese officials are able to facilitate business. China has a long tradition of bureaucratic control of and participation in business, as well as respect for people in positions of power. Because Pointer had been president of the Australia–China Chamber of Commerce and Industry, and had been in many government-led delegations through the sister-city agreement, he was able to use his official position to further his business.

As managing director, he personally undertook to develop his company's China business rather than leave it to a subordinate. Because of the Chinese respect for those in positions of authority, managing directors have a special role to play in negotiations. Large companies should ensure that managers at a high level take an active role in meeting their Chinese counterparts. This has always been the case at the Australian company Pacific Dunlop, where not only the managing director but also the chairman undertake relationship-building in China on a regular basis.

Titles are sometimes downplayed in English-speaking countries, but they are very important in China. The whole consciousness of hierarchy is expressed in the exchange of business cards—originally a Chinese tradition—which clearly state one's position in the company. In the past, China's business cards were of different sizes. A very large one, 60cm by 30cm, was used to herald the arrival of a high-ranking imperial official. Symbols of status can be identified today: the mayor (a very powerful person in today's China) will wear a well-cut suit of high-quality fabric; top Chinese business people use business cards embossed with traditional characters rather than the Communist-introduced simplified characters. Such symbols are dictated by the Chinese sensitivity to status and reputation.

We saw how much power bosses have over subordinates when the Chinese negotiating team refused point blank to change the terms of reference that had been decided by top officials and approved by the State Council. It is understandable, then, why the officials Pointer met in Nanjing and Shanghai were able to arrange for him to buy silk noiles and angora rabbit hair.

## 3 Build credibility: take their questions seriously

The Chinese have excellent networks, large numbers of people to do research, a tradition of playing one competitor off against another, and a training in patient attention to detail. They bring all these things into play in assessing what a foreign negotiator tells them. Since they are rarely in a great hurry—unlike most westerners—they are prepared to spend a lot of time questioning and double-checking the answers. When they find a discrepancy, they will use it to pressure the foreign negotiator.

Pointer's way of handling such incidents is to say, 'I don't know the answer to that, but I will research it and let you know.' This is the best way to avoid giving incorrect answers and thus undermining your credibility, or opening yourself to Chinese pressure tactics as they exploit inconsistencies.

The questions themselves can give the foreign negotiator clues about what is important to the Chinese. If you think about what they ask and how they ask it, you will be able to discover what is important to them, or what their goal is. Never dismiss the questions as a nuisance, as the engineers did. Knowing Chinese aims can help you structure your case to meet their objectives and, furthermore, not to do so too cheaply.

## 4 Follow the Chinese bargaining process: meet face and Chinese interests

Pointer demonstrated the Chinese bargaining process: begin with an ambit claim and negotiate it step by step. Never say 'yes or no' or paint yourself or them into a corner. Their attitude is that the whole world wants to do business with them. If you go in too hard and the Chinese negotiator loses face, he can do the business with someone else.

This was particularly important in the Commodity Inspection Bureau incident, as Pointer had nothing to gain by proving that the bureau people were in the wrong. Because Pointer understands the system and the Chinese need to avoid publicly embarrassing anybody, he was able to deal with the situation in a calm and friendly manner, but *without giving in.*

Pointer's strategy was rather 'Chinese': he acknowledged the Chinese demands but also got something back. This is negotiating around face. Teresa Chung does exactly the same thing. She always tries to get something back without turning the situation into a federal court case.

The bargaining process takes time. If you are in too much of a hurry, it is impossible to manage things so you get the outcome you want. Pointer spent three weeks on his initial negotiation with the Chinese, and noted another Chinese characteristic: 'If they know you are there for days, it will take days.' This is why many foreign business people give the Chinese a false departure date to try to bring the decision making forward.

The intensity and thoroughness of the bargaining process have forced Pointer to prepare his case in detail before leaving for China; to search for all the facts and information relevant to the market or the particular business, as well as what his competitors are doing; and to be crystal clear about his bottom line. He is determined never to go below that. When to do business means he will lose money, he goes home without the business. If you use a 'loss leader', the Chinese will take that as the benchmark and you will find it difficult to bring future business up to a profitable level.

## 5 Know your own benefit

The tactic of using 'regulations' to convince foreign negotiators to go the Chinese way is similar to another common Chinese influence tactic: telling foreigners they are 'our old friend'. A Chinese article on negotiation recommends '[using] psychological stimulation to get the opponent to accept your offer by taking advantage of the customer's expectation of long-term trade, a "big head" or a big company's self-importance, and the willingness of a customer to agree based on old friendship' (Li 1989). Pointer's acute comment, 'That is a good way to get somebody to sell them something at a discount,' goes to the heart of the strategy. Unfortunately this 'old friend' approach has made many negotiators feel special and induced them to drop their normal standards of good business practice.

No negotiator should accept his opponent's word as to any future benefit or the content of any 'regulation'. The Chinese team leader will make almost any claim to influence the westerner to accept his version of the situation, because impressing his own team with his efficacy is far more important to him than what the foreign negotiator may think. Everything needs to be checked out and dispassionately examined from a bottom-line perspective.

It is all too easy in China to do things because of potential, rather than actual, growth or profit. The Chinese are skilled at being charming and gracious, offering the potential of their huge market and putting all doubts to rest! Victoria, Pointer's home state, did in fact undertake a 'goodwill' construction in Nanjing to impress the Chinese with the skills and quality of their construction industry. The building, paid for by the Victorian building industry, was handed over to the Chinese, who used it thereafter for their own purposes, not as a showcase for Australian building skills. No Victorian has ever set foot in it since, and no contracts came out of it. In return, the Chinese built the Facing Heaven Gateway, a traditional wooden gate, in Melbourne's Chinatown at a minuscule fraction of the cost of the Australian building. Such are the rewards for accepting Chinese promises of future business. I do not blame the Chinese because of this, but only use the example to warn western negotiators that 'goodwill' can blind them to Chinese agendas.

## 6 Keep an emotional distance: accept some things with good humour

Pointer did not make a fuss when the Chinese illegally tapped into his telex call to Europe. He should have known that there is no confidentiality in China. Chinese office staff inform their bosses about expatriate salaries and correspondence that passes through their hands. Any workman coming into a manager's office has the right to look through any correspondence that happens to be lying on the manager's desk. I would recommend Bill Purves's inside account of managing a joint venture in Guangdong, *Barefoot in the Boardroom*, to anyone who wants to know how little privacy there is in China, and how a Chinese general manager's office really operates. You have to recognise that the Chinese will use anything against you (particularly if it is a weakness).

## 7 Use informal occasions to check facts and assumptions

Because the foreign negotiator is excluded from approaching the Chinese in their offices or at their homes, as he might do if he were negotiating in his own country, banquets and other entertainments are a rare opportunity to talk informally with them. As Pointer found, at such events a Chinese team member will often give a hint on what his side is thinking.

The contract written on the tablecloth was the largest contract Pointer ever drew up in China, so the informal setting did not inhibit the Chinese from doing the deal. Sometimes they will suddenly announce at a banquet that they agree to do a deal when formal discussions have seemed to be getting nowhere.

The use of such occasions to influence the Chinese side in the nicest possible way should never be underestimated. It is just another example of relationships being a cornerstone of negotiation success.

## 8 Take control

Pointer followed this maxim in two different ways in this case study. He took control at the beginning of negotiations to put his point of view and move the agenda in the way he wanted it to go. He also took control of the time, suggesting to the Chinese on one occasion that they bring forward the meeting from Wednesday week to Saturday, and on another by insisting his contract be completed that night because he was leaving China the next day. In each case he fully played up the fact that he was a guest, and that the Chinese always try to look after guests. If they do not, they lose face.

# 9    Taking control

One of the most difficult negotiations in China is to establish a joint venture which meets current western standards for the recruitment of staff, their performance and remuneration, as well as the technical aspects of the business. What the western negotiator wants to achieve is invariably contrary to Chinese business practice and to many Chinese goals.

The Chinese partners will wish to put as many of their staff on the payroll as possible, while the western partner, in line with international productivity benchmarking, will want to employ as few people as possible. The Chinese will want control over who is assigned to the joint venture, while the foreigner will want to base hiring practice on experience and ability, without regard to a person's connections. The Chinese will want to maximise their profit and the amount of foreign currency brought in, while the westerner will be intent on maximising efficiency and technical excellence.

The result is inevitably confrontation. In this type of situation the Chinese give full play to their characteristic negotiation tactics, in particular the use of 'regulations', the use of threats and psychological pressure, slowness and demands for lengthy explanations and justification. Members of the bureaucracy often do not want to negotiate at all: they simply want you to accept their decrees, not only on small matters but on matters central to the success of the enterprise.

The case study in this chapter shows how these pressures can be handled effectively despite the frustration and anger they arouse in western negotiators.

## CASE STUDY 4: 'WE KEPT BRINGING IT BACK TO WHAT WAS FAIR'

TNT, an international transport company, began negotiating to set up an express freight joint venture in China in 1988. The venture was to provide an express delivery service, using long-distance road freighters, between Shanghai and Shenzhen. Paul Goode, general manager corporate projects, headed TNT's negotiation team.

Although TNT's immediate partners were keen to get the joint venture established, the bureaucracy was not so helpful. Goode spent five years negotiating in Shanghai, Beijing and Shenzhen before agreement was reached in 1993.

TNT knew that the Chinese had fixed ideas about how a joint venture should be established and managed, but it did not wish to accept them. It wanted to establish the business according to its own standards of profitability and efficiency. TNT put certain items into its negotiating strategy on which it was determined not to compromise. Chinese willingness to agree on these points would determine whether or not the company would go ahead with the joint venture. One of the most important issues concerned the recruitment and salary of the Chinese deputy general manager. At the time, it was the accepted thing that the Chinese would be solely responsible for appointing the deputy general manager, without any input from the western partner or from the expatriate general manager.

Goode's view was that if the deputy general manager was not chosen on merit, the business would be paying for something for which it was getting no value. He says, 'There is a difference between the cost of doing business and getting robbed! Paying such a huge salary with no regard to the value of the deputy general manager is just another way of siphoning money off the joint venture. We had to define the ongoing principle we wanted to have here. It is the same as in Australia. The deputy general manager would get paid for his experience and on performance. If he was no good, then "thanks for coming, we'll see you later".

'We wanted to have that principle in from the start. And that is what we had to keep hammering at them: you had to pay for something that was real. They would say, "This is the way it is done in China and you'll do it." We said, "No, we won't," and we didn't.' Goode dealt with pressure from the

Chinese side by putting it into perspective. He said, 'I don't think the Chinese are different from anybody else. If they can get you to move from your position to theirs, they will continue to try doing that.'

One of the Chinese negotiators, a Party representative, consistently took a hard, antagonistic line. He insisted on the Party's position that all personnel, from the deputy general manager down to the workers, should be paid salaries calculated at a fixed percentage of the expatriate general manager's salary. He never shifted from this position, and Goode never shifted from his: that workers should be paid on the basis of ability and what they could bring to the joint venture. The Party man ended up being moved on. Goode kept reiterating that the concept of fair play is not just a western concept, that performance and ability must be the criteria, and nothing else.

It was clear to Goode that the Chinese had very little experience of the bases on which managers in the west are compensated and promoted. As a way of convincing them of the rightness of his position, he brought the Chinese to Australia, showed them what people in various positions did, explained how they were graded on experience, performance and ability, and pointed out how their salary reflected this grading.

The size of the salaries was also an issue. The Chinese practice was for the deputy general manager to be paid 75 to 80 per cent of the general manager's salary. Many expatriate general managers had salaries as high as $US500 000. Although the Chinese expected $350 000 to $400 000 for their man, he would receive only a small fraction of this sum, because another regulation stipulated that the salary was to be paid to the Chinese partner organisation which would keep most of it and give him the rest. Goode showed the Chinese the salary of the executive who was to run the venture. Because the job did not warrant a top manager, he was to come from the ranks of middle management. Far from earning $500 000 a year, he was to be paid just $65 000.

Goode also wanted all salaries, including the general manager's, to be paid by the joint venture, not by TNT. The Chinese tried to put the cost of the expatriate manager on to TNT, saying, 'If you must have someone of this status, with such expensive housing, then you should pay for it.' TNT insisted that these were part of the costs of the joint venture, and that what the Chinese were paying for was western knowledge and technology.

TNT repeatedly put forward their point of view that they would teach the Chinese so that eventually they could run the joint venture on their own. Often in joint ventures, the foreign company invested only capital and kept all the knowledge and technology secret, so that the business fell over when the expatriate manager left. TNT intended to share its management knowledge and technology, as well as provide capital.

If the discussion did not go the way the Chinese wanted, they would expect Goode to concede because he was running out of time. He would say, 'Well, we can't proceed on this. We will come back to it later.' He acted as if he had all the time in the world. He made it clear that he was committed to his point of view, and that if he did not succeed this time, he would next time.

Although some of the issues made the negotiation very difficult, they were integral to the philosophy of TNT. Goode wanted to surmount them, and so did his immediate Chinese partners—although not necessarily the bureaucracy. Both sides had made a big investment of time and neither wanted to say, 'Oh well, we just can't settle this one, so that's it. We'll pack our bags and go home.'

As time passed, the role of the Party representatives and the bureaucracy became less and less important. In the end, the Chinese accepted that the deputy general manager would be appointed in consultation with the general manager, that his salary would be performance-based and at a lower rate than the mandated 75 per cent, and that it would be paid directly into his bank account, without a percentage being retained by the authorities.

They also accepted that other workers in the joint venture would be recruited by the general manager and paid on the basis of their skills, and not on a flat percentage rate. This discussion on salaries took eighteen months, and was conducted for periods of two to three weeks every three months.

When Goode was discussing building a new freight terminal, the Chinese once again tried to push him into what served their needs, not his. He handled the enormous pressure with firmness and a low-key manner. Even so, he admits that it was not at all easy.

'We had to have a new building built for the freight terminal.

I had to get them to build it the TNT way. That was difficult. What we call a "freight terminal" in Australia—a shed with a single-span roof, docks for trucks to back up to, room for a forklift to move about in—had nothing to do with what the Chinese call a "freight terminal". They would think of a two-storey building with concrete posts every three metres. If there was a dock it certainly would not be level with the truck floor . . . they'd have made sure of that! An articulated vehicle wouldn't have room to manoeuvre and there would be no room for expansion. Our whole reputation in the express freight business is built on the fact that we *move* freight, we do not store it. In China they say that if 100 packages go through a terminal in a day, all they would move would be maybe 25, so there would have to be room to store 75.

'In meetings with their engineers and planners there would be one person in the room who knew what I was talking about, but we were outnumbered by all the bureaucrats who wanted to build these bloody buildings with concrete columns every 3m, and 2m to 2.5m ceilings. To try to explain to them the concept of an open shed with a single span, the use of rolled-steel joists in the ceiling and a translucent roof (their roofs are concrete because it is cheap) . . . you are looking at two days before anybody in the room has even a basic understanding!

'First, they do not want to understand the concept because they think you are crazy. And then, as you try to explain it, they revert to the defensive position. They say, "Well, that is the way you build it in Australia, but here we do it like this." Then I have to make sure that I remain calm while I remind them that I am there because they recognise TNT as the expert in express freight, and ask if they are still willing to accept our point of view. I was responsible for representing the company correctly, and for setting up the joint venture for the long term. I had to show them a different way of doing things. It was very difficult. I can understand why a lot of western business people give up, because the Chinese process wears you down.'

Goode says the Chinese he dealt with often lost their temper, although he found the main negotiators reasonable enough. They did not agree with him about many things, but they were reasonably consistent and he could usually argue logically with them. Occasionally they would bring in a bureaucrat who would lose his patience with Goode. He would be patronising and say

that the Chinese know what is best for China. Even when he
believed the Chinese were wrong, Goode had to sit through it
and listen. He would remind them that they invited him, and
that if they recognised TNT as the expert, then, since he was
the company's representative, they should listen to him.

On every item, the Chinese would push for things to be
done according to their custom. Goode protected himself from
this pressure by making certain items, such as the recruitment
and salary issues, and the completion of the freight terminal,
non-negotiable.

The second slice of TNT's capital investment was tied to
the terminal's completion. When the Chinese said, 'The terminal
is complete,' he said, 'We need a certificate of practical
completion.' In China, there is no equivalent, so they said,
'When we say it is finished, you will pay the money.' He said,
'No, when you say it is finished, we will apply the definition
of practical completion and we will get some experts to come
to China who understand our concept, and if they say it is
complete, we'll pay the money.' His attitude was that you can
never afford to just say, 'When in Rome . . .' and play it 100
per cent by their rules. He says, 'If it is a joint venture, then
by definition you are asking them to accept 50 per cent of
what you want to do.'

All the way through the negotiations, Goode insisted on
auditing the investment inputs from both sides. As in most joint
ventures, TNT was putting in foreign currency, which was easy
to document, and the Chinese were investing in kind: the land
and the buildings, whose value was not so easily documented.

This difference in inputs protracted the negotiations. Goode
kept trying to assess what the Chinese share was worth. He
had to work out the equivalent in dollars, and decide what was
fair. He says, 'You can't say the land is worth three times what
it is just to make it equal to the foreign contribution. They
understand the concept "equal". It doesn't mean "Let's pretend
it is equal", it must really be equal.' He insisted on an auditable
record of all the joint venture's capital contributions to make
sure the equity was valid. This demanded a great deal of time
and stamina, but was satisfactorily achieved in the end.

To help bridge the gap between the Chinese negotiators'
ideas and his own, Goode often invited them to dinner at his
hotel, using the opportunity to get a feel for what they were

thinking and give them a better understanding of his own position. He would do the same when they invited him out.

Slowness in negotiations is a major complaint of western business people in China. Goode explains what happened in his case: 'If you and I were going to discuss the deputy general manager's salary package, maybe if I thought it was going to be real tough, I'd allow a day . . . it took us 18 months! So my expectation was wrong. Probably if you went to the Chinese at the start and asked, 'How long will it take to discuss the deputy general manager's salary?', they would probably say half a day, because as far as they are concerned it is simple: you pay him 75 per cent of the expatriate general manager's salary. I wanted to change the rules completely, yet I still had an expectation that we could knock it over in one meeting . . . wrong! You have to understand what their expectations are.

'As part of that, you learn just how far apart our culture is from theirs. "Urgent" for us doesn't mean the same for them. A short-term strategy for us is this week or this month or at least in this year's business plan. When our negotiations started the people from China said, "We will do everything we can to make sure this is dealt with quickly. They explained to us they meant *five years*, and in fact it did take five years. So far as the Chinese are concerned they did pretty well. As far as we are concerned, we can't believe that it has taken this long to do things!'

The fact that every conversation had to be translated added immeasurably to the time required to negotiate and to the level of understanding. Goode recalls, 'You put your argument. It goes through into interminable interpretations. The Chinese side has a discussion, then they are about to say something . . . by this time you are lucky if you can remember what you said originally. You have to focus on who you are talking to and what the interpreter is saying against a background of people coming and going, and discussions going on in other parts of the room. It is a very difficult process. What we might have done in ten or fifteen minutes if we shared the same language, would take a minimum of two hours.

'When you say something you include gestures, nuances and body language. You may think you have done pretty well, because you know exactly what you have said. But although the interpreter might be good at literal translation, he may not understand where you are coming from or the whole context.

So he will then tell you what they said, and it is clear that they have not understood quite what you meant. The process is just so protracted.'

In 1988 the Chinese economy was entirely centralised. Any formal agreement had to have the seal of approval from Beijing. Goode would discuss something with his Chinese partners. It then went to the bureaucrats in Shanghai, who gave it their approval, then it would go to Beijing for another stamp. He says: 'The most difficult thing is the debilitating effect of the bureaucracy and the sheer numbers of people. We know there are differences when we go up there, and we see them as soon as we arrive, but you have to actually work within the system to feel the grinding effect that it can have on you. It was very time consuming: lots of meetings, lots of explanations, lots of going round and round and over and over the same ground all the time. The bureaucrats' attitude was that they were in charge of the rules and regulations, so you should just do as you were told and wait your turn.'

One of the most frustrating experiences Goode had was explaining the concept of express delivery to members of the bureaucracy: that his company would pick something up and get it to the destination much faster than the Chinese were currently doing. This idea was completely new to the Chinese. Their freight cycle was three to four weeks. He told them, 'We are bringing in this type of truck and we can get the trip down to 40 hours, but let us say 48 hours. So we can pick up on Monday afternoon and deliver on Thursday morning.'

One of the Chinese team asked, 'Why would you want to do that?' Goode replied that as the Chinese economy developed, the transport chain would speed up. This had no meaning for the Chinese. He says: 'They looked at me like, "This is novel" . . . like selling a refrigerator in Alaska!' He realised that not only did they not understand, but they suspected there was something in it for TNT that he was not telling them. Goode explained the idea as honestly and as well as he could, but he could see it did not make sense to them. He was unprepared for this kind of frustration, because usually he is questioned about the services or products his company provides, not the rationale behind them.

On a number of occasions, Goode left his Chinese partners to deal with the bureaucracy over such matters as pulling down a building or clearing the building site. But when he returned to China for the next negotiating session, the job would not have been done. His partners would either have gone to the ministry or council and made no headway, or not have gone at all.

He would say to them, 'Now we are going to see the ministry, and this is what we want. Sock it to them. Don't sit back and let us get railroaded again.' He added that this was part of their responsibility to the joint venture. They agreed to go, but told Goode that if he really wanted some action he would have to go with them. They asked him to sit there looking angry while they did the talking. He says, 'If that's the way you play the game, and ultimately everybody gets what they want, you do it!' Although he did not know what they were saying, he assumed it was something like, 'This was supposed to be done, it hasn't been, and so-and-so from TNT is up here now, and the whole joint venture is in jeopardy.' In any case, it achieved the desired result.

One of the biggest problems for TNT was gathering the information on which the joint venture's financial projections would be based. Goode says, 'I have never been anywhere in the world where if you don't ask absolutely the right question, you will not get the right answer. At home if you ask a simple question about directions, you'll probably get all the information and an alternative route.

'In setting up the joint venture I would ask, "How much is a truck driver paid?" I wanted to know how much it will cost the joint venture to hire such a person. What they would tell me is either what the most expensive driver gets, or what the least expensive driver gets, and they would not tell me that I have to provide housing and other things I would not equate with the company's responsibility in Australia. The result was that without the right information I would understate the cost by miles. I would go back and say, "You didn't tell me that I should double that figure because there is an accommodation cost," and they would reply, "Well, you didn't ask us that!"'

Goode believes that in asking questions in China, westerners need to be very detailed, precise and specific. He ended up gathering trustworthy information from other foreign companies in a similar business. Since there were no reliable statistics available in China, he found compiling his own more reliable than taking statistics from overseas and trying to adjust them for Chinese conditions.

# DISCUSSION

## 1 Negotiate around Chinese 'regulations': define the issue and look for alternative solutions

This case study illustrates how the Chinese use appeals to false authority and to their way of doing things to pressure foreigners to give in to them on certain issues. Goode came under considerable psychological pressure to fall in line with Chinese 'regulations'.

It is noteworthy that during the five-year negotiation period, the balance of power was changing in China, and this was to TNT's advantage. The Party representatives who spent endless hours pressuring Goode to obey 'regulations' gradually disappeared from the negotiations. This has been noted by many negotiators over the past fifteen years, as the Communist left wing has lost power in China and the economic reformers have gained power.

Effective influence strategies are needed to move the Chinese away from their demands and to open alternative solutions to difficult issues. Because all things in China are negotiable, the Chinese are open to the force of argument. Goode used several different strategies, depending on the issue.

### 1.1 Determine your own benefit: non-negotiable items

TNT had clear objectives for this negotiation, and it signalled them early to the Chinese side. These non-negotiable items gave Goode a number of focal points on which he could stand against Chinese pressure. He succeeded in changing many positions taken by the Chinese: on the recruitment and salary issues, on the building of the freight terminal, on payment of capital on Chinese say-so that the terminal was complete, on the Chinese evaluation of their investment in kind.

The Chinese approach was always that these things were mandated and not open to negotiation. You could say that Goode was quite Chinese in the way he negotiated around the non-negotiable! Also notable is that he was able to achieve this without a breakdown in relations.

However, making items non-negotiable will not in itself lead to a successful outcome. Influence strategies are needed to bring the Chinese around to your way of thinking.

## 1.2 Use first principles

When the Chinese used the forcing tactic, 'This is the way it is done in China,' Goode went back to first principles. He reminded them that they had invited TNT to China, and that since they acknowledged TNT as an expert in express freight, they should defer to TNT's point of view.

In a study of foreign companies in China, 50 per cent said they had been invited to China because of their expertise (Eitman 1990). The study found that this fact did not deter the Chinese from trying to override foreign expertise by insisting on the superiority of the Chinese way. This indicates two hidden motives driving the Chinese: that foreign capital is as important, if not more important, to them than technology (which most western companies focus on); and that many Chinese lose face when westerners flaunt their superiority in technology and systems. Negotiators should not forget to look for the unspoken motives on the Chinese side.

## 1.3 Use 'fair play' notions

In the discussions on the deputy general manager's recruitment and salary and on auditing the Chinese equity, Goode appealed to the Chinese sense of fairness. This tackled head-on their preference for making special rules for their own in group and other rules for members of out groups.

## 1.4 Use documentary evidence and outside experts

This can be extremely effective in China, because there are usually many people on the Chinese side who have input into decision making but are not present in the face-to-face negotiations. They need to be convinced behind the scenes. Using documentary evidence and experts is helpful here, and also addresses the Chinese preoccupation with trickery. They are always afraid that the other side is being devious and, without concrete evidence, never feel they can trust what is said to them.

By showing the Chinese the salaries and performance criteria of Australian managers, and explaining how the Chinese managerial jobs compared with them, Goode provided irrefutable evidence that his proposals were reasonable and not a way to cheat the Chinese. He achieved a similar result when he brought in international experts to adjudicate on the completion of the freight terminal. Both actions removed the issue from simply being a difference of opinion.

### 1.5 Alter the power balance: change location

Bringing the Chinese to Australia to let them see for themselves the levels of management, and the responsibilities and remuneration that went with them, shifted the balance of power which had been weighted to the Chinese side by holding the negotiations in Shanghai and Beijing. As most westerners are obliged to negotiate in China, this makes them all the more susceptible to Chinese pressure tactics. It gives strength to Chinese negotiators, especially those who have never travelled abroad and therefore accept Chinese custom as the only way to solve issues.

Goode broke Chinese control over the negotiation. He was also able to bring in other people to lend authority to what he was saying. This made it harder for the Chinese to insist that things be done their way.

## 2 Give explanations that are in line with Chinese interests

Negotiating in China generally involves far more explanation than in most other countries. One of Goode's strengths is his ability to explain his point of view in a thorough and reasonable way.

When the Chinese wanted TNT to pay for the salary package and accommodation of the expatriate general manager by saying, 'if you must have someone of that status, who has to have that level of accommodation . . .' Goode pointed out that TNT was already contributing unacknowledged benefits to the project by bringing in its expertise and technology—in line with China's economic goals. Similarly, when he was faced with bureaucrats who doubted the usefulness of express freight, he was able to control his frustration and explain the underlying reasons for introducing such a business to China and the benefits this would bring.

An ability to answer criticisms and allay doubts by thorough explanation is essential for any negotiator going to China. If you are unable to do this without dictating or being arrogant, you had best find someone else to represent your company.

## 3 Allow time: controlling head-office expectations

Goode was extremely fortunate because his company, TNT, did not see the China project as urgent. It was prepared to make a modest investment, but was more preoccupied with reorganising its other international business and its head office. It did not trumpet the China investment to the press, which would have put extra pressure on Goode and given an advantage to the Chinese negotiators.

This lack of pressure from head office gave Goode the time he needed to secure the difficult but crucial non-negotiable elements in TNT's strategy. One of the speakers quoted in the Introduction emphasised the importance of time. In his view it gave the Chinese 'total comparative advantage'. In case study 5, the American negotiator says, 'The number one requirement for negotiating in China . . . is patience.' In fact, one of his handicaps was that the people in America had no idea of this and by their impatience put him into a pincer movement—the Chinese pressuring him on one side, the Americans on the other.

When executives go to China with a game plan devised at head office, they unwittingly diminish their negotiating strength. The plan is unrealistic because it has been decided on by people far from the reality of China and, often, ignorant of the win–lose game Chinese negotiators are happy to play. Executives whose performance is being assessed by senior people at home who have no experience in China are sometimes forced to concede unnecessarily to the Chinese, just so they can return home with a contract. This gives the venture a very shaky foundation, as the Chinese will use any weakness to press their advantage, often at the ultimate cost of seeing the joint venture fail.

## 4 Allow time: bureaucracy and new ideas

Goode lamented the time needed to translate English into Chinese and back again, which was only increased by the need to make detailed explanations, particularly to the bureaucracy, and to introduce them to totally new concepts. As he says, 'I wanted to change the rules completely, yet I still had an expectation that we could knock it over in one meeting . . . wrong!'

Accepting new ideas involves looking at the world in a new way and changing well-established notions, including the organisational framework that supports them. This cannot be done overnight. A recent survey in Australia found that corporate culture change was the greatest cause of stress in executives. What looks to westerners in China like a Chinese cultural problem is often the same response to change seen all over the world. It only seems to be a Chinese problem because westerners are convinced of the rightness of their position, and cannot imagine things being done in any other way.

Part of Goode's strategy for handling the delays caused by assimilating new ideas was to leave China after discussing a major new initiative, so the Chinese could discuss the matter among themselves and come to a decision. Goode would return after two months and broach that subject again. This also gave the Chinese time to come to terms with the new issues he had introduced.

## 5 Use a go-between: the Chinese partner

As Goode became more familiar with the Chinese partner's team, he used them to negotiate with the bureaucracy. In doing so, he shifted the negotiation from a confrontation between the Chinese side and the western side to a joint Chinese–western approach to the Chinese authorities in the interests of the joint venture. Being on the same side in an argument does a great deal to advance the joint venture.

Even before this shift takes place, arguing in the interests of the joint venture rather than those of the parent company can help diffuse conflict in the negotiation. The Chinese always identify the interests at stake as either 'Chinese' or 'foreign'. Because of the insider–outsider consciousness, this can push the negotiation into conflict mode. By appealing to the joint interests of both sides, western  negotiators can pull the rug out from under the dialectical, us-vs.-them approach.

Using the Chinese partner to negotiate with the bureaucracy also saved Goode time because those particular negotiations were able to be done entirely in Chinese, shortcutting the tedious interpreting process with its inbuilt potential for misunderstandings.

## 6 Build personal relationships

Goode took the initiative of inviting members of the Chinese team to eat with him at the hotel. In this environment he was able to discuss things on a personal level. Often in China this is difficult. Many Chinese refuse invitations because they cannot reciprocate, or because they do not want to leave themselves vulnerable to criticism from their own side.

When the negotiators visited Australia, Goode invited them to dinner at his home, further consolidating the personal relationship. His company was also generous in paying for several senior managers not directly involved in the negotiations to visit Australia before and during the negotiations. Initiatives like this force the Chinese to see the western negotiators as real people, rather than stereotypes. This makes it harder for them to ignore the westerners' arguments.

Goode had a trump card not mentioned in the case study: the consultant Stephen FitzGerald, a former Australian ambassador to China, who spoke excellent Chinese. Goode says, 'His ability to understand the culture and language of both sides was an extraordinary benefit. I don't know how many times he helped the Chinese interpreter with Chinese words. They genuinely liked him. Because he understands Chinese culture, he had no difficulty in putting our position, because he knew how to put it without insulting them.'

## 7 Alter the power balance: use domineering tactics

Goode identified something quite 'Chinese' when he said to his joint venture partners, 'Sock it to them. Don't sit back and let us get railroaded again.' The Chinese are susceptible to a different kind of influence strategy from westerners. Competitive, domineering strategies succeed with the Chinese, whereas problem-solving, integrative strategies are more successful with westerners (Graham *et al.* 1988).

This is not a surprising finding, given the didactic approach the Chinese take not only to education but to mediate disputes, advising the parties on how they should think, directing them on the concessions they should make and frequently using moral principles to force a resolution (Wall 1993). This is at odds with the western concept of mediation, in which the mediator guides the disputing parties to propose their own settlement conditions.

Domineering tactics can work well with competitive negotiators like the Chinese. Two factors in Chinese life probably account for this. One is that Chinese are much more willing than westerners to accept the dictates of people in high positions. As we saw in Chapter 2, one study of this trait found that on a 100-point scale the scores were: UK 35, Australia 36, US 40, compared with China 56, Taiwan 58, Hong Kong 68 and Singapore 74 (Hofstede 1980, and Lai and Lam 1986).

The other reason for the success of domineering tactics is that the Chinese are used to living with lots of other people and having to shout above one another to be heard. On many occasions when Chinese acquaintances have been battering me with their demands, I have just shouted across the top of them without waiting for them to finish. From the first time I tried it, to my continuing surprise, it has worked! They have listened to me and taken my point of view on board. You would have to be careful about shouting in a formal negotiation, but the raised voice may have its place as a tactic for taking control of the discussion.

One domineering tactic is to spell out the ultimate consequences if the other party does not do as you ask. Goode's Chinese partners used their own version of 'ultimate consequences' by saying to the bureaucrats, 'This was supposed to be done, it hasn't been . . . and now the whole joint venture is in jeopardy.'

## 8 Keep an emotional distance: gathering information

As we have seen, gathering information in China is difficult. Frustration at not getting sufficient information in reply to questions is an experience mentioned over and over by western negotiators. Apart from the fact that China is a 'closed' society in which much information is closely guarded by the bureaucracy, difficulties may arise when the Chinese assume a westerner has certain background knowledge (for example, that it is customary for the company to provide housing and other benefits) and so see no point in mentioning it.

There is also a certain vagueness about answers in China. This stems from the need to preserve face: not wanting to say anything that will upset the enquirer or get the answerer into trouble. I have experienced it many times in China. Once I asked a straightforward question, 'Is the hospital far?' and got the answer, 'Just up around the corner.' I set off, but eventually abandoned my search after an hour of fast walking (in the pouring rain, as I recall!) with no hospital in sight.

A lot of misinformation comes about because many Chinese are not streetwise. They have worked all their lives in government enterprises where everything is provided for them, including group holidays; they've been assigned to their job, and they have never had to seek information in an alien environment. They genuinely do not know a lot of things westerners take for granted, or how to find them out.

# *10* Stepping back

Stepping back and watching the game is particularly useful when negotiating in China because it preserves the face of both the Chinese and the western negotiator.

Losing your temper will make you lose credibility and could bring the whole endeavour to an end. What makes people lose their temper in China? Case study 5 shows how left-field tactics can mislead western negotiators to such an extent that they end up in deadlock and in face-losing confrontation. Chinese pressure tactics such as the invocation of 'regulations' and 'the Chinese way' also create frustration because it is hard to argue logically against them. The common Chinese response, 'We will have to refer that back,' makes time drag and gives westerners the feeling that they have lost control over the negotiation process. It forces them to 'sit on their hands', not a familiar or comfortable experience for most western business people.

This case study has two parts. In the first part we see a westerner responding unthinkingly to the Chinese use of left-field tactics, unreasonable demands, failure to abide by the conditions of the contract, and face-saving behaviour that disguises true motives.

In the second part, the negotiator has learnt to step back and view the Chinese tactics with a reasonably objective eye. This results in a much better outcome with less anguish.

## CASE STUDY 5: 'THE MORE WE TALKED ABOUT FRIENDSHIP, THE DEEPER THE TROUBLE'

# I

John Hoover, an American, went to China in 1980 to bring an acrobatic troupe on a tour of the US. He had a high profile and a good reputation for promoting innovative theatre and tours, and he was familiar with the ins and outs of negotiating business agreements in his own country. With him was his business partner, also well known and well respected in the business of theatre.

Hoover recalls their first meetings with the Chinese. 'We said, "This is who we are, this is what we want, this is how many performances we want, and this is how much we can afford to pay. Here's our budget." We were absolutely open with them.

'The Chinese took that as an opening gambit, because that is how they are used to working. But it was not an opening gambit at all! That is exactly how we dealt with other theatrical entrepreneurs in America. We would lay it all out on the table so that we could do the deal quickly and efficiently. In China, that turned out to be disastrous. We were on the back foot all the time because they were thinking, "If they can offer $2000 a performance, they can really afford $5000," which we really could not.

'When the troupe got to America, they kept coming up with demands for money which were not included in the original contract. There was a clause that said "the company will participate in all reasonable publicity as requested by management". We got them onto a Saturday night variety show on television. But a young adviser from the embassy told them he'd read that when people go on television in America they get $30000. We told them this was not true. One does not get paid for appearing on a TV show. It just gives good national exposure and publicises the tour.

'Our explanation made no difference. They still demanded a fee for going on the TV show. They refused to get on the bus to take them to the studio. They just said, "No, we are not going unless you pay us." We came back at them that the contract says you will do this, we have asked you to do it, it is a formal request. We got to the point where there was only

half an hour to go before their appearance on the show and
the adviser from the embassy was still demanding they get paid.
By this time he had got the price down to $1000.

'It was absolute blackmail. It was clearly in breach of
contract. I think they knew it, but they were being advised by
the fellow from the Chinese embassy. In the end we paid them.
Their appearance went smoothly, and no one watching would
have had any idea of the agony going on in the background.
After the show we had a meeting. We told them we would
deduct the $1000, which was in breach of contract, from their
weekly fee, which we did.

As the tour went on, Hoover says, the Chinese made other
demands not covered in the contract. 'Suddenly one morning
they said that they wanted chocolate: one kilo per person per
day. It was absolutely stupid. Half the troupe did not even like
chocolate! I would come up with every possible reason, such
as, they could not carry it all home in their suitcases because
they would be 40kg overweight. But rational arguments had
nothing to do with it. It had become a symbol of something.
It led to total misunderstanding on both sides, total obduracy.
They would say, "This is our position, this is our position."

'We would explain why that position was inconsistent,
illogical, wrong, perverse, illegal, immoral. We would speak
ourselves hoarse for an hour, and they would say, "This is our
position." Once you have given away all your counter-
arguments, you make it very hard for yourself the next time.

'The last of the tour payments was made at interval during
their last performance. They refused to go back on stage
afterwards. They wanted the $1000 for the TV appearance to
be refunded to them. We had a 40-minute interval. They were
screaming at me.

'It was a big mistake on our side to have ever said they
were in breach of contract. It was a very serious accusation,
even though it was absolutely true. We went in very hard as
you do in the west in a similar situation. The problem was the
officials who were with them, who were hard-line party people.
I had to write a cheque for them because we had 10 000 people
out there in the concert hall, and the interval had run out.
Once I'd done that they went back on stage and the final
performance was a stunning success.'

## II

Six years later, Hoover was chosen to negotiate the contract for an exhibition of China's archaeological treasures that was to tour a number of US cities. The mayor of one city and the Chinese Minister for Culture had signed an agreement that China would send the exhibition as a goodwill gesture to mark the establishment of sister-city ties. The official announcement was given extensive media coverage.

But when Hoover came to settle the details, the Chinese were no longer willing to send the exhibition as a gift. They had realised that these were priceless treasures, and they wanted to make money out of them. Suddenly they demanded an exorbitant fee.

Hoover now drew on his previous experience with the Chinese. He knew it would be difficult, particularly as it was to be negotiated at a high level of the central bureaucracy in Beijing. There were two years before the exhibition opened, so he took his time to negotiate, much as he had seen the Chinese do before. Every month he would meet with officials from the Ministry of Culture. He says, 'The process was very illuminating. It demonstrated the number one requirement for negotiating in China, which is patience.'

Hoover's strongest bargaining point in this negotiation was that the exhibition had been agreed to publicly at ministerial level. When the Chinese put up terms that he thought were outrageous (which they did regularly), he would appeal to the principle that this was China's gift, and that it is not customary to charge for gifts. Not that he usually got anywhere with his appeal that China had agreed to do this for free. The Chinese Minister for Culture had said yes to the original proposition—that it would be a mark of friendship to have the exhibition—without considering the details. This made it very difficult for both sides but slightly more so for the Chinese, since they had offered the gift.

Meanwhile Hoover's own side were also putting pressure on him because they wanted a commitment that the exhibition would go ahead. They told him to speed the process up because they had to get all the marketing in place. When the Chinese learned that one American gallery was building a special new exhibition space at a cost of millions of dollars, it made it harder for him to negotiate reasonable terms.

Hoover kept assuring the American promoters, 'Of course

the exhibition will arrive, because the Minister for Culture has said it is coming. We will sign an agreement as it is being loaded onto the plane . . . if we are lucky.' From experience he knew that the Chinese string out negotiations until the last second. But the promoters kept telling him that was not good enough. They did not understand the process, nor the cost of what they were being asked to give away. Hoover believed that the money the Chinese would have made out of the exhibition, which was meant to go to preserving archaeological sites and treasures, would have been used to buy more Mercedes-Benz cars for vice ministers. He wanted proper safeguards put into the agreement.

He says 'The Chinese were not prepared to allow any monitoring of how the money was spent. They just wanted basically to have it handed over, and said that what they did with it was their business, "China's internal affairs". I kept saying, "That is unacceptable because it is American money."'

At each monthly meeting, Hoover and the three Chinese negotiators would talk about friendship and tell each other what they had done since they had last met. Then they would go through the draft contract clause by clause. When an objection came up that they could not resolve, they would put it aside and agree to come back to it after they had referred it to their superiors.

The negotiations were always amicable. Hoover learnt in dealing with the Chinese to play the same games: 'Sometimes I would try to be a mirror at a meeting. If they were dilly-dallying and didn't want to talk about the main issue, I was happy to dilly-dally and talk about last week's soccer match. When we were in trouble we'd talk about friendship between our two peoples, and the more pots of tea and the more we talked about friendship, the deeper the trouble.'

The Chinese would try to get Hoover to put out his cards first by asking, 'What are you prepared to offer?' He would respond with, 'Well, what are *you* prepared to offer?' He would keep this up until the Chinese realised that if they wanted to move forward they would have to offer something, and that he would then offer something in return. Sometimes they would negotiate for weeks on all sorts of side issues: Which airline should they travel on? What publicity would they get out of it? How much business would this bring in for the airline? Could they ask for free flights? How many could they ask for? All these issues were quite irrelevant to the choice, safety and display of the treasures.

A stumbling block for a long time was which company the Americans would insure the exhibition with. The Chinese said, basically, that they could insure with anyone they liked provided it was the Chinese People's Insurance Company. The People's Insurance Company was quite happy to provide insurance at an astronomical price, but it would not cover the exhibits in the event of malicious damage, which was a key consideration. The American side had to go through all the fine print, cable their colleagues at home for information, and pass on the details of every conversation. They not only commented on what was said but on what they thought the intention behind it was. Sometimes the interpreters would approach Hoover outside a meeting and tell him what the problem was and how he might get around it. Hoover would also use banquets and other social occasions to give the Chinese an informal explanation of American business customs while steering clear of the obstacle itself.

With the insurance, he made no headway until he got international brokers to quote on it. Then he could say, 'So-and-so's insurance policy is $1.5 million, whereas the People's Insurance Company wants $2 million, and so-and-so's covers malicious damage and yours does not.' The Chinese would reject the less costly policies, saying it was 'mandatory' that national treasures be insured with the People's Insurance Company. The Americans said they were happy for that company to do it, provided it could match the international brokers' premium and terms. In the end, despite the 'regulations', the exhibition was insured by an American company, Hoover explains cynically, 'A lot was tied up with insurance, and there was a lot to be gained by China having one of the damned things broken while the exhibition was in the US.'

He came to understand the negotiating process well after a while. He recalls, 'When we came to a contentious issue we dropped it. In the west, if you have a bone like that, you want to chew it to death, have that meeting and get it resolved then and there. In China, you don't do that. You say, "OK, we agree to disagree on that. Let's leave it."

'Provided you give the impression that you too have all the time in the world, they know you have to resolve a given problem eventually. So they will come back to it. You can come back to it yourself at the next meeting and say, "OK, we had a problem last time, what are your views?" And you see if there has been a bit of ground given. You try and give something yourself, so you can make progress. So there is give and take.'

Some of the discussions were very technical—for example about curators: who was allowed to come, how many there would be, what their responsibilities would be, why new curators had to be flown out (when Hoover had already agreed to have a number of curators accompany the exhibition throughout the tour), whether or not American museum staff would be allowed to handle the exhibits. The official party was to go to the US for the opening. Then the Chinese wanted other official groups to visit the exhibition. One of the things the Chinese like is overseas trips. Senior people say, 'We have done all this and we have worked at the ministry for 30 years. We want a trip to America.' The American team really had to do their homework. How much it would cost? Could they afford it? Did they want it? Was there a benefit? They might decide they would give the minister a ticket and pay for the assistant's accommodation, but ask the Chinese to buy the tickets for any other officials. So they had certain items up their sleeve to give away.

Hoover reflects: 'We did the negotiations and the give-aways month by month. We were aware that we should not open with all our high cards. We'd do the negotiation and see where we had got to. We knew we would have to go back next time with something to give them. What was it going to be? And what should we ask in return? The permutations and combinations were immensely complicated. We had to do a lot of work before we went into a negotiation session, and then we had to be prepared to come back empty-handed. Sometimes we would walk out and after a cooling-off period, say, "Let's try again."

'We would look for something to concede. We had to give them something so they could go back to their masters, and say, "We won this point. We have got this much more money than we thought we were going to get." I think you do have to try and actually see what they want. Write that down, do the exercise from their side.'

The Chinese changed negotiators a number of times. As Hoover said, 'We would have just thought we had reached an understanding about something, and the next month they would say, "I'm sorry, Mr Li has gone off somewhere, so I am doing it today. I don't know where you got to last time, so shall we start again?" Someone up the line had obviously said, "We have to win this point." Mr Li may well have been in the next room, but he wasn't trotted out.'

When they changed negotiators, there were often differences in personality. Sometimes, particularly depending on the political swings, it would be a stonewaller who would say, 'No, Mr Li did not agree to that. I think you misunderstood that.' In the middle of it all, the Vice Minister changed, which made it complicated. There were hardliners and people changing positions.

All the meetings were conducted in two languages. In official meetings, even Chinese people who speak impeccable English will only deal through interpreters. Hoover believes this is because it leaves an area of ambiguity. The Chinese can always say, 'No, what I really said was . . .' Usually Hoover was alone on his side, except for the interpreter, while the Chinese side had a senior official, an interpreter and two observers. He found it very hard to read their faces, especially that of the official.

American laws sometimes helped Hoover's case. He would say, for example, 'No, you cannot do that, because all exhibits have to be cleared by US Customs, whether that is acceptable to you or not. I agree with you it is unacceptable, but they will get off the plane at the other end, and the customs will impound them. It does not matter what I say or what is in our agreement. That is the law.'

Sometimes the negotiations would be punctuated by a change of venue, a banquet, or meetings on other subjects. Over lunch, which would come in the middle of a negotiating day, Hoover would be 'all sweetness and light'. But he would use the relaxed atmosphere to give the Chinese clues as to why he was taking a certain stance. He would talk around the issue (without ever mentioning it) and explain an aspect of American society or law or custom that showed what his position was based on.

At crucial points, the Chinese would try delaying, going into defensive mode, focusing on irrelevancies. Hoover got used to waiting for them to introduce these red herrings. 'I would just think that I was getting somewhere and some totally irrelevant demand would come out of left field . . . something totally out of keeping with whatever it was we were discussing. My immediate reaction would be "Shock! Horror! Outrage!", which is exactly what they wanted, and I'd get all wired up and finally concede the point. Then I would think, "OK, we've conceded that, now you guys must concede something that is central to what we are discussing."'

They also avoided difficult decisions by appealing to higher authority: 'We will have to ask the director or the minister,' 'We have to refer that back.' Hoover never knew who was being asked or referred to, and was therefore unable to influence the powerful person in question.

In his own work in America he could often see exactly where the block was: a bureaucrat who did not want something to happen, for example. He could name the person and think, 'I can go round him'. His difficulty in dealing with the Chinese bureaucracy was that a negotiator could retreat into it and he would get no signals as to who was opposing him. It usually was not the person negotiating with him, but some of the higher officials. Many times he had the Chinese negotiator repeating the same thing over and over again, no matter what he said.

Negotiations went on right up to the day the exhibition was due to be loaded on the plane. Then the Chinese would not let it be loaded. The Americans wanted to use a US airline to avoid potential damage from poor loading practices. The Chinese wanted to use China Airlines. A week later the exhibition finally took off—on a US airline.

Hoover reflects, 'The negotiation required a very clear set of objectives and a great deal of patience. Living there helped that. I had two years before the exhibition was due to leave China. So many negotiators who go to China have five days set aside, and they get nowhere.' He thinks the Chinese had no clear strategy during the negotiations, but changed tack according to how things were going. 'They are masterful at it,' he says. 'They do it instinctively.'

Despite all the problems, Hoover was pleased with the outcome. The exhibition did tour the US, and the terms were reasonable. Hoover also managed to get guarantees that the money would be spent on archaeological preservation—but only after an *additional* two years of negotiations!

## DISCUSSION

This case study demonstrates that it is possible to learn how to negotiate successfully in the Chinese manner, even after an exceptionally bad start.

## 1 Keep an emotional distance: define the issue and look for alternative solutions

It is a big temptation for foreigners to lose their temper in China. As we discussed in Chapter 2, westerners inherit a history of superior attitudes to the Chinese. When the Chinese refuse to go along with what they want, they start to dictate and demand compliance.

This can result in a deadlock, as we saw when the acrobats refused to get on the bus to go to the TV studio and then refused to go back on stage after the final interval. And they won—in the end the $1000 had to be paid to them twice!

In the second set of negotiations, Hoover insisted on a cooling-off period, so he would not be under pressure to conclude the negotiation in a hurry. Since he had two years to reach agreement, he paced himself, leaving two- to three-week breaks between sessions.

Cultural clashes also contribute to the tendency for westerners to lose their temper. Breaking a contract, as in the first of Hoover's negotiations, is regarded as normal in China but dishonourable in the west (not that western business people never break contracts!). And in the second negotiation, Hoover had trouble convincing the Chinese that archaeological preservation was a better use for the money than luxury cars.

It is easy to imagine why the Chinese negotiators were so tough in this negotiation, as there is great resentment in China about the US habit of criticising issues such as human rights, which China insists are its own affair and none of the US's business. Hoover's belief that the Chinese side hoped one of the treasures would be broken so they could get the insurance is another example of a cross-cultural ethical judgment.

## 2 Follow the Chinese bargaining process: leave room to negotiate

An essential part of the bargaining process in China is to start high and gradually make concessions. You must always leave room to negotiate. As Hoover found, you simply cannot expect to complete a negotiation in one go, as would happen in the west.

Apart from the tradition of haggling, there is the Chinese suspicion of outsiders. Hoover was not a long-term associate of the Chinese. The negotiation over the acrobats was the first time the Chinese group concerned had dealt with him, and they probably expected they were being cheated. Fabulous stories circulate in China of the wealth of the US (which is true in terms of the private income and possessions of ordinary Americans compared to the Chinese). If you ask young people there what they want to do, most say they want to go to America to make their fortune. They do not always fully understand the economics behind western business, and therefore what they ask for can seem shockingly exorbitant—as in the case of the acrobats' demand for a $30 000 TV appearance fee.

Because in this first negotiation Hoover had not planned for the give-and-take of Chinese bargaining, he kept nothing in reserve to give and made a loss on the tour. He handled the second negotiation very well; not accepting the initial Chinese price and preparing early and rationally the concession-making stage. Negotiating is a dynamic process. As things change, opportunities open up, and the Chinese are very skilled at identifying and taking advantage of them. It is therefore important to build a range of concessions in to any strategy and to pad the price.

## 3 Prepare for negotiations after the contract

In both negotiations, Hoover found that the Chinese wanted more than they originally agreed to. In the first negotiation, he did the worst possible thing when this occurred—he confronted them and accused them publicly of dishonourable behaviour. At every level of business, the Chinese habit of trying to change the original agreement causes a breakdown of relationships with westerners. It is simply not part of our business ethic to demand things not in the contract after it has been signed. If there needs to be a change to the contract we signal it differently, not suddenly from out of left field, as in this case. For the Chinese, on the other hand, ongoing relationships are an endless negotiation of the rules.

Hoover had learnt by the second negotiation not to react emotionally when such moments came, but to use the initial agreement with the Chinese Minister of Culture, that the exhibition be sent as a goodwill gesture, to persuade the Chinese negotiator to moderate his demands. He also conceded some points on the understanding that the Chinese would have to concede points to him. He never gave in without getting something in return.

## 4 Negotiate around demands: preserve face and look for hidden needs

In international negotiation theory, demands are like wishful thinking—they set a target and they represent only one way to reach that target. The western negotiator need only search for what will satisfy the demand—he need not necessarily meet it. He may meet the demand part way, or substitute something else for what is asked for. In China, a demand may conceal a wish which is not immediately apparent and will not be acknowledged in public.

When the Chinese team demanded $30 000 and the chocolate, they were only indicating that they wanted something more than was stated in the contract, not necessarily what they specifically asked for. The fact that the embassy official was prepared to reduce the demand from $30 000 to $1000 shows how far it was above his satisfaction point. But Hoover, never having come across this tactic before, was so appalled he could not stand back and see that the Chinese were merely testing the limits. The chocolate demand, on the other hand, was so ridiculous it was obviously hiding some other expectation.

Hoover learnt a very important lesson in his first negotiation: to step back and give himself time to think about the issue strategically. As he said, 'In the west, when you have a bone like that, you want to chew it to death, have that meeting and get it resolved then and there. In China, you don't do that. You go away and come back next time and you just see if there is a bit of ground been given. You try and give something yourself, so that you can make progress.'

## 5 Allow time: control head office pressures

In the second set of negotiations, Hoover was very aware of the problems created for him by his bosses in the US, who were not familiar with Chinese pressure tactics. Unless a negotiator is able to control head office demands, he will find himself in a vulnerable position negotiating with the Chinese. They have the advantages of time and being on the spot.

Hoover's two-year timetable gave him the luxury of being able to walk out of a negotiation session empty-handed. When negotiators feel they have to prove to head office that they are making progress or that they will definitely return with a contract, they make themselves vulnerable to Chinese pressures.

## 6 Negotiate around fixed positions and Chinese 'regulations'

In the second negotiation Hoover repeatedly came under pressure to accept the Chinese position. Initially, when the Chinese demanded a high fee for the exhibition, he reminded them that they had previously agreed to send the exhibition free. He eventually succeeded in lowering the fee.

When the Chinese insisted that it was mandatory for the People's Insurance Company to insure the exhibition treasures, Hoover produced, in writing, the charges of international insurance brokers. Since the American side was to pay the insurance premium, he had some leverage. However, it was still up to him to resist the claim of Chinese 'regulations'.

It is interesting that the Chinese at times wanted to do things that were contrary to American Customs law, and that they persisted with these demands, not realising that regulations in the US really cannot be got around. Hoover had to resist their pressures, detailing what would happen if they sent the objects without proper documentation.

Chinese Customs is noted for its toughness, but it is generally under the control of local power brokers, and any regulations can be dodged with the right connections. This, and the fact that the regulations vary from one place to the next, make it hard for the Chinese to come to terms with the unified and uncompromising nature of American laws. Americans and other westerners, in turn, find it hard to believe how flexible Chinese 'regulations' can be.

## 7 Look for hidden needs in concession making

Concession making is affected by the Chinese sensitivity to face. Hoover looked at the hidden motivations of the Chinese side—the self-esteem of the negotiators themselves, and their need to show superiors and fellow team members that they had wins from time to time. So he never said a straight no. Concessions were deliberately planned in to his negotiation strategy.

Hidden motivators are often neglected in negotiation planning. They include not only the importance of approval by superiors and peers and the fear of punishment for failure, but also the typical Chinese reluctance to make a decision. To overcome this obstacle you need to build in assurances and sweeteners, such as trips overseas. These are legal. Giving financial incentives is not, and could result in long gaol terms for the recipients.

Hoover's account of the multiplicity of issues brought up by the Chinese side demonstrates the amazing attention Chinese negotiators pay to small details. He imitated Chinese practice by calculating the costs of all concessions and systematically analysing them with the back-up team in the US.

## 8 Keep an emotional distance: coping with changing tactics

Because this negotiation centred on the galvanising question of foreign currency, and because it took place only within the bureaucracy, the Chinese side used every possible tactic to disorient and pressure Hoover. They regularly changed negotiators, each time throwing out all previous understandings. With every change in negotiator came a change in personality. This good guy–bad guy tactic is used in China quite often. It can be effective with foreigners already under strain from culture shock, solitude, and the isolation of being unable to speak Chinese. The 'bad guy' wears down the negotiator's resolve, then the 'good guy', by being sympathetic, gets him to let slip information that helps the Chinese side. More than a few westerners subjected to such tactics have abandoned the negotiations.

The Chinese have a goal, they have a huge team assigned to the negotiation, and they can vary the up-front negotiator when they are not moving towards that goal. As Hoover mentions, at the time of his second set of negotiations there were political shifts going on behind the scenes between the 'open door' advocates and conservatives. Among the latter were many former Red Guards and inquisitorial zealots of the Cultural Revolution, both groups strongly antipathetic to the west, and particularly the US. These changes were reflected in the Chinese negotiation tactics.

At this level of negotiation it was difficult for Hoover to build a bridge to the other side. The interpreters came to him outside the formal negotiation with information which gave him some clues to the attitudes of the Chinese side and the issues he could address to overcome an objection.

In appealing to higher authority and to 'regulations', Hoover mirrored the tactics of the Chinese themselves, thus protecting himself or forcing them to make a conciliatory gesture. He did, though, always look for ways to signal that he was willing to cooperate. This is of absolute importance in negotiating with the Chinese, who always expect a level of benevolence in negotiations with developed countries.

All the way through this negotiation Hoover made an effort to remove himself from emotional involvement in the drama, to step back and watch. We can see how dramatically different the outcome in this case was from that of his entanglement with the acrobatic troupe, where he gave full rein to his natural responses, with disastrous results. Having learned to his cost what this could lead to, in the second negotiation he generally kept control over his own emotions, or at least left when things were difficult. He was watching and assessing the behaviour of the other side all the way through. In a negotiation he closely observed the faces of the people not speaking, and he went along with the other side's dilly-dallying when they were unprepared to move along discussion of substantive issues.

Even at the very end, when the Chinese suddenly refused to load the exhibits on the plane, Hoover gave them time to sort out the problem (which was probably an internal dispute). In such situations, using the threat of ultimate consequences as described in Chapter 3, or offering a concession deliberately held back until the last moment, can help bring the negotiation to a close.

# *11* Demonstrating commitment

The great lure of the Chinese market and its abundant cheap labour creates a highly competitive business environment as companies from all over the world seek opportunities to expand their markets or to export cheap goods. As we know, the Chinese regularly play competitors off against one another in negotiations. How can any business make a place for itself in such a competitive environment?

The executives in the next case study faced just such a predicament. They were in the shoe business, one of the most competitive buying markets in China, which produces 80 per cent of the world's shoes. Giant shoe companies from Europe and the US have enormous clout in the Chinese market because their orders can consume the output of hundreds of factories. This gives them a great deal of leverage in asking for price discounts. In 1994, China exported to the US 700 million shoes out of its production of 4 billion. Smaller companies are thus faced with a problem. How can they influence Chinese negotiators to prioritise their comparatively modest orders and give them price reductions that will not disadvantage them in their home market?

This case study demonstrates not only how one group of western executives developed the skills to influence Chinese negotiators, but how their respect for the Chinese, their commitment, and the long-term approach they took to negotiations in China, led to an ever increasing flow of opportunities for their company.

## CASE STUDY 6: 'ONCE YOU'RE IN . . . '

Pacific Dunlop is a diversified Australian-managed manufacturer and marketer of footwear, clothing, optical fibre cables, tyres and batteries. In 1995, it had sales of $A7 billion worldwide. In the 1970s, it started buying football boots, work boots and sandshoes from China. It later expanded into yarn, clothing and textiles, and in 1980 started to move its footwear and clothing manufacturing operations to China. It now manufactures optical fibre cable there as well. The company has gone from strength to strength in China, partly thanks to the influence of one man—Paul Winestock.

Paul Winestock is an Australian with a middle-European Jewish background. His first job was buying Chinese textiles through the mail for a small textile importing company. Some years later he took over the company, and was invited to visit China. From this small beginning he has built a large network there.

Winestock says of his success and influence in China, 'It is a question of evolution, it is not a question of it suddenly happening.' He built his reputation by going to China regularly, right through the 1960s and 1970s when few foreigners were there because of the Cultural Revolution, negotiating footwear and textile purchases in Shanghai, Beijing, Nanjing and Tianjin. He would stay in hotels where there was no heating, no shop and no dining room because all the staff were attending political meetings. His support on these nights would be a bottle of whisky brought in from Hong Kong.

He dealt with the same officials year after year and became very widely known. Because the officials he negotiated with as a young man have moved through the bureaucracy into positions of power, he is now known to officials at the highest level. One of these men is Li Haoran.

Li was an official in the Textile Import–Export Corporation, and he worked with Winestock for many years when Winestock was a selling agent for the corporation. Later he was appointed managing director of the Animal By-Products Import–Export Corporation, which dealt in leather shoes. When Winestock asked to be the exclusive wholesaler and distributor of Chinese leather shoes in Australia, Li organised this for him. Under the centralised system, the ministry in Beijing controlled the footwear factories and sold all output through the import–export corporation, which decided how to tackle any market, and had the power to award exclusive selling rights.

Winestock was given control of 25 per cent of China's shoe exports. He had agreements with the corporation's offices in Beijing and Shanghai. These areas produced the best shoes and officials there had well-developed trading systems and hundreds of factories under their control.

Winestock believes that a major concern of the Chinese is the reputation of the western negotiators and companies they deal with. They ask themselves, 'Can we trust these people?' Only if they are confident they can, he says, is it possible to do business with them. 'If you promise something and do not do it, you will lose face, and lose their confidence in you.'

He believes that westerners will succeed in China if they can show the Chinese that their business will bring China gains and foreign currency. He told the Chinese that if they let individual Australian retailers go out to the provinces to buy from the factories, they would play one factory off against another, and so force the prices down. If that happened China would lose foreign currency. Winestock gave them a plan for maximising their profit. If they made him the sole wholesaler and retailer of their leather shoes in Australia, they would get price stability and make more money. He promised to buy from them on a regular basis, but warned that if they opened the market up to retailers, they would lose control of it. Retailers were unreliable. They might buy from China one year but not necessarily the next. Without commitment to China, they would simply follow the cheapest prices around Asia, South America and Eastern Europe.

Arguing this way from the late 1960s, Winestock was able to keep the exclusive rights to retail Chinese footwear in Australia until his company was bought out by Pacific Dunlop in 1982. During the years he was building up his shoe business in China, says George Preston, whom he later trained, 'Winestock's reasoning was this: when you made money in the good days, you had to remember that when the Chinese needed to sell at a higher price. You *had* to be able to give it to them somehow.

'Winestock had an advantage: he ran his own private company. He didn't have to report to a board. There was enough fat in his company that it didn't make any difference to him whether he had a bad year or a particularly good year.

He was able to take a long-term view. So he had the freedom to say, "Well, I don't need to make so much profit this year. I can live with not making $2 million this year. It's going to cost me half a million this year, but I know I'm going to get it back." If he was really convinced that the Chinese representatives were up against a wall and couldn't lower the price, he would move to their position on the understanding if the price had gone up by the next time they negotiated he was to be paid back.

'Winestock would say "You've got to have a feeling for your business." It isn't "OK, I'm giving you 2 per cent and I want 2 per cent back." You can't judge a price and your profit down to a percentage. It is never anything like that, but he would find some way of getting something back.'

Among his western business associates, Winestock is known as a very aggressive businessman: direct and tough to the point of ruthlessness. But in China he is a different person. He knows that behaving in his usual way will get him nowhere. So he pays attention to face.

He knows that no matter how you might do business in the rest of the world, China is different. It really sees itself as 'the Middle Kingdom', superior to all other countries. Winestock believes you have to understand this. In any negotiation there is an underlying notion that the Chinese really do not need to do business with you at all, that there will always be someone else who wants to do business with them. If you push them too far, they will think, 'Why should I deal with this guy? I've got my job anyway. It doesn't matter to me.'

Winestock negotiates in the Chinese way. He says, 'I negotiate as it goes. When I started getting my first agencies in garments and shoes in the 1960s, I was performing for days and days. We would sit at the table and go over the issues point by point, then go back over it all again. Sometimes you couldn't reach a conclusion, so we'd leave it. I'd come back two months later. Some contracts took me a week, some took me a year, coming and going.'

At the end of a series of negotiating sessions Winestock is able to say, quite bluntly, 'That's my price and I'm going.' His bluntness amazes other westerners who see him in action. It is a sign of the depth of his relationship with the Chinese that they do not take offence. He says, 'I can tell them off and they take it from me. But before I do, I think.' He sticks by his own interests because he believes it is impossible to penetrate the thinking of the Chinese side. He never loses his temper because he knows the Chinese will freeze and it will be the end of the business.

Because he has been going to China for so long, and is so widely known, he is also able to tell the Chinese what prices he should be paying for shoes and textiles. But he never squeezes them too much, because he has a good idea of what is possible for them. He knows a great deal about China's economy, manufacturing and enterprise management, and as a result he does not ask, as many westerners do, for what is technically impossible for them. Even so, there have been times when he has had to take losses, when the Chinese would be late in delivering shoes and a whole consignment would miss the fashion season. His business would be on the brink of going under. The Chinese, seeing this, would support him by supplying shoes at cost until his business was profitable again. And his business has been exceedingly profitable over the long term.

A vital part of Winestock's approach is putting time into public relations. He never expects to fly in, stay a day, and fly out with a deal. He believes China is 'not a level playing field' when it comes to negotiating business agreements. Hosting banquets is important to success. The Chinese love to go to banquets because they can eat food of a kind they never eat at home. When a Chinese group visits Winestock he holds banquets for them every night, although he does not much like going out to restaurants himself. He also stresses that giving respect to everyone from the managing director to the clerk is important. It is a matter of face.

When Pacific Dunlop bought out Winestock, he toured China with the top managers of Pacific Dunlop to ensure that the Chinese would continue to honour their original agreements with him. These agreements were passed to Pacific Dunlop and stayed in place until 1989, when the centralised trading system broke down and Hong Kong Chinese went into the provinces and did new deals that allowed them to sell directly to the big shopping chains in Australia.

Pacific Dunlop's success in China was built on Winestock's contacts and experience. He trained its executives to negotiate with the Chinese after the buyout. Preston says of Winestock's way of dealing with the Chinese, 'He is the embodiment of the principle of mutual benefit. Mutual benefit is just words to a lot of people, but he really lives by it in all his dealings with them. Without Paul Winestock, I don't think Pacific Dunlop would have learnt that lesson at all.'

After the buyout Pacific Dunlop's shoe sales increased 140 per cent in four years, far more than its executives had envisaged. This huge success gave managing director Philip Brass the idea of using China as a base to develop Pacific Dunlop's US business.

In China Pacific Dunlop could buy at a significant price advantage over the Americans, who tended to buy in Taiwan and rarely had good relationships with the Chinese. They were very combative. The Chinese did not like their style of banging on the table and saying, 'You've got to make a decision now because we're flying out tomorrow.' The result would often be a power struggle between the Chinese and the Americans.

Pacific Dunlop's top managers and Winestock had a yearly roadshow. They visited all the major ministries and export corporations, outlining what they were going to do for China in selling shoes, and showing how they were going to develop the market. They said, 'We're going to buy one million pairs of x shoe, the market is growing by y per cent, our share is z per cent, and shoes will grow at q per cent.'

The Chinese would pressure Pacific Dunlop, saying, 'If you want to retain the exclusive agency for the Australian market, you've got to sell 1.5 million.'

John Gough, the chairman, Brass and Winestock would say, 'No, no, no. It's got to be the traditional thing—900 000, but the target will be 1.2 million.' When they discussed the matter at head office in Beijing, representatives of the Light Industry Export Corporation, who operated from the provinces, would say 'What are we getting out of this? We've got a customer who says he's going to buy 100 000. If you let us sell individually you would end up with more than you're getting from Pacific Dunlop.'

The company won these arguments—and the continuation of their contracts—with the cogent points that when they took over from Winestock they took 1 million pairs of shoes a year, they had increased this to 1.2 million pairs, and they were now adding the US business.

As Pacific Dunlop's Australian and American markets grew, leather supply and quality control became serious issues. Local factories would make the shoes with whatever skins were available. To solve this problem, the company put Preston in charge of the feasibility study for building a tannery on the outskirts of Shanghai. It was to be the largest tannery in the world. As part of the study, Preston brought in some Spanish people whose family had run tanneries for 400 years.

The Spanish found it very difficult to deal with the Chinese. Before leaving for China they would telex an outline of all the things they wanted to do and send a rough timetable. But when they arrived, everything would be changed. They would not be able to see the person they particularly wanted to talk to because he was not there, so they could not determine essential matters such as how much the water would cost. At meetings in Shanghai they would ask if they could visit Sichuan to see the collecting points for the skins. The Chinese would say yes but then make the trip impossible.

The Spanish got extremely frustrated, but Preston was able to see both sides of the situation. The key problem was that they were dealing with a trading corporation based in Shanghai, when most of the skins came from hundreds of kilometres away in Sichuan, Anhui or Jiangsu. China's huge size created problems in communication. Policies were set by the Communist Party in Beijing. The delegate to the Party Congress would have to relay decisions to the local Party organisation, which in turn would relay them to the corporations and individual operations, mostly by word of mouth. It could take a year for a decision to reach the individual.

Complicating the approval process, the central government had begun to change the structure and responsibilities of the trading and industry corporations. In the midst of all this, people in the Animal By-Products Corporation in Shanghai did not know exactly what was happening, so they were wary about making decisions. They were responsible to the trading corporations, which still answered to the Ministry of Foreign Affairs and Trade (MOFERT), whereas tanneries reported to the Light Industry Corporation, which reported in turn to the Ministry of Light Industry.

Further complications arose from the trend for provincial governments to become more independent and seek control of their local companies' earnings, so they could get more foreign exchange. The mayor of Shanghai was soon to become Party secretary, so the Shanghai government was approving initiatives from the By-Products Corporation and various industry corporations in Shanghai rather than sending to Beijing for approval. There was bureaucratic chaos.

Much of what Preston and the Spanish were doing in the feasibility study was new to the Chinese. Each time Preston arranged to meet with the Chinese project managers from the Animal By-Products Corporation, he would have to assure them that this was only a feasibility study, he was not negotiating, he just wanted information. But they were reluctant to give it because they thought it would undermine them when they came to negotiate the contract. Preston needed to know the cost of water, coal, and other inputs in different locations. It was very difficult for the Chinese to find a way through the system to get him that information. No matter where he wanted to locate the factory, the local county would have its own special laws and charges.

The initial investment was to be $US10 million in capital and $5 million in working capital and stock, with projected losses of $2–3 million over the first two to three years. The Chinese could not agree to taking on such losses. In the end, they could not even guarantee that they could get the two million skins that would make the tannery viable. Because of this, the tannery project was abandoned.

Preston says 'If you put it to a Chinese corporation, even now there would be nobody there to say, "I'm prepared to take on those losses." Only China International Trust and Investment Corporation (CITIC) or someone fairly high up would be prepared to take the responsibility to advocate a joint venture whose feasibility study says we are going to lose money.'

Most people setting up businesses in China find that the central bureaucracy is a major stumbling block, particularly when it comes to getting permits. Pacific Dunlop, however, uses the subsidised and centralised system to its advantage. Because the whole system is controlled, Preston has found that 'Once you're in, you are the people the Chinese are going to do business with.' The Chinese have approached Pacific Dunlop to set up many new ventures, not all of which it has agreed to.

While he was negotiating about the tannery, Preston was also negotiating to set up a sock factory and a factory to make shoe heels and soles. He says, 'Our partners in the joint venture were our trading partners, and because we took over from Winestock, there was an enormous fount of goodwill there. I was the principal negotiator and I'd been talking and negotiating in China since 1982. We'd talked in 1984, '85 and '86 about these things, so we had a fair amount of understanding about what we'd be up against.

'Philip Brass, the managing director, was always there with me negotiating on major initiatives, so the Chinese knew we had a long-term strategic commitment. They knew we weren't going to rush off and buy from Taiwan if there was a pricing problem.' Because of this, Pacific Dunlop was able to initiate new kinds of ventures. The shoe components factory was taxed at low export rates, even though its product was not exported but sold to shoe factories in China.

The company's next venture came about because it was buying socks out of Beijing and started talking with a mill about doing something on a bigger scale. Some time later an official from MOFERT said on a visit to Australia that his ministry would be interested in trying to develop the sock business. So Pacific Dunlop set up a company in Hong Kong with the Beijing International Investment Trust Corporation to invest in socks and some other areas. One of the shareholders was China Silk.

China Silk is a very powerful corporation which controls every aspect of the silk industry, from production to manufacturing and export, and which reports to the State Council. Two men whom Winestock had known for years were now managing director and deputy managing director of China Silk. They had worked in the footwear corporations and had also known the Pacific Dunlop people in their early trading days. They took a shareholding to help get the sock investment program going.

The contracts for the sock mill were breakthroughs at that time. Pacific Dunlop was able to get the Chinese to accept that capital would be committed in two stages and that the second stage of investment would depend on the success of the first. Preston believes that his company was only able to achieve this because of its long relationship with the Chinese—at least in Beijing and the north. Had it tried to set up the same joint venture in the west or south, where it was not well known, it would have had much more trouble.

Rather than do all the organisation themselves, Pacific Dunlop's executives relied upon their Chinese partners to bring other Chinese groups into the joint venture to provide the labour and find the factories. They have learnt always to work through the Chinese network to learn whom they should talk to and whom they ought to involve. This has been far more reliable than using western government agencies and outside consultants. Having partners with inside knowledge makes all the difference in how fast a joint venture can be established. Most of the company's joint-venture contracts have been negotiated in six to eighteen months, compared with the three to five years usual for companies new to China.

In building the sock factory, Pacific Dunlop let its Chinese partners handle many of the negotiations with the locals. The factory was to be built on land where rice was grown, so the partner (in this case the district) negotiated with the village on giving up the land, and on compensation. These were both complex negotiations that the company considered would be better handled by the Chinese.

When there was a serious cost overrun on the building, once again Pacific Dunlop let its Chinese partners negotiate with the contractor. They took a strong view, saying, 'We are not going to finalise the price of the building because it isn't finished and we don't think this is fair.' The cost in the original contract was 4 million RMB. It ended up being 7.5 million. The Chinese negotiated it down to 6.5 million with all sorts of compromises.

In setting up the sock factory, Pacific Dunlop did not want to become an employer of Chinese labour. It had seen how Chinese factories were organised. If you asked how many employees a factory had, its manager would tell you '900'. But when Pacific Dunlop people walked around the factory they would see only about 200 people actually working there. Nine hundred would turn out to be the number that the factory had been told it had to employ by the local labour unit, which in turn had got the figure from head office in Beijing. The number of people employed had no relationship to the factory's output.

Pacific Dunlop said it would show the Chinese partners how to use the machinery and get the sort of productivity expected in the west, but it would not employ vast numbers of people. Officials from the No. 1 Sock Factory and the Beijing government came to Australia to look at Pacific Dunlop's factories.

Throughout the negotiations, the Pacific Dunlop negotiators held the line that initial productivity should be 50 per cent of that expected in Australia. Twice as many people as would normally operate the machinery were trained, but with the expectation that after a certain start-up period, productivity levels would rise to international best practice. That has been achieved.

Because Pacific Dunlop was always introducing new business concepts and using western contracts with which the Chinese were unfamiliar, they had to spend inordinate amounts of time explaining the technical terms. Some contracts would be 30 pages long. They would hope to get through at least half of the contract in five days, but would get bogged down in the preamble.

Preston would say, 'Look, let's not worry about that. Let's get to the substantive issues.' When, on the day he left, all the key issues would come out, he would try to give them an answer or insist, 'That is our position.' The big difference between the the Americans saying this and leaving and Preston doing the same was that the Chinese knew, without doubt, that Preston would be back to continue negotiating, whereas if the Americans did not get their way they would go elsewhere. Preston usually chooses a point on which to end the discussion, then goes away and thinks about it and perhaps comes back to it the next day. He doesn't think there is any point in trying to force an issue and then flying out of the country. If possible he stays in China until he resolves an issue.

His approach to negotiating is to focus on the major points he needs to gain, rather than on the vast number of small details the Chinese like to go through. He knows this approach is part of their negotiating system and lets it take its course. 'When we are trying to negotiate shoe prices, if the Chinese representative says, "I'm in real trouble with $5.75 a shoe, I need to go back to that factory and pay them more," then you've got to make a judgment and say, "OK, perhaps I'll go to $5.90." But if he says "$6.25", the technique that really works for me is to show him the figures, and prove I can't move on the price. If I reply to his request with a blunt, "I'm not going to do it," at the end of the day he's going to walk away and I know he will inflate next season's prices.'

One tactic Preston has often encountered is for the Chinese to blame price hikes on unspecified costs or overheads. They might say, 'It has gone up 30 per cent because of the leather.' The Pacific Dunlop buyers would look at the leather markets and find that prices had gone up only 5 per cent. When they told the Chinese this, the Chinese would say, 'Oh yes, but there are other things too.' With the Taiwanese, on the other hand, it is possible to work through all component costs because the agents have a stakeholding in the factory and know such details.

The Chinese representatives would not know the costs of individual parts of the shoes. Pacific Dunlop's negotiators would then have to go through a bargaining process with them, looking at the leather, insoles, and PVC, even though they had no idea how the Chinese were pricing these elements. They would try to trade an increase in one component for a decrease in another. They could also fall back on the fact that the company had a commitment to China and vice versa.

Because Preston has a wide perspective on all Pacific Dunlop's trading relationships, he can always find areas where he can concede advantages to the Chinese. If, in buying shoes, he needs to give way somewhere, he may use his knowledge that women's shoes can be discounted because men's shoes are selling well. Someone who was solely responsible for women's shoes might want to fight to retain a certain profit, wondering at the concessions that Preston makes.

Pacific Dunlop's commitment was shown in the flexible way it negotiated prices. For example, a drop in the value of the Australian dollar means a windfall saving for the Australian buyer. If this happened, Pacific Dunlop would adjust its price if the Chinese were finding it a problem, just as Winestock had always done.

Preston says: 'Our experiences are probably coloured by the fact that we've been trading with them a long time and have a long-term view of it and we have experience in the slowness of doing business there. It is very much a process of giving way when they are in trouble, but at the same time, they have got to take that on board the next time around should you need some help. Sometimes we remind them of our long-term commitment. Where they won't give way we may say, "We're committed to you and we think that we've done a good job over the years, and we'll continue to do so. We are not going to other markets, by and large, and you have got to take that into consideration." Indeed, the company forbade its employees to go to Taiwan even if they could sometimes buy a shoe there more cheaply than in China. The Americans would say Pacific Dunlop was not competitive enough, but the company saw that as taking a short-term view.

Preston says, 'If you are going to deal in China you have to be able to make a commitment. Of course, just as in any business partnership, you cannot go under water with them, but you must be flexible and be able to see a problem from their point of view and have a position of mutual benefit. All successful arrangements came down to that in the long term—and to personal relationships.'

Preston describes his company's approach to its Chinese partners as 'rather Japanese'. A contract can only go so far, he says. Flexibility is important. The worst thing possible is to walk in with a lawyer who wants to dot all the i's and cross the t's. 'In doing a joint venture contract,' he goes on, 'You try to get the really hard things worked out and agreed to, but then you throw the contract away. If your partner continually says to you, "This is what the contract says," you've got the wrong partner and the arrangements aren't working. You're better off to get that partner out the door or walk away yourself, because that's not how you deal in any business anywhere, but particularly with the Chinese.'

If a problem arises in Australia, such as a shipment arriving late, the Chinese will not answer fax or phone enquiries about it. So Preston and his fellow negotiators have learnt that they have to get on a plane immediately—the next day—and go and talk to them face to face.

Paying attention to personal relationships has helped Pacific Dunlop in many ways. One senior manager says: 'The whole networking thing is far more important than most western businessmen understand. You speak to people and they say, "We know someone who can get us in here and can get us in there," but that's a quarter of it. It's the connections, it's very wide. You don't appreciate it until you've spent a bit of time there . . . and I don't mean going there for a weekend every now and again! You've really got to get to know the Chinese themselves. We have had people assigned to us in starting up new businesses who are so well connected, and therefore so powerful, that when they walk into a room all the other Chinese fall silent. We have also benefited from the advice of well-connected people in recommending marketing managers for us. These marketers have been crucial in gaining us substantial contracts in regions of China where we had no experience.'

All Pacific Dunlop enterprises in China have been drawn into one of the first holding companies ever to gain approval in China. It allows the company to balance losses in one operation with profits in another, and it may one day be able to be listed on the Chinese Stock Exchange.

Three other developments demonstrate the benefits of

making a long-term commitment to China and having a wide network of personal relationships there. The same executives who took over from Paul Winestock in shoe negotiations have now negotiated to establish ice-cream production in ten Chinese provinces, with full access to the Chinese market. This makes Pacific Dunlop the largest manufacturer and marketer of ice-cream in China. The new chairman of the ANZ Bank, John Gough, a former managing director and now chairman of Pacific Dunlop, has won the right for ANZ to become the first Australian bank to operate in China. And in 1990 the then mayor of Shanghai, Zhu Rong-ji, invited Pacific Dunlop's then managing director, Philip Brass, to join his city's International Economic Advisory Committee.

## DISCUSSION

### 1 Become known and build trust

Paul Winestock sums up an important truth about the Chinese business world when he says, 'It isn't a level playing field.' In China, who you and your associates are is more important to success than the mere excellence of your product or your competitiveness.

The Chinese are fiercely loyal to their own groups, as we have seen. The individual they are dealing with is more important than his company. Chinese business reflects Chinese social life: it is highly personalised.

When a new western manager goes to China, the Chinese want to test him out before they agree to do business with him. No matter what company he represents, if he himself is unacceptable to them, they will agree, nod politely at his suggestions, but do nothing. It's the face-saving way of saying no. The reason Winestock accompanied the Pacific Dunlop managers when they visited China after the buyout of his business was to signal to his Chinese associates that the new people should be treated as insiders. He also made sure the company sent its top executives: the chairman and the managing director, because status is very important in China.

Winestock worked to make himself an insider with the Chinese. He went there regularly, even during the Cultural Revolution. I suspect that he would not have run scared to the international airport, like many foreign businessmen, during the Tiananmen incident.

He kept his promises. As he says, 'If you promise something and do not do it, you will lose face, and they will lose their confidence in you.' This is a critical point because Chinese notions of friendship are based on action. It is also a measure of how reliable you are as a business associate, critical information in the flexible Chinese business environment where law does not protect you very adequately. Winestock met Chinese requirements in these areas: he took losses at times without abandoning the Chinese corporations, and helped his old friends establish a textile mill. In return, the Chinese supported him in different ways: giving him the exclusive right to retail Chinese shoes in Australia, and selling to him at cost when their deliveries were late and his business was placed in jeopardy. The Chinese are much less forgiving of people who fail to demonstrate their reliability as friends than most westerners.

We have seen how important it is to personalise negotiations, so that you break through the Chinese stereotype of the exploitative, cunning foreigner. It is also much harder for them to use stonewalling tactics when they know you as a person. Banquets are one of the activities Winestock used to build his credibility with the Chinese. Even though he is a private person who usually avoids restaurant socialising, he makes an exception for the Chinese. Willingness to host banquets which give face to Chinese business associates is one of the measures by which the Chinese judge a westerner a friend.

Having a good reputation in China as a reliable business partner willing to help, has resulted in many advantages for Winestock and Pacific Dunlop. Apart from the exclusivity agreement, for Pacific Dunlop it has meant a speeding up of the negotiation process: six to eighteen months compared with three to five years for most Chinese–foreign joint ventures; a continuing string of business proposals from the Chinese side; support for new initiatives such as the shareholding by China Silk in the sock factory and the assignment of powerful people to help the company penetrate Chinese markets; the approval of new joint-venture conditions, such as the shoe components factory's tax regime and the sock venture's two-stage capital investment; and approval for a holding company in Shanghai. Because powerful Chinese know Pacific Dunlop chairman, John Gough, the bank of which he is now also chairman, ANZ, was given priority treatment in Shanghai. The invitation to managing director Philip Brass to join the mayor of Shanghai's economic advisory committee is another demonstration of how the Chinese personal network operates.

Business delegations from China visiting other Australian companies have asked, 'Is this a Pacific Dunlop company?' They have heard about Pacific Dunlop and know it is a company that can be relied upon.

## 2 Follow the Chinese bargaining process and save face

Winestock adjusted his normal business behaviour to suit the Chinese. He thought about the effects of confrontation on face, he acknowledged that the Chinese could do business with anyone in the world and that forcing them would only lead to the loss of his business with them, and he understood that since decisions in China are made by a group, he should make his point and then let them recess. He also followed normal Chinese bargaining style: going through the contract point by point and exchanging concessions—as he puts it, 'giving a little bit here and a little bit there'.

Preston followed his lead and, to cope with the tediousness of the process, identified a number of major issues on which he would stand firm which he kept as mental signposts through the bargaining process.

It is important to be able to give concessions to the Chinese when they need them for their own internal reasons (which are kept hidden from outsiders). This takes time. The shoe price bargaining illustrates this point, and the need to insist that the other side give something back at another time. The Chinese do this when they do business with one another, and western negotiators should follow suit, otherwise negotiations can easily end in deadlock or, as Preston pointed out, a 'payback' at a later date.

## 3 Argue in the interests of the joint business

In devising his negotiation strategy to gain his initial exclusivity contracts for Australia, and later to retain them, Winestock focused on the goal that was most important to the Chinese, to maximise their foreign currency earnings. The Pacific Dunlop executives followed the same strategy, and explained their proposal in terms of the advantages it would bring to the Chinese.

They also pointed out how reliable they had been in the past, and how they would continue to pursue joint gains.

In his shoe-buying and joint-venture negotiations, Preston reiterated his company's ongoing commitment to China. This underlined the point that Pacific Dunlop would deliver its promises to the Chinese and had their interests at heart. While emphasising the benefits of staying with Pacific Dunlop, he and his fellow negotiators also explained that the Chinese would lose money if they did not follow the Pacific Dunlop strategy. This tactic of 'ultimate consequences' was often used to push negotiations to a close.

## 4 Allow time

Many western business people grumble about Chinese slowness and stalling, attributing it to evil motives. Preston describes in detail the factors that slowed his tannery negotiations. Having travelled extensively in China, he has seen the backwardness of provincial manufacturing and experienced the problems caused by poor infrastructure, waiting in airports for hours after his plane's officially scheduled departure time, for example. He has also done business in areas far from the main cities and come across the suspicion between provinces and their focus on local interests. As he says, every county has its own special laws and charges, and business takes three to four times longer to do in the provinces than in Shanghai.

Negotiators must take into account China's stage of development, as well as the fluid lines of responsibility. In the tannery negotiations, decision making was devolving from the central bureaucracy to the local level. There were hold-ups because the tanneries and the Animal By-Product Corporation reported to different bureaucracies, and there were changes in personnel.

This case study illustrates that China is not a monolith but a collection of competing regions and bureaucracies. Liberalisation of the economy has accelerated this tendency, bringing both advantages—that business can be done locally without always going through the central bureaucracy, for example—and disadvantages, such as the great variations between regulations in different districts and the time it takes for foreign business people to solve these problems and get approval.

The tannery negotiations failed because of internal problems on the Chinese side. The Animal By-Products Corporation in

Shanghai could not guarantee that the provinces, over which they had no control, would be able to supply the number of skins necessary. In all negotiations in China, foreigners should be aware of the difficulties created by the Chinese system. In my experience too many business people go to China with unrealistic expectations and then blame the Chinese when negotiations fall apart.

The other major reason for slowness in the tannery negotiation, and an ingredient in its failure, was that Pacific Dunlop was proposing a financial structure that was new and unacceptable to the Chinese. Despite many hours of explanation, in the end, it was too radical for the Chinese bureaucracy's responsibility system. The Chinese have been prepared to accept other new proposals, but only after exhaustive explanation and assurance. Preston says he might spend five days just explaining the technical terms in a contract's preamble, because western legal concepts and legalese are new to China. But if he did not do this he found it difficult to move discussion on to more substantive issues.

## 5 Use go-betweens

The western negotiator must know when to use a Chinese go-between. In both this case study and the TNT study, the negotiators used their partners when third parties (such as the local authorities) were involved. The partners were thus induced to abandon their individual interests and adopt the interests of the joint venture. This benefits the western partner in a number of ways. The Chinese know how to negotiate with one another. There is no shortage of people on the Chinese side, they are on the spot, and they can devote the necessary time to it without the costs incurred by a foreigner staying in China.

## 6 Breaking deadlock: Use documentary evidence

Preston showed his bottom-line figures to the Chinese representative in the shoe pricing negotiations when he was being pressed to lift his offer. This tactic helps overcome Chinese distrust of what foreigners tell them. Once the bottom line is established, it is possible to negotiate around it. However, one must not start with the bottom line, only move to it if necessary.

## 7 Breaking deadlock: expand the options

When you must meet Chinese demands, being able to move between issues or parts of a negotiation is crucial to avoiding a breakdown. If a breakdown occurs, the Chinese will do the business with someone else or get their own back in future negotiations. Preston gave the Chinese the price they wanted on the women's shoes because he knew he could make up the difference on men's shoes.

## 8 Prepare for post-contract negotiations

The Pacific Dunlop executives' approach to post-contract problems is clear and unequivocal: they renegotiate. If a problem arose while they were in Australia, Preston and his fellow negotiators would get on a plane the next day. Because of face, the Chinese would not tell the Australian head office what had gone wrong. The executives could only find that out by going to China. And they did it immediately, so they could resolve the problem before it hurt their business operations. Post-contract problems have occurred regularly in all their joint venture and trading operations, but are always solved by further discussion.

Delivery and quality problems are common complaints of western business people in China: late delivery, and quality that bears no resemblance to the standard or sample—as we saw in the case of the rabbitskin jackets in Chapter 1. These problems are due to poor infrastructure, the low level of development, and management problems.

Winestock and Pacific Dunlop use the normal Chinese method of dealing with failure to fulfil the contract: negotiating for some recompense, and stressing their ongoing commitment to China.  Hard-line legal approaches to contract breaking involving punitive action either fails to secure proper compensation or leads to a total breakdown in the business relationship. The key is to 'get something back'. Lawyers have played no part in dealing with contract infringements at Pacific Dunlop, the renegotiation is always done by executives who are well known to the Chinese.

The post-contract negotiation involves the same amount of explanation as the initial negotiation, and this requires a good-natured negotiator, able to see the long-term benefits of the association with the Chinese and prepared to put in the time and effort to achieve it.

Because of the post-negotiation problems that regularly come up with the Chinese, it is vital to have a long-term relationship in mind, during which losses in one year may be offset against gains in another year. It is far better to go into a negotiation understanding that there will be problems and making allowances for dealing with them, than to go in unaware and pay the price later.

# *12* Conclusion

Throughout this book one question has hung without being explicitly stated: 'Do Chinese negotiation practices differ fundamentally from negotiation practices in the west?' My conclusion is that although many aspects are shared, underlying conditions push Chinese behaviour at the negotiating table in directions that are not frequently encountered in the west. During the encounter westerners find their cherished values challenged and their confidence shaken. This chapter identifies the underlying conditions that shape the Chinese negotiating style, thus making it possible to integrate all the different facets into a comprehensible whole.

## THE STAGES OF A NEGOTIATION

Negotiations cannot be successfully pursued in a vacuum. When westerners go to China and expect to negotiate a mutually satisfactory agreement within a short time-frame, they are inevitably frustrated by the degree of resistance they encounter. Negotiations are too often seen as simply that interval of time when two teams sit opposite one another and discuss the desired agreement. Hawkins and Hudson (1991) define negotiations as a process that begins long before the formal negotiation period and extends after it. They consider the pre-negotiation period an important influence period. Shell supports this view of pre-negotiation when it advises its negotiators in China to 'exchange views with partners before formal negotiation'.

The greatest mistake westerners make in China is to believe

that the goals of the Chinese will be the same as their own. Because neither side is generally well known to the other (if at all), they hold views about the other side that are not related to reality. Furthermore, often the Chinese negotiators believe the relationship will be short term, and that once the immediate goal has been achieved, the westerners will leave China and they will have no further responsibilities to them. This expectation leads to bazaar haggling with its dubious ethics (Raffia 1982). This explains why the overseas Chinese emphasise building personal relationships and mutual commitment prior to negotiation. The Chinese adherence to their own group goals reinforces the win-lose mentality of bazaar haggling.

Proper use of the pre-negotiation period can minimise problems that might arise during the formal negotiation period. It is useful for establishing your reputation and that of your company, searching for areas of common ground, and determining the attitude of the Chinese side and whether or not the Chinese team has authority to negotiate. It should also be used to probe how familiar the Chinese team is with the technology or service that is to be negotiated. Their degree of unfamiliarity will determine how difficult it will be to gain acceptance for your plan and whether it can be implemented successfully. If you are establishing a precedent, the Chinese need time to accept it and you will need to build a long negotiation period into your planning (Rojot 1991).

The Chinese use the pre-negotiation period to assess how 'soft' you are. In the opening pages of this book, Tony Kosky, with his rabbit skin jackets, went to great lengths to demonstrate that he was not 'soft' and would not accept unfair treatment. Thereafter the Chinese modified their use of outsider ethics with him.

Chinese and western expectations differ about the implementation period after formal negotiations. The Chinese expect to renegotiate many items the western side thought had been agreed to. The implementation process itself will also throw up many new issues, and these will involve further negotiations. Some hard truths may come to light that were hidden during the formal negotiation. It is necessary to prepare for the extra demands and changes to the contract, as well as many unforeseen problems that arise in implementing the contract. Finance can be held in reserve, implementation can be planned as a series of stages, each dependent on the successful completion of the preceding stage, a steering committee can be set up or go-betweens used to get at the truth and to save face.

## TEAM NEGOTIATING AND TEAM DECISION-MAKING

The people across the table or around the room are but the tip of the iceberg that is the Chinese negotiating side. Behind them are many more controlling teams and stakeholders who devise strategy and control decision-making. The extent of this complexity is reported in the following advice to Chinese chief negotiators:

> As chief negotiator you must bear the pressure and objectives of the leading group. This is more troublesome than the pressure of the foreign side. You must not follow the line of least resistance simply because the leading group has a particular agenda. When there is a difference of opinion between the negotiating team and the leadership, it is most important to gain the support of the intermediate leading group. Once that is obtained, write a report for the leadership which analyses and weighs all factors and ask the leadership to write comments on it. When the leadership sees that your opinion is based on thorough and balanced analysis, it will, in most circumstances, take it into account (Li 1988).

The western negotiator must deal with this diffusion of responsibility and reluctant decision-making. You have to convince a multitude of people, not just the one sitting opposite you as chief negotiator. Appropriate strategies are to give detailed explanations to the team facing you, and provide documentary evidence that can be passed on to the groups behind the scenes. Frequent recesses allow issues to be discussed with the controlling groups. The reasons for hold-ups can be uncovered by the use of a go-between or discussion on informal occasions. When an inflexible position is taken on one particular item, that item should be put aside and returned to later.

The large number of people having input also affects the style of the negotiation. Items can be brought up suddenly, without any apparent logic. An adversarial atmosphere can easily develop. But the most obvious effect of so many people being involved on the Chinese side is the time negotiations take. Western negotiators need time to explain, time to answer questions and objections, time for the other side to discuss matters, time to go behind the scenes and avoid embarrassing individuals publicly, and time for a decision to be made.

Techniques for bringing the negotiations to a close that are particularly useful in China include appeals to fairness and to loyalty, as well as explanations of the ultimate consequences of not making a speedy decision.

## BUREAUCRATIC CONTROL

The conundrum in China is that although government guidelines seem clear, obtaining approval proves to be complex, uncertain and frustrating. Since the bureaucracy has the power of approval, and there is a certain flexibility in the way the guidelines are applied, efforts must be exerted to encourage those with power to view the proposal favourably. Of most importance is to provide thorough but uncomplicated documentary evidence that helps them to decide in your favour without fear that they have left themselves open to criticism. According to Gibbons (1996), if you provide too much complex information, the official may '(a) do nothing (then he or she cannot make a mistake); (b) shuffle it sideways to another department (pass the problem to someone else, who will lose it, or not do anything about it); or (c) return it not approved.'

The Chinese partner can do the negotiations with the bureaucracy on your behalf, as long as they are thoroughly briefed by you. Third parties, highly regarded 'foreign friends' and 'foreign experts', political representatives and Chinese power-brokers (such as mayors, deputy mayors and provincial governors) can intercede on your behalf. They will provide the necessary security for individuals in the controlling bureaucracy to make the decision.

Finally, approval will be given according to economic policy guidelines. In the 1980s the guidelines were directed at gaining capital, technology and business management skills through foreign investment in joint ventures. These priorities resulted in China receiving outdated technology, and multinationals like Volkswagen dominating the domestic market. As a result, Chinese priorities for the late 1990s are technology intensive industries, import substitution, infrastructure and agricultural projects. The emphasis is on large projects which introduce advanced technology and expert management skills. National goals, which change in response to evolving Chinese needs, will be reflected in approvals issued by the controlling bureaucracies.

## THE HAGGLING TRADITION

I have already touched on two elements that contribute to a style of negotiation that bears close resemblance to marketplace haggling. These are the belief that relations with foreigners will be short term, and the input of many individuals in teams at different levels of the hierarchy. Also of relevance is the Chinese historical experience of western countries and companies. Hostility, fear and distrust are the results of this experience. Western negotiators in China frequently report that their Chinese counterparts who are motivated by these feelings use the following strategies: stonewalling (a refusal to budge), attacking (to intimidate and make you uncomfortable) and trickery (to dupe you into giving in) (Ury 1991).

The haggling formula followed is fairly standard. It begins with broad principles and unrealistic demands, and proceeds with exaggeration of Chinese compromises and minimisation of those yielded by the opposition, pressure for the opponent to make a quick compromise to gain consensus, 'muddying the water' with irrelevant issues and cross-examination based on previously noted replies and comments, the use of information from competitor companies to extract more benefits from foreign companies, and serious negotiation only when the Chinese believe they are close to your bottom line. A certain tendency to use what might be described as 'sharp practices' is evident throughout the negotiations.

Dealing with such a style requires clarity about what you want to achieve and flexibility in dealing with the changing tactics. There are so many distractions placed in the way of the foreign negotiator, it is essential to think strategically rather than emotionally. Emotions can be the negotiator's undoing. The most effective response is to be sympathetic, fair and controlled. Much depends upon a negotiator's ability to exert control without causing resentment.

## HIDDEN AGENDAS

There are logical reasons for all Chinese negotiating positions, although the logic may not be apparent because Chinese negotiation style is to keep their group's motivations hidden from strangers. It may also be a logic that differs from that of western business practice.

The foreign negotiator must always be aware that there is a public face and a private face, and that most problems are solved by operating in the private arena. The Chinese side often signals that they are open to finding a solution but unfortunately these signals are not received by the western side because of cultural differences. With experience, it is possible to be alert to such signalling. What is really important here is that many problems can be solved with discretion. This may be best done by using a third party, a typical Chinese device. The Chinese must not be made to look like failures in public or seen to be disobeying the instructions of their superior officers.

Although *Getting to Yes* (1979) and *Getting Past No* (1991) were apparently best sellers in the US, their advice that 'face-saving is at the core of the negotiation process', and that 'helping an opponent save face is vital to securing his co-operation', is rarely employed in public negotiations between the US and China. The result is the confrontation and mutual ill-will that not infrequently glares out at us from the media.

## ETHNOCENTRICITY AND HISTORICAL INFLUENCES

Throughout the writing of this book I was tugged at different times to one or other pole of the western experience in China—to those whose experience was such that 'the delay, the apparent deceit and misrepresentation, and the intrigue' brought about 'sadness, and sometimes utter hopelessness' (Gibbons 1996) versus those who saw the Chinese as 'nice people' who paid on time and acted honourably. What I was experiencing was just what westerners in China experience: the effect of ethnocentricity.

In cross-cultural encounters when things do not go according to expectations, the natural human response is to label what is unfamiliar or contrary to one's own wishes as 'bad'—to judge it morally—in contrast to one's own values and actions which are seen as 'good'. One then goes on to stereotype all members of the foreign culture as sharing those detested qualities. On reflection it is possible to see that people of one's own culture can act in exactly the same way as the foreigners, but obviously one does not go on to stereotype everyone in that culture as 'bad'. In China, as in business transactions anywhere, the people involved are as varied as their agendas and their ethics.

Westerners want to make a profit in China, and bring that profit home. When the Chinese have a different aim, to profit themselves, and pursue it with vigour, western business people often feel that the Chinese have no right to do so. For their part, the Chinese feel that the west has no right to dictate terms to them—Chinese negotiators see themselves as representatives of a sovereign state with a rich civilisation and an illustrious history (which includes long periods of great innovation, wealth and power). The incompatibility of each side's point of view, and the ethnocentrism associated with it, not infrequently constitutes the greatest stumbling block to successful Chinese–western negotiations.

A knowledge of Chinese negotiation practices and their underlying rationale can help bring balance to the judgments western negotiators make. So too can appreciation of the ethno-centric factors that influence both sides.

# Bibliography

Bergère, Marie-claire 1989, *The Golden Age of the Chinese Bourgeoisie 1911–1937*, Cambridge University Press, Cambridge

Blackman, C. 1995, *Australian Executives in China: The Management Challenge. A Survey Report*, Australia–China Chamber of Commerce and Industry, Melbourne

—— 1993, *Strategies for Venturing in Asia*, CEDA, Melbourne

Breth, Ron and Jin, Kai-ping (n.d), *Business Negotiations with the People's Republic of China*, Victoria College Press, Melbourne

Chen, Derong and Faure, Guy 1995, 'When Chinese companies negotiate with their government', *Organizational Studies*, vol. 16 no. 1, pp. 27–54

Druckman, Daniel 1973, *Human Factors in International Negotiations: Social-Psychological Aspects of International Conflict*, Sage Publications, Beverly Hills

Dutton, Michael R. 1992, *Policing and Punishment in China. From Patriarchy to 'the People'*, Cambridge University Press, Cambridge

Eiteman, David K. 1990, 'American executives' perceptions of negotiating joint ventures with the People's Republic of China: Lessons learned', *Columbia Journal of World Business*, Winter 1990, pp. 59–67

Fisher, Roger and Ury, William 1979, *Getting to Yes: Negotiating Agreement Without Giving In*, Houghton Mifflin, Boston

FitzGerald, C.P. 1985, *Why China? Recollections of China 1923–1950*, Melbourne University Press, Melbourne

FitzGerald, Stephen 1986, '"Genuine friendship, genuine frankness": Some frank comments on our friendly economic relations', J. Fincher and C.L. Pan *In Business with China: Planning and Managing Sino-Australian Economic Cooperation*, Australian National University, Canberra

Gibbons, Russell 1996, *Joint Ventures in China: A Guide for the Foreign Investor*, Macmillan Education, Melbourne

Graham, John L. and Sano, Yoshihiro 1984, *Smart Bargaining. Doing Business with the Japanese*, Ballinger, Cambridge, Mass.

Grow, Roy F. 1989, 'Acquiring foreign technology: What makes the transfer process work?' in D.F. Simon and M. Goldman eds, *Science and Technology in Post-Mao China*, Harvard University Press, Cambridge

Harwitt, Eric 1992, 'Foreign passenger car ventures and Chinese decision-making', *Australian Journal of Chinese Affairs*, no. 28 July, pp. 141–66

—— 1995, *China's Automobile Industry: Policies, Problems and Prospects*, ME Sharpe, New York

Hawkins, Leo and Hudson, Michael 1991, *Effective Negotiation*, ENS Business Publications, Kew

Hofstede, Geert 1980, *Culture's Consequences. International Differences in Work-Related Values*, Sage Publications, Beverly Hills

Hsu, Immanuel C.Y. 1986, *The Rise of Modern China*, Oxford University Press, Hong Kong

Huang, Yao-sheng 1985, 'Guanyu yu waishang qiatan yewude jidian benhui' (A few personal experiences regarding negotiation with foreign traders), *Jingji guanli yu yanjiu* (Economic Management and Research), vol. 5, pp. 57–58

Hutcheon, Robin 1990, *First Sea Lord: The Life and Work of Sir YK Pao*, Chinese University Press, Hong Kong

Kreisberg, Paul H. 1994, 'China's negotiating behaviour', TW Robinson and D Shambaugh eds, *Chinese Foreign Policy: Theory and Practice*, Clarendon Press, Oxford

Kristof, Nicholas D. and Wudunn, Sheryl 1994, *China Wakes: The Struggle for the Soul of a Rising Power*, Nicholas Brealey, London

Lai, T.L.G. and Lam, Y.W.C. 1986, 'A study on work-related values in the People's Republic of China' Parts 1, 2, 3, *The Hong Kong Manager* Dec/Jan, Feb/March, June/July

Lall, Arthur 1968, *How Communist China Negotiates*, Columbia University Press, New York

Lampton, David M. 1986, *Paths to Power: Elite Mobility in Contemporary China*, University of Michigan, Ann Arbor

—— 1992, 'A plum for a peach: Bargaining, interest and bureaucratic politics in China', K.G. Lieberthal and D.M. Lampton eds, *Bureaucracy, Politics and Decision-making in Post-Mao China*, University of California Press, Berkeley

Leung, Thomas and Yeung, L.L. 1995, 'Negotiation in the People's Republic of China: Results of a survey of small business in Hong Kong', *Journal of Small Business Management*, vol. 33, no. 1, pp. 70–77

Li, Guo-qing 1989, 'Shangwu tanpan gejieduande shiyongxing wenti chutan' (An initial exploration of practical issues of different stages during business negotiation), *Shangye yanjiu* (Business Research), vol. 9, pp. 29–31

Li, Yu-feng 1988, *Waimao tanpan celue yu fangfa* (Foreign trade negotiation strategy and method), Meitan Gongye Chubanshe, Beijing

Li, Zhi-sui 1994, *The Private Life of Chairman Mao*, Random House, New York

Liao, Kuang-sheng 1984, *Antiforeignism and Modernization in China, 1860–1980, Linkage Between Domestic Politics and Foreign Policy*, Chinese University Press, Hong Kong

Lieberthal, Kenneth G. 1980, *Revolution and Tradition in Tientsin, 1949–1952*, Stanford University Press, Stanford

Lu, Han-chao 1995, 'Away from Nanking Road: Small stores and neighbourhood life in modern Shanghai', *Journal of Asian Studies*, vol. 54, no. 1 February, pp. 93–123

Macleod, Roderick 1988, *China, Inc. How to Do Business with the Chinese*, Bantam Books, New York

MacNair, H.F. 1913, *Modern Chinese History: Selected Readings*, Shanghai, quoted by I.C.Y. Hsu 1983, *The Rise of Modern China*, 3rd ed., Oxford University Press, Hong Kong

Mann, Jim 1989, *Beijing Jeep: The Short Unhappy Romance of American Business in China*, Simon & Schuster, New York

Morse, Hosea Ballou 1910–1918, *The International Relations of the Chinese Empire. Vol. I: The Period of Conflict 1834–1860; Vol. II: The Period of Submission 1861–1893; Vol. III: The Period of Subjection 1894–1911*, Longmans, Green, London

Naughton, Barry 1992, 'Hierarchy and the bargaining economy: Government and enterprise in the reform process', K.G. Lieberthal and D.M. Lampton eds, *Bureaucracy, Politics and Decision-making in Post-Mao China*, University of California Press, Berkeley

Nixon, Mary Anne 1994, 'Building grain storage facilities in China—International contract negotiation', *Cost Engineering*, vol. 36, no. 5 May, pp. 7–11

Purves, Bill 1991, *Barefoot in the Boardroom. Venture and Misadventure in the People's Republic of China*, Allen & Unwin, Sydney

Pye, Lucian W. 1982, *Chinese Commercial Negotiating Style*, Oelgeschlager, Gunn and Hain Publishers, Cambridge, Mass.

—— 1985, *Asian Power and Politics: The Cultural Dimensions of Authority*, Belknap Press of Harvard University Press, Cambridge, Mass.

—— 1986, 'The China trade: Making the deal', *Harvard Business Review* July–August, pp. 74–80

—— 1995, 'Factions and the politics of Guanxi: Paradoxes in Chinese administrative and political behaviour', *The China Journal*, no. 34 July, pp. 35–53

Raffia, Howard 1982, *The Art and Science of Negotiation*, Belknap Press of Harvard University Press, Cambridge, Mass.

Rojot, Jacques 1991, *Negotiation: From Theory to Practice*, Macmillan, London

Shapiro, James E., Behrman, J.N., Fischer, W.A. and Powell, S.G. 1991, *Direct Investment and Joint Ventures in China. A Handbook for Corporate Negotiations*, Quorum Books, New York

Silin, Robert H. 1976, *Leadership and Values. The Organization of Large-scale Taiwanese Enterprises*, Harvard University Press, Cambridge

Smith, Richard J., Fairbank, John K. and Bruner, Katherine F. eds, 1991, *Robert Hart and China's Early Modernization. His Journals, 1863–1866*, Council on East Asian Studies, Harvard University, Cambridge

Triandis, Harry C. 1990, 'Theoretical Concepts that are Applicable to the analysis of ethnocentrism', R.W. Brislin, *Applied Cross-cultural Psychology*, Sage Publications, Newbury Park

Tse, David K., Francis, June and Walls, Jan 1994, 'Cultural differences in conducting intra- and inter-cultural negotiations: A Sino-Canadian Comparison', *Journal of International Business Studies*, vol. 25, no. 3, pp. 537–555

Ury, William 1991, *Getting Past No*, Random Century, London

Walder, Andrew G. 1986, *Communist Neo-Traditionalism, Work and Authority in Chinese Industry*, University of California Press, Berkeley

Wall, James A. Jr 1993, 'Community mediation in China and Korea: Some similarities and differences', *Negotiation Journal: On the Process of Dispute Settlement*, April, pp. 141–153

Yang, Bo 1991, *The Ugly Chinaman and the Crisis of Chinese Culture*, trans. by Don J. Cohn and Jing Qing, Allen & Unwin, Sydney

Yang, Mayfair Mei-hui 1989, 'Between state and society: The construction of corporateness in a Chinese socialist factory', *Australian Journal of Chinese Affairs*, no. 22, July, pp. 30–59

—— 1994, *Gifts, Favors and Banquets. The Art of Social Relationships in China*, Cornell University Press, Ithaca

Zhang, Jiashen ed. 1993, *Waishang touziqiye shiwu shouce* (A Practical Guide to Joint Ventures), Jingji Guanli Chubanshe, Fuzhou

Zweig, David, Hartford, Kathy, Feinerman, James and Deng, Jianxu 1987, 'Law, contracts, and economic modernization: Lessons from the recent Chinese rural reforms', *Stanford Journal of International Law*, vol. 23, no. 2, pp. 319–364

# Index

adversarial bargaining, xi
  atmosphere, 54–5, 115, 192
ambit claim, 52, 58–9; *see also*
  bargaining
American executives, ix
American Motor Corporation, ix
anti-foreignism
  negative stereotypes, 28, 30,
    184
  propaganda, 25, 55
approvals, 60–2, 37–8, 193
arbitration, 68–9
*Art of War, The*, 7, 12
aspiration points, 59
assumptions, 23, 50, 116–18,
  136; *see also* perceptions
authority, *see* hierarchy

banquets, 12, 47, 98, 136–7,
  184
Baoshan Iron and Steel Plant,
  28
bargaining
  bureaucratic, 8, 138
  ethics, 7–8, 191
  iron law of, 9
  persistence, 6
  step-by-step process, 5, 52,
    134, 164, 185
  tactics of, 194; *see also* ambit
    claim; individualistic

  bargaining; win–lose;
    win–win
benevolence, 26, 169
bird cage economics, 29
body language, 93
bribery, 16
Britain, 11, 24–5
bureaucracy
  codes, 88–9
  in delay, 60–1
  wrangling, 39; *see also* stalling

Canton Trade (Spring) fair,
  16, 27, 132
Cantonese, xiii
case studies
  commodities trading, 123–32
  cultural tours, 156–63
  importing, 98–102
  mining company, 107–13
  Pacific Dunlop
    manufacturing joint
    ventures and exporting,
    171–83
  TNT express freight joint
    venture, 139–46
change; *see* precedents
changing levels, 84–5
chief negotiator, 85–6, 90, 117,
  192
China-centredness, 69

# interrogating TEXTS

General Editors
PATRICIA WAUGH AND LYNNE PEARCE

To 76305
and all the other lines I've hung on

# *Reading* DIALOGICS

**LYNNE PEARCE**
Lecturer in English, Lancaster University

Edward Arnold
A member of the Hodder Headline Group
LONDON   NEW YORK   MELBOURNE   AUCKLAND

© 1994 Lynne Pearce

First published in Great Britain 1994

Distributed in the USA by Routledge, Chapman and Hall, Inc.
29 West 35th Street, New York, NY 10001

*British Library Cataloguing in Publication Data*
Pearce, Lynne
 Reading Dialogics. — (Interrogating
 Texts Series)
 I. Title  II. Series
 801.95

ISBN 0–340–55052–X

*Library of Congress Cataloging in Publication Data*
Pearce, Lynne
 Reading dialogics / Lynne Pearce.
  p.    cm. — (Interrogating texts)
 Includes bibliographical references and index.
 ISBN 0–340–55052–X : $16.95
 1. Literature — Philosophy.  2. Criticism.  3. English literature —
19th century — History and criticism.  4. English literature — 20th
century — History and criticism.  5. American literature — 20th
century — History and criticism.  I. Title.  II. Series.
PN49.P39  1994
801′.95 — dc20                                          93–43946
                                                            CIP

Typeset in 10/11 Palatino by Hewer Text Composition Services,
Edinburgh. Printed and bound in Great Britain for
Edward Arnold, a division of Hodder Headline PLC,
338 Euston Road, London NW1 3BH by
Biddles Ltd, Guildford and King's Lynn

# CONTENTS

vi  *Contents*

# GENERAL EDITORS' PREFACE

*Interrogating Texts* is a series which aims to take literary theory – its key proponents, debates, and textual practices – towards the next century.

As editors we believe that despite the much vaunted 'retreat from theory', there is so far little material evidence of this supposed backlash. Publishers' catalogues reveal 'theory' (be it literary, cultural, philosophical or psychoanalytic) to be an expanding rather than a contracting market, and courses in literary theory and textual practice have now been established in most institutions of Higher Education throughout Europe and North America.

Despite significant improvements to high school syllabuses in recent years, however, most students still arrive at University or College ill-prepared for the 'revolution' that has shaken English studies in the past twenty years. Amid the welter of increasingly sophisticated and specialized critical works that now fill our libraries and bookshops, there is a pressing need for volumes like those represented by this series: volumes that will summarize, contextualize and *interrogate* the key debates informing contemporary literary theory and, most importantly, assess and demonstrate the *effectiveness* of the different approaches in the reading of literary texts.

It is, indeed, in its 'conceptual' approach to theory, and its 'interrogation' of theory *through* textual practice, that the series claims to be most strikingly new and distinctive. Instead of presenting literary theory as a series of 'approaches' (eg., Structuralism, Marxism, Feminism) that can be mechanistically 'applied' to any text, each volume will begin by examining the epistemological and conceptual frameworks of the theoretical discourse in question and examine the way in which its philosophical and political premises compare and contrast with those of other contemporary discourses. (The volumes on *Postmodernism* and *Dialogics* both consider their epistemological relation to the other, for example.) Each volume, too, will provide a historical overview of the key proponents, texts, and debates represented by the theory, as well as an evaluative survey of the different ways in which the theory has been appropriated and deployed by literary critics. Alongside this informative and evaluative contextualization of the theory, each volume will perform readings of a selection of literary texts. The aim of these readings, as indicated earlier, is not simplistically to demonstrate the way in which the theory in question can be 'applied' to a text, but to question the suitability of certain aspects of the theory *vis-à-vis* certain texts, and ultimately to use the texts to *interrogate the theory itself*: to reveal its own inadequacies, limitations and blindspots.

Two of the most suggestive theoretical keywords of the 1980s were *dialogue* and *difference*. The *Interrogating Texts* series aims to (re)activate both terms in its attempt to map the great shifts and developments (the 'continental drift'?!) of literary theory over the past twenty years and into the twenty-first century: the differences both within and between the various theoretical discourses, and the dialogues that inhere and connect them.

Eschewing the mechanical association between theory and practice, it should also be pointed out that the individual volumes belonging to the series do not conform to any organizational template. Each author has been allowed to negotiate the relationship between theory and text as he or she thinks best, and in recognition of the fact that some of our theoretical categories will require a very different presentation to others.

Altough both the substance and the critical evolution of the theoretical discourses represented by this series are often extremely complex, we hope that the perspectives and interrogations offered by our authors will make them readily accessible to a new generation of readers. The 'beginnings' of literary theory as a revolutionary threat and disruption to the Academy is fast receding into history, but its challenge – what it offers each of us in our relentless interrogation of literary texts – lives on.

Lynne Pearce
Patricia Waugh
1993

# ACKNOWLEDGEMENTS

Since many of my friends and colleagues seem to be under the impression that this book was written remarkably quickly, I'd like to record that it's now ten years since I first started working with Mikhail Bakhtin's dialogic theory as part of my Ph.D. on John Clare. My first thanks are therefore due to a number of people from the Birmingham years: in particular, my supervisor Mark Storey, and to David Lodge, Deirdre Burton and Adrian Stokes (the postgraduate student who first said the word 'polyphony' to me!).

The conception of this particular project, meanwhile, dates back to 1988 and was inspired, in part, by my reading of Jane Rule's novel *This is Not For You* (1970). Written entirely in the second person, this 'dialogue' with an erstwhile friend of many years who was almost (but never quite) a lover, fed into many of my own gestating thoughts on what Jeanette Winterson has referred to as the 'private language' of women (*Sexing the Cherry*, 1989): those forms of intimate address which privilege certain audiences and exclude others through a subtle arsenal of irony, ellipsis and intonation. These ideas took me straight back to Bakhtin, and in the following year a book which would combine my interest in dialogic theory and contemporary women's writing began to take shape. I was by then lecturing at Durham University, and the project was finally launched as part of the *Interrogating Texts* series I was invited to coedit with Patricia Waugh. So, to Pat, and to Christopher Wheeler at Edward Arnold, many thanks for your support and encouragement throughout.

The actual composition and writing of the book belongs, however, to my first three happy years at Lancaster University, and I would like to extend my gratitude to all the members of the Department of English and the Centre for Women's Studies who have given the project intellectual and practical support, in particular: Richard Dutton (who, as Head of Department, allowed me a term's study leave to get the book written); Jackie Stacey (who offered an enormous amount of helpful and supportive advice on the first draft); Celia Lury (for her intervention in the Introduction and Conclusion: your observations are recorded!); Sarah Franklin (who also added her voice to the early draft); and Tony Pinkney (for useful bibliographic and other information).

Other significant contributors to the writing of the book were: Sara Mills (who, like Jackie, worked extremely hard on the first draft and offered much useful guidance); my coeditor, Pat Waugh (also a supportive reader); and Rowena Murray (for supplying the book's title and other inspirations, as well providing practical instruction in the 'chronotope of the sea-voyage': see Chapter 5 for details!).

Meanwhile, at the risk of becoming predictable, my final 'heartfelt gratitude, etc., etc.' must once more go to Sarah Oatey, whose eighteen-year long (collusive/antagonistic/ribald/ironic/intimate but *never* conciliatory) dialogue with me fulfils all the criteria described in this book – and more.

The author would like thank the US journal *Criticism* for granting permission to reprint (in slightly revised form) the essay which appeared in their publication under the title 'John Clare's "Child Harold": A Polyphonic Reading' (*Criticism*, **31**, 2, 1989, pp. 139–57).

# INTRODUCTION

## I
### The Dialogic Principle

I remember exactly where I was when I found out about my husband's adultery – I was sitting in the loo on the first floor landing, a tiny box of a room with walls and ceiling covered in speckled wallpaper. It was like crouching inside a Christmas wrapper. The phone had rung in the kitchen below – a call from his cameraman in Germany. I had answered the phone myself, had a chat, passed it over to him and gone upstairs to the loo.

You can always tell who is talking at the other end of the line. With the Germans he adopts a jokey tone that echoes their Bavarian accents, lots of *ja* sounds and Germanic inflections punctuated with exclamation marks. Then suddenly his voice changed. He spoke in a tone he had never used before, not with me, not with anyone, a voice like a hot tongue. It made me dizzy just to hear it through the floor. In that instant I understood everything – who she was, what had happened between them . . . Longing and warmth vibrated up the pipes. I didn't hear what was said. You didn't need to. Dazed, I waited until he had put down the phone (Jennifer Potter, *Guardian*, 5 August 1992).

A word is a bridge thrown between myself and another. If one end of the bridge belongs to me, then the other depends on my addressee. A word is a territory shared by both addresser and addressee, by the speaker and his interlocutor (V. N. Voloshinov, *Marxism and the Philosophy of Language*, 1929, p. 86).

I t may seem rather surprising to you (a reader whom I shall presently identify) to open a book on literary theory and be confronted with an account of adultery. Rereading it alongside the second quotation, however, you might begin to guess the set of connections I am about to make in my attempt to communicate the key principles of dialogic thought.

The decision to approach my subject of study tangentially, through this description of an overheard telephone conversation, derives from the explanations I have found myself offering whenever I tell people I am writing a book on dialogic theory. To the question 'What is dialogics?', my original floundering attempts at a conceptual definition have now been replaced by the quotation from *Marxism and the Philosophy of Language* cited above, and a discussion of what happens when we use the telephone.

The telephone, I argue, is a uniquely suggestive metaphor for coming to terms with the central tenets of dialogism. It is, like the word/bridge analogy in the Voloshinov quotation, an instrument of communication that can *only* function through the interaction of two people: the caller can speak only when the person being dialled picks up the receiver.

For central to the dialogic philosophy of the Bakhtin group, and present in their discussions of language, literature and human subjectivity, is a recognition of the impossibility of saying, meaning or, indeed, *being*, without the reciprocating presence of an addressee.[1]

What I would like to do in these preliminary remarks, then, is explore further the conditions of spoken dialogue present in telephone conversations and indicate how these relate to some key principles of dialogic theory. This will be followed by a section describing the ways in which dialogics has achieved the status of an epistemology (i.e., 'a theory of the grounds of knowledge': how we 'make meaning'), and what the key features of this epistemology are. The third section will then confront the *politics* of dialogic thinking: both the way in which Bakhtin's own writings have been appropriated by the 'liberal' and 'radical' wings of academia, and the role of dialogism in our understanding of contemporary world politics. The fourth section, 'Dialogic Theory and Textual Practice', will explain the rationale for this volume, and this will be followed by a chapter-by-chapter guide on how the material is organized. The Introduction concludes with a postscript addressed to you, the reader, exploring some of the special features of the text–reader relationship. Before proceeding with the telephones, I should perhaps also suggest that readers unfamiliar with Bakhtin's work may prefer to turn to sections two and three of the Introduction once they have worked through the rest of the book. Since one of the purposes of this chapter is to conceptualize and contextualize Bakhtin's ideas at a more abstract level, these readers might find it more suitable as a conclusion than an introduction.

As I indicated above, the telephone conversation exemplifies the Bakhtinian concept of dialogicality by being predicated on the *active* communication of two participants: the speaker and his or her addressee.

---

1   Mikhail Mikhailovich Bakhtin was born near Moscow in 1895 and with his brother, Nikolai (later a professor of linguistics at Birmingham University), enjoyed a broad university education at St Petersburg and other prerevolutionary centres of learning. From 1918 onwards he was surrounded by a group of friends especially interested in contemporary German philosophy, and with certain of these – in particular Valentin Voloshinov and Pavel Medvedev – formed what has come to be known as the 'Bakhtin group'. Recognition of the intellectual collaboration of this group, as their interests transferred from 'abstract' philosophy to an engagement with contemporary theories of language, literature and psychoanalysis, is important. Although published under their separate names, there has long been been a suspicion that many of the early works of the group (in particular, *Freudianism* (1927), *The Formal Method* (1928) and *Marxism and the Philosophy of Language* (1929); see Further Reading for full details) were *coauthored* (although others argue for them being authored entirely by Bakhtin). I discuss these problems of attribution in more detail at the beginning of Chapter 1, but readers will be aware from my own allusion to texts 'by' Voloshinov and Medvedev, and by my frequent references to 'the work of the Bakhtin circle', that I have chosen to retain the possibility of these other writers also contributing to the group of writings now referred to as 'Bakhtinian'. For further details of Bakhtin's life, see K. Clark and M. Holquist, *Mikhail Bakhtin* (Cambridge, MA: Harvard University Press, 1984) or M. Holquist, *Dialogism: Bakhtin and His World* (London and New York: Routledge, 1990).

While in a face-to-face conversation between two people one may remain silent, the addressee of a telephone conversation is usually obliged to signal her presence/attention through some form of verbal utterance, be this merely a 'hmm' or a 'uh-huh'. This process of verbal exchange, the means by which any individual's 'utterances' are made in anticipation of another's response, is central to Bakhtin's conception not only of how we communicate but also how we *mean*.[2] The grunting party at the other end of the telephone line may therefore be seen as the symbolic (dis)embodiment of 'the one who is always there' in some (often unidentified) shape or form. Although, as Voloshinov observes in *Marxism and the Philosophy of Language* (see Chapter 1, Section III) we may not necessarily have a named interlocutor in mind when we make our utterances (spoken or written), a discursive recipient of some kind is always present:

> Utterance, as we know, is constructed between two socially organized persons, and in the absence of a real addressee, an addressee is presupposed in the person, so to speak, of a normal representative of the social group to which the speaker belongs. The word is oriented towards an addressee, toward who that addressee might be: a fellow member or not of the same social group, of higher or lower standing . . . someone connected to the speaker with close social ties (father, brother, husband, and so on) or not. There can be no such thing as an abstract addressee, a man unto himself, so to speak.[3]

At the same time that the telephone conversation is an apposite symbol of the contract between speaker and addressee on which, according to the Bakhtin group, all thought/utterance is predicated, so does the answering-machine provide a complimentary metaphor for how it is impossible to speak into silence. Unless practised in the art, most of us find it extremely difficult to leave messages of any length on other people's answering-machines. What we do attempt, moreover, often comes out as hesitant, awkward and embarrassed; without a reciprocating presence at the other end of the line, we find it hard to order and communicate our ideas. In their essay, 'The telephone: a neglected medium', Guy Fielding and Peter Hartley explain the public's general dislike of answering-machines in what are effectively dialogic terms.[4] Connections to answering-machines, just as much as the inability actually to 'get through', tend (according to their research) to be perceived as 'failed calls'. This, indeed, accords with the Bakhtinian theory that, even when we are not aware of it, our thoughts and utterances are *structured* by the reciprocating presence of our addressee.[5] So that while most of us,

---

[2] 'Utterance', according to Holquist (*Dialogism*, p. 60), is 'the fundamental unit of investigation' in Bakhtin's work. Although the terms bears the connotations of spoken discourse, it may also refers to 'units of communication' in written texts.
[3] V. N. Voloshinov, *Marxism and the Philosophy of Language* (1929), trans. L. Matejka and I. R. Titunik (Cambridge, MA: Harvard University Press, 1986), pp. 85–86. Further page references to this volume will be given after quotations in the text.
[4] G. Fielding and P. Hartley, 'The Telephone: A Neglected Medium', *Studies in Communication*, ed. A. Cashdan and M. Jordan (Oxford: Basil Blackwell, 1987), pp. 110–24.
[5] 'The word in living conversation is directly, blatantly oriented towards a future answer word. It provokes an answer and structures itself in the answer's direction'. M. Bakhtin, *The Dialogic Imagination*, ed. M. Holquist, trans. C. Emerson and M. Holquist (Austin, TX: University of Texas Press, 1981), p. 280.

given a few seconds to collect our thoughts, are able to compensate for the temporary absence of our telephonic addressee by imagining them receiving our message at some future time, our initial sense of panic and confusion betrays just how much we were anticipating their response.

The conditions determining the use of the telephone, then, may be seen as symbolic of the 'dialogic contract' which, for the Bakhtin group, pre-empts any utterance, written or spoken. While in *Marxism and the Philosophy of Language* and the later essays attributed to Voloshinov (see Further Reading), this dependence of speaker upon addressee is analysed at a primarily linguistic level (see Chapter 1) in Bakhtin's work in *Problems of Dostoevsky's Poetics* (1929) and *The Dialogic Imagination* (1934–41) (see Further Reading) it is used to analyse the interanimation of voices and consciousnesses in literary texts, and to explain stylistic features such as stylization, parody and a special variety of 'doubly voiced discourse' called 'hidden polemic' (see Chapter 1, Section VI). Meanwhile, in addition to its verbal/textual manifestations, the dialogic contract is also presented by the Bakhtin group as a model of 'subject acquisition': because the Bakhtinian subject is an incontrovertibly *social* subject, he or she is formed through an ongoing process of dialogic exchange with his or her various interlocutors (see Chapter 1).

Implicit in all the Bakhtin group's writings on the dialogic interdependence of speaker and addressee there is, moreover, the recognition that this is a dynamic inscribed by *power*. Acknowledgement of this fact is, I feel, vital to a radical, politicized understanding of the dialogic principle, and its avoidance by some commentators is responsible for the 'wet liberal' view of Bakhtin's theory that has emerged in some quarters (see discussion in the next section). Returning to the example of the telephone conversation, I would like to point to where this power dynamic is most explicit in Bakhtin's writings: namely, with respect to *intonation*. Intonation (whether in actual speech or in its textual representation) is, according to Katerina Clark and Michael Holquist, 'the purest expression of values assumed in any utterance . . . for the reason that [it] always lies at the border of the verbal and the non-verbal'.[6] In this pronouncement, they are alluding to the way in which, in everyday speech, the *tone of voice* we use in our address always supplements its semantic communication in some way. Intonation may reinforce the apparent sincerity of a statement or, as in the case of irony, reveal a sentiment entirely at odds with it. It will also reveal much about the relationship between the speaker and addressee: whether it is professional or intimate, for example; whether it is friendly or adversarial; and which of the interlocutors, in this particular exchange, holds the balance of power. As Clark and Holquist also observe, 'Intonation clearly registers the other's presence, creating a sort of portrait in sound of the addressee to whom the speaker imagines she is speaking' (ibid.).

Intonation, then, is the means by which the power dynamic present in *all* dialogic exchange most effectively reveals itself. This is illustrated most poignantly in the description of 'telephonic adultery' quoted at the beginning of the section. As Clark and Holquist have observed, the

6  Clark and Holquist, *Mikhail Bakhtin*, p. 12.

telephone is the perfect instrument for demonstrating how our intonation, rather than our actual words, will betray the nature of (power-inscribed) relationships: 'A common illustration of this tendency is when we hear someone talking on the telephone to another person whose identity we do not know, but whose relation to the speaker we can guess from the speaker's speech patterns' (ibid., pp. 207–208).

In the *Guardian* extract, it will be remembered, the wife perceives her husband's adultery not by attending to the details of the conversation ('I didn't hear what was said. You didn't need to'), but by registering the (shocking) intimacy of his tone: 'Then suddenly his voice changed. He spoke in a tone he had never used before, not with me, not with anyone . . .'. In an instant, the wife recognizes the status in which her husband's interlocutor is held. His voice betrays an intimacy expressive of possession: the speaker has recognizable (sexual) power over his addressee and she (could we overhear her voice at the other end of the line) possibly has a similar power over him.

To conclude, then, the telephone conversation provides us with a highly suggestive symbolic expression of the key constituent features of Bakhtin's dialogic principle. It helps us focus, first, on the *dialogic contract* in which all of us are engaged in our effort to speak, to 'mean', to 'be'. All these activities require the reciprocating presence of an addressee in the same way that a telephone call requires the presence of someone else at the other end of the line. Secondly, through the magnified significance of *intonation* brought about by a form of communication in which there is no other 'extraverbal context' (see Chapter 1), we are alerted to the way in which all dialogues reveal a 'portrait in sound' of the power-inscribed relationship between speaker and addressee. This profoundly interdependent view of human communication is central to much of Bakhtin's thought; even those areas of his philosophy not directly concerned with language and literature.[7] And while, if we are searching for a more comprehensive vision of Bakhtin's work we would do well to heed Ken Hirschkop's warning that not all his thinking can be reduced to the model of 'ordinary (i.e., spoken) dialogue', there is no question that a great deal of his linguistic and literary analysis does originate with this conceit.[8] The quotation from Voloshinov with which I opened ('A word is a bridge thrown between myself and another') is reproduced, in various forms, many hundreds of times in the work of the Bakhtin group, and its simple elucidation of human communication as a reciprocal relationship is most certainly what has fuelled the multidisciplinary espousal of dialogic thinking the world over.

[7] A new insight into Bakhtin's philosophical thought has been provided by the publication of his early essays in the volume *Art and Answerability*, ed. M. Holquist and V. Liapunov, trans. V. Liapunov (Austin, TX: University of Texas Press, 1990). Page references to this volume will be given after quotations in the text.
[8] K. Hirschkop, *The Higher* (Times Newspapers), 1 May 1992, p. 27.

## II
## Dialogics as Epistemology

As I indicated at the beginning of this Introduction, dialogism has infiltrated Western intellectual thought at many different levels. Not only is it an area of literary theory and textual practice which cuts across other approaches and positionings (structuralism/poststructuralism/marxism/feminism/psychoanalysis), but it has also been espoused as a new model of academic debate and, in its most grandiose aspect, presented itself as a new epistemology.[9] As Michael Holquist has put it: 'Dialogism is also implicated in the modern thinking about thinking'.[10] In this section I would like to focus, briefly, on the nature of this dialogic epistemology: both its roots in Bakhtin's own writings and how it relates to other recent revisionings of knowledge production such as Einstein's 'theory of relativity' and postmodernism.

The first thing to make clear is that Bakhtin was not himself responsible for raising dialogics to the level of a metanarrative. Although all his works share in a broad philosophical continuum whose integrity scholars are only now beginning to recognize, the works on which his reputation have been founded in the West are very discipline specific: *Dostoevsky's Poetics*, *The Dialogic Imagination* and *Rabelais and His World* (1965) are all, primarily, works of literary criticism. The representation of dialogics as an epistemology is a result, rather, of the Bakhtin industry: of the hundreds of readers and critics from a broad spectrum of disciplines within the human and social sciences who have perceived in this relational model of text/self/world a means of tempering the apocalypticism of postmodernist discourse. As I observe at the end of Chapter 2, dialogism 'may possibly be regarded as the theoretical balm we need to heal a world split open by the contemporary obsession with "difference"' (p. 111).

If an epistemology is to be found in Bakhtin's own writings it needs to be identified and constructed by his *readers* and, as Clive Thomson has indicated in his essay, 'Mikhail Bakhtin and Shifting Paradigms' (1990), this movement is now underway.[11] Michael Holquist's books and essays have long struggled to relay the 'essence' of 'dialogic thinking about thinking', and the publication of the early philosophical essays, *Art and Answerability* (1990; see Further Reading), has provided scholars with a new foundation on which to raise the epistemological superstructure. What these recent commentators have observed is that across the writings of the

---

[9]  'A new model of academic debate': Don Bialostosky has proposed that we have, in Bakhtin's dialogic principle, an alternative to the 'dialectical' and 'rhetorical' models of traditional literary and philosophical thought. Noting that 'the best generic model for this kind of discourse is the symposium', Bialostosky draws a picture of literary criticism which will democratically 'converse' with earlier readers and critical positions without 'reducing them' to its own argument. See D. Bialostosky, 'Dialogics as an Art of Discourse in Literary Criticism', *Publications of the Modern Languages Association* **101**, 5, October, 1986, pp. 788–97.

[10]  Holquist, *Dialogism*, p. 15.

[11]  C. Thomson, 'Mikhail Bakhtin and Shifting Paradigms', *Mikhail Bakhtin and the Epistemology of Discourse*, *Critical Studies* (special issue), **2**, 1–2, 1990, pp. 1–12.

Bakhtin group (whether these be texts focused on literature, linguistics or theories of the subject), the focus on relationality between binary terms remains constant. As I illustrated in the last section, all meaning depends on the presence of a reciprocating other: a contract that, in Bakhtin's early philosophical writings, is expressed through the concept of *answerability*. A succinct summation of how this principle pervades all Bakhtin's thought is provided by Holquist in the introduction to *Art and Answerability*:

> But what is essential for Bakhtin is not only the categories as such that get paired in author/hero, space/time, self/other, and so forth, *but in addition the architectonics governing relations between them*. What counts is the simultaneity that makes it logical to treat concepts *together*. The point is that Bakhtin honours *both* things and the relations between them – one cannot be understood without the other (p. xxiii).

Identifying a nascent epistemology in Bakhtin's work also requires acknowledgement of his philosophical precursors. Ken Hirschkop has argued that dialogism will be liable to all manner of misappropriation if we do not attend to Bakhtin's own philosophical mentors such as Emmanuel Kant and Martin Buber.[12] Michael Holquist has also emphasized the significance of contemporary German thinkers such as Hermann Cohen and Richard Avenarius who formed the 'academic mainstream' of Bakhtin's own early intellectual experience.[13]

Before proceeding to a discussion of the difference between a dialogic epistemology and that of other contemporary thinkers and intellectual movements, it is first necessary to indicate what such thinking *shares* with other early twentieth-century discourses.

Unquestionably the most central of these discourses is structuralism. As will be seen in the analysis of *The Formal Method* (1928) in Chapter 1 (see Further Reading), much of the writing of the early Bakhtin group is in explicit or implicit dialogue with Ferdinand de Saussure and, aside from the similarities and differences between the two parties on the nature of language *per se*, both share the same relational epistemology.[14] This common root is aptly expressed in Terence Hawkes's representation of Saussure's position: 'The true nature of things may be said not to lie in the things themselves, but in the relationships we construct, and then perceive, between them'.[15] Structuralism, like dialogism, posits 'meaning' as the relationship *between* differences, and both systems tend to see these differences in terms of binary oppositions. In this last respect, indeed, dialogism is very clearly on the side of structuralist rather than poststructuralist thinking.

Another obvious comparison may be drawn between dialogic epistemology and the 'new' physiscs of Albert Einstein. Einstein's theory of relativity (1905) was also a theory of *relationality*, as Holquist has illustrated with reference to Einstein's work with moving objects:

---

[12] See Hirschkop, *Higher*, p. 27. Also Holquist's introduction to *Art and Answerability*, pp. xi–xvi.
[13] Holquist, *Dialogism*, p. 16.
[14] For a useful summary account of the similarities and differences between Bakhtin and Saussure see ibid., pp. 42–47.
[15] T. Hawkes, *Structuralism and Semiotics*, New Accents (London: Methuen, 1978), p. 17.

The observer's ability to see motion depends on one body changing its position *vis-à-vis* other bodies. Motion, we have come to accept, has only a relative meaning. Stated differently, one body's motion has meaning only in relation to another body; or – since it is a relation that is mutual – has meaning only in dialogue with another body (*Dialogism*, p. 20).

As with the example of the telephone, Einstein's experiments prove that the conditions necessary for the production of meaning involve the simultaneous and reciprocating presence of two terms.

The other discourse one would expect dialogism to have much in common with is Marxism, yet because of all the effort that has been expended in trying to disentangle Bakhtin's work from the marxist/communist intellectual environment in which he worked, this obvious point is easily missed.[16] While contemporary dialogics may be far removed from the 'grand narrative' of Marxism, however, in the architecture of Bakhtin's own work it is most certainly one of the central pillars (if not also the outside wall).

As will be seen in the discussion of *Marxism and the Philosophy of Language* in Chapter 1, the dialogic principle is explicitly Marxist to the extent that it is predicated upon a *social* contract between speaker and addressee. All utterance (spoken or written) is made from within a concrete sociohistorical context and is therefore profoundly ideological. As Michael Holquist has observed:

> There is, then, in Bakhtin's aesthetic an emphasis on the primacy of lived experience in all its bewildering specificity. It is an emphasis that accords with the most classical Marxist emphasis on the priority of historical experience *vis-à-vis* all ideational representations of it, as in the programmatic statement of Marx and Engels themselves in *The German Ideology*: 'The production of notions, ideas and consciousness is from the beginning directly interwoven with the material activity and material intercourse of human beings, the language of real life' (*Art and Answerability*, p. xliv).

Holquist has pointed, too, to the connection between Bakhtin's early work on speech relations and Marx's theories of 'value' and 'exchange' (p. xli). In this respect an obvious comparison may be drawn between the dialogic contract and the Marxist analysis of capitalist labour relations, in which profit depends upon workers 'reciprocating' the demands of their employers. This model of economic production, like the dialogic model of knowledge production, is based on a power-inscribed (i.e., 'unequal') 'dialogue' between two fixed terms.

Moving on to post-Althusserian Marxism, a salient comparison may also be drawn between the speaker and addressee in the dialogic contract and the workings of ideology. As Louis Althusser argues in his famous essay on 'Ideological State Apparatuses', ideology works through the 'interpellation' ('hailing') of individuals.[17] Once again, 'meaning' is made/

---

16   Some of the most vigorous attempts to disassociate Bakhtin from Marxism have been by Gary Saul Morson and Caryl Emerson. See *Rethinking Bakhtin: Extensions and Challenges*, ed. G. S. Morson and C. Emerson (Evanston, IL: Northwestern University Press), pp. 2–3.

17   L. Althusser, 'Ideology and Ideological State Apparatuses' in *Lenin and Philosophy and Other Essays*, trans. B. Brewster (London: New Left Books, 1971). See note 11 to Chapter 1 for further explication of Althusser's theory of ideology.

enforced/communicated through the *active participation* of two subjects or terms. To return to the earlier metaphor: ideology would not work if we (its subjects) failed to pick up the receiver. Beyond this model of 'contractual engagement' there are, however, significant differences between Althusser and Bakhtin on the *extent* to which subjects are able to accept/resist their ideological inscription (inasmuch as Althusser's subjects have sometimes been seen to be the passive 'dupes' of their society's ruling ideologies). I will say more about the differences between the two thinkers on the question of the *agency* of the subject (i.e., how 'active' is 'active'?) in Chapter 2.

I want to move on now to a consideration of the status of dialogics in more recent intellectual thought – in particular, its position both within and against the epistemology of postmodernism.[18] The first point to make about the connection between dialogics and postmodernism is that they are historically coterminous, both going into popular intellectual circulation in the 1980s. Barry Rutland has argued, indeed, that the belated reception of Bakhtin's work in the West is of particular significance in this instance, since it has meant that his dialogic theories of language and textuality were interpreted 'through and against the body of writings indicated by the names of Lacan, Derrida, and Foucault'.[19]

Aside from this historical/intellectual contingency, what the discourses of dialogism and postmodernism most obviously share is a newly relational view of language (with its roots in Saussurean linguistics), and a theory of subjectivity that rejects the humanist principles of 'wholeness' and 'autonomy'. This said, there is a significant difference in the way the two systems handle this 'deconstruction' of metaphysical values. While, for example, the dialogic subject may share the same sense of *provisionality* as the postmodern subject (in the sense that she is made not once, but over and over again), she will not share his sense of irrevocable 'fragmentation' since she is always in the process of 'reconstituting' through interaction with others.[20]

These contrasting models of the subject compare, too, with the subtle but clear distinction between Bakhtin and Jacques Derrida on the question

---

[18] For an accessible and highly informative introduction to postmodernist epistemology see P. Waugh, *Practising Postmodernism/Reading Moderism, Interrogating Texts* (London and New York: Edward Arnold, 1992). I am aware that I am representing only one 'version' of postmodernism in the following remarks, but see this as the (admittedly problematic) consequence of dealing with discourses at this level of 'metanarrative'.

[19] B. Rutland, 'Bakhtinian Categories and the Discourse of Postmoderism', *Mikhail Bakhtin and the Epistemology of Discourse, Critical Studies*, **2**, 1–2, 1990, pp. 123–36.

[20] For a characterization of the postmodern subject see P. Waugh, *Feminine Fictions: Revisiting the Postmodern* (London and New York: Routledge, 1989), pp. 6–16. Waugh writes: 'Postmodernism situates itself epistemologically at the point where the epistemic subject characterized in terms of historical experience, interiority, and consciousness has given way to the "decentred" subject identified through the public, impersonal signifying practices of other similarly decentred subjects. It may even situate itself at a point where there is no "subject" and no history in the old sense at all. There is only a system of linguistic structures, a textual construction, a play of differences in the Derridean sense. "Identify" is simply the illusion produced through the manipulation of irreconcilable and contradictory language games' (p. 7).

of 'difference'.[21] Like Derrida, Bakhtin was obsessed with the notion of difference and plurality: 'the mystery of the one in the many'. As Clark and Holquist note: 'A question that fuels Bakhtin's whole enterprise . . . is, What makes differences different?' (*Mikhail Bakhtin*, p. 9). It is Bakhtin's answer to this question, meanwhile, that ultimately distinguishes him from Derrida. In simple terms this may be explained by realizing that whereas for Derrida differences (between signifier and signified, subject and object, self and other) are perpetually *alienated* through the process of 'deferral' (see note 21), for Bakhtin they are perpetually *related* through simultaneous dialogue. This concept of *simultaneity*, significant at every level of Bakhtin's thought, is of extreme importance here since it provides the context in which differences can be reconciled. As Clark and Holquist explain, Bakhtin's concept of difference depends not on a dialectical 'either/or' but a dialogic 'both/and' (ibid., p. 7). By means of this reasoning, signifiers and signifieds, subjects and objects maintain their difference but are nevertheless able to communicate with one another.

Reading out from these key distinctions between dialogic and post-structualist/postmodernist theories of language and subjectivity, it is possible to glimpse some of the ways a dialogic epistemology differs most substantially from a postmodernist one. First there is the obvious but important point that dialogics, unlike postmodernism, has the confidence to proclaim itself a 'grand narrative'.[22] It presents us with a theory of knowledge that admits *we can* make sense of the world we inhabit providing we allow that such meaning is provisional, dynamic and constitutive of two (reciprocating) terms. This is in stark contrast with postmodernist thinking in which language, as a system of difference and deferral *but not relation*, allows us to see and know nothing beyond 'the play of [its own] linguistic structures' (see note 21). Whereas the Derridean formation of language denies us the possibility of 'meaning' to ourselves or to others, in the Bakhtinian universe we can, as Clark and Holquist have observed, 'mean' – but only within the reflexive bounds of an interlocutory relationship. While no longer possessing the authority of the Cartesian subject ('I think, therefore I am') the dialogic subject can nevertheless achieve a provisional and dynamic perception of the self/world through the refractive mirror of his or her addressee:

> I *can* mean what I say, but only indirectly, at a second remove, in words I give and take back to the community according to the protocols it observes. My voice can mean, but only with others – at times in chorus, at best of times in dialogue (*Mikhail Bakhtin*, p. 12).

21    Derrida's theorization of difference led him to invent a new term, *différance*, which combined connotations of difference and deferral. As Chris Baldick summarizes: 'The point of this neologism is to indicate simultaneously two senses in which language denies us the full presence of any meaning: first, that no linguistic element (according to Saussure's theory of the sign) has a positive meaning, only an effect of meaning arising from its differences from the other elements; second, that presence or fullness of meaning is always deferred from one sign to another in an endless sequence.' C. Baldick, *The Concise Oxford Dictionary of Literary Terms* (Oxford and New York: Oxford University Press, 1990), p. 58.
22    See Thomson, 'Paradigms', p. 8. Thomson writes: 'Postmodernism, unlike dialogism, is unable to theorize itself'.

## III
## Dialogics, Politics and Power

To speak of language, without speaking of power, in a Bakhtinian perspective is to speak meaninglessly, in a void. For Bakhtin, language is thus everywhere imbricated with assymmetries of power. Patriarchal domination and economic dependency make sincere interlocution impossible. There is no 'neutral' utterance; language is everywhere shot through with intentions and accents; it is material, multiaccentual, and historical, and is densely overlaid with the traces of its historical usages.

These Bakhtinian formulations have the advantage of not restricting liberatory struggle to purely economic or political battles; instead, they extend it to the common patrimony of the utterance. Bakhtin locates ideological utterance at the pulsating heart of discourse, whether in the form of political rhetoric, artistic language, or everyday language exchange.[23]

My first reaction to Bakhtin was to become seduced by his theory of dialogism since it seemed to offer a utopian ground for all voices to flourish; at least all voices could aspire to internal polemic and dialogism. Yet Bakhtin's blind spot is the battle. He does not work out the contradiction between the promises of utopia or community and the battle which is always waged for control.[24]

These quotations, from two critical studies of the late 1980s, both assert the central significance of *power* in Bakhtin's dialogic theory. They disagree, however, on the question of whether Bakhtin himself was aware of the power dynamic implicit in each and every dialogic encounter. For Bauer, the fact that dialogue is the 'site of battle' was one of Bakhtin's chief 'blind spots'; Stam, on the contrary, perceives him to have been acutely aware that 'language is . . . everywhere imbricated with assymmetries of power'.

My own general inclination is to agree with Stam rather than Bauer. As was graphically illustrated through the example of the telephone in the previous section, the great emphasis on *intonation* in the Bakhtin group's analysis of spoken utterance is a testimony to the way in which all dialogic exchange is power inscribed. Our interlocutors are always very precisely situated on a socioeconomic scale *vis-à-vis* ourselves (see the quotation in Chapter 1, pp. 73–74) and this, together with the degree of formality/intimacy inherent in the relationship, will determine who holds the balance of power (see my discussion of John Clare's poem, 'Child Harold', in Chapter 3 for an illustration of this). It is important to recognize, too, that this power dynamic is not restricted to Bakhtin's writings on spoken language: his stylistic analysis of the novel, in particular his discussions of polyphony, heteroglossia and doubly voiced discourse (see Chapter 1) are all implicitly concerned with the question of power. Textual voices, no less than actual ones, are shot through with the registers of nationality, race, class and education.

23  R. Stam, *Subversive Pleasures: Bakhtin, Cultural Criticism and Film* (Baltimore, MD, and London: Johns Hopkins University Press, 1989), p. 8.
24  D. Bauer, *Feminist Dialogics: A Theory of Failed Community* (Albany, NY: State University of New York Press, 1989), p. 5.

Bauer's complaint about Bakhtin's work would seem to me to be more effective as a complaint against his followers: a complaint against the many readers and critics who, as will be seen in Chapter 2, have chosen to define 'dialogue' as a conciliatory exchange between two purportedly equal parties. While it is true that a great many descriptions of the dialogic contract emphasize *reciprocity*, it is important not to confuse this with an unproblematized democratization of the interlocutory contract. There are plenty of instances, as I shall signal in my review of the key Bakhtin texts in Chapter 1, in which we are expressly alerted to the inequalities between the terms/subjects under consideration.

It is, however, important to examine *why* the democratic/conciliatory model of dialogism has been so popular among Bakhtin's followers. For Ken Hirschkop it is explained as part of the general 'depoliticization' of Bakhtin's works by the liberal wing of his followers.[25] 'The dialogue', divested of notions of power and inequality, is set up as a utopian model of humanist values in which individuals engage in polite, respectful and conciliatory exchange with one another:

> For dialogue, after all, does depend upon a rather peculiar model of language. It envisages language as a series of one-on-one encounters, encounters between speaking subjects who could in theory be evenly matched . . . It is the combination of this model of language with the political ideas of individual autonomy and respect for others which gives the claims of dialogue such force.[26]

This reading is, according to Hirschkop, not only a myth but also a dangerous myth: an equation of linguistic dialogue and liberal democracy that takes no account of the 'uneven structuring of language' (see below). It ignores the fact that in any exchange between two or more persons/discursive positions a power dynamic is inevitably involved; or, indeed, that dialogues in different contexts and different media are qualitatively different things:

> To use the face-to-face conversation as a model for the TV broadcast, the government directive, the religious service or cultic ceremony, the written record or the literary text is wrong-headed and restrictive, for all these forms must appear deficient to the extent they make impossible the relations of dialogue. Not only do such discursive structures often entail some kind of internal unevenness, such as a clear and irreversible distinction between speaker and listener, the relations between them are likewise uneven. Writing, then print, then the electronic media of the twentieth-century have endowed certain speech acts with a force unavailable to others; conversely face-to-face conversations often have a flexibility unavailable to the more durable utterance.[27]

Positing the spoken dialogue as a model appertaining to all acts of communication therefore denies the specificity of each medium and conceals power differentials and other political interests. For Hirschkop, as

---

25   See K. Hirschkop, 'Is Dialogism for Real?', *Social Text*, **30**, 1992, pp. 102–13 and the Introduction to *Bakhtin and Cultural Theory*, ed. K. Hirschkop and D. Shepherd (Manchester: Manchester University Press, 1989).
26   Hirschkop, 'Dialogism', p. 111.
27   Ibid., p. 112.

has already been observed, the best way this liberal/apolitical appropriation of Bakhtin can be countered is through the newly historicized reading of his work which recognizes, for instance, that 'dialogue' does not have a fixed or monolithic meaning. Taking the Bakhtin texts as a whole, 'dialogism' is not always coterminous with 'dialogue' and is by no means the utopian model of communication that some readers have desired it to be.

While I have much respect and sympathy for Hirschkop's argument that the depoliticization of Bakhtin's work is partly the result of the mass appropriation of his terms out of context, one of the purposes of this book is to endorse the fact that dialogism *is* a discourse which has now outgrown its origins in Bakhtin's own writings. That this has been a reactionary/liberal appropriation of dialogism in some quarters cannot be denied, but that it has offered a radical, thoroughly politicized new framework for textual analysis in others cannot be denied either. As Robert Stam (himself one of the most admirably political of Bakhtin's followers) concludes:

> Although Bakhtin has had a world-wide impact on cultural studies, affecting not only the Soviet Union but also Western Europe, Japan, North America, and South America, it is not always clear which 'Bakhtin' is having the impact. Each country and school seems to nurture its own Bakhtin, and often multiple Bakhtins can be seen to co-exist within the same country. The last few years have witnessed, in fact, a kind of posthumous wrestle over the soul and legacy of Bakhtin. As an extraordinarily complex, contradictory and at times even enigmatic figure, Bakhtin has been appropriated by the most diverse ideological currents. In political terms we find Bakhtin the populist, Bakhtin the Marxist, Bakhtin the anti-Marxist, Bakhtin the social democrat, and Bakhtin the anti-Stalinist. There is a left reading of Bakhtin (Frederic Jameson, Terry Eagleton, Tony Bennett etc) and a liberal reading (Wayne Booth, David Lodge, Tzvetan Todorov) (Stam, *Subversive Pleasures*, p. 15).

So, if the 'right' of the academy have won one portion of the 'soul' of Bakhtin, the 'left' have won another; and, as will be seen in Chapter 2, some of the most radical appropriations of the dialogic principle have been in the area of feminist criticism.

As I conclude at the end of my survey of recent feminist engagements with Bakhtin and dialogic theory, the inherently political status of *all* feminist criticism means that its authors have simply no investment in a depoliticized reading of the key concepts. While not all feminist writers have chosen to interpret dialogue as the 'site of battle' as Dale Bauer has (see quotation at the beginning of this section), all the discussions of the representation of voice/utterance/discourse in literary texts are implicitly or explicitly concerned with questions of power, be this the dynamic present in the exchange between male and female interlocutors (including the relationship between text and reader) or the complex positionings enacted between members of all-female communities. Similarly, feminists have been among the most outspoken critics of a naïvely politicized reading of Bakhtin's 'carnival', arguing that the temporary suspension of class hierarchies in carnivalized texts does not necessarily mean the suspension of patriarchy.

I want to move on now from this brief discussion of how Bakhtin's own works have been politically conceived and appropriated to a consideration of how dialogics has provided us with a useful framework through which to read contemporary history and world politics.

For the Bakhtinian scholars Robert Stam and Barry Rutland, suggestive parallels can be drawn between the dialogic principle – in particular, its emphasis on *multivocality* – and the carnivalized nature of the postmodern world. Stam writes:

> For Bakhtin, as we have seen, entire genres, languages, and even cultures are susceptible to 'mutual illumination'. His insight takes on special relevance in a contemporary world where communication is 'global', where cultural circulation, if in many respects assymmetrical, is still multi-voiced, and where it is becoming more and more difficult to corral human diversity into the old categories of independent cultures and nations. Third World culture, as I suggested earlier, is by definition a multi-voiced field of intercultural discourse, and some would argue that it is the proleptic site of postmodern collage culture (*Subversive Pleasures*, p. 192).

Stam's vision of the postmodern world as one in which a 'heteroglossia' of nationalities and cultures are finding new independence through the collapse of nineteenth-century imperialism and yet, at the same time, are dialogically *connected* through the network of global communication that represents an interesting conflation of the dialogic and postmodern epistemologies discussed in the previous section. The distinctly utopian colouring to such a scenario, with its suggestion that the world of the twentieth century has become a vast international marketplace in which all voices/nations engage harmoniously with one another, is also a feature of Rutland's text. Focusing, in particular, on the 'carnivalized' disintergration of Europe following the collapse of the Berlin Wall, Rutland draws this dialogic analogy:

> Bakhtin and his circle do not set out a political agenda but their writings are instinct with political implications. It is a very basic politics of popular desire that at the time of writing is manifest in the streets of Leipzig, Prague and Bucharest, where uprisings of a markedly carnival character have destabilized systems of the most relentless administrative thoroughness, even in the teeth of death. Bakhtinism taps directly into the abiding macrostate condition of society and culture, the dialogic flux of collective desire as the ultimate conditioning factor of all particular monologizing microstates. In this perspective, postmodernity is a condition of 'permanent revolution' in that the dialogical modality of carnival is at work consistently and ubiquitously through the mass media, flooding the margins into the centre, opening new spaces of discourse and empowerment. We have witnessed Stalinist monology fail utterly in the face of postmodern aspiration. It remains for transnational capitalism to be devoured by the tiger it rides so smugly.[28]

This reading of contemporary European history through a dialogic lens seems, to me, to make the same mistake as those textual analyses cited earlier which characterize 'multivocality' as an inherently democratic phenomenon. It overlooks the fact that a hundred 'small voices' (or nations/communities) will vie for power in the same way as two big

---

[28]   Rutland, 'Bakhtinian Categories', pp. 132–33.

ones. Polyphony is not, in itself, any guarantee of fair and equal representation.

Robert Stam, despite the evident utopianism of the earlier statement and a belief that 'Bakhtinian categories . . . display . . . a built-in affinity for the oppressed and the marginal' (*Subversive Pleasures*, p. 21) also recognizes the potential for this sort of confusion; and his solution is to correct the egalitarianism implicit in the category of the polyphonic with the complementary connotations of heteroglossia (see Chapter 1): 'The notion of polyphony, with its overtones of harmonious simultaneity, must be completed by the notion of heteroglossia with its undertones of social conflict rooted not in random individual dissonances but in the deep structural cleavages of social life' (ibid., p. 232). This acknowledgement that *all* national and ethnic groups, like all utterances, will be socially and culturally competitive in their dialogic exchange is a crucial point evidenced in the more recent history of European balkanization. With this sobering example in mind, one can only wonder whether, three years on from the events in Prague and Hungary he describes, Rutland would now be quite so sanguine about the 'carnivalesque' eruption of the microstates of Eastern Europe where the utopian vision of dialogic harmony has given way to nationalistic factionalism and civil war. What the 'application' of Bakhtinian theory to world politics might finally be seen to prove is that dialogue is, indeed, a far more volatile, more potentially 'aggressive' category than has been allowed in readings of literary texts. Certainly *vis-à-vis* Rutland's own sortie into the affairs of Eastern Europe, Dale Bauer's image of dialogue-as-battle would seem sadly more apposite than that of the symposium.[29]

# IV
## Dialogic Theory and Textual Practice

In the previous sections we have seen how dialogics has become a discourse with theoretical claims far in excess of those in Bakhtin's own writings: how it has been raised to the level of an epistemology (a theory of the production of knowledge itself), and how it has provided a framework through which to read the decentred global politics of the postmodern world. The origins of dialogic thought remain, however, with Bakhtin's own readings of *literary* texts and, despite the growth of the discourse beyond this function, by far the greatest utilization of dialogics has been in the area of textual analysis. What needs to be established immediately, however, is the distance that now separates Bakhtin's own readings of Dostoevsky and his 'literary history' of the birth and development of the novel, with the dialogic textual practice which has spread through literary and cultural criticism in the last ten years. While Bakhtin, as will be seen in the overview of his major works offered in Chapter 1, saw dialogue (both at the level of the individual word and between the larger units of

[29] 'Symposium': see note 9 above.

'utterance' and 'discourse') as a feature of particular authors/texts/genres, his followers have now engaged the dialogic principle to analyse almost anything. Dialogics has thus moved from being a feature of specifically novelistic discourse to a general *reading strategy*. It is possible to perform a 'dialogic reading' on any chosen text in the same way that it is possible to perform a Marxist, feminist or psychoanalytic one; and the eclecticism of critical practice at the present time means that the dialogic approach is frequently combined with various other theoretical/political perspectives (e.g., feminism). In the same way, then, that this book has aimed to locate the discourse of dialogism in its broadest philosophical and cultural context, so too, through the review of recent dialogic textual criticism provided in Chapter 2, does it attempt to pay tribute to the multifarious deployment of dialogics as a reading strategy. To this extent, Chapters 1 and 2 exist in interesting tension with one another, with Bakhtin's own author-specific claims (e.g., Dostoevsky was the 'inventor' of the polyphonic novel) juxtaposing ironically with the multigeneric, multidisciplinary locations of dialogic activity in the work of contemporary critics. At the same time it should be noted, however, that Bakhtin's own dialogic specifications became increasingly liberal as his work progressed: concerning polyphony, for example, what began as the unique invention of Dostoevsky was later recognized to be a feature of 'the novel' (i.e., all novels), and then of 'novelized discourse' in general (thus including 'novelized' poetry and drama). Similarly, some of Bakhtin's followers have chosen to be more genre specific than others, with writers like David Lodge choosing to focus on the stylistic features of dialogism (e.g., 'doubly voiced discourse') as peculiar to the novel.[30]

What has resulted from the widespread engagement of Bakhtin's theory in so many different areas of textual practice is a refinement and redefinition of many of the key concepts. Even as the 'dialogic principle' has itself been expanded through its acontextual invocation, so have the categories of carnival, chronotope and the various species of doubly voiced speech (see Chapter 1) been challenged and reviewed. 'Carnival' is, indeed, probably the best example of how a Bakhtinian term has been reworked in this way. As we shall see in Chapter 2, many critics have been attracted to 'carnival' as a means of describing the polyphonic and anarchic quality of certain texts, but have been unhappy with Bakhtin's presentation of it as a *temporary* reversal of the normal hierarchy, doubting that this can represent any significant lasting political revolt for the 'folk' involved. Instead of dispensing with the concept entirely, however, feminist critics like Clair Wills and Nancy Glazener (see Chapter 2, section III) have suggested ways in which it may be revised to become politically acceptable.

This last point brings me on to the rationale behind my own book which, like the other volumes in the *Interrogating Texts* series, combines explication of a particular theoretical discourse (in this case, dialogics) with readings of literary texts with the purpose of interrogating both text *and* theory. This is to say that my readings in Part Two are intended both to demonstrate the

---

30   David Lodge's essays using Bakhtinian theory are now collected together in the volume *After Bakhtin: Essays on Fiction and Criticism* (London and New York: Routledge, 1990).

usefulness of the key dialogic concepts in the the reading of literary texts and to reveal the extent to which they need to be revised and modified. Like the work of many of those critics reviewed in Chapter 2, my own readings are, at times, improvising of Bakhtin's own theses and formulas, in response to the demands of the particular text I am working with. I will return to the ethics of this 'rewriting' of Bakhtin's work in the conclusion, but would argue, at this point, for it being endemic to the spread of dialogics as a reading strategy.

## V
## A Guide to *Reading Dialogics*

For those readers who have not already deduced the fact from an examination of the list of contents, the discussion in the last paragraph should have revealed that this book falls into two parts. Part One comprises an overview of the major works produced by the Bakhtin group between the 1920s and the 1970s (Chapter 1), followed by a review of how the dialogic principle has been taken up and reworked in more recent literary and cultural criticism (Chapter 2). Part Two (Chapters 3, 4 and 5) offers paired readings of six literary texts, these being grouped according to the three categories of 'genre', 'subject' and 'gender', which also provide the framework for the discussion in Chapter 2. Since I describe the rationale behind my choice of literary texts (together with a summary of the central theses and aspects of dialogic theory explored in each chapter) in the Preface to Part Two, I shall concentrate here on explaining more about the presentation of material in Part One.

Chapter 1, as I have already explained, takes the form of an overview of all the major works produced by Bakhtin and his circle. I deal with these texts chronologically although, as I note at the beginning of the chapter, readers should be aware of the discrepancy between the dates when the books and essays were originally written and their publication dates, both in the Soviet Union and in the West (see Further Reading for full details). Mention of the Bakhtin circle also alerts us to the confused and disputed authorship of many of the major works: as I explain in the chapter, the last ten years has seen much heated dispute over whether the books and essays published under the names of Voloshinov and Medvedev were partly or wholly authored by Bakhtin. While many Bakhtin scholars remain unconcerned by this problem of attribution, others (notably those who want to present Bakhtin as a anti-Marxist) have worked hard to prove their point. The extent to which dialogic thought espouses or rejects Marxist philosophy and politics is, indeed, another problem in its own right, and my own tendency is to affirm rather than to deny the affiliation. While there is little question that early works like *Freudianism* (1927), *The Formal Method* (1928) and *Marxism and the Philosophy of Language* (1929) are written out of a Marxist ideology, Bakhtin scholars like Michael Holquist, Gary Saul Morson and Caryl Emerson have argued that some of these positionings can be explained as 'window-dressing' to appease the State censor.[31] This attempt to turn the texts on their ideological heads has, I argue, been taken to dubious lengths in some instances. While there is clear biographical evidence that Bakhtin's life was, indeed, plagued by his poor relations with the communist authorities, this is not necessarily to deny his Marxism. Neither should the a-Marxist appropriations of dialogic theory by contemporary critics prevent such a realignment in the future.

As I acknowledge at the beginning, the explication of the work dealt with in Chapter 1 does not pretend to be exhaustive but focuses principally on those concepts and arguments that may be situated within the discourse of dialogism. That is to say, there may be a reading of Bakhtin *other* than a dialogic one, and any thorough-going exploration of 'Bakhtinism' would have to consider this possibility. One term that is the focus of my own readings and yet does not obviously present itself as part of the dialogic continuum, however, is *chronotope*. Chronotope, as I explain in Chapter 1, is Bakhtin's name for the representation of time/space in the literary text. His own engagement with the term is largely via literary history, appointing different chronotopes to different literary genres (e.g., the 'adventure chronotope', the 'idyllic chronotope'). It is a concept, then, that has nothing obviously to do with verbal dialogue except that, like the Bakhtinian model of the utterance, it is structured as a *relationship* between two fixed terms. In my own readings, however, I discover a further point of connection in the structural similarity between the polyphonic text and what I describe as the *polychronotopic* text (Chapter 5), thus proving that Bakhtin's dialogic principle is not confined to purely linguistic representations.

I would like to conclude this introduction to Chapter 1 with a brief summary of the principal fields of interest represented by Bakhtin's texts. These are: (1) *language* (the linguistic analysis of spoken and written utterance); (2) *literature* (author- and genre-specific analyses of the literary text, focusing both on the macrocosmic construction of those texts (e.g., 'polyphony') and more local stylistic features (e.g., 'doubly voiced discourse'); (3) *literary history* (Bakhtin's impressive overviews of the birth, growth and development of the novel as featured in parts of *Dostoevsky's Poetics* and *The Dialogic Imagination*); and (4) *subjectivity* (where the dialogic model of the utterance, with its emphasis on relationality and social situatedness, is also made the model for the construction of the human subject). I should also signal, however, those areas which Bakhtin's work are very expressly *not* concerned with: notably *gender* and the dialogic role of the *reader* in the production of textual meaning.

The absence of gender awareness in all areas of Bakhtinian theory is one of the key issues that this book will be concerned with, both in the theoretical background and in the readings in Part Two, four of which (i.e., Chapters 4 and 5) are centrally concerned with a regendering of the dialogic formations of subjectivity and chronotope. Dialogic theory, as will be seen

---

[31] See Morson and Emerson, *Rethinking Bakhtin*, pp. 31–49, for a full account of this debate.

in Chapter 2, has proven especially attractive to feminist critics looking for alternative models of sexual/textual identity, but much work has had to be done rewriting Bakktin's scripts to include this gendered dimension. Meanwhile, although the dialogic relation between text and reader is not a total blind spot in Bakhtin's work, it is surprisingly underdeveloped both in the writings of the Bakhtin circle and in the work of their followers. While an obvious parallel exists between the relationship of speaker-addressee *in the text*, and that of text and reader, little explicit reference is made to the latter. This is an issue I will return to in Chapter 2 and, again, in the Conclusion.

I want to move on, finally, to discuss how I have structured my survey of contemporary dialogic criticism in Chapter 2. Chapter 2 is divided into three sections – genre, subject and gender – these being the subject headings under which I discovered most recent critical engagements with dialogic theory to be grouped. Under the heading of 'genre' I look at the ways in which recent critics have utilized Bakhtin's own genre-specific accounts of dialogic activity to read a wide range of texts and point, in particular, to the way in which the 'application' has spread beyond the novel into readings of poetry and drama, as well as to other media such as film. What one must conclude from this is clearly that, whatever the limits on Bakhtin's own definition of the 'novelized text', in contemporary literary circles the distinction between poetry and fiction has become something of a red-herring. The books and articles I review in this section are concerned with the textual representation of dialogism at both a macro- and a microcosmic level; that is to say, both with the polyphonic and heteroglossic structuration of texts, and with dialogism at the level of the individual word and utterance.

The section on 'the subject', meanwhile, brings together the growing body of books and essays which have appropriated dialogic theory to construct a new model of the subject. Most of these studies still function as literary criticism (that is to say, they analyse representations of the subject in *literary texts*), but what emerges – and what I attempt to profile – is a new definition of subjectivity itself. The dialogic subject, as will be seen in my own reading of Virginia Woolf's *The Waves* (1931) in Part Two, may be perceived as an alternative to certain psychoanalytic models of gender acquisition. This survey, like the one of gender which follows, is of particular importance in showing the growth and development of dialogics away from its Bakhtinian source, since the model of the dialogic subject which emerges in these textual analyses is far more clearly defined than the one that may be inferred from the original writings.

Gender, as I noted above, is without question the most serious blind spot in Bakhtin's own formulation of dialogic relations, be these linguistic, textual or interpersonal. Indeed, I open this section of Chapter 2 by voicing the question already raised by a number of feminist writers: if Bakhtin's work is so overwhelmingly silent on the issue of gender, why should we bother? And if we do, isn't it problematic to simply 'add' gender to the other criteria of dialogic analysis? These are, indeed, serious questions, but the fact remains that dialogic theory, in its many facets, has proven immensely popular to feminists. Nancy Glazener, and Dale Bauer and

Susan McKinstry (Chapter 2) are among those who have attempted to specify what those attractions are, but by way of introduction it would perhaps be best simply to say that dialogics has provided feminist critics with both a means of analysing the complex relationship between masculine and feminine discourses and with a way of accounting for the specificity of women's writing. On this last point, recognition of how the reader is gendered in the text–reader relationship has proven vitally important, with some critics (myself included) suggesting that our definition of women's writing should move away from questions of content and authorship to that of *address* (i.e., who a text is written *for* – see Chapter 2).

The way in which Bakhtin's key concepts have been adopted, adapted and rewritten by his followers reveals some interesting problems, problems both with the theory itself and with its role within textual practice. Rather than deal extensively with these problems as they present themselves in Chapter 2, however, I have chosen to save my 'trouble-shooting' for the Conclusion where I can include a retrospective on my own readings in Part Two. This conclusion, as will be seen, itself takes the form of a dialogue of questions and answers, and beyond the rather clichéd applicability of such a format in a book on dialogics, it is my hope that the questions might be representative of some of the concerns that you, the reader, will have accumulated in the course of reading this book. Certainly, they are questions that have been based, in part, on the comments of my own 'readers' (see the Acknowledgements for details), as well as on the general queries raised by my students on the literary theory course at Lancaster University. To all concerned: my thanks.

# VI
## You: The Reader

> It hurts to tell it over, over again. Once was enough: wasn't once enough for me at the time? But I keep on going with this sad and hungry and sordid, this limping and mutilated story, because after all I want you to hear it . . . Because I'm telling you this story, I will your existence. I tell, therefore you are.[32]

In a book espousing the theory that our ability to 'mean' depends entirely on the existence of a reciprocating 'other', it would be remiss to end this Introduction without acknowledging you, the reader of my text. As the Atwood quotation recognizes, to 'tell a story' is to inscribe textually the presence of an interlocutor: to 'will' them into existence. So by writing the story of dialogics I have effectively willed myself an addressee – but who is she?

The first thing to recognize, of course, is the fact that 'you' are not singular. Books like this one, although marketed to a fairly small, specialized audience, nevertheless suppose it to be of 'worthwhile' proportions. As

---

[32]  M. Atwood, *The Handmaid's Tale* (London and New York: Jonathan Cape, 1986), p. 279.

Atwood's narrator consoles herself elsewhere in *The Handmaid's Tale*, 'You can mean thousands' (p. 50). According to Bakhtin, however (see Chapter 1), neither your plurality nor your hypothetical status can deny the fact that I have a fairly particularized communicant in mind. The same factors of social and educational profiling apply as if I were addressing myself to a single, identified interlocutor in a spoken dialogue.

Acknowledging this, it is fairly obvious that I have constructed 'you' as an academic audience: a group of readers with a certain familiarity and interest in literary criticism; readers who have had, or are receiving, the benefits of higher education. This is the point, however, at which your homogeneous identification ends, and here I would like to supplement Bakhtin's own rather fixed and unitary model of the dialogic contract (between two socially 'fingerprinted' interlocutors) with one which allows for a more dynamic exchange of positionings between text and reader, speaker and addressee.

It is clear, for example, that most academic books of this kind identify their audience as a mixture of students (both undergraduate and postgraduate) and lecturers. As a consequence, you will find that many texts which are ostensibly meant for the student market (this being the remit of the publisher) are more obviously 'in dialogue' with fellow academics 'in the field'. This, it seems to me, is an especially amusing instance of Bakhtin's 'hidden polemic' (see Chapter 1: the variety of 'doubly voiced speech' in which the speaker – here, the author – has one ear anxiously directed to the authoritative scorn/approval of his or her peers!). Such anxiety, in short, is why so many texts meant to be 'student oriented' are anything but: their authors are more concerned with 'proving' their knowledge/skills than in sharing them in the most accessible way. While I hope that *this book* will not alienate its student readers in this fashion, neither will I pretend that I have ignored the 'future answer word' of the 'expert' entirely. It is likely that Bakhtin scholars (including several cited in the text) will read this book as well as their students, and beyond named individuals it is also inevitable that my words will be directed towards discourses and debates (issues of 'ethnicity' and 'essentialism', for example) which are politically sensitive.

By now you, the reader, whether student or senior academic, may well be wondering how such 'split-address' manifests itself. The answer, I would suggest, is that the reader is being *constantly* repositioned and redefined. As Martin Montogmery discovered in his discourse analysis of radio DJs, speakers and texts are 'continually addressing different segments within [their audience]'.[33] This means that for a portion of a text/address a certain addressee will be acknowledged (e.g., 'anyone listening in Edinburgh'), before being replaced by others (i.e., those listening in Glasgow). This system of *shifting address* also allows for the possibility of two or more groups being addressed simultaneously. So, returning to my own example, it is quite possible that in the course of a discussion I will conceptualize my addressee as first 'student', then 'expert', before eliding the two.

[33] M. Montgomery, 'D-J Talk', *Media, Culture and Society*, **8**, 4, 1986, pp. 421–40.

Aside from the public and anonymous recipients of my discourse, there will also be the more intimate 'unofficial' readers: friends and colleagues who I have positioned as 'allies' rather than as 'adversaries', and whose dialogic contribution to this book (both direct and indirect) will exist as a subtext only they recognize.[34] This *exclusivity of address*, the way in which a text can 'identify' a particular group or individual and exclude others through the mechanism of shared knowledge/intimacy, is something I have explored in my own work on women's writing (see Chapter 2, section III).[35] The existence of such subtexts in academic works is not something usually acknowledged, but they are surely present in the work of most authors. This points to a degree of complexity perhaps lacking in Bakhtin's own construction of the utterance (spoken or written): a recognition that the positioning of our immediate 'addressee'/'object of utterance' will be overlaid with a history of other relationships.[36] When I write about the telephone in the opening section of this Introduction, for example, I do so from a position which mixes theoretical and personal experience, thus extending my audience to include a subtextual 'other' (who, in reading this, will recognize herself immediately).

I should conclude this address to my readers with a word on their gender. While it will be clear from what I have already said that all my readers (public/intimate; antagonistic/supportive) are likely to share a broad, socioeconomic grouping, there is an inevitable distinction between the male and female members of this group in terms of their textual positioning. I say this not because I set out to discriminate consciously *against* male readers but because, by acknowledging that *all* texts gender their readers (though not all do so self-consciously or consistently), I must include my own.[37] In simple terms of its marketing, it is likely that *Reading Dialogics* will solicit a predominantly (though not exclusively) female audience. As a study with a self-proclaimed interest in issues of gender, and including readings of five texts by women writers, it will, it is hoped, prove especially interesting for feminist readers and critics. For this reason, you, the reader, will be correct in assuming that I have quite explicitly positioned you as female on more than one occasion, although at other times I have made a special effort to acknowledge the presence

---

34   In her book on Virginia Woolf and Christa Wolf, Anne Herrmann discusses the way in which the two authors position their readers as (male) adversaries and (female) allies respectively. See A. Herrmann, *The Dialogic and Difference: 'An/Other Woman' in Virginia Woolf and Christa Wolf* (New York: Columbia University Press, 1989). There is a full discussion of this and other aspects of Herrmann's work in Chapter 2.

35   See my essay 'Dialogic Theory and Women's Writing' in *Working Out: New Directions for Women's Studies*, ed. H. Hinds, A. Phoenix and J. Stacey (Brighton: Falmer Press, 1992), pp. 184–93.

36   Don Bialostosky defines the Bakhtinian 'object of utterance' as follows: 'Every instance of intonation is oriented in *two directions*: with respect to the listener as ally or witness and with respect to the object of the utterance [i.e., the thing being spoken about] as the third, living participant whom the intonation scolds or careses, denigrates or magnifies'. See D. Bialostosky, *Making Tales: The Poetics of Wordsworth's Narrative Experiments* (Chicago, IL, and London: University of Chicago Press, 1984).

37   'Speaking figuratively, the listener is normally found *next to* the author as his ally.' M. Bakhtin, *Bakhtin School Papers*, ed. A. Shukman, *Russian Poetics in Translation*, No. 10 (Oxford: RTP Publications, 1983), pp. 23–24.

of my male readers through the strategic use of mixed personal pronouns. To any of the latter who, by this open admission of their marginalization are already feeling affronted (!), I would claim simply to be redressing a gender imbalance that has been in *covert* operation in academic discourse for too many years.

After this polite confrontation with my male readers, it obviously behoves me to position the majority of you, of either sex, as friends and allies: interlocutors who (in Bakhtin's own words) are 'positioned alongside the author' and, despite varying degrees of theoretical and critical knowledge, will feel 'engaged with' rather than 'talked at'.[38] For whatever the shifting dynamics of class, education and intimacy that inform any dialogic encounter, the one thing that Bakhtin's theory makes absolutely clear is the integral power of the addressee. Without your reciprocating presence, it should be remembered, I could not have got beyond the first page of what follows.

[38]  For various discussions of the way in which (all) texts gender their readers see *Gendering the Reader*, ed. S. Mills (Hemel Hempstead: Harvester Wheatsheaf, 1994).

# Part One

# THEORETICAL BACKGROUND

# 1

# BAKHTIN AND THE DIALOGIC

This chapter aims to present the reader with a broad overview of Bakhtin's writings as they relate to the dialogic principle. This is to say that my accounts of each of the key texts, although reasonably thorough, will not explicate the full range of philosophical, linguistic, literary and political issues represented by that text, but only those that are, either implicitly or explicitly, part of the 'dialogic continuum'. I will consider all the major works produced by Bakhtin and the Bakhtin school in the chronological order of their first publication, though readers should be aware that these dates differ considerably from their first translation and publication in the West (see Further Reading for full details).

There is also, of course, the problem of attribution which is proving a heated and long-running saga among Bakhtin scholars, especially (in recent years) to the extent that the authorship of the individual texts *matters*. After a period of fairly relaxed policy in which the majority of critics were happy to argue that our own poststructuralist views of authorship, combined with the collaborative working practice of the Bakhtin group itself ought to make questions of the individual attribution of the early texts (notably *Freudianism* (1927), *The Formal Method* (1928) and *Marxism and the Philosophy of Language* (1929)) irrelevant, there is now a countermove among scholars like Caryl Emerson and Gary Saul Morson to disassociate Bakhtin's name from texts they feel he almost certainly *was not* the author of. Their justification for insisting on a more rigorous investigation into the attribution is that, by associating Bakhtin with these early texts, certain key factors in his development as a thinker and critic are obscured and distorted. In addition, his political stance – namely, to what extent he was ever a Marxist – will be profiled very differently depending upon whether or not such works are included. Emerson and Morson write: 'The work of the Bakhtin group offers us a real *choice* between a Marxist and non-Marxist interpretation of a new view of language and culture; readers can only lose by collapsing this dialogue into an elaborate hoax to elude the censor.'[1] This reference to 'the

[1]  *Rethinking Bakhtin: Extensions and Challenges*, ed. G. S. Morson and C. Emerson (Evanston, IL: Northwestern University Press, 1989), p. 3.

censor' highlights Emerson and Morson's dispute with Michael Holquist who presents the Marxist orthodoxies of the three disputed early texts as mere 'window dressing' included to appease the communist authorities.[2] While they would have it appear, however, that their disassociation of Bakhtin from the work of Medvedev and Voloshinov would be an advantage to those critics who want the Marxism of those texts to be 'taken seriously' (p. 40), their more urgent agenda is clearly to absolve Bakhtin of any Marxist tendencies. The arguments they put forward in this respect are, in my opinion, as tenuous as they are desperate, and include the presentation of Bakhtin's critique of 'dialectics' in his 'Notes' from 1971 as evidence of his life-long opposition to Marxism.[3] While it is evidently true that Bakhtin suffered badly at the hands of the Soviet authorities, one wonders whether Emerson and Morson's anxiety to 'clear his name' has more to do with current anticommunist feeling than with the attribution of the early works. In a post-Soviet world it seems to have been necessary for these critics to make a clean break with Marxism as well as communism, whereas earlier commentators were quite happy to tolerate the ambiguity of the (early) Bakhtin being one (i.e., Marxist) but not the other (communist).

The extent to which the attribution of the early texts 'matters' will also depend upon whether the reader is concerned with a proper historical contextualization of Bakhtin's writings. In his recent work Ken Hirschkop has argued convincingly that such historicism is necessary if we are to establish a proper understanding of Bakhtin's key concepts (such as dialogism) and to prevent them from being randomly appropriated by critics of all political persuasions.[4] This was, of course, one of the key problems associated with the current 'fashion' for dialogics that I discussed in the Introduction, but here it intersects with issues of authorship and chronology. Hirschkop's concern, for example, over Bakhtin's emphasis on the 'concrete materiality' of 'the word' in *Marxism and the Philosophy of Language* could (according to Emerson and Morson) be resolved by disclaiming Bakhtin's association with that particular text, and a different profile of author and concept would emerge as a consequence.

While Hirshkop's arguments for a proper historicization of Bakhtin's work are powerful, particularly in an attempt to prevent a depoliticization of the key concepts, my own project, which constitutes an overview of the 'dialogics industry' (see Chapter 2) as well as Bakhtin's works must necessarily forgo such purism, although in this chapter I do endeavour to reflect some of the changes and developments in Bakhtin's dialogic thinking in the different texts. I have also taken a pragmatic approach to the 'attribution' debate, for the reason that the majority of secondary critical sources that I review in the next chapter are themselves ultimately unconcerned about whether their textual source is Bakhtin, Voloshinov or Medvedev. In my defence, I would, at this point, like to invoke

[2]   K. Clark and M. Holquist, *Mikhail Bakhtin* (Cambridge, MA: Harvard University Press, 1984), p. 168.
[3]   Morson and Emerson, *Rethinking Bakhtin*, p. 30.
[4]   *Bakhtin and Cultural Theory*, ed. K. Hirschkop and D. Shepherd (Manchester and New York: Manchester University Press, 1989), pp. 1–38.

the sentiments of one of the most skilful (and politically self-aware) of Bakhtin's appropriators, Robert Stam, who writes:

> Such a preoccupation [i.e., in the work of Morson and Emerson] shows insensitivity to what Allon White calls the 'hybrid and collaborative composition' chosen by Bakhtin and is diametrically opposed to Bakhtin's view of writing as always dialogical, impure, citational. For the purposes of this text, therefore, the name Bakhtin will be used stenographically, to refer to Bakhtin himself together with his close collaborators, under the assumption that the works in question represent a mingling of voices, a view that strikes us as perfectly in keeping with the Bakhtinian conception of authorship.[5]

This is, of course, an easy way out of the problem that the majority of those critics 'working with Bakhtin' (as opposed to 'working on him') would be more than happy to accept. In my own discussions I, like Stam, will be using Bakhtin's name generically in many instances (i.e., to refer not only to him but also to the extended Bakhtin school), but I have also chosen to refer to the authors of the early texts by their published titles (i.e., Bakhtin and Medvedev, *The Formal Method* (1928), Voloshinov, *Freudianism* (1927) and *Marxism and the Philosophy of Language* (1929) – see Further Reading). While there is the clear possibility that critics like Emerson and Morson on the one hand, and Hirschkop on the other, may, in the future, persuade us that such scholarly indeterminacy is harmful to dialogic criticism as well as Bakhtin scholarship, most of that which has been practised to date has been only minimally concerned with the attribution or chronology of the texts in which the key principle is lodged.

In the following discussion I deal with the full spectrum of texts associated with the Bakhtin school now available in English translation with the exception of the early philosophical essays included in the volume *Art and Answerability* (1924) (see Further Reading). Although the editors, Michael Holquist and Vadim Liapunov, and critics like Ken Hirschkop have argued for the importance of these essays in establishing an authentic profile of Bakhtin's intellectual and political development, I am excusing myself on the grounds that these are very much philosophical writings that would prove extremely difficult and unrewarding for the general or student reader, and that although they do, indeed, contain the germs of many of Bakhtin's key concepts (Holquist identifies, for example, the origins of Bakhtin's 'I/Other' dichotomy), these are not presented in a linguistic or literary context.

I have endeavoured to make my explication of the texts and their concepts as lucid and accessible as possible without, it is hoped, sacrificing too much of the complexity of Bakhtin's own argument and examples.

[5] R. Stam, *Subversive Pleasures: Bakhtin, Cultural Criticism and Film* (Baltimore MD, and London: Johns Hopkins University Press, 1989), p. 3.

# I
## *Freudianism: A Critical Sketch*
### *V. N. Voloshinov, 1927*

Although most commentators now preface their comments on *Freudianism* with the remark that it is insufficiently sensitive to the complexities of Freud's theory, there is no denying that it represents one of the earliest and most spirited critiques of the ahistoricism of psychoanalysis.[6]

*Freudianism* is a brisk, 'no-nonsense' tract which clearly assumes that the blindnesses and limitations of Freud's hypotheses are so blatantly manifest that they need little explication. In terms of the polemical style of this book, it is also worth noting Holquist's point that 'Bakhtin' (and he assumes the author *is* Bakhtin and not Voloshinov) was here seeking a more populist audience than he had done hitherto, and that the book was an opportunity for him to present some of the 'fundamental' philosophical criteria that he had been exploring in the *Architectonics* in a more accessible form (for example, the relationship between the 'inner' and 'outer' body).[7] Crucial to the development of Bakhtin's theory of the dialogic is the emphasis placed on *context* and *situatedness* and, according to Holquist, this occurs in *Freudianism* under the guise of Bakhtin's rewriting of the doctor–patient relationship. The latter, together with an an acute sense of the role of *language* in both Freud's 'treatments' and his failed attempt at a 'scientific objectivity', look forward to many of the points expounded in *Marxism and the Philosophy of Language*.

The text opens with a bid to expose 'the basic ideological motif of Freudianism', and this is summed up in the popular cliché that 'everything is reducible to sex':

> A human being's fate, the whole content of his life and creative activity – of his art, if he is an artist, of his scientific theories, if he is a scientist, of his political programs and measures, if he is a politician, and so on – are wholly and exclusively determined by the vicissitudes of his sexual instinct. Everything else represents merely the overtones of the mighty and fundamental melody of sex (p. 10).

The author's (who I am naming as Voloshinov) first and most pressing critique, then, is that Freudian theory sees a person's consciousness as being shaped by his 'biological being' rather than 'his place and role in history – the *class, nation, historical period* to which he belongs' (ibid.). The limitations of this biological/sexual determinism are made to appear self-evident.

Voloshinov's speculations on the intellectual context which made this ahistoricism possible relate to the still-popular reading of 'modernism'

---

[6]   See, for example, the opinions expressed by J. W. Vetch in the Foreword to the English translation of V. N. Voloshinov, *Freudianism: A Critical Sketch*, trans. I. R. Titunik and ed. in collaboration with N. H. Bruss (Bloomington, MN, and Indianapolis, IN: Indiana University Press, 1976), pp. viii–ix. Further page references to this volume will be given after quotations in the text.

[7]   Clark and Holquist, *Bakhtin*, p. 172.

which sees the early twentieth century as a period which turned its back on history. He argues that psychoanalysis may be seen as an early twentieth-century reaction to a world in 'crisis and decline': a characteristic retreat into comforting belief that *'Man is above all an animal'* (p. 11).

Chapter 2 of *Freudianism* examines 'Two Trends in Modern Psychology', namely, 'Subjective Psychology' and 'Objective Psychology', citing the key proponents and basic methodological assumptions (and limitations) of each. This is followed by an exploration of the grounds for a relationship between psychology and Marxism, which establishes (not surprisingly) that the 'objective trend' (i.e., the belief that the 'behaviour of a living organism is wholly accessible to *external, objective apprehension'* p. 20) is more commensurate with the principles of dialectical materialism. Marxism, argues Voloshinov, does not deny the existence of the 'subjective-psychical' but merely insists that it 'cannot be divorced from the material basis of the organism's behavior' (pp. 21–22): this is, of course, another way of restating the maxim that everything, in the last analysis, is reducible to the economic base. Marxism will also insist that human psychology is not the psychology of the individual *per se*, but of that individual within society: *'human* psychology must be socialized' (p. 22). With these provisos in place, Voloshinov makes it clear that a 'marriage' between Marxism and psychology *is* possible, and he cites contemporary psychologists like A. B. Zalkind to show that such work has already been pursued in the Soviet Union.

As far as Freud's psychoanalytic method is concerned, however, an accommodation within Marxism is vastly more problematic. Here the focus of Voloshinov's critique – and this is the part of the thesis that looks forward most interestingly to Bakhtin's later works – is that Freud was ignorant of the role of language and ideology in both the constitution of the human psyche and his treatment of it. According to Voloshinov, what Freud failed to see was that all conscious and supposedly 'unconscious' thought is 'ideological through and through' (p. 24). While many subsequent theorists have argued that Freud, far from being 'ignorant' of the psychic role of language, was obsessed with it, it was clearly not a linguistic consciousness socially grounded enough for Voloshinov's taste.

Part II of the book consists of an exposition of Freudian thought up to 1927 which is a date, as Holquist has observed, extremely early in Freud's career, and excludes work that would answer many of Voloshinov's criticisms. Although there is little purpose in my reproducing an account of this survey, I shall observe those aspects of Freud's work that Voloshinov chooses to focus on, namely, the role of the unconscious and Freud's treatment of 'repression'; an account of the sexual drives (including a summary of the Oedipus complex); an account of the basic tenets of Freud's psychoanalytic method (focusing on the use of free association, the interpretation of dreams, jokes, Freudian slips, etc.); and, finally, a review of Freud's 'philosophy of culture', in particular his understanding of art and religion. What is interesting about this catalogue is that it *does* represent a fairly comprehensive profile of the 'essential Freud' that is still popular in the West today and that while, in such a brief overview (all this is achieved in only 35 pages) the account is necessarily sketchy and lacking in subtlety, it is reasonably accurate in all the important technicalities (for example, 'how dreams work'). What betrays the author's impatience is not so much polemical interjection or veiled subplot but the way in which all the 'grand theories' are reduced to such a cursory list of points.

In the final section of the book (Part III), Voloshinov expands on those criticisms brought forward in Chapter 2 of Section I. The first of these is a return to what he perceives to be Freud's false distinction between the 'conscious' and 'unconscious' mind. Here he uses irony to question how a psychic mode ostensibly 'outside' language and reason could effect such logical connections:

> Let us turn attention to the operation of censorship. Freud considers the censorship a 'mechanism' that operates completely *unconsciously* (the conscious, as the reader will recall, not only does not control the work of the censorship but does not even suspect its existence). Yet, how delicately the 'unconscious mechanism' detects all the logical subtleties of thoughts and the moral nuances of feelings! The censorship demonstrates enormous ideological erudition and refinement; it makes purely logical, ethical, and aesthetic selections among experiences. Can this possibly be compatible with its unconscious *mechanical* structure? (p. 70).

Some pages later he concludes emphatically: '*The whole of Freud's psychical "dynamics" is given the ideological contamination of consciousness*. Consequently, *it is not a dynamics of psychical forces but only a dynamics of various motives of consciousness*' (p. 77). From this conclusion (which looks forward to the whole body of Bakhtin's later work) Voloshinov proceeds to expound the crucial role of *context* and *situation* in all verbal utterance – the dialogic conditions which make every use of language, written or spoken, a profoundly social act:

> Not a single instance of verbal utterance can be reckoned exclusively to its utterer's account. Every utterance is *the product of an interaction between speakers* and the product of the broader context of the whole complex *social situation* in which the utterance emerges (p. 79).

In terms of Freud's psychoanalytic treatments, moreover, the special context in which doctor and patient are brought together is bound to give a special ideological direction to the patient's responses. Far from her utterances being an expression of her 'repressed unconscious' they are, according to Voloshinov, a dialogic response to both her interlocutor (her doctor) and the situation she finds herself in:

> Between doctor and patient there may be differences in sex, in age, in social standing, and moreover there is the difference of their professions. All the factors complicate their relationship and the struggle between them.
> And it is in the midst of this complex and very special social atmosphere that the verbal utterances are made . . . (ibid.).

What Voloshinov demonstrates in this artful turnround is that the 'resistance' associated with the psychoanalytic method is not the result of the trauma experienced by a patient when she is brought face to face with her unconscious, but a response to the peculiarly charged social context in which she finds herself. Psychoanalysis is not predicated on a psychic dialogue between the conscious and unconscious mind, but a more literal one between doctor and patient. This reformulation brings a whole new dimension to the notion of a 'talking cure'.

In the final chapter, Voloshinov attempts to put a further nail in Freudianism's coffin by displaying it as a *symptom* of a depraved and disintegrating bourgeoisie. What Freud's analysis exposes is not the unconscious desires of individuals but those of a whole society in malaise. Indeed, his description of the *contradictory* nature of 'behavioural ideology' (the Bakhtin group's term for Freudian psychology) at the beginning of the twentieth century anticipates that of later Marxists such as Raymond Williams, who challenged the notion of ideology as the preserve of society's ruling group and presented, instead, a complex vision of societies and individuals in which dominant ideologies were constantly in the process of being challenged by alternative and oppositional ideologies.[8] Arguing along similar lines, Voloshinov equates the so-called 'unconscious' of Freud's patients with a set of oppositional ideologies which have emerged because of the imminent demise of society's ruling group:

> Other levels, corresponding to Freud's unconscious, lie at a great distance from the stable system of the ruling ideology. They bespeak the disintegration of the unity and integrity of the system, the vulnerability of the usual ideological motivations (p. 89).

What Freud calls the 'unconscious', then, is no more than the expression of a dissident voice that is in the process of becoming an alternative or, indeed, 'revolutionary' ideology (p. 90). It is, however, interesting to observe some political ambiguity in Voloshinov's argument at this point: although, on the one hand, he is positing the existence of such alternative ideologies as the *symptoms* of a degenerate society, on the other they are clearly welcomed as agents of change and revolution. Equally interesting is the way in which such statements have been interpreted by Bakhtin's more liberal commentators, like Holquist, as veiled challenges to the totalitarian Soviet regime, when they can more obviously be read as a traditional Marxist critique on the degeneracies of late capitalism.[9] What is, however, undisputed in their account of Freud is the Bakhtin group's refusal to countenance a psychology that is not a *social* psychology, and a view of human consciousness (including Freud's purported 'unconscious') that is not ideological.

Although it nowhere introduces the concept of dialogism *per se*, *Freudianism*'s great emphasis on the importance of the social situatedness of *all utterance* (including the utterances exchanged in therapy), anticipates many of the foundational principles of language and literary discourse

[8]   See R. Williams, *Marxism and Literature* (Oxford: Oxford University Press, 1977), p. 125. Williams argues that, in addition to its dominant ideology, any society in any given historical moment will produce additional and competing ideologies which he classifies into four main types: alternative (coexisting with the dominant ideology); oppositional (challenging the dominant ideology); residual (formed in the past, but still active in the cultural process); and emergent (the expression of new groups outside the dominant group).
[9]   Clark and Holquist, *Bakhtin* 'Bakhtin [Voloshinov] thus translates Freud's metaphor of censorship into a recognizably Russian scenario. The unconscious operates like a minority political party opposed to certain aspects of the reigning politics of a culture' (p. 184).

explored in *Marxism and the Philosophy of Language* and the later Bakhtinian texts.

## II
### *The Formal Method*
#### *P.N. Medvedev, 1928*

Although the object of *The Formal Method* is ostensibly a critique of the Formalism represented by Shklovsky and the OPOIAZ group, from the very first page it is also a covert tribute to the new scientific rigour the Formalists brought to the study of literature.[10] Medvedev admits this most directly at the end of the first section, which is itself a rather defensive manifesto of 'The Objects and Tasks of Marxist Literary Scholarship':

> It can be said that poetics in the Soviet Union at present is monopolized by the so-called 'formal' or 'morphological' method. In their short history, the formalists have managed to cover a wide range of problems in theoretical poetics. There is hardly a single problem in this area that they have not touched upon somehow in their work. Marxism cannot leave the work of the formalists without exhaustive critical analysis.
>
> Marxism can even less afford to ignore the formal method because the formalists have emerged precisely as specifiers, perhaps the first in Russian literary scholarship. They have succeeded in giving great sharpness and principle to problems of literary specification which makes them stand out sharply and to advantage against the background of flabby eclecticism and unprincipled academic scholarship (p. 36).

Inasmuch as Marxist scholarship demanded a new emphasis on 'the concrete' (a favourite word among the early Bakhtin group), the Formalists were seen to offer a desirable set of new analytic tools, and the task of *The Formal Method* was partly to make an inventory of them for the purposes of its own 'sociological poetics'. The fact that this documentation is preceded by the chapter defending the work of Marxist literary scholarship can therefore be seen as either more 'window dressing' for the State censor (see the discussion on *Freudianism* above), or as an indication of the genuine

---

10   P. N. Medvedev/M. M. Bakhtin, *The Formal Method in Literary Scholarship: A Critical Introduction to Sociological Poetics*, trans. A. J. Wehrle (Baltimore, MD, and London: Johns Hopkins University Press, 1978). Page references to this volume will be given after quotations in the text.

For a brief definition of 'Russian formalism' see C. Baldick, *The Concise Oxford Dictionary of Literary Terms* (Oxford and New York: Oxford University Press, 1990): 'A school of literary theory and analysis that emerged in Russia around 1915, devoting itself to the study of literariness, i.e., the sum of 'devices' that distinguish literary language from ordinary language. In reaction against the vagueness of previous literary theories, it attempted a scientific description of literature (especially poetry) as a special use of language with observable features. This meant deliberately disregarding the contents of literary works, and thus inviting strong disapproval from Marxist critics, for whom formalism was a term of reproach' (pp. 195–96).

For a summary of the work of Viktor Shklovsky and the OPOIAZ group see T. Hawkes, *Structuralism and Semiotics* (London: Methuen, 1977).

insecurity of Marxist critics faced with a compelling new conceptualization of the literary text. Yet whatever the motive, there is a clear sense that Medvedev is in desperate need to convince both himself and his reader of the intrinsic social and historical nature of all works of art:

> But this effect of literature on literature [a reference, here, to the Formalists' focus on intertextuality] is still a sociological effect. Literature, like every other ideology, is social through and through. If the individual work of art does not reflect the [economic] base, it does so at its own risk, in isolation and detachment from all the rest of literature (p. 28).

By tying the text to the economic base 'in the last analysis', Medvedev, like Louis Althusser, grants Marxist literary criticism the necessary permission to share with the Formalists a new focus on the individual text and its constituent devices.[11] The importance of forging this initial connection between the formal and the ideological is understood most clearly if one looks at Bakhtin's later works like *Problems of Dostoevsky's Poetics* (1929) which owes its key theoretical formulations to a close, formalist acquaintance with an individual author and his or her works. One might even go so far as to say that 'polyphony' and 'the double-voiced word' would not have been 'discovered' by Bakhtin were it not for the methods of distinguishing and analysing a text's formal design that he learnt from his early acquaintance with Formalism.

Medvedev's solution to the problem of how to combine the desirable specificity of the 'formal method' with the Marxist insistence that every word of literature is ideological 'through and through' does not, however, become clear until the end of Chapter 6 ('Material and Device as Components of the Poetic Construction'). It is at this point that he directly confronts the question of *how* 'external form' is to be related to 'intrinsic ideological meaning' (p. 118), citing the Formalists' retreat into the theory of the 'transrational word' and their assimilation of 'material' to 'device' as evidence only of their failure. The crucial missing element, he argues, is *social evaluation*: it is this which 'unites the material presence of a word with its meaning' (p. 119).

'Social evaluation' as Medvedev explains it here may be best defined as the manner in which each and every 'word utterance' (poetic and nonpoetic) exists as a social event and act of communication:

> Every concrete utterance is a social act. At the same time that it is an individual material complex, a phonetic, articulatory, visual complex, the utterance is also part of social reality. It organizes communication oriented towards reciprocal action, and itself reacts; it is also inseparably enmeshed in the communication event. Its individual reality is already not that of a physical body, but the reality of a historical phenomenon. Not only the meaning of the utterance but also the very act of its performance is of historical and social significance,

---

11  See L. Althusser's essay, 'Ideology and Ideological State Apparatuses' in *Lenin and Philosophy and Other Essays*, trans. B. Brewster (London : New Left Books, 1971). Althusser delivered an important challenge to traditional Marxist thinking when he argued for the 'relative autonomy' of 'ideological state apparatuses' (such as religion, education and the family) in the perpetration of a society's ruling group, while acknowledging that these institutions nevertheless remained connected to the 'economic base' (the source of capitalist power) 'in the last instance'.

as, in general, is the fact of its realization in the here and now, in given circumstances, at a historical moment, under the conditions of the given social situation (p. 120).

In anticipation of the theory of language worked through in *Marxism and the Philosophy of Language*, the 'word' is inescapably social and historical. Its materiality (which Formalist 'specification' had brought to new recognition) is not to be understood merely as an expression of its formal autonomy but through its situated engagement in a unique social/linguistic context. In this specification, Medvedev's analysis very closely foreshadows the central tenet of the dialogic principle: all verbal/textual meaning is ultimately determined by a word's relationship to 'a future answer word'. Dialogicality is, in other words, the *context* which causes a word's material presence to become commensurate with its meaning:

> It is this historical actuality, which unites the individual presence of the utterance with the generality and fullness of its meaning, which makes meaning concrete and individual and gives meaning to the word's phonetic presence here and now, that we call social evaluation (p. 121).

Later in the same chapter Medvedev struggles, rather less convincingly, to take his argument one step further and account for the difference between 'poetic' and 'practical' language according to the same formula. Although the exact nature of the distinction is extremely hard to convey, some sense of his intention may be grasped through the metaphor of 'completion' he employs to describe it. In practical speech, social evaluation (in the sense of the socially defining context in which an utterance is made) may not fill or 'penetrate' all aspects of the linguistic material, so that the utterance remains, in some ways, 'incomplete'. In poetic language, however, 'social evaluation is complete in the utterance itself' (p. 127); the context is commensurate with the word. Another way of expressing this would be to say that the poetic word is somehow more totally imbued with its social and historical context than the practical word, though because Medvedev offers no examples it is difficult to imagine how the difference would appear in the written text.

Beyond this central theoretical preoccupation of how the material presence of the word/text may be united with its ideological meaning, *The Formal Method* constitutes a fairly detailed account of the history of the Western European and Russian Formalist movements and an inventory of the methods of critical analysis employed by Shklovsky and his followers. While this is not the place to reproduce full details of the latter, there are a few points in Medvedev's critique which represent significant anticipations of Bakhtin's evolving dialogic theory.

The first point of importance, which occurs almost incidentally in the section on early Formalism in Russia, concerns the role and status of *the author vis-à-vis* the literary text. Here Medvedev praises the Formalists for the new emphasis they put on the 'poet as craftsman', but criticizes the implication that this is *all* he [sic] is: 'The artistic work is not only created, but also made. But for the formalists it is only made' (p. 63). As will be seen in the later discussion of *Dostoevsky's Poetics*, the exact role of the author in the production of the dialogic/polyphonic text was to prove a difficult problem for Bakhtin, who was torn between a wish to celebrate Dostoevsky's own innovatory 'genius' (he supposedly 'invented' the polyphonic novel) and the cognition that the author/narrator of such texts is characterized by his *lack* of authority. In a lengthy and somewhat laboured passage in *Dostoevsky's Poetics*, Bakhtin finally discovers a formula for preserving a sense of the author's creativity, but it is clear that in terms of the actual orchestration of the polyphonic text his function is more obviously that of the craftsman (see below).

The second area in which Medvedev's commentary significantly fore-shadows Bakhtin's later work is his insistence on the social and reciprocal orientation of *all utterance*. Indeed, a large part of Medvedev's critique of the Formalists' methodology is a challenge to their concept of 'literariness' and here, again, we see that the crux of his argument depends upon a burgeoning dialogic principle: poetic and practical utterances (despite the difference he struggles to define in the section discussed earlier) are the same to the extent that they exist as communicative acts: as a response to, or anticipation of, another's word:

> If we take the word 'communicative' in its widest and more general sense, then every language and utterance is communicative. Every utterance is oriented on intercourse, on the hearer, on the reader, in a word, on another person, on social intercourse of any kind whatever (p. 93).

Following on from this account of the similarity between poetic and practical speech, Medvedev shows how many of the 'devices' that the Formalists' account specifically 'literary' are, in fact, elements in the dialogic exchange between the text and its *reader*: this is to say, their *motivation* is communicative, even if their function within the text appears to be self-consciously aesthetic. Medvedev sees such devices as a textual expression of '*speech tact*':

> Speech tact has a practical importance for practical language communication. The formative and organizing force of speech tact is very great. It gives form to everyday utterances, determining the style and genre of speech performances. Here tact should be understood in a broad sense, with politeness as only one of its aspects . . .
>
> Under certain circumstances, in certain social groups, speech tact creates grounds favouring the formation of utterances having characteristics the formalists consider typical of poetic language: brakings, evasions, ambiguities, crooked speech paths . . .
>
> The form is that of a concealed or overt dialogue with the reader, a game with him. This applies to *Tristram Shandy* and other works, and to the parts of Gogol and Dostoevskii that the formalists enlist to prove, or more precisely to illustrate, their theoretical positions (pp. 95–96).

By suggesting that the most avant-garde literary devices may be thought of as items of exchange between text and reader in this way, Medvedev, once again, points to *dialogue* as the fundamental structuring principle of the literary text.

*The Formal Method* ends with three chapters on the Formalists' approach to genre and literary history, and in many respects Medvedev's critique here simply reproduces earlier criticisms on a macrocosmic scale. On the issue of genre, for example, he attacks the Formalists' definition of it as a 'specific grouping of devices with a defined dominant' (p. 129) and argues that such a rigidly autonomous view of the text ignores its social orientation: 'In the first place, the work is oriented toward the listener and perceiver, and toward the definite conditions of performance and perception' (p. 131).[12] This means that each genre is defined by its specific communicative purpose: hence the ode originated as part of a 'civil celebration', while the lyric had its origins in religious worship. To describe genres simply as groupings around dominant aesthetic devices is, from this perspective, to miss completely the significance of their dialogic contextualization.

Medvedev's criticism of the Formalists' conception of literary history is similarly focused on what he perceives to be a false notion of textual autonomy (albeit an *intertextual* autonomy). While welcoming their attempt to free literary criticism of the 'psychologically subjective interpretation of the artistic work as the expression of the inner world or "soul" of the artist' (p. 145), Medvedev rejects an objectification of the text which takes no account of the 'ideological environment' in which it was produced (ibid.), thus repeating earlier comments on the importance of socially contextualizing the individual utterance.

As we shall see, this movement from microcosmic to macrocosmic linguistic and/or literary spheres is a feature of Bakhtin's dialogic system: what is true of the smallest unit ('the word') is also true of the utterance, the discourse, the text and the historical-literary genre. Throughout the spectrum of textual events, the same conditions of dialogic engagement apply: 'Every utterance, including the artistic work, is a communication, a message, and is completely inseparable from intercourse' (p. 151).

## III

### *Marxism and the Philosophy of Language*

*P.N. Voloshinov, 1929*

Voloshinov's *Marxism and the Philosophy of Language* is the text in which dialogism breaks conceptually into the writings of the Bakhtin group, and it contains some of the most frequently quoted phrases and passages on the subject.[13]

In the same way that *Freudianism* and *The Formal Method* are Marxist critiques of contemporary trends in psychology and literary criticism respectively, so is *Marxism and the Philosophy of Language* a response to

---

12   The formalist critic, Roman Jakobson, argued that all literary texts may be distinguished by their 'dominant' stylistic devices, and that literary history may thus be characterized by a reactionary process in which new texts displace the 'dominant' of their predecessors. For an account of Jacobson's theory, see Hawkes, *Structuralism and Semiotics*, pp. 76–87. See also the discussion following.

13   P. N. Voloshinov, *Marxism and the Philosophy of Language*, trans. L. Matejka and I. R. Titunik (New York: Seminar Press, 1973). Page references to this volume will be given after quotations in the text.

the challenge of Saussurean linguistics. The early part of the study is hence an attempt to resituate Saussurean theories of signification within an acceptable materialist framework. This, according to Voloshinov, requires that 'the sign may not be divorced from the concrete forms of social intercourse' (p. 21): the same dictum, precisely, that we have already seen espoused by Medvedev concerning the poetic word in *The Formal Method*. In *Marxism and the Philosophy of Language*, however, the social context from which all signs and subjects extract their meaning takes on the flesh of a fully fashioned *dialogic community*. Although the word 'dialogic' is not invoked directly (as it is in Bakhtin's later writings), Voloshinov lays repeated emphasis on the concepts of *relation* and *interaction*:

> Every sign, as we know, is a construct between socially organized persons in the process of their interaction. Therefore, the forms of signs are conditioned above all by the social organization of the participants involved and also by the immediate conditions of their interaction (p. 21).

In Part II of *Marxism and the Philosophy of Language* Voloshinov develops this notion of dialogic context to propose a new theory of language. This theory rejects both what he refers to as the 'Individual Subjectivist' (neo-Kantian) and 'Abstract Objectivist' (Saussurean) schools of language, and argues, instead, that all individual speech acts exist as a function of dialogue between their participating subjects.[14] Such an all-determining emphasis on *context* is necessarily concomitant with an emphasis on the *performative* function of language: the speech act or utterance. As Holquist has written, for Bakhtin this is the 'fundamental unit of investigation'.[15] It is extremely important, however, to distinguish such 'utterance' from Saussure's notion of *parole*. Apart from anything else, Bakhtinian utterance is not associated exclusively with the spoken word (an utterance may be spoken or *written*) and it does not carry with it the same notion of free will on the part of the speaker. According to Holquist, the dialogic utterance 'is always achieved in the face of pre-existing restraints'.[16]

Adjectives habitually associated with the concept of the utterance in Voloshinov's and Bakhtin's vocabulary are 'concrete' and 'particular'. Both of these adjectives emphasize the specificity of language and the way it operates. The force of this specificity is recorded in the following paragraph:

> The linguistic consciousness of the speaker and of the listener-understander, in the practical business of living speech, is not at all concerned with the abstract system of normatively identical forms of language, but with language-speech in the sense of the aggregate of possible contexts of usage for a particular

[14] For a useful summary account of the 'Individual Subjectivist' and 'Abstract Objectivist' schools of linguistics, see M. Holquist, *Dialogism: Bakhtin and His World* (London and New York: Routledge, 1990). Holquist writes: 'Abstract objectivism treats language as a pure system of laws governing all phonetic, grammatical, and lexical forms that confront individual speakers as inviolable norms over which they have no control. Another tendency opposed by dialogism, 'individual subjectivism', is the polar opposite of the first . . . It denies pre-existing norms and holds that all aspects of language can be explained in terms of each speaker's voluntarist intentions' (p. 42).
[15] Ibid., pp. 59–63.
[16] Ibid., p. 60.

linguistic form. For a person speaking his native tongue, a word presents itself not as an item of vocabulary but as a word that has been used in a wide variety of utterances by co-speaker A, co-speaker B, co-speaker C and so on, and has been variously used in the speaker's own utterances. A very special and specific kind of orientation is necessary if one is to go from there to the self identical word belonging to the lexicological system of the language in question – the dictionary word (p. 70).

Voloshinov's fundamental disagreement with the Saussurean language system, then, is its relative indifference to the social speech act.

The central tenets of dialogism in its expressly linguistic sense are to be found in the chapter on verbal interaction. This chapter contains, in my opinion, some of the most suggestive passages in the whole Bakhtinian archive: theories about the dialogic nature of all human communication upon which the reader may meditate endlessly. The first such proposition I would like to explore in some detail is that all utterances are determined by their *'immediate social situation'* (p. 85) – a theory that we have already seen foreshadowed in Medvedev's critique of Freud. Voloshinov writes:

Utterance, as we know, is constructed between two socially organized persons, and in the absence of a real addressee, an addressee is presupposed in the person, so to speak, of a normal representative of the social group to which the speaker belongs. The *word is oriented towards an addressee*, toward *who* that addressee might be: a fellow-member or not of the same social group, of higher or lower standing (the addressee's hierarchical status), someone connected to the speaker by close social ties (father, brother, husband, and so on) or not. There can be no such thing as an abstract addressee, a man unto himself, so to speak. With such a person, we would indeed have no language in common, literally and figuratively. Even though we sometimes have pretensions to experiencing and saying things *urbi and orbi*, actually, of course, we envision this 'world at large' through the prism of the concrete social milieu surrounding us. In the majority of cases, we presuppose a certain typical and stabilized *social purview* toward which the ideological creativity of our own social group and time is oriented, i.e., we assume as our addressee a contemporary of our literature, our science, our moral and legal code.

Each person's inner world and thought has its stabilized *social audience* that comprises the environment in which reasons, motives, values, and so on are fashioned. The more cultured a person, the more closely his inner audience will approximate the normal audience of ideological creativity; but, in any case, specific class and specific era are limits that the ideal of the addressee cannot go beyond (pp. 85–86).

Crucial in this formulation of how utterances are produced is not only the recognition of the a priori existence of the addressee but also the role of *power* in determining the quality of the utterance. Most suggestive are the particular examples Voloshinov uses to illustrate his point. By naming relationships between friends and family, between persons of 'higher or lower social standing', he alerts us to the power dynamic that is present in every verbal (spoken or textual) exchange. Every utterance is determined fundamentally by the degree of intimacy, formality or social hierarchy that informs our relationship with our addressee. Even more revealing, however, is Voloshinov's insistence that this dynamic operates even when we believe we are addressing our thoughts 'to no one in particular': to 'ourselves', to 'the world and large'. According to Voloshinov, such utterances are *profoundly* social and interactive. In the absence of a named addressee, we direct our utterances towards a culturally specific 'social purview'. We may not be addressing an individual, but we are most certainly interacting with a particular discursive set. In the case of a personal diary, this might be a discourse informed by the cultural codes, values and interests of the social group to which we belong; in the case of an academic textbook, this will almost certainly be a particular subgroup of the academic community. *Vis-à-vis* this last point, Voloshinov also makes the important observation that all utterances are class specific. The sociocultural competency possessed by a speaker and her interlocutor will be intrinsic to the utterance.

Following through the theory that *all* utterances, even the most apparently private and solipsistic are, in fact, inescapably social, Voloshinov makes a similar claim for subjectivity by collapsing the difference between 'self' and 'other': what he calls the 'self-experience' and the 'we-experience'. Self-experience, contrary to its representation in post-Romantic thought and literature, is not solitary and asocial. In the same way that all our utterances are made in anticipation of a future answer word which is socially accountable, so are even the most apparently solitary of our experiences determined by our sense of ourselves in relation to others. Implicit in Voloshinov's claim is the notion that our post-Romantic celebration of this particular brand of individualism (the ability, say, to have a sublime experience alone at the top of a mountain) depends crucially on a firm sense of ourself as part of a particular community: a particular cultural and socioeconomic subgroup that enjoys doing such things. Our sense of self depends upon the confidence we do or do not possess about our role within the wider community. The implications of this dialogic view of the subject will be discussed in greater detail in the next chapter.

In the chapter on 'Verbal Utterances' Voloshinov includes an important coda on the nature of dialogue, namely, that it is not an exclusively *spoken* phenomenon:

> Dialogue, in the narrow sense of the word, is, of course, only one of the forms – a very important form, to be sure – of verbal interaction. But dialogue can also be understood in a broader sense, meaning not only direct, face-to-face, vocalized verbal communication between persons, but also verbal communication of any type whatsoever. A book, i.e., *a verbal performance in print*, is also an element of verbal communication. It is something discussable in actual, real-life dialogue, but aside from that, it is calculated for actual perception, involving attentive reading and inner responsiveness, and for organized *printed* reaction . . . Moreover, a verbal performance of this kind also inevitably orients itself with respect to previous performances in the same sphere, both those by the same author and those by other authors (p. 95).

This notion of *intertextuality*, which is now commonplace in poststructuralist literary criticism, is central to Bakhtin's later work in *Dostoevsky's Poetics* and *The Dialogic Imagination* (1934–41), where it is given a more complex elucidation (see the discussion following).[17]

Another phenomenon that Voloshinov introduces at this point and which attains a special importance in the later writings is the importance of *extraverbal context* in all verbal communication. In the 1926 essay on the crucial role of *intonation* in the dialogic construction of meaning, 'Discourse in Life and Discourse in Poetry' (see the discussion following), Voloshinov shows how a host of extraverbal factors (along with intonation) have to be taken into account if we are to understand properly the import of a given utterance. This supercontextualization of 'the word' is here articulated by Voloshinov as follows:

> An important problem arises in this regard: the study of the connection between concrete verbal interaction and the extraverbal situation – both the immediate situation and, through it, the broader situation . . . *Verbal communication can never be understood and explained outside of this connection with a concrete situation.* Verbal intercourse is inextricably interwoven with communication of other types, all stemming from the common ground of production. It goes without saying that the word cannot be divorced from this eternally generative, unified process of communication. In its concrete connection with a situation, verbal communication is always accompanied by social acts of a nonverbal character (the performance of labor, the symbolic acts of a ritual, a ceremony etc.), and it is often only an accessory to these acts, merely carrying out an auxillary role (p. 95).

The significance of linguistic *context* is addressed, again, in the final chapter of *Marxism and the Philosophy of Language* where Voloshinov considers 'the difficult problem of meaning' (p. 99). He begins by making the commonsense point that an utterance as superficially unambiguous as 'what time is it?' will nevertheless mean different things in different concrete historical situations: the significance of the whole utterance (what he calls the 'theme') is variable. There are, however, elements within every utterance which are *'reproducible* and *self-identical'* (p. 100) in all instances of repetition ('the meanings of words, the forms of morphological and syntactic union, interrogative intonations' (ibid.)) and these may be referred to as the 'meaning' of the utterance. It will be clear from all the earlier discussion, however, that 'meaning' in this narrowly defined 'linguistic' sense is very much an artificial category and that, in practice, 'no absolute, mechanistic boundary can be drawn between theme and meaning. There is no theme without meaning and no meaning without theme' (ibid.). Voloshinov concludes by returning us to the fundamentally dialogic condition of all utterance:

> Therefore, there is no reason for saying that meaning belongs to a word as such. In essence, meaning belongs to a word in its position between speakers; that is, meaning is realized only in the process of active, responsive understanding. Meaning does not reside in the word or in the soul of the speaker or in the soul of the listener. Meaning is the *effect of interaction between speaker and listener produced via the material of a particular sound complex.* It is like an electric spark which occurs only when two different terminals are hooked together (pp. 102–103).

[17]   It is also worth noting that this concept was first made popular by Julia Kristeva when she worked with Bakhtin's texts in the 1970s. See the chapter on 'Word, Dialogue, and Novel' in *Desire in Language*, ed. L. S. Roudiez (New York: Columbia University Press, 1980).

The contents of Part III of *Marxism and the Philosophy of Language*, 'Toward a History of Forms of Utterance in Language Construction', I will not discuss in detail, since the text here does no more than follow through the implications of the earlier sections in terms of their practical application to the study of (Russian) syntax. It will be clear from this overview, however, that *Marxism and the Philosophy of Language* offers a bold challenge to many of the traditional presuppositions of linguistic and literary study, and establishes 'dialogue' as the basic building block of all spoken and written utterance. I end my discussion with what I consider to be one of the most eloquent expressions of dialogism to be found in the writings of the Bakhtin school:

> Orientation of the word toward the addressee has an extremely high significance. In point of fact, *word is a two-sided act*. It is determined equally by *whose* word it is and *for whom* it is meant. As word, it is precisely *the product of the reciprocal relationship between speaker and listener, addresser and addressee*. Each and every word expresses the 'one' in relation to the 'other'. I give myself verbal shape from another's point of view of the community to which I belong. A word is a bridge thrown between myself and another. If one end of the bridge depends on me, then the other depends on my addressee. A word is a territory shared by both addresser and addressee, by the speaker and his interlocutor (p. 86).

## IV
### *Problems of Dostoevsky's Poetics*
#### *M. M. Bakhtin, 1929*

As I indicated in the Introduction, I regard *Dostoevsky's Poetics* as the pivotal Bakhtinian text: the dialogic nerve centre from which all the other books and essays, all the key concepts and theories, may be seen to radiate.[18] Most certainly it is the text in which the dialogic principle, brought to conceptual consciousness in *Marxism and the Philosophy of Language*, is given its official launch: *dialogue, dialogism, polyphony* and *double-voiced discourse* at this point enter the Bakhtinian vocabulary and, indeed, the vocabulary of literary criticism. *Dostoevsky's Poetics* also has the virtue of being more accessible than the essays which comprise *The Dialogic Imagination* and is, for that reason, the first place to which I direct student readers of Bakhtin.

For today's reader, one of the most amusing things about this text is the way in which 'the discovery' of a new 'polyphonic' literary form is attributed exclusively to the Russian novelist, Dostoevsky:

> We consider Dostoevsky one of the greatest innovators in the realm of artistic form. He created, in our opinion, a completely new type of artistic thinking, which we have provisionally called *polyphonic*. This type of artistic thinking found its expression in Dostoevsky's novels, but its significance extends far beyond the limits of the novel alone and touches upon several basic principles of European aesthetics. It could even be said that Dostoevsky created something

[18] The edition of *Dostoevsky's Poetics* I shall be using here is *Problems of Dostoevsky's Poetics*, ed. and trans. C. Emerson (Minneapolis, MN: University of Minnesota Press, 1984). (Page references to this volume will be given after quotations in the text.) This edition is based on Bakhtin's 1963 revised version of the text and Appendix II includes his notes, 'Toward a Reworking of the Dostoevsky Book' (1961). Another translation of the text was published in 1973: *Problems of Dostoevsky's Poetics*, trans. R. W. Rotsel (Michigan, Ardis 1973).

like a new artistic model of the world, one in which many basic aspects of old artistic form were subjected to a radical restructuring (p. 3).

What is clear to all of us now, of course, is that it was Bakhtin (if anyone) who 'invented' the polyphonic novel by bringing its form to theoretical consciousness: as the author himself later concedes, polyphony is a *tendency* inherent in all novelistic discourse – Dostoevsky is simply an exemplary exponent of the form.[19] Since Bakhtin's own dialogic consciousness was developed in relation to a particular author, however (that is to say, as a piece of *literary criticism*), something of Dostoevsky's special qualities need to be acknowledged, not least his difference from purportedly monologic authors like Tolstoy. It is impossible to ignore the fact that Bakhtin's notion of the polyphonic, as represented by Dostoevsky, became visible because of its apparent deviation from the standards of narratorial authority and closure represented by other 'classic' novelists. We should probably compromise, therefore, and acknowledge both Dostoevsky and Bakhtin as (dialogic) coproducers of the new dialogic 'model of the world' in which Dostoevsky is the catalyst, Bakhtin the enthusiastic exponent.

Bakhtin follows his opening statement on Dostoevsky being the originating architect of the polyphonic novel with the corollary that his own treatment of the novelist will focus on his 'literary technique' rather than on the philosophic 'content' of his work. In crude terms one might even go further and suggest that *Dostoevsky's Poetics* is, essentially, a *formalist* study; but such a harsh distinction between form and content is, in other ways, inimical to the spirit of dialogism. It could certainly be argued, however, that it was the close study of literary form undertaken by the Bakhtin group during work on *The Formal Method* that made the distinctiveness of Dostoevsky's approach first visible to Bakhtin (see above).

A large part of the first chapter of *Dostoevsky's Poetics* is taken up with Bakhtin's dialogue with Dostoevsky's own critics and commentators. In the 1963 edition this includes an account of the more recent criticism on Dostoevsky's work, including essays by A. Lunacharsky and Viktor Shklovsky which were written after the publication of the first edition of the book. Bakhtin has some interesting conversations with these later critics, but his attitude towards the early commentators is that they were all – in their different ways – seeking to 'monologize' Dostoevsky's work (p. 8). What is interesting about this chapter, however, is not the particulars of Bakhtin's disagreements with Dostoevsky's other critics, but the statements on the originality of Dostoevsky's artistic form that emerge as a result of the disputes. This first chapter – presumably because it was based on Bakhtin's first, excited discovery of Dostoevsky's stylistic innovation – is an infectious and compulsive read: Bakhtinian hyperbole at its very best. While in *The Dialogic Imagination* Bakhtin's tendency to repetition becomes rather tedious (although it does have the virtue of helping the reader through difficult concepts!), here the exuberant protests of Dostoevsky's genius, the hasty brushing aside of commentators who were blind to this

19   See Bakhtin, *Dosteovsky's Poetics*, p. 44. note 4. Here Bakhtin concedes: 'This does not mean, of course, that Dostoevsky is an isolated instance in the history of the novel, nor does it mean that the polyphonic novel which he has created was without predecessors.'

or that point, and the conviction that he – and we – are truly dealing with an earth-moving innovation – a new *Zeitgeist* – are utterly compelling. Even now, after many years of rereading the text, I am surprised at how this first chapter always seduces me into reading it once more.

Bakhtin opens his chapter by observing how many of Dostoevsky's commentators have been bewildered by the number of 'contradictory philosophical stances' (p. 5) represented in his novels. This difficulty is, he argues, the direct result of one of the primary criteria of the polyphonic text: the independence of characters from their narrator. The multiple voices and characters of Dostoevsky's novels are not subsumed in the worldview of the author-narrator: they are fully independent and, as Bakhtin puts it, 'equally valid' (p. 7). This representation of multiple voices and multiple points of view leads, inevitably, to a different structuring of the polyphonic novel: a linear development of plot and character culminating in exposition and closure is replaced by texts which are far more contradictory and indeterminate. Bakhtin concedes that from the perspective of the 'monologic European novel' (p. 8) Dostoevsky's novels may appear 'chaotic', but he claims for them the 'higher unity' of the polyphonic novel. Later in the chapter Bakhtin focuses on one of the ways in which Dostoevsky's novels disappoint traditional expectations of unity and closure in their resistance to notions of growth, evolution and dialectic. In this respect they deviate sharply from the classic realist text described (and advocated) by the more orthodox Marxist critics like Christopher Caudwell.[20] He writes:

> The unified, dialectically evolving spirit, understood in Hegelian terms, can give rise to nothing but a philosophical monologue . . . In this sense the unified evolving spirit, even as an image, is organically alien to Dostoevsky. Dostoevsky's world is profoundly *pluralistic* (pp. 26–27).

It is interesting to observe that in celebrating the explicitly anti-Hegelian spirit of Dostoevsky's novels, Bakhtin might have been treading on thin ice as far as the Soviet censor was concerned; a few pages later, however, he goes even further by declaring that Dostoevsky's worldview not only rejected a synthesizing dialectic but it also turned its back on (technological) 'history':

> In Dostoevsky's thinking as a whole, there are no generic or causal categories. He constantly polemicizes, and with a sort of organic hostility, against the theory of environmental causality, in whatever form it appears . . . he almost never appeals to history as such, and treats every social and political question on the plane of the present day (p. 29).

If we recall the statements made in *Freudianism* and *Marxism and the Philosophy of Language* on the dangers of ahistoricism in contemporary society, such approval for Dostoevsky's 'journalistic' method seems remarkable. The reader gets the impression, however, that Bakhtin

---

[20]  See C. Caudwell, *Illusion and Reality*, 2nd ed. (London: Lawrence and Wishart, 1946). According to Caudwell's prescription, the 'classic realist' text worked for Marxism by producing 'reflections' on contemporary bourgeois society which were then available for socialist critique.

realized this emphasis on 'coexistence and simultaneity' in Dostoevsky's work to be so central to its polyphonic structuration that its ideological implications had to be swept aside. Certainly, these aspects of the novels give rise to some of Bakhtin's most animated writing:

> The fundamental category in Dostoevsky's mode of artistic visualizing was not evolution, but *co-existence* and *interaction*. He saw and conceived his world primarily in terms of space, not time. Hence his deep affinity for the dramatic form . . . (p. 28).

It is worth observing how abstract Bakhtin's own formulation becomes at this point. Although ostensibly writing about Dostoevsky and Dostoevsky's novels, it is plain to see that what he is really doing is constructing his own 'worldview'.

Towards the end of the first chapter, Bakhtin's theorizing on the 'essential nature' of the polyphonic novel takes another turn. In conversation with Viktor Shklovsky (who by the time of the 1963 edition had already written a response to Bakhtin's ideas, see p. 46) he makes an important connection between the polyphonic and the dialogic with the statement: '*The polyphonic novel is dialogic through and through*' (p. 40). This conjunction of, yet distinction between, the two terms is important since many commentators – Michael Holquist included – have assumed them to be fully interchangeable: 'The phenomenon that Bakhtin calls "polyphony" is simply another name for "dialogism"'.[21] Although it is true to say that, on many occasions, the two terms do, indeed, seem to be virtual synonyms in Bakhtin's discourse, I have always felt that it is useful to maintain a distinction whereby 'polyphony' is associated with the macrocosmic structure of the text (literally, its 'many voices') and 'dialogue' to reciprocating mechanisms *within* the smaller units of exchange, down to the individual word. Something of this distinction is expressed in the following paragraph:

> Dostoevsky could hear dialogic relationships everywhere, in all manifestations of conscious and intelligent human life; where consciousness began there dialogue began for him as well . . . Thus all relationships between external and internal parts and elements of his novel are dialogic in character, and he structured the novel as a whole as a '*great dialogue*'. Within this 'great dialogue' could be heard, illuminating it and thickening its texture, the compositionally expressed dialogues of the heroes; ultimately, dialogue penetrates within, into every word of the novel, making it double-voiced, into every gesture, every mimic movement of the hero's face, making it convulsive and anguished; this is already the '*microdialogue*' that determines the peculiar character of Dostoevsky's verbal style (p. 40).

There will be more detailed examination of what is referred to here as 'microdialogue' later in this section.

In Chapter 2 of *Dostoevsky's Poetics*, Bakhtin develops his ideas on 'The Hero, and the Position of the Author with Regard to the Hero in Dostoevsky's Art'. There is little in this chapter that substantially advances the basic premises proposed *vis-à-vis* the hero's 'independence'

21   Clark and Holquist, *Bakhtin*, p. 242.

and 'unfinalizability' as it is expressed in the opening chapter, but – as always with Bakhtin – the reframing of an idea in a different context, seen from a slightly different perspective, lends a new suggestiveness to his ideas. I shall therefore pick up on some of the points expounded in this chapter which seem the most thought provoking and controversial.

Following through the idea already expressed in Chapter 1, Bakhtin identifies the hero's 'self-consciousness' as the 'dominant' of Dostoevsky's novels (p. 50). 'The dominant' is a term invented by the Russian Formalist critic, Roman Jakobson, to describe that aspect of a work of art which is its controlling or 'dominant' characteristic.[22] According to Jakobson's theory, art advances and renews itself by reacting against the 'dominant' of earlier works. Thus in poetry, for example, Imagism may be seen as a reaction to Symbolism (p. 13). According to Bakhtin's argument here, the self-consciousness of the hero has become the feature of Dostoevsky's texts that most obviously distinguishes him from his predecessors such as Gogol. This self-consciousness is part of the total polyphonic and dialogic design of the Dostoevskian novel inasmuch as it is commensurate with the hero's independence. The problem of where such absolute independence of character leaves the author was not lost on Bakhtin either; and, in anticipation of the criticisms of his more pedantic readers, he is careful to defend himself against accusations of Barthesian extremism ('the author is dead') by arguing for a difference between 'creation' and 'invention': the author of the polyphonic novel cannot be said to 'invent' his or her characters because they are defined by the 'logic' of their own self-consciousness, but he or she does 'create' the work of art which allows those characters their being (pp. 64–65).[23] This is a somewhat desperately argued point which suggests that Bakhtin had, indeed, driven himself into a cul-de-sac by granting his characters this much autonomy. It is interesting to observe how much stronger his argument becomes when he moves on to a model in which the author–character relationship is described not in terms of independence but of dialogue. This, for me, is the most suggestive part of Bakhtin's meditation on the author–character relationship. In one especially lyrical passage he presents his case as follows:

> Thus the new artistic position of the author with regard to the hero in Dostoevsky's polyphonic novel is a *fully realized and thoroughly consistent dialogic position*, one that affirms the independence, internal freedom, unfinalizability, and indeterminacy of the hero. For the author, the hero is not 'he' and not 'I' but a fully valid 'thou', that is, another and autonomous 'I' ('thou art'). The hero is the subject of a deeply serious, *real* dialogic mode of address, not the subject of a rhetorically *performed* or *conventionally* literary one. As this dialogue – the 'great dialogue' of the novel as a whole – takes place not in the past, but right now, that is in the *real present* of the creative process (p. 63).

Two points are worth extracting from this passage: first, the idea that author and character are bound together in the polyphonic text in a

---

[22] See note 12 above.
[23] See Roland Barthes's famous essay, 'The Death of the Author', in *The Rustle of Language* (Oxford: Basil Blackwell, 1986), pp. 49–53.

reciprocal relationship of exchange (in which, for the author, the hero is always subject and never object of the address); and second, that the 'life' of this relationship depends upon the fact that it is being negotiated and renegotiated 'in the *present tense* of the creative process': that is to say, as the text is being written. This model of exchange and interaction seems, to me, to accord with Bakhtin's dialogic worldview far better than his image of autonomy, although it is clear that the latter was a necessary move in establishing the multiple centres of consciousness present in the polyphonic text.

One final aspect of the Dostoevskian hero worth commenting on in Bakhtin's analysis is his or her own 'unresolved' psychological state. The self-consciousness of Dostoevsky's characters does not bring them to a moment of sudden, epiphanistic insight since 'Dostoevsky always represents a person *on the threshold* of a final decision, at the moment of *crisis*, at an unfinalizable – and *unpredeterminable* turning point for his soul' (p. 61). In the provisional, interactive world of the polyphonic text everyone, and everything, is in a state not of being but of becoming. The implications of this will be discussed in the section on subjectivity in the next chapter.

Bakhtin's chapter on 'The Idea in Dostoevsky' anticipates his key philosophical point about 'the word', namely that, in the polyphonic text, neither words nor ideas exist independently but in dialogue with other words and consciousnesses: 'the idea is inter-individual and inter-subjective' (p. 88). Because of the rather vague notion of what Bakhtin means by 'idea', this is admittedly one of the occasions where the concept of dialogue seems to be stretched almost to the point of banality: characters, texts, and now the abstract concept of 'the idea' are subject to the same 'master' principle. When commenting on the so-called 'ideological monologism' of other authors, however, Bakhtin gives us more of a sense of how keenly political such differences between texts can be: the monologic structuring of a text wherein the author's views invade and dominate those of his or her characters is clearly associated, in Bakhtin's mind, with a totalitarian intolerance, against which Dostoevsky's polyphonic texts are liberatingly democratic. Towards the end of the chapter, Bakhtin uses extracts from Dostoevsky's texts to show how – through the dialogic exchange of many characters – there is no attempt to fix or privilege a particular position or viewpoint: his own 'ideology' does not emerge as the ruling voice (p. 85). While later Marxist critics like Althusser would undoubtedly question the possibility of ideological 'neutrality' in any text, Bakhtin does select some convincing passages from Dostoevsky to illustrate his point, including a piece of journalism entitled 'The Environment'. In this text, the narrator advances his ideas as a series of statements and rejoinders between himself and other voices (see the discussion on 'hidden polemic' later in this section), and Bakhtin concludes:

> Everywhere his thought makes its way through a labyrinth of voices, semi-voices, other people's words, other people's gestures. He never proves his own positions on the basis of other abstract positions, he does not think thoughts together according to some referential principle, but juxtaposes orientations and amid them constructs his own orientation (p. 95).

Bakhtin also makes the small, but revealing, point that Dostoevsky's writing is completely devoid of aphorism: that the polyphonic text is intrinsically opposed to 'thinking in separate rounded-off and self-sufficient thoughts which were purposefully meant to stand independent of their context' (p. 96).[24]

The long chapter in *Dostoevsky's Poetics* on 'Genre' introduces us to an aspect of Bakhtin's writing that we have not seen to date, namely, the literary-historical research exemplified most spectacularly by *Rabelais* (1965) and the essays in *The Dialogic Imagination*. Even in the relatively short space allocated to this task in *Dostoevsky's Poetics*, Bakhtin offers a stunning historical overview of all the literary-historical genres – from classical times to the present – which have, in his opinion, foreshadowed the polyphonic novel. The genres he focuses on in particular are the Socratic dialogue, the Menippean satire and what he refers to as the 'tradition of carnivalized literature', all of which are characterized by a rejection of 'stylistic unity':

> Characteristic of these genres are a multi-toned narration, the mixing of high and low, serious and comic; they make wide use of inserted genres – letters, found manuscripts, retold dialogues, parodies on the high genres, parodically reinterpreted citations; in some of them we observe a mixing of prosaic and poetic speech, living dialects and jargons (and in the Roman stage, direct bilingualism as well) are introduced, and various authorial masks make their appearance (p. 108).

The long section on *carnival* is an excellent introduction to this most popular of Bakhtinian theories, and – I would suggest – a better place to start than the almost burdensome scholarly account in *Rabelais*. This discussion includes some concise and typically suggestive accounts of the main properties of carnival (e.g., 'decrowning activity', eccentricity, laughter, parody, profanation and 'doubling').

Following this lengthy exposé of carnival and the literatures to which it has given rise, Bakhtin provides evidence of the tradition in Dostoevsky's own works. Negotiating the problem of to what extent Dostoevsky was *conscious* of working in such a tradition, Bakhtin is, however, careful to point out that the early carnivalesque literatures are inherited by modern writers as part of their *total* literary inheritance; that what Bakhtin did was reactivate an anarchic tendency that had been repressed and largely dormant between the seventeenth and the nineteenth centuries. He hastily concludes, however, that 'authentic polyphony' (p. 178) was very much Dostoevsky's own invention.

The final chapter of *Dostoevsky's Poetics*, 'Discourse in Dostoevsky', is very much the linguistic 'microchip' of Bakhtin's whole dialogic project. In this chapter Bakhtin explores, in depth, the workings of dialogic discourse. Although this has the appearance of linguistic analysis, Bakhtin is clear to establish, in his opening comments, that his object of study – 'language in its concrete living totality' (p. 181) is not at all the same as that of most

---

[24] This avoidance of aphorism may be contrasted with a writer like Jeanette Winterson (see Chapter 5) whose texts are littered with blunt, often humorous, aphoristic statements and declarations.

contemporary linguists who are concerned not with the study of language in its social context but with the operation of abstract systems. Bakhtin's analysis of 'dialogic speech' (p. 183) is, by their standards, a species of *metalinguistics*. This argument will be familiar to those who have already read the account of *Marxism and the Philosophy of Language* (see above) and, indeed, it is in this section of *Dostoevsky's Poetics* that we see the most obvious connections between the two texts.

Before we proceed with a summary of Bakhtin's analysis of dialogic discourse, however, it is first necessary that I clarify the connection between this detailed analysis of language use and Bakhtin's conception of the polyphonic novel as a whole. Probably the best way of understanding this is through the micro/macrocosmic relationship that I cited earlier to distinguish between the use of the terms 'dialogic' and 'polyphonic'. If polyphony is allowed to refer, in its most literal sense, to the coexistence of 'many voices' within a particular text, then 'dialogue' is concerned with the articulation of the relationship *between* those voices and, indeed, *within* the individual voice. This is because, as we shall see, Bakhtin's theory of dialogic activity is projected beyond what he refers to as the exchange of 'relatively entire utterances': it may also be a feature of the individual word. Bakhtin's own account of the micro/macrocosmic nature of the dialogic is best summed up in the following paragraph:

> Dialogic relationships are possible not only among whole (relatively whole) utterances; a dialogic approach is possible toward any signifying part of an utterance, even toward an individual word, if that word is perceived not as the impersonal word of language but as a sign of someone else's semantic position, as the representative of another person's utterance; that is, if we hear in it someone else's voice. Thus dialogic relationships can permeate inside the utterance, even inside the individual word, as long as two voices collide within it dialogically (microdialogue, of which we spoke earlier) (p. 184).

What Bakhtin is arguing here is that *all* units of speech, from the sentence down to the individual word, are dialogic if they exist in relation to 'someone else's voice' or word. Thus we may find, in a sample section of text, dialogic activity at a number of different levels: between two identified interlocutors (i.e., characters within the text), between the utterance and an unidentified *other* text/interlocutor, between each of the individual *words* and others existing either inside or outside the text. Bakhtin's classification of these different types of dialogic activity, as they appear in the novelistic text, has been usefully summarized by David Lodge in the table reproduced below, which is itself a simplification of the one presented by Bakhtin (see *Dostoevsky's Poetics*, p. 199):

I   *The direct speech of the author.* This means, of course, the author as encoded in the text, in an 'objective, reliable, narrative voice'.

II   *The represented speech of the characters.* This may be represented by direct speech ('dialogue' in the non-Bakhtinian sense): or by the convention of soliloquy or interior monologue: or in those elements of reported speech which belong to the language of the character rather than the narrator in free indirect style.

III   *Doubly-oriented or doubly-voiced speech.* This category was Bakhtin's most original and valuable contribution to stylistic analysis. It includes all speech which not only refers to something in the world but which also refers to another speech act by another addresser. It is divided into several sub-categories, of which the most important are stylisation, *skaz* [definition follows], parody and hidden polemic.[25]

'Monology', as represented by category I, refers to those texts in which (to quote Lodge) 'the authorial narrator does not merely impose his own interpretive frame on the table, but makes the characters speak the same language as himself' (p. 19). Bakhtin, as we have already seen, associates this type of authorial hegemony largely with prenovelistic discourse, although it is also a tendency in the classic-realist novel fronted by the so-called 'omniscient narrator'. Category II, meanwhile, refers to the ostensibly 'free speech' of the individual characters within a text, together with the existence of other 'nonauthorial' discourses (e.g., a cited political or religious way of thinking which is very clearly not the author's). According to Bakhtin's classification, however, such voices are not truly dialogic unless they can be seen to be completely free of narratorial control. Although there may be varying degrees of objectification in the represented speech of such characters, in many instances they are still *the object of the author's intention* and therefore another instance of 'single-voiced discourse' (p. 189). As we saw earlier, independence from authorial control is a prerequisite for characters (and their speech) in Bakhtin's blueprint of the polyphonic novel.

After dispensing, somewhat laboriously, with these two categories of 'single-voiced discourse characteristic of the monologic text', Bakhtin moves on to examine an exciting array of 'doubly voiced discourses'. In his own classification table, Bakhtin subdivides double-voiced discourse into three main types:

I   Unidirectional double-voiced discourse (represented chiefly by *stylization* and *skaz*).

II  Varidirectional double-voiced discourse (represented chiefly by *parody*).

III The active type (represented by variations of *dialogue, hidden dialogue* and *hidden internal polemic*). (This is a paraphrase of Bakhtin's own text.)

I will consider each of these categories in turn. According to Lodge's summary, 'Stylization occurs when the writer borrows another's discourse and uses it for his own purposes – with the same general intention as the original, but in the process "casting a slight shadow of objectification over it"' (p. 19). Such a discourse, although the product of strict authorial control, is nevertheless double voiced because 'in keeping with its task, [it] must be perceived as belonging to someone else' (p. 189). The author has, as it were, control over the purpose to which the voice is being put, but he or she has to respect its independence. *Skaz* is a Russian term used to describe narration which bears characteristics of *oral discourse* and was first coined by Boris Eikenbaum (see ref., ibid.). Bakhtin observes that *skaz*, according to this criterion, is a common and important type of novelistic discourse, but argues with Eikenbaum over its strictly 'oral characterization', preferring

[25]   See D. Lodge, 'Lawrence, Dostoevsky, Bakhtin', *Renaissance and Modern Studies*, **29**, 1985. Reproduced in D. Lodge, *After Bakhtin: Essays on Fiction and Criticism* (London and New York : Routledge, 1990), pp. 59–60.

the notion that '*skaz* is above all an orientation toward *someone else's speech*, and only then, as a consequence, toward oral speech' (p. 191). The subtlety of this point may be clarified by observing that in modernist literature (e.g., the writing of Virginia Woolf), narration which bears traces of a character's speech becomes common, although this is often a representation of their 'inner speech patterns' rather than of their oral communications.[26] What both stylization and *skaz* have in common, however, is that they are unidirectional: it is the prerogative of the author to 'make use of someone else's discourse in the direction of its own aspirations' (p. 193); that is to say, 'it does not collide with the other's thought, but rather follows in the same direction' (ibid.). (Lodge's own illustration of these types of speech in Lawrence's writings are discussed in Chapter 2.)

Parody, on the other hand, is a more fully dialogized form of discourse inasmuch as it 'introduces . . . a semiotic intention that is directly opposed to the original one' (p. 193). In what Bakhtin classifies 'varidirectional discourse', 'The second voice, once having made its home in the other's discourse, clashes hostilely with its primordial host and forces him to serve directly opposing aims. Discourse becomes an arena of battle between two voices' (ibid.). In parody, then, the author presents the stylizations of another's discourse in such a way that is opposite to the intention of the original, often with the purpose of ridicule. As will be seen in the readings which follow in Part Two of this book, texts which may be designated polyphonic in the macrocosmic sense (i.e., comprising many, 'independent' voices) invariably make extensive use of stylization, *skaz* and parody. The double-voiced discourse of the third type, however, *hidden dialogue* and *hidden polemic* is a rarer and, for Bakhtin, more precious commodity: one might go so far, indeed, as to cast 'hidden polemic' as the 'secret weapon' of the polyphonic text – the quintessential expression of dialogicality.

In contrast to stylization and parody, in which the discourse of the 'other' is *passive* in the hands of the author, in hidden polemic (and its attendant forms) it is *active*:

> This third variety, as we see, differs sharply from the preceding two varieties of the third type. This final variety might be called *active*, in contrast to the preceding *passive* varieties. And so it is: in stylization, in the narrated story and in parody the other person's discourse is a completely passive tool in the hands of the author wielding it. He takes, so to speak, someone else's meek

---

26   This type of narration is known by some narratologists as free indirect discourse (FID). It is, according to narratologist Shlomith Rimmon-Kenan, a type of discourse (typically associated with modernist 'stream-of-consciousness' writers like Virginia Woolf) which is 'grammatically and mimetically intermediate between indirect and direct discourse' (see S. Rimmon-Kenan, *Narrative Fiction: Contemporary Poetics* (London and New York: Routledge, 1983, p. 110). FID combines the third-person 'reporting' of the narrator with the direct discourse of the character being represented. The following passage from Virginia Woolf's *To the Lighthouse* is a classic example: 'For he [Charles Tansley] was not going to talk the sort of rot these people wanted him to talk. He was not going to be condescended to by these silly women. He had been reading in his room, and now he came down and it all seemed to him silly, superficial, flimsy . . . They did nothing but talk, talk, eat, eat, eat. It was the women's fault' (V. Woolf, *To the Lighthouse* (London: Dent, 1978), p. 99.

and defenseless discourse and installs his own interpretation in it, forcing it to serve his own new purposes. In hidden polemic and in dialogue [i.e., 'hidden dialogue'], on the contrary, the other's words actively influence the author's speech, forcing it to alter itself accordingly under their influence and initiative (p. 197).

Bakhtin's classification then draws a distinction between those types of active discourse which are visible or present in the text (i.e., they belong to named interlocutors or stated positions) such as 'a rejoinder to a dialogue' or 'any discourse with a sideward glance at someone else's word' (p. 199) and the 'hidden' varieties ('hidden dialogue' and 'hidden internal polemic') in which the interlocutor is not named in the text but whose presence may be inferred. One of the best ways to understand the latter is through the example of the overheard telephone conversation cited by Katerina Clark and Michael Holquist.[27] As I observed in the Introduction, one of the most intriguing things about a telephone dialogue is the fact that one only needs to hear one side of the conversation to divine the presence/status of the other party, and of the relationship between the two speakers. This, according to Bakhtin, is also the means by which we can divine the 'hidden dialogues' of the literary text:

> Imagine a dialogue of two persons in which the statements of the second speaker are omitted, but in such a way that the general sense is not at all violated. The second speaker is present invisibly, his words are not there, but deep traces left by these words have a determining influence on all the present and visible words of the first speaker. We sense that this is a conversation, although only one person is speaking, and it is a conversation of the most intense kind, for each present, uttered word responds and reacts with its every fiber to the invisible speaker, points to something outside itself, beyond its own limits, to the unspoken words of another person (*Dostoevsky's Poetics*, p. 197).

In 'hidden internal polemic' the presence of the 'invisible other' is revealed by a similar mechanism, although here the inferred discourse is posited as antagonistic or hostile:

> In a hidden polemic the author's discourse is directed toward its own referential object, as in any other discourse, but at the same time every statement about the object is constructed in such a way that, apart from its referential meaning, a polemical blow is struck at the other's discourse on the same theme, at the other's statement about the same object . . . The other's discourse is not itself reproduced, it is merely implied, but the entire structure of the speech would be completely different if there were not this reaction to another person's implied words . . . In hidden polemic . . . the other's words are treated antagonistically, and this antagonism, no less than the very topic being discussed, is what determines the author's discourse (p. 195).

Bakhtin's own illustrations of these instances of hidden dialogue and hidden polemic are taken from Dostoevsky's *Notes from the Underground*. The story of the 'Underground Man' is the story of a man haunted and hunted by a persecutory 'other': all his words are made 'under the influence of the other's anticipated [negative] reaction' (p. 228):

[27] Clark and Holquist, *Bakhtin*, pp. 207–208.

I am a sick man . . . I am a spiteful man. An unattractive man. I think that
my liver hurts. But actually, I don't know a damn thing about my illness. I am
not even sure what it is that hurts. I am not in treatment and never have been,
although I respect both medicine and doctors. Besides, I am superstitious in the
extreme; well, at least to the extent of respecting medicine. (I am sufficiently
educated not to be superstitous, but I am.) No, sir, I refuse to see a doctor
simply out of spite. Now, that is something that you probably will fail to
understand.[28]

While in the opening words of the text 'the internal polemic with the other is
'concealed'" (p. 228), Bakhtin shows how its presence may nevertheless be
inferred and how, by the middle of the paragraph, the 'polemic has broken
out into the open' as the narrator addresses himself to an anonymous 'you'
whose influence is felt both implicitly and explicitly for the remainder of
the text.

Needless to say, in terms of Bakhtin's overall thesis, Dostoevsky
emerges as the most revolutionary exponent of double-voiced discourse
to have yet put pen to paper (see p. 203). Referring back to our earlier
descriptive distinction, Bakhtin makes it clear that Dostoevsky's novels
are dialogic/polyphonic in both a micro- and a macrocosmic sense: they
are structured on a principle of freedom and independence of character
(represented in the text as 'many voices'), and they allow for maximal
exchange *between voices* through a complex and varied use of dialogized
discourse. In terms of the development of Bakhtin's own philosophy,
moreover, it was clearly his work with Dostoevsky that set up the
framework for his own revolutionary worldview in which every term
is, of necessity, defined in terms of a reciprocating 'other'.

# V

## *Rabelais and His World*

### M. M. Bakhtin, 1965

Bakhtin's study of Rabelais, which began life as the author's doctoral
thesis, is the home of what has become perhaps his most popular and
clichéd concept: *carnival*.[29] As I indicated in the section on *Dostoevsky's
Poetics*, the latter is perhaps a better place for the new reader to begin
familiarizing herself with the literary-historical origins of the phenomenon
since Bakhtin there compresses into twenty pages what his analysis of
Rabelais's carnivalesque inheritance takes a lengthy book to accomplish. A
similarly pragmatic move would be to focus on the Introduction to *Rabelais*: a
substantial sixty-page account of the origins of carnival, its transmission into
literature and the significance of related key concepts such as the 'grotesque
body'. Such an unashamedly exploitative approach to the text will explain,

28   F. Dostoevsky, *Notes from the Underground* (1864) (New York: Bantam, 1981), pp. 1–2.
29   The Rabelais book was not finally published until 1965, although Bakhtin had been
working on it since the 1930s. See M. Bakhtin, *Rabelais and His World*, trans. H. Iswolsky
(Bloomington, IN: Indiana University Press, 1984). Page references to this volume will be
give after quotations in the text.

however, *why* concepts like the carnivalesque have become such empty signifiers in contemporary criticism: removed from their original scholarly critical context, Bakhtin's keywords become convenient catch-alls for all manner of textual practice (see Chapter 2 for evidence of this). And while the purpose of this book is partly to legitimate such appropriation, it is equally true that we should be aware that in 'gutting' Bakhtin's texts in this way we are inevitably distorting and diluting what he meant by his favoured terms (see the beginning of this chapter for more discussion of this problem).

The proper context of Bakhtin's exploration of the carnivalesque is Rabelais: a writer whom he holds up as much undervalued and misunderstood in the contemporary West. For Bakhtin, Rabelais is the 'father' of popular culture: a culture which is, itself, rooted in the 'folk humour' of the Middle Ages.

Bakhtin opens his investigations by outlining three forms of 'folk humour' that circulated widely in the medieval world. These are:

I   *Ritual Spectacles*: carnival pageants, comic shows of the marketplace.
II  *Comic Verbal Compositions*: parodies both oral and written, in Latin and the vernacular.
III *Various genres of billingsgate* ['Billingsgate' means 'abuse and violate invective': the term has its etymological origins in the fishwomen of Billingsgate Market, London]: curses, oaths, popular blazons (p. 5).

In understanding Bakhtin's emphasis on the radical and subversive nature of this 'folk humour' it is important to grasp that his concept of the carnivalesque (as present *in literature*) has its origins in *actual* carnival (see category I above). The medieval carnival was, he claims, something that existed at the 'borderline of art and life' (p. 7) and which represented the 'second life' of the common people. Its special *political* significance was the way it temporarily suspended and upturned the orthodox hierarchy and allowed, quite literally, the people their 'voice(s)':

> The suspension of all hierarchical precedence during carnival time was of particular significance. Rank was especially evident during official feasts . . . It was a consecration of inequality. On the contrary, all were considered equal during carnival. Here, in the town square, a special form of free and familiar contract reigned among people who were usually divided by the barriers of caste, property, profession, and age . . . People were, so to speak, reborn for new, purely human relations. These truly human relations were not only a fruit of imagination or abstract thought; they were experienced. The utopian ideal and the realistic merged in the carnival experience, unique of its kind.
>
> This temporary suspension, both real and ideal, of hierarchical rank created during carnival time a special type of communication impossible in everyday life. This led to the creation of special kinds of marketplace speech and gesture, frank and free, permitting no distance between those who came into contact with each other and liberating from norms of etiquette and decency imposed at other times. A special carnivalesque, marketplace style of expression was formed which we find abundantly represented in Rabelais's novel [*Gargantua and Pantagruel*] (p. 10).

On this last point, a clear connection may be drawn, too, between the type of dialogic interaction permitted by the unique social context of the carnival and the polyphonic and heteroglossic interanimation of voices Bakhtin describes in his favoured nineteenth-century novelists like Dostoevsky and Dickens (see the discussion in the section on *The Dialogic Imagination* below). Indeed, as we saw in our review of *Dostoevsky's Poetics*, carnivalesque literature from the Middle Ages onwards is one of the key originating sites of the modern novel: the novel has its deepest tap-root in a popular, oral (i.e., specifically nonliterary) tradition.

In the Introduction, Bakhtin also presents us with the specificity of 'carnival laughter', which is then explored in more detail, and in relation to Rabelais, in Chapter 1. What is significant in the following description is the emphasis placed on the *mixed* 'spirit' of laughter which is simultaneously 'gay' and 'triumphant', 'mocking and deriding'. It is also a *dialogic laugher* in that it mocks the begetter as well as the object of ridicule:

> Let us say a few initial words about the complex nature of carnival laughter. It is, first of all, a festive laughter, therefore it is not an individual reaction to some isolated 'comic' event. Carnival laughter is the laughter of all the people. Second, it is universal in scope; it is directed at all and everyone, including the carnival's participants. The entire world is seen in its droll aspect, in its gay relativity. Third, this laughter is ambivalent: it is gay, triumphant, and at the same time, mocking, deriding. It asserts and denies, it buries and revives. Such is the laughter of carnival (p. 12).

Bakhtin further points out the difference between this wholesome, 'regenerative' laughter and the cynical humour of later, literary parody. It is a difference extended to the type of 'comic verbal compositions' (see the categories reproduced above) produced during the medieval period itself, which were also of a qualitatively different type to those that followed in that they retained an element of the joyous and the festive. The third expression of folk humour, what Bakhtin dubs 'billingsgate', is a special form of abusive banter predicated upon familiarity, intimacy and an (implicit) anti-authoritarianism.

In the second part of the Introduction, Bakhtin moves on to a discussion of the comic imagery associated with the culture of the carnival and, in particular, the *grotesque body*. This is another area of Bakhtin's work that has been widely appropriated and contested by critics, most notably in its gendered implications. In his frequently cited article on 'Bakhtin and the Challenge of Feminist Criticism', Wayne Booth threw down a gauntlet to feminists eager to work with Bakhtin by pointing out the terrible misogyny of the *Rabelais* book.[30] Feminists have, themselves, subsequently objected to the patronizing way in which this 'discovery' was made for them, and argued, sensibly, that it is quite possible to utilize aspects of Bakhtin's work on carnival and the body without condoning the misogyny implicit in some parts of the discussion.[31] Robert Stam also points out that we should observe a distinction between the misogyny of Rabelais as *reported*

---

[30]   W. Booth, 'Freedom and Interpretation: Bakhtin and the Challenge of Feminist Criticism', *Critical Inquiry*, 9, 1, 1982, pp. 45–76.

[31]   See discussion in Chapter 2 which refers to several feminist critics who have both worked with and problematized the concept of carnival.

by Bakhtin and the lacunae in his own conceptualization of the body.[32]

Bakhtin's definition of the grotesque body as it is represented by Rabelais emphasizes its 'positive, assertive nature' (p. 19), its universality and communality (it is not 'private' property, ibid.) and its anti-classicism (where it is, of course, opposed to the humanist bodily ideal of the Renaissance). Its political function is one of *degradation*: though, once again, Bakhtin has to cleanse the term of its perjorative connotations. The degradation performed by the grotesque body is in the spirit of carnival; it is focused on the liberation of the repressed, the overthrowing of existing hierarchies:

> The people's laughter which characterized all the forms of grotesque realism from immemorial times was linked with the bodily lower stratum. Laughter degrades and materializes . . . Degradation here means coming down to earth as an element that swallows up and gives birth at the same time. To degrade is to bury, to sow, and to kill simultaneously, in order to bring forth something more and better (pp. 20–21).

For Robert Stam (cited above in connection with the misogyny debate), Bakhtin's 'grotesque body' is inherently androgynous and bisexual: 'Bakhtin lauds the androgynous body of carnival representation . . . Bakhtin's account, in those terms, has certain affinities with Cixous's positing of the ideal of bisexuality' (p. 163). While most feminist readers will be suspicious of this easy conflation of androgyny and bisexuality, Stam does proceed to make some interesting and convincing observations on the 'dialogic construction' of Bakhtin's 'body': in particular, the fact that its sexual and reproductive functions exist in relation to its other material functions (e.g., eating, drinking, excretion) and that this inevitably diffuses the emphasis on sexuality and gender *per se*:

> Rather than privilege sexual difference *between* bodies, with the phallus as the ultimate signifier, Bakhtin discerns difference *within* the body. For Bakhtin, all bodies are self-differentiating; every body is a constantly expanding and contracting universe . . . There is no privileging of the male term over the female, no positing of lack, no dynamism contrasted with atrophy.
>
> Bakhtin's view of the body is not phallocentric or even cephallocentric. He throws down, in this sense, the tyranny of the head and the phallus. Bakhtin privileges not only the genitals, but also the bowels, the swallowing, devouring body, the 'gaping mouth' and the anus, corporeal zones quite neutral from the standpoint of sexual difference, zones where the male–female binary opposition becomes quite simply non-pertinent (p. 162).

In the Introduction to *Rabelais*, Bakhtin follows his conceptual introduction of 'the body' with another periscoped literary history which traces its legacy in the 'Romantic grotesque' through to twentieth-century Modernism. While such a sketch will, doubtless, provide an adequate introduction for many readers, in terms of Bakhtin's thesis is, of course, mere *context* for the discussion of Rabelais that follows. For the purposes of my own overview, I have chosen to comment only on those aspects of the study which are of special significance to the evolution of Bakhtin's dialogic theory.

Considering how much heated debate there has been in recent years over the so-called 'disputed texts' (see discussion at the beginning of this chapter), it is

---

[32] See Stam, *Subversive Pleasures*, pp. 162–64. Further page references are given after quotations in the text.

surprising that no one has pointed out the obvious fact that Bakhtin sounds *least* like 'Bakhtin' in *Rabelais and His World*. Although, as we have already seen, it utilizes concepts which may be conceived in terms of dialogicality, *Rabelais* invokes none of the familiar vocabulary of 'polyphony', 'unfinalizability', 'novelness' or 'heteroglossia'. Even in the chapters most centrally concerned with language (Chapter 2 on the 'Language of the Market Place' and Chapter 6 on 'The Material Bodily Lower Stratum'), Bakhtin's discussion only very tangentially implies the dialogic and relational models of discourse and utterance used so extensively (indeed, so repetitively!) elsewhere. Of course, the reader already familiar with the dialogic model can, and will, *infer* parallels (see Robert Stam's analysis of Bakhtin's 'grotesque body' cited above, for example) – but they are nowhere obvious. *Rabelais* is an exception among Bakhtin texts in that its focus is *visual* rather than aural (the chapters are structured around different sets of imagery), and the author's method is descriptive rather than analytic. Although *Rabelais* is a formidable work of scholarship (like the essays in *The Dialogic Imagination*, it demonstrates Bakhtin's breath-taking grasp of the history of Western European literature), it does not speculate and polemicize in the same way as the other central texts, and its philosophy is cultural-historical rather than linguistic. Indeed, in his concluding section Bakhtin only expends six pages on the uniqueness of Rabelais's language (compared to a whole book on Dostoevsky), and focuses on just two key characteristics: its saturation in an oral tradition, and what he refers to as the 'dual tone' of popular speech. It is this last feature that I want to posit as the most significant contribution to dialogic thought offered by the *Rabelais* book: a particular species of 'double-voicedness' that Bakhtin does not deal with elsewhere.

In his celebration of the 'dual tone' of Rabelais's representation of popular speech, Bakhtin is referring to the interactive expression of *praise* and *abuse* inherent in the language of Rabelais's characters. He first explores this feature in his discussion of the litany Panurge addresses to Friar John on the question of marriage. Central to the dialogue between the two men is the repeated use of the word *couillon* ('cock') (it is, in fact, repeated 303 times), the connotations around which are essentially ambiguous (p. 418) and oscillate between 'praise' and 'abuse'. Bakhtin sees the passage as representative of a basic peculiarity of Rabelais's language: a language which 'always combines . . . the praise-abuse image and is always addressed to the dual-bodied world of becoming' (p. 420). Such ambivalence of expression is, according to Bakhtin, a feature of colloquial speech (the 'language of the marketplace') where it takes the form of a coded defiance of official discourse. It is also a powerful sign of familiarity and intimacy between the interlocutors:

> This style is characterized by the absence of neutral words and expressions. It is colloquial speech, always addressed to somebody or talking for him, or about him. For this other party there are no neutral epithets and forms; there are either polite, laudatory, flattering, cordial words, or contemptuous, debasing, abusive ones . . . The more official the speech, the more are these tones differentiated, for the speech rejects the established social hierarchy . . . But the more unofficial and familiar the speech, the more often and

substantially are those tones combined, the less distinct is the line dividing praise and abuse . . . Whenever conditions of absolute extra-official and full human relations are established, words tend to this ambivalent fullness. It is as if the ancient marketplace comes to life in closed chamber conversation. Intimacy begins to sound like the familiarity of bygone days, which breaks down all barriers between men (p. 421).

Although Bakhtin does not use the vocabulary of dialogism in this context, it is clear that we are dealing with a typically dialogic formation. The (manifestly patriarchal) praise-abuse system is predicated upon *actual* dialogue (it occurs as a dialogic exchange between two or more interlocutors) and, on a theoretical level, the two terms exist *only* in reciprocal relation to one another. What is especially striking about this instance of double-voiced language, however, is its political situatedness: it is the dialogue of 'the people' against authority:

Thanks to the duality of tone, the laughing people, who were not in the least concerned with the stabilization of the existing order and of the prevailing picture of the world (the official truth), could grasp the world of becoming as a whole. They could thus conceive the gay relativity of the limited class theories and the constant unfinished character of the world – the constant combination of falsehood and truth, of darkness and light, of anger and gentleness, of life and death.

In the official philosophy of the ruling classes such a dual tone of speech is, generally speaking, impossible: hard, well-established lines are drawn between all the phenomena and these phenomena are torn away from the contradictory world of becoming, of the whole. A monotone character of thought and style almost always prevails in the official spheres of art and ideology (pp. 432–33).

The power relation expressed in this 'dual tone' language does not exist *internally*, between the speakers using it: it is present rather in the relationship between the interlocutors and an (absent) ruling group. And while in Bakhtin's formulation this 'popular rebellion' is blantantly patriarchal (a game for 'the boys' only), the linguistic conspiracy of the oppressed group can be used, in other circumstances, to explain the specificity of female dialogue. I will return to this factor in section III on 'gender' in Chapter 2.

The *Rabelais* book, then, does not employ the same vocabulary of dialogism that we find in *Dostoevsky's Poetics* and the essays of *The Dialogic Imagination*. Yet there is no doubt that Bakhtin's 'carnival' is an inherently dialogized concept: both actual carnivals and the languages and literatures associated with them are manifestly polyphonic and heteroglossic, sites upon which all manner of voices and languages break free from hierarchical/authorial control. The text's focus on the 'language of the marketplace' also lends an important new political dimension to our conceptualization of the dialogic, reminding us that the social context in which a voice is heard is never politically neutral, and that all utterances are inscribed by a power dynamic. The voices of carnival are exceptional in that they are addressed both *explicitly* to their allies (the people of the marketplace) and *implicity* to the absent authorities. The ribald and abusive language thus signifies intimacy in one direction, and ridicule in another.

Carnival uses its double-voiced language simultaneously to honour and deride.

# VI

## *The Dialogic Imagination*

*M. M. Bakhtin, 1934–41*

The four essays collected together under the title of *The Dialogic Imagination* provide a major stylistic and historical overview of the European novel. Now it is not a single author (Dostoevsky or Rabelais) but the novel itself which becomes 'the hero' of Bakhtin's text.[33] From the point of view of Bakhtin's evolving dialogic theory, the essays which are of most interest are the much anthologized 'Discourse in the Novel', and 'Forms of Time and Chronotope in the Novel'. I shall therefore spend the largest part of this section discussing these, though it is necessary to pay some tribute to Bakhtin's impressive literary-historical scholarship with a few words on 'Epic and Novel' and 'From the Prehistory of Novelistic Discourse'.

The main thesis of 'Epic and Novel' is an attempt to distinguish the novel from other literary modes and genres (for example, poetry and epic). It is, in the first instance, a *historic* distinction: while all other literary genres are accounted fixed and dead, the novel is plastic and evolving. It is a contemporary form in the process of definition. And Bakhtin makes it clear that it was a particular conjunction of historical factors that caused the novel to emerge when it did, even though, as we shall see in the next essay, its prototype may be traced back to medieval and ancient literature. In its mature form, however, the novel must be seen as the product of the modern European nation state: the interlingual 'trade' between countries that was the consequence of the Renaissance.

After briefly accounting for the novel's origins, Bakhtin proceeds to detail the key differences between it and the epic. Quintessential to the latter is what he describes as a valorization of 'the absolute past' which is conceived in terms of 'national beginnings and peak times' (p. 15). The novel, by contrast, is the genre of the historic present. Another crucial difference obviously resides in the epic's use of official and elevated language, which is to be compared with the mixed social registers ('heteroglossia') of the novel. And where the primary 'theme' of the epic is 'tradition' itself, the novel is the first genre to detail the ongoing processes of everyday life, a criterion linked to yet another difference: the epic's emphasis on closure and completeness, which may be fundamentally contrasted with the 'unfinalizability' of the novel. Where, too, the epic is a genre of 'high moral seriousness', the novel (as we shall see in the discussion of the next essay) is the genre of *laughter*; and where the epic is profoundly monologic, the representation of a single, authoritative voice, the novel is inherently dialogic. (Bakhtin introduces this reference to the dialogic with a section on the Socratic dialogue which repeats, in abbreviated form, what is written in *Dostoevsky's Poetics*.)

33   M. Bakhtin, *The Dialogic Imagination: Four Essays by M. M. Bakhtin*, ed. M. Holquist and trans. C. Emerson and M. Holquist (Austin, TX : University of Texas Press, 1981).

Two other factors, that Bakhtin expounds in this essay which are worth noting are the ways in which the novel *involves its readership* in a way that was prohibited by the various distancing devices of the epic, and also the differential representation of the individual character. *Vis-à-vis* the former, Bakhtin comments on the specific danger inherent in 'the novelistic zone of contact' (p. 32) inasmuch as 'we might substitute for our own life an obsessive reading of novels' (!) (ibid.). Although the concept of dialogue is not directly invoked here, it is clear that this is an interesting sociological expression of the dialogic relationship between text and reader. Writing on the novel's representation of character, Bakhtin compares the 'unfinalized' nature of the novel's form and, in particular, its 'zone of contact with the inconclusive present' (p. 37) with the 'provisional' nature of the novel hero who is generally 'human' and 'inadequate', and thus very different from the 'fully finished and completed being' of the epic (p. 34).[34]

'From the Prehistory of Novelistic Discourse' opens by restating and reworking many of the ideas already familiar to us from *Problems of Dostoevsky's Poetics* – in particular, the dialogic (and often ironic/parodic) relation of the author to the language of his or her characters. In this instance, Bakhtin uses extracts from Pushkin to illustrate the difference between poetic and novelistic discourse (p. 44 ff.). As in *Dostoevsky's Poetics* Bakhtin also feels compelled to find an image of an author whose dialogic relation to the heterogeneous voices/characters in the texts is in danger of rendering him or her invisible. In this instance, he presents the author as a sort of architect: 'The author (as creator of the novelistic whole) cannot be found at any one of the novel's language levels: he is to be found at the center of organization where all levels intersect' (p. 49).

Once he has established the principle distinguishing features of novelistic discourse – the 'objectification' of language/utterance, the multiplicity of styles, registers and voices, and the author's dialogic relation to them – Bakhtin proceeds to demonstrate how the characteristics were foreshadowed in the novel's prehistory:

> Novelistic discourse has a lengthy pre-history, going back centuries, even thousands of years. It was formed and matured in the genres of familiar speech found in conversational folk language (genres that are as yet little studied) and also certain folkloric and low literary genres. During its germination and early development, the novelistic word represented a primordial struggle between tribes, peoples, cultures and languages – it is still full of echoes of this ancient struggle (p. 50).

What is especially interesting in this particular sketch is Bakhtin's use of images of conflict and struggle which vie with the more conciliatory representations of dialogic activity that we find in his writings and which, by and large, have been the more widely promulgated by his followers.[35]

---

[34] This repeats the point made about the novelistic hero that Bakhtin makes in *Dostoevesky's Poetics*: 'For in fact Dostoevesky always represents a person *on the threshold* of a final decision, at a moment of *crisis*, at an unfinalizable – and *unpredeterminable* – turning point for his soul' (p. 61).

[35] The most significant exception to the 'conciliatory' school of dialogics is Dale Bauer in *Feminist Dialogics: A Theory of Failed Community* (Albany, NY: State University of New York Press, 1989). This work will be discussed in detail in Chapter 2.

Bakhtin begins his analysis of the prehistory of the novel with a focus on *parody* which is, as we saw in the section on *Dostoevsky's Poetics*, one of the key types of double-voiced discourse to be found in the modern novel (see above). Bakhtin's argument here is that, since these earliest times, every genre of literary (and, indeed, nonliterary discourse) has had its own 'parodying and travestying double', such as the Roman satyr play which, in the Roman theatre, followed upon and mocked the preceding tragic trilogy (see p. 55). Bakhtin also emphasizes both the *polyglossic* and *heteroglossic* nature of ancient literatures. Polyglossia is the term used to describe the linguistic and cultural mixing of national languages: for example, the complex interaction of Greek, Latin and adjacent oriental languages. Heteroglossia, on the other hand, refers to the 'internal differentiation' and 'stratification' of different registers *within* a language: in particular, the struggle between official (ideologically dominant) and nonofficial registers. As we will see in our later discussion of the essay on 'Discourse and the Novel', heteroglossia becomes one of the key criteria for Bakhtin's analysis of the struggle between voices of different *social classes* in authors such as Charles Dickens.

In the final section of this essay, Bakhtin moves from the Ancient World to the Middle Ages, the historical epoch upon which a great deal of his dialogic hypothesizing is focused. He sees, indeed, a direct line of development from a Roman to European medieval literature – added to which the Middle Ages is characterized as an irreverent, anti-authoritarian period of history (see p. 72). In his analysis of medieval literature, Bakhtin's primary stylistic focus is again *parody*, especially in relation to its irreverent dethroning of religious discourses. From the Middle Ages, Bakhtin's 'prehistory of the novel' proceeds swiftly to the Renaissance and the origins of the modern novel in the work of Rabelais and Cervantes (p. 80). At this point we witness, in Bakhtin's writing, a return to the hyperbole that characterizes *Dostoevsky's Poetics*. The hero of the text this time is 'the spirit of the age' through which 'the parodic-travestying word' broke through all remaining boundaries. The Renaissance is presented as the metamorphic moment at which the long history of novelistic discourse finally yielded up its ultimate expression: the modern novel.

From this brief overview of the two essays of literary history, I move on now to a discussion of 'Discourse in the Novel' which has become Bakhtin's best-known piece of writing. Since much of this text is a reiteration of the principles of dialogue and polyphony contained in *Doestoevsky's Poetics*, I shall avoid dwelling on those theoretical criteria that have already been explicated and concentrate, instead, on what new or supplementary items enter Bakhtin's vocabulary at this point, together with those – like *heteroglossia* – which are substantially developed.

Heteroglossia – meaning most simply a 'social diversity of speech types' (p. 263) is, according to Bakhtin, the most distinctive feature of the novel as a genre:

> The novel can be defined as a diversity of social speech types (sometimes even diversity of languages) and a diversity of individual voices, artistically organized. The internal stratification of any single national language into social dialects, characteristic group behaviour, professional jargons, generic languages,

languages of generations and age groups, tendentious languages, languages of authorities, of various circles and passing fashions, languages that serve specific sociopolitical purposes of the day, even of the hour (each day has its own slogan, its own vocabulary, its own emphases) – this internal stratification present in any language at any given moment of its historical existence is the indispensable prerequisite for the novel as a genre. The novel orchestrates all its themes, the totality of the world of objects and ideas depicted and expressed in it, by means of the social diversity of speech types and by the different individual voices that flourish under such conditions. Authorial speech, the speeches of narrators, inserted genres, the speech of characters are merely those fundamental compositional unities with whose help heteroglossia can enter the novel; each of them permits a multiplicity of social voices and a wide variety of their links and interrelationships (always more or less dialogized) (pp. 262–63).

Heteroglossia, from the perspective Bakhtin is adopting here, is, indeed, *the* distinguishing feature of the novel. While in *Dostoevsky's Poetics* the originality of novelistic discourse is located rather in the *articulation* of different centres of consciousness (the independence and freedom of the characters), in this essay Bakhtin sees such formal innovation as the mere *vehicle* for the realization of the novel's a priori feature: a profound intermixture of linguistic social registers. By failing to observe this factor, moreover, traditional stylistic analyses of the novel have failed to recognize its generic uniqueness, and have concentrated analysis on its language in a strictly *poetic* sense (the study of its imagery, its 'force', 'clarity', etc.) without acknowledging at all the multiplicity of voices and linguistic 'dialects' that make up the whole (p. 263). It should be observed that Bakhtin's description of heteroglossia in the preceding quotation is very similar to his account of the operation of 'speech genres' in his late essay on that subject (see below). We will be returning to Bakhtin's practical demonstration of heteroglossia in the novel later in the discussion. From this damning opening account of the limitations of traditional stylistic analysis in understanding the novel, Bakhtin proceeds to a critique of modern linguistics and its failure to recognize the inherently social ('ideological') and dialogic nature of *all* language. His argument here repeats in briefer, though even more confident terms, the principles first expounded in *Marxism and the Philosophy of Language*. The blindness of 'linguistics, stylistics, and the philosophy of language' has been to search for a false *unity* in their object of study: hence, 'real ideologically saturated "language consciousness"' has remained outside 'their field of vision' (p. 274).

In the subsection 'Discourse in Poetry and Discourse in the Novel', Bakhtin elucidates what he means by the 'inner-dialogicality of language' with a series of pronouncements that echo the classification of 'double-voiced discourse' found in *Dostoevsky's Poetics*. Although the discussion in the present essay does not substantially advance the views put forward in *Dostoevsky's Poetics*, it is interesting to register the change in Bakhtin's own vocabulary in writing on the subject. With 'dialogicality' replacing 'Dostoevsky' as the *object* of study, Bakhtin's assertions become at once more subtle *and* more extravagant – perhaps because his own words are, here, addressed to an (adversarial?) community of linguists rather than the fellow literary critics who form the collective 'we' of *Dostoevsky's Poetics*. Without a previous reading of the earlier text it is my experience that students find the more abstract, less well contextualized statements of this essay less accessible than the easy-flowing discussion in *Dostoevsky's Poetics*, but as a complementary text, the essay provides some wonderfully suggestive and, indeed, emotive, passages on the dialogicality of the 'living' word:

> The word in living conversation is directly, blatantly, oriented toward a future answer-word: it provokes an answer, anticipates it and structures itself in the answer's direction. Forming itself in an atmosphere of the already spoken, the word is at the same time determined by that which has yet not been said but which is needed and in fact anticipated by the answering word. Such is the situation in any living dialogue (pp. 279–80).

However, the attempt to distinguish between poetic and novelistic discourse is, in my opinion, one of Bakhtin's red-herrings. As I observed while working on my Bakhtinian analysis of John Clare's poetry in the 1980s, few of the literary critics then turning to Bakhtin as a theoretical model were constrained by his vilification of poetry as 'inherently monologic', finding as many examples of dialogicality in Wordsworth or Walter Stevens as in Dickens.[36] While it is clearly true that during the nineteenth and twentieth centuries the 'novelization' of poetry accounted for a major break with its earlier epic and lyric modes, it is equally questionable whether *any* literary text can be fully (or even predominantly) monologic. Hence it is not surprising that in this essay Bakhtin is constantly qualifying his comparison between novel and poetry with phrases like: 'In genres that are poetic *in the narrow sense*' (my italics). It would seem, indeed, that his poetic discourse is no more than a hypothetical (and ultimately false) polarity against which to pit the dialogicality of the novel. And behind the awkwardness of this distinction lies the larger problem of the tension between historic/generic specificity and conceptual generalization in Bakhtin's work generally. Throughout his writings we find him making the grandest of claims for the dialogicality of *all* utterance, at the same time as arguing for its absence from a particular literary form.

One of the sections of this essay that students find most useful is Bakhtin's *demonstration* of heteroglossia (see the earlier discussion for a definition of this) in comic fiction. In his discussion he focuses on four principle means by which heteroglossia is incorporated and organized in the novel: stylization, the direct speech of characters, a third-person representation of the character's inner speech and the incorporation into the text of other literary genres (e.g., songs, poetry, fairy-tales). Especially illuminating is the reading of the various stylizations and parodic stylizations which abound in Dickens's *Little Dorrit* (1855–57), of which Bakhtin writes:

36   L. Pearce, 'John Clare and Mikhail Bakhtin: The Dialogic Principle – Readings from John Clare's Manuscripts 1832–1845', unpublished Ph.D. thesis, University of Birmingham, 1987. See also D. Bialostosky's book on Wordsworth from this period, *Making Tales: The Poetics of Wordsworth's Narrative Experiments* (London: University of Chicago Press, 1984) and G. L. Burns in *Wallace Stevens: The Poetics of Modernism*, ed. A. Gelpi (Cambridge: Cambridge University Press, 1986). The applicability of dialogic theory for genres other than the novel will be discussed in detail in Chapter 2.

His entire text is, in fact, everywhere dotted with quotation marks that serve to separate out little islands of scattered direct speech and purely authorial speech, washed by heteroglot waves from all sides. But it would have been impossible actually to insert such marks since, as we have seen, one and the same word often figures both as the speech of the author and as the speech of another – and at the same time (pp. 307–308).

This conflation of two voices or social dialects in one utterance Bakhtin refers to as a *hybrid construction* typical of the comic novel. Thus, in a single sentence of Dickens's text we might find the language of the author combined with a clause parodying the language of ceremonial speeches (see pp. 303–306 for a discussion of this). Such analysis is, of course, based on the classification of double-voiced discourse first worked out in *Dostoevsky's Poetics*, though the emphasis here on different social-class registers (the anarchic juxtaposition of the languages of official discourse with that of the common people) gives Bakhtin's argument a slightly new emphasis.

In the subsection of the essay on the role of the 'speaking person' in the novel, Bakhtin focuses on the role of language in the 'ideological becoming' of subjects (p. 341) in a way that anticipates Louis Althusser's theory of interpellation.[37] He writes: 'The ideological becoming of the human being, in this view, is the process of selectively assimilating the words of others' (p. 341). Allowing that all language is ideological (a point frequently repeated in this essay), Bakhtin writes suggestively about the struggle of 'alien voices' within each individual and, in particular, the role of what he describes as the *internally persuasive word* in developing and redirecting our consciousness:

The importance of struggling with another's discourse, its influence in the history of the individual's coming to ideological consciousness, is enormous. One's own discourse, and one's own voice, although born of another or dynamically stimulated by another, will sooner or later begin to liberate themselves from the authority of another's discourse. This process is made more complex by the fact that a variety of alien voices enter into the struggle for influence within an individual's consciousness (just as they struggle with one another in surrounding social reality) (p. 348).

What distinguishes Bakhtin's theory from Althusser's, however, is the degree of freedom and resistance he allows his subjects: although they, like Althusser's are subjected to a battery of competing ideological discourses, they are also in a perpetual process of renegotiating their relation to those discourses. This is achieved through a process of objectification that is often heard in the subject's voice as a stylization or parody of the authoritative word. This struggle for the objectification of another's word is, according to Bakhtin, quintessential to the drama of the novel, and he cites the fiction of Pushkin and Dostoevsky as exemplary of this sort of conflict.

Characteristic of this part of the essay is, indeed, Bakhtin's perpetual slide between the language of everyday speech and the language of the novel;

[37] Interpellation: the term invoked by Louis Althusser to describe the way in which individual subjects are 'called up', 'hailed' or 'recruited' by the ideologies circulating in their society. See note 11 above for reference.

between real people and fictional characters – in acknowledgement of which he draws a subtle distinction between the *transmission* of another's word in real-life conversation and 'extra-artistic discourse', and the representation of another's word in the literary text. What distinguishes the literary 'word' is its *conscious and intentional* hybridization: the 'mixture of two social languages within the limits of a single utterance' (p. 385). Such 'hybridization' occurs 'organically' and 'unconsciously' in all language, but in the literary text it is, itself, made the 'object' of representation. Implicit in Bakhtin's conceptualization of the speaking subject in the novel, then, is his or her closeness to the speaking subject in the 'real world' – both historical subject and literary character are animated and defined by their inscription in the languages of others: 'Discourse in the novel is structured on an uninterrupted mutual interaction with the discourse of life' (p. 383). The novel, by extension, may be seen as a graphic dramatization of the process through which the languages of the different speaking subjects infect one another to the extent that this becomes the chief preoccupation of the novel:

> The plot itself is subordinated to the task of co-ordinating and exposing languages to each other . . . What is realized in the novel is the process of coming to know one's own language as it is perceived by someone else's language, coming to know one's own belief system in someone else's system (p. 365).

Bakhtin concludes the essay on 'Discourse in the Novel' with another potted literary history, this time comparing what he has identified as the two different stylistic lines of development in the European novel. The first line, which he traces back to the 'Sophistic Novel' and classic Chivalric Romance 'leaves heteroglossia' outside itself (p. 374) to the extent that 'non literary' languages are allowed into the text only once they have been abstracted and stylized. The second line – represented by Rabelais, Cervantes and the development of the Baroque novel – 'parodically reverses' (p. 386) the avoiding strategies of the first line by rooting its texts in the heteroglossia of the marketplace. Bakhtin's discussion here obviously grows out of his earlier historical overviews in 'Epic and Novel' and 'From the Prehistory of Novelistic Discourse', but the categorization into two distinct blood lines is new, as is his reading of them specifically in terms of heteroglossia.

Bakhtin concludes his essay with some 'methodological observations' on novelistic analysis, the most ironic of which concerns the competence of the critic! Indeed, after having followed Bakhtin through his exhaustive archaeology of the novel's hybrid origins, and having attended to his passionate defence of its heteroglossic 'nature', one should, perhaps, be amused to find that the wonders of novelistic discourse still ultimately depend upon a sensitive reader in order to be rendered visible. *Identifying the different social registers present in a text is no easy task* (especially when dealing with a text from an earlier century or different culture), and it is interesting to see how, in tacit acknowledgement of this, Bakhtin resorts to words like 'feel' to describe the reader's task (e.g., 'This process has to do with the "feel" we have for distancing . . .' p. 419). This must inevitably alert us to the dialogic relationship that is least well explored in Bakhtin's work on the novel: that between text and reader. As with his work on Dostoevsky, Bakhtin has once again underplayed his own role in the analytic process, ascribing innovations to the texts (polyphony, heteroglossia) that are partly the innovations of his own methodology, scholarship and readerly competence. This begs the question of whether the heteroglossic nuances Bakhtin finds in Dickens's texts *are* the common property of those texts and their readers, or whether they are visible to only a very specialized reader with particular literary competence. So attuned to the significance of dialogue in almost every aspect of life and literature, Bakhtin's modesty seems to have prevented him from seeing the dynamics of his own relationship to his object of study.

In the final part of this review of *The Dialogic Imagination*, I will deal with the essay 'Forms of Time and Chronotope in the Novel'. Until recently, chronotope was one of the least discussed and least utilized aspects of Bakhtin's theory of the novel although, as we shall see, it forms an important complement to his work on polyphony, and is a profoundly suggestive additional concept through which to explore the poetics of fiction.

Chronotope is a term Bakhtin derived from Einstein's 'theory of relativity'. Meaning, literally, 'time-space', Bakhtin defines chronotope as: 'the intrinsic connectedness of temporal and spatial relations that are artistically expressed in literature' (p. 84). What drew Bakhtin to Einstein's theory was that it saw time and space as somehow inseparable, and this, he reasoned, was very manifestly the case in the representation of time and space in the novel:

> In the literary artistic chronotope, spatial and temporal indicators are fused into one carefully thought-out, concrete whole. Time, as it were, thickens, takes on flesh, becomes artistically visible; likewise, space becomes charged and responsive to the movements of time, plot and history (ibid.).

Having acknowledged the inseparability of the two terms, however, it is fair to say that Bakhtin's *own* literary analysis is more concerned with the representation of time than space, since time is the 'dominant' element in literary chronotope.

What is difficult for readers engaging with Bakhtin's concept of chronotope for the first time, especially in creating for themselves a suitable working definition of the term, is that he uses it both to refer to the *general principle* of how time-space is represented in the novel and to label different subcategories: for example, the 'adventure chronotope' or the 'chronotope of meeting'. These last two examples could presumably be translated into 'the handling of time/space in adventure narratives' and 'the conjunction of time/space in the literary motif of the meeting'. The best way of understanding the term, however, is through the different contexts in which Bakhtin uses it, several of which are the subject of the discussion which follows.

Like 'Epic and Novel' and 'The Prehistory of Novelistic Discourse', this essay approaches its theoretical and stylistic concerns through a historical overview of the novel and its attendant genres. Bakhtin's starting point this time is the Greek romance which he sees as the prototype of the *adventure chronotope*; a form which has played a central role in the development of the European novel. According to Bakhtin, what is distinctive about this type of chronotope is that between the official start and finish of the textual action (traditionally represented by the meeting of the lovers and their marriage), time, effectively, stands still: 'We have an extratemporal hiatus between two biological moments – the arousal of passion, and its satisfaction' (p. 90). Such texts present no record of *passing time*: of the sequence of seasons and years, of character development, of human ageing:

> In this kind of time, nothing changes: the world remains as it was, the biographical lives of the heroes do not change, their feelings do not change, people do not even age. This empty time leaves no traces anywhere, no indications of its passing. This, we repeat, is an extratemporal hiatus that appears between two moments of a real time sequence, in this case one that is biographical (p. 91).

Once again, Bakhtin's use of a poetic vocabulary – the notion of an 'empty time' – holds many resonances for contemporary readers and critics with two centuries of fiction-writing behind them. Without too much trouble, we can all think of texts in which the 'real time sequence' is suspended to dramatic effect or, conversely, where the passing of biographical/historical time is recorded in minute detail. Instead of the passing of 'real time', what we find inside the adventure chronotope is, according to Bakhtin, a 'series of short segments' (adventures within adventures) connected by 'random contingency' (p. 92). In such texts, events are moved on by something happening 'suddenly' or 'unexpectedly' and great emphasis is placed on what he describes as 'simultaneity' (e.g., chance meetings) and 'chance rupture' (chance 'nonmeetings', i.e., people not turning up). Chance and fate and the intervention of all manner of irrational and divine forces are, indeed, the prime movers in the adventure chronotope: causality dependent upon character or external historical forces are entirely absent. To complement the impersonality of the temporal action, space in such texts is similarly abstract: although a bold geographical canvas is needed upon which the action can be painted (e.g., seas for requisite shipwrecks), no details of place are given. This is because what Bakhtin refers to as 'concretization' would 'introduce its own rule-generating force' (p. 100).

Closely associated with the adventure chronotope is the type of text that Bakhtin has designated the *adventure novel of everyday life*, owing to its conflation of the adventure chronotope with 'everyday time'. Bakhtin cites Apuleius's *The Golden Ass* as the classic example of this kind of text (of which there are very few) since it encapsulates the 'life story' of Apuleius *within* his two metamorphoses, which are the functional equivalent to the start and finish of the action (meeting and marriage) in the traditional Greek romance. In this particular text, 'everyday life' is represented by what Bakhtin designates the 'chronotope of the road': the pilgrimage the hero is obliged to make on the way to metamorphosis or self-realization. Especially interesting in the discussion of this variety of chronotope is the emphasis that is placed on the spatial dimension of the correlative:

> An individual's movement through space, his pilgrimages, lose that abstract

and technical character that they had in Greek romance . . . Space becomes more concrete and saturated with a time that is more substantial: space is filled with real, living meaning, and forms a crucial relationship with the hero and his fate . . . The concreteness of this chronotope of the road permits *everyday life* to be realized within it (p. 120).

In terms of the structure of the text as a whole, however, the representation of time in these episodes from everyday life (the time when Lucius was an ass) is 'scattered, fragmented, deprived of essential connections' (p. 128) and is therefore not *intrinsic* to the hero's transformation (which takes place as the result of a magical event). In the adventure novel of everyday life, the chronotope of everyday life is not without bearing on the life of the hero (Lucius regards his time spent as an ass as an important experience), but it is not central to his 'becoming' in the way it is in Bakhtin's third example from ancient literature: biography and autobiography. Jeanette Winterson's *Sexing the Cherry* (to be discussed in Chapter 5) is an interesting contemporary example of a text which mixes 'adventure' and 'everyday' chronotopes in this way.[38]

Bakhtin sees in the biographies and autobiographies of the Greeks and the Romans many important seeds of novelistic development, not least a new articulation of the chronotope. Although most of the earliest auto/biographies were very much expressions of the 'public self-consciousness of a man' (p. 140) which excluded the possibility of any authentic 'becoming', certain texts (e.g., ironic self-characterizations in verse by Homer and Ovid) began to expose a private self-consciousness which brought with it a new, 'evolutionary' exposition of character *through time*.

While Bakhtin's analysis of chronotope in chivalric romance so closely models that of the adventure chronotope of Greek romance that I shall not go into its subtleties here, his observations on the time-space inhabited by the 'rogue, clown, and fool' in the early novel are worth observing. The fool, according to Bakhtin, is a subversive figure not merely because of his inversion/questioning of traditional morals and values but also because he occupies a different chronotope to the other characters: 'The rogue, the clown and the fool create around themselves their own special little world, their own chronotope' (p. 159). In the later development of the novel, this possibility of certain characters existing *outside* the main spatiotemporal action (so as to be in a position to comment critically upon it) is of vital importance, and looks forward to the complex multilayering of place and time (the simultaneous *coexistence of chronotopes*) that is a feature of the modern (and, indeed, postmodern) fictional text.

Moving on to the Renaissance period, Bakhtin attributes another innovation in the development of the literary chronotope to Rabelais. Rabelais's writing, he argues, was instrumental in purging the spatial and temporal world of a 'transcendent world-view' (p. 168) and valorizing the 'here and now'. This is reflected, thematically, in his excessive/obsessive emphasis on *materiality* and *corporeality* (Bakhtin shows how *Gargantua and Pantagruel* is structured through a series of bodily related functions), and this, in turn, required a new order of chronotope: 'A new chronotope was

[38]  J. Winterson, *Sexing the Cherry* (London: Bloomsbury, 1989).

needed that would permit one to link real life (history) to the real earth. It was necessary to oppose to eschatology a creative and generative time, a time measured by creative acts, by growth and not destruction' (p. 200). The chronotope that Rabelais devised had its roots, according to Bakhtin, in *folkoric time*. It is characterized, principally, by its emphasis on *collective time* and *collective life*:

> This time is collective, that is, it is differentiated and measured only by the events of *collective life*; everything that exists in this time exists solely for the collective. The progression of events in an individual's life has not yet been isolated (pp. 206–207).

It is also a time measured by *labour*, in particular, the phases of agricultural labour. Its roots in farming mean that it is consequently a time associated with 'productive growth': a time that 'in its course binds together the earth and the laboring hand of man' (p. 208). Bakhtin nevertheless points out that the profound organicism of Rabelaisian time can only be properly appreciated when it is compared with the chronotopes of later literature:

> . . . when the time of personal, everyday family occasions had already been separated out from the time of the collective historical life of the social whole, at a time when there emerged one scale for measuring the events of a *personal life* and another for measuring the events of history (ibid.).

This fracturing and fragmentation of the chronotope as a consequence of the multiple centres of individual consciousness contending with one another in the modern novel is, indeed, a feature of both the texts analysed in Chapter 5, and it is clear that Bakhtin regards Rabelais's organicism as representative of a lost anti-bourgeois ideal in which the time-space continuum was experienced collectively. Rabelais's chronotope was prevented from being proto-Marxist, however, by its failure to associate growth with *historical progress*: instead, the folkloric time on which Rabelais's model is based is 'profoundly cyclic', thus denying 'growth . . . an authentic "becoming"' (p. 210).

Also essentially cyclical in its representation of time is the species of chronotope associated with the *idyll*. Bakhtin sees the idyll as another important influence on the development of the novel: a lingering fantasy of a past 'Golden Age' in texts reluctant to engage with contemporary history. What is theoretically unique about the idyllic chronotope, according to Bakhtin, is that *unity of place* (idylls are set in a single, familiar place, cut off from the rest of the world) gives rise to *unity of time*:

> This unity of place in the life of generations weakens and renders less distinct all the temporal boundaries between individual lives and between various phases of one and the same life. The unity of place brings together and even fuses the cradle and the grave . . . (p. 225).

In the development of the novel, it is nostalgia for this immortality that causes the treatment of such themes as nature, love, family, childbearing and death to become 'elemental': to 'undergo sublimation at a higher philosophical level' (p. 230) thus divorcing them from their proper historicity. Equally important, however, are those texts (mostly appearing in the late eighteenth and early nineteenth centuries) which mark the destruction of the idyll in their direct engagement with emerging capitalism and the disappearance of the agrarian society on which the idyllic chronotope was based.

In terms of its theoretical implications, the most interesting part of Bakhtin's essay is his concluding remarks (written in 1973). Here he directly addresses many of the questions implicit in the historical survey, including the relationship of the generic chronotopes (the principle literary forms that have been dealt with, e.g., adventure romance, folktale, Rabelaisian novel) to the equally important subcategories of chronotope (e.g., the 'encounter chronotope', the 'chronotope of the road'). He also quickly sketches in some of the new types of chronotope associated with the nineteenth- and twentieth-century novel, including the 'castle chronotope' of Gothic fiction, the 'salon chronotope' and the 'provincial-life chronotope' ('day in, day out the same round of activities are repeated', p. 248), and the 'chronotope of the threshold' (his principal exemplar here is Dostoevsky). Since these are the chronotopes with which modern readers will be most familiar, one rather regrets that there is not a more lengthy exposition of these recent mutations. However, such a wish is to misunderstand Bakhtin's project in these essays which is very much that of the literary historian and scholar.

To return to the question of the relationship between the generic chronotope and its subcategories, it is in his concluding remarks that Bakhtin begins to explore the possibility of *multiple* chronotopes coexisting within a single text. This gives rise to a very particular kind of dialogic relationship that is witnessed by author and reader, but cannot (of necessity) be 'known' by the characters/consciousnesses locked up in their own, individual chronotopic worlds:

> Within the limits of a single work and within the total literary output of a single author we may notice a number of different chronotopes and complex interactions among them, specific to the given work or author: it is common moreover for one of these chronotopes to envelop or dominate the others (such, primarily, as those we have analysed in this essay). Chronotopes are mutually inclusive, they co-exist, they may be interwoven with, replace or oppose one another, contradict one another or find themselves in ever more complex interrelationships. The relationships themselves that exist *among* chronotopes cannot enter into any of the relationships contained *within* chronotopes. The general characteristic of these interactions is that they are *dialogical* (in the broadest use of the word). But this dialogue cannot enter into the world represented in the work, nor into any of the chronotopes represented in it: it is outside the world represented, although not outside the work as a whole. It (this dialogue) enters the world of the author, the performer, and the world of the listeners and readers. And all these worlds are chronotopic as well (p. 252).

This presentation of chronotopes as multiple and coexistent (what I refer to in Chapter 5 as *polychronotopic*) is very important for all readers working with modernist and postmodernist fiction, as is the notion of *position* and *hierarchy* implicit in Bakhtin's observation that in most texts one chronotope usually 'dominates' the others. It is the means by which this domination is challenged, together with the way that characters in certain postmodern texts *are* allowed to invade consistently each other's chronotopes that I shall be especially concerned with in Chapter 5.

## VII
### *Essays and Notes*
*The Bakhtin Circle, 1925–52*

I would like to conclude this overview of the work of Bakhtin and the Bakhtin school – in particular, its evolving principle of dialogicality – with brief mention of some of the notes and essays now available in translation. The ones I want to focus on here are 'The Problem of Speech Genres' and 'The Problem of the Text' from the collection *Speech Genres and Other Late Essays,* and an essay by Voloshinov – 'Discourse in Life and Discourse in Poetry' – which appears in the *Bakhtin School Papers.*[39]

The essays which comprise the *Speech Genres* collection were first published in the Soviet Union in 1979 in a volume entitled *The Aesthetics of Verbal Creation,* which includes a wide and rather random selection of Bakhtin's work, early and late.[40] *Speech Genres* reproduces *only* the later works, including the title essay, the transcript of an interview Bakhtin gave to *Novy Mir* in 1970, an essay on the *Bildungsroman* (focusing on Goethe), and two sets of working notes: 'The Problem of the Text', which I deal with here, and other fragments from Bakhtin's notebooks of 1970–71. All these late pieces which, as Michael Holquist observes, show Bakhtin to be preoccupied with the same key concepts right until the end of his life, form an important coda to the discussions found in the major texts.

The essay on 'Speech Genres' is an important supplement to the theory of language worked out by Voloshinov in *Marxism and the Philosophy of Language* and the discussion of heteroglossia in *The Dialogic Imagination.* Here, Bakhtin expands and refines some of the principal ways in which a dialogic study of the utterance – taking into account the context in which it is made, and to whom it is addressed – is immeasurably superior to the 'grammatical analysis' of such language carried out by structural linguists who focus on the *sentence* as an acontextual unit of communication.

Bakhtin defines the speech genre as the 'sphere in which language is used' (p. 61). Each individual utterance (spoken or written) belongs to a 'microcommunity' or genre defined by its social context and addressee. While literary genres have been studied extensively, little attention has been paid to the 'speech genres' of everyday life which, although literally 'boundless' in their wealth and diversity (p. 60), are nevertheless accountable in their specificity. The relationship between primary speech genres and secondary ones (e.g., those represented by literary genres)

---

39   *Speech Genres and Other Late Essays,* ed. C. Emerson and M. Holquist, trans. V. McGee (Austin, TX: University of Texas Press, 1986); *Bakhtin School Papers,* ed. A. Shukman, *Russian Poetics in Translation, No. 10* (Oxford: RTP Publications, 1983).
40   *Estetika slovesnogo tvorcestva (The Aesthetics of Verbal Creation)* (Moscow: Iskusstuo, 1979). Michael Holquist discusses the composition of the *Speech Genres* collection in the Introduction to that volume.

is also important, since the latter often incorporates the former. Indeed, they could be said to exist in a dialogic relation with one another.

Most suggestive in this essay is Bakhtin's extended commentary on the factors which condition the choice of a particular speech genre (pp. 78 ff.) and his detailed characterization of the role of the addressee, both in actual dialogue and in the literary text. *Vis-à-vis* the former, he discusses the way in which we make our selection of speech genre in any given situation from a huge 'repetoire' of oral and written genres:

> Speech genres organize our speech in almost the same way as grammatical (syntactical) forms do. We learn to cast our speech in generic forms and, when hearing others' speech, we guess its genre from the very first words; we predict a certain length (that is, the approximate length of the speech whole) and a certain compositional structure; we foresee the end; that is, from the very beginning we have a sense of the speech whole, which is only later differentiated during the speech process. If speech genres did not exist and we had not mastered them, if we had to originate them during the speech process and construct each utterance at will for the first time, speech communication would be almost impossible (pp. 78–79).

Ability to select the appropriate genre for a given situation, and then to communicate in it, is also a skill commensurate with power. None of us has knowledge of all possible speech genres, and our ability to communicate in some and not others is often a sign of our particular social class and education:

> Many people who have an excellent command of a language often feel quite helpless in certain spheres of communication precisely because they do not have a practical command of the generic forms used in the given spheres. Frequently a person who has an excellent command of speech in some areas of cultural communication, who is able to read a scholarly paper or engage in scholarly discussion, who speaks very well on social questions, is silent or very awkward in social conversation. Here it is not a question of impoverished vocabulary or of style, taken abstractly: this is entirely a matter of the inability to command a repertoire of genres of social conversation, the lack of a sufficient supply of those ideas about the whole of an utterance that help one cast one's speech quickly and naturally in certain stylistic forms . . . (p. 80).

Although Bakhtin is referring here to 'everyday' conversation, the texts I will be considering in Part Two supply plenty of this sort of evidence, representing characters whose age/class/gender/sexual orientation determines their fluency in some speech genres and their exclusion from others.

A feature of Bakhtin's essays is that they often supply illustrations of theoretical points lacking in the major texts. In his presentation of the role of the addressee in the characterization of the speech genre, for example, he paints a vivid picture of just how multiple and various the addressee is – how the relationship between speaker and addressee may vary:

> An essential (constitutive) marker of the utterance is its quality of being directed to someone, its *addressivity* . . . This addressee can be an immediate participant-interlocutor in an everyday dialogue, a differentiated collective of specialists in some particular area of cultural communication, a more or less differentiated public, ethnic group, contemporaries, like-minded people, opponents and enemies, a subordinate, a superior, someone who is lower,

higher, familiar, foreign, and so forth. And it can also be an indefinite, unconcretized *other* . . . Both the composition and, particularly, the style of the utterance depend on those to whom the utterance is addressed, how the speaker (or writer) senses and imagines his addressees, and the force of their effect on the utterance. Each speech genre in each area of speech communication has its own typical conception of the addressee, and this defines it as a genre (p. 95).

By alerting us to the specificity of each and every addressee, actual or textual, Bakhtin is also reminding us of the power dynamics that operate in each and every act of communication (written or spoken). In the subsequent discussion he focuses, in particular, on the constraints imposed on communication in which there is a disparity in 'social position, rank and importance' (p. 96), and (obversely) on the *lack of constraint* in 'familiar' and 'intimate' relationships. His comments concerning the latter have important implications for the role of dialogue/dialogism in the construction of subjectivity, and for the special familiarity/intimacy associated with gender-specific language (see the discussion in Chapter 2).[41] Here he writes:

Finer nuances of style are determined by the nature and degree of *personal* proximity of the addressee to the speaker in various familiar speech genres, on the one hand, and in intimate ones, on the other. With all the immense differences among familiar and intimate genres (and, consequently, styles), they perceive their addressee in exactly the same way: more or less outside the framework of the social hierarchy and social conventions, 'without rank', as it were. This gives rise to a certain *candor* of speech (which in familiar styles sometimes approaches cynicism). In intimate styles this is expressed in an apparent desire for the speaker and addressee to merge completely . . . Intimate genres and styles are based on a maximum internal proximity of the speaker and addressee . . . Intimate speech is imbued with a deep confidence in the addressee, in his sympathy, in the sensitivity and goodwill of his responsive understanding. In this atmosphere of profound trust, the speaker reveals his internal depths. This determines the special expressiveness and internal candor of these styles (as opposed to the loud street-language candor of familiar speech) (pp. 96–97).

Bakhtin concludes this essay with a comment on the immense importance of the 'speech addressee' for the study of literature:

Each epoch, each literary trend and literary-artistic style, each literary genre within an epoch or trend, is typified by its own special concepts of the addressee in the literary work, a special sense and understanding of its reader, listener, public, or people (p. 98).

Literary genres, like the speech genres of everyday life upon which (according to Bakhtin) they are predicated, are expressions not of particular 'themes' or 'styles' but of a particular set of relationships between speaker and addressee, author and audience. This rare consideration of the role of

---

[41] It is important to recognize that in this discussion Bakhtin is distinguishing *between* familiar and intimate speech, as well as marking ways in which *both* differ from formal or official speech. 'Intimate speech' is characterized by a sympathetic/empathetic relation between speaker and addressee; 'familiar speech' by jesting, ribaldry and a communal 'billingsgate'.

the reader/audience in the dialogic process I will return to in the conclusion (pp. 205–207).

The piece of writing known as 'The Problem of the Text' is, as Michael Holquist has observed, 'not so much an essay as a series of entries from the notebooks in which Bakhtin jotted down his thoughts' (p. xvii). As such, it is a script without a single theme or argument and, along with the 'problem' of texts – what they are, the relations between them – includes a string of thoughts on many of the major intellectual preoccupations of Bakhtin's career. Two of the most interesting addenda, which I want to focus on here, are Bakhtin's thoughts on authorship and the role of what he calls the *superaddressee* in the presentation of any utterance.

The issue of authorship was something Bakhtin never properly resolved in his earlier writings. As we saw in the discussion of *Dostoevsky's Poetics*, Bakhtin's celebration of texts which granted freedom and autonomy to the characters, and which shunned any monolithic ideological point of view, tended to reduce the role of the author-narrator to that of mere puppet-master. In these late notes, Bakhtin refines his position a little by acknowledging the difference between authors and narrators, and by discussing the different roles played by the latter in different types of texts. More recent narratologists' models of the 'real' and 'implied author' are mirrored in Bakhtin's dichotomy of the 'pure author' and 'the partially depicted, designated author who enters a work' (p. 109).[42] However, Bakhtin also transfers his dialogic model of the utterance to the author's 'word', arguing that it can never be the sole property of the author. The words of any author (as of any individual) are made in partial anticipation of another's response: 'To see and comprehend the author of a work means to see and comprehend another, alien consciousness and its world, that is, another subject ("Du")' (p. 111). In short, Bakhtin's observations on the author in this late work make his (or her) role even more partial and provisional: a presence who has only limited powers of control in the text he or she produces, and whose words are occupied by the 'alien consciousnesses' of his addressees (i.e., both his or her readers, and the characters within the text). Whether or not Bakhtin had read Barthes's essay on 'The Death of the Author' by this time is unknown, but it is clear that his own views of authorship were moving in a poststructuralist direction.[43]

The most useful coda produced in these late notes is the expanded discussion of the role of the addressee in the dialogic performance of the utterance. Bakhtin's first move here is to revise the model of the utterance

---

[42] Wayne Booth's identification of the 'implied author' in *The Rhetoric of Fiction* (Chicago, IL: University of Chicago Press, 1961) was developed and refined by Seymour Chatman in *Story and Discourse* (Ithaca, NY: Cornell University Press, 1978), who produced the following, well-known model of narrative transaction:

Real Author > Implied Author > (Narrator) > (Narratee) > Implied Reader > Real Reader

Rimmon-Kenan, *Narrative Fiction*, writes that: 'More than just a textual stance, Booth's implied author appears to be an anthropomorphic entity, often designated as the author's second self' (p. 86). According to this view, the implied author is the governing consciousness in the work.

[43] Barthes, 'The Death of the Author', see note 23 above.

as a relationship between two terms – speaker and addressee – and propose, instead, a 'tripartite unity' in which the first two are supplemented by the third category of the *intertext*: 'Those whose voices are heard in the word before the author comes upon it' (p. 122). This is to say that the speaker's utterance will be styled and conditioned not only in relation to his or her immediate addressee (actual or textual), but also as a response to the many other voices that will, at some time, have passed comment on the subject under discussion. If we venture a political opinion about something, for example, we will do so not only in anticipation of the response of our immediate addressee but also with an ear to all the comments we have heard passed on the subject.

In a later part of the discussion, Bakhtin explores how some of the 'other voices' that determine the reception of a text may materialize into a second interlocutor whom he calls the *superaddressee*. Separate from the actual addressee, Bakhtin's superaddresse is the virtual equivalent of the reader-response theorists' 'ideal reader': the hypothetical presence who fully comprehends the speaker's words and hence allows his or her utterance to be made despite doubts about whether the 'actual' addressee will understand and/or respond:

> But in addition to this addressee (the second party), the author of the utterance, with a greater or lesser awareness, presupposes a higher superaddressee (third), whose absolutely just responsive understanding is presumed, either in some metaphysical distance or in distant historical time (the loophole addressee). In various ages and with various understandings of the world, this superaddressee and his ideally true responsive understanding assume various ideological expressions (God, absolute truth, the court of dispassionate human conscience, the people, the court of history, science, and so forth) . . . Each dialogue takes place as if against the background of the responsive understanding of an invisibly present third party who stands above all the participants in the dialogue (partners) (p. 126).[44]

The notion of a 'loophole addressee', present in some distant historical time, is exemplified by a text like Margaret Atwood's *The Handmaid's Tale* (1985) in which the heroine directs her address not only to her lost communicants of the past (mother, husband, friends) but also to one outside the present Gileadean time: a superaddressee in the future who will understand all that she says.[45] I will also invoke the concept of the 'superaddressee' in my own reading of *Wuthering Heights* (1847) in Chapter 3, where I relate it to the question of whether or not that text can be said to include 'hidden dialogue' and 'hidden polemic' in its reported dialogues.

---

44 For a discussion of the 'implied' and 'ideal' reader, see, in particular, W. Iser, *The Implied Reader: Patterns of Communication in Prose Fiction from Bunyan to Beckett* (Baltimore, MD: Johns Hopkins University Press, 1974) and *The Act of Reading: A Theory of Aesthetic Response* (Baltimore, MD: Johns Hopkins University Press, 1976).

45 Atwood, *The Handmaid's Tale*. At several points in the text the narrator, Offred, directly addresses the reader in the following manner: 'But if it's a story, even in my head, I must be telling it to someone. You don't tell a story only to yourself. There's always someone else.

Even when there is no one.

A story is like a letter. *Dear You*, I'll say. Just *you*, without a name . . .' (pp. 49–50).

I move on now to Voloshinov's essay in *The Bakhtin School Papers*. 'Discourse in Life and Discourse in Poetry' is an important text in expanding our understanding of the role of *extraverbal context* and *intonation* in the dialogicality of the utterance. Following on from his brief treatment of these issues in *Marxism and the Philosophy of Language* (see Section III above), Voloshinov here argues that all discourse is crucially dependent on extraverbal context for its 'judgements and evaluations' to be realized: 'Discourse itself taken in isolation, as a purely linguistic phenomenon, cannot of course be either true or false, bold or modest' (p. 10). He demonstrates this with reference to a short narrative describing the exchange of a single word between two people sitting alone in a room:

> A couple are sitting in a room. They are silent. One says, 'Well!' The other says nothing in reply. For us who are not present in the room at the time of the exchange, this 'conversation' is completely inexplicable. Taken in isolation the utterance 'well', is void and quite meaningless. Nevertheless the couple's peculiar exchange, consisting of only one word, though one to be sure which is expressively inflected, is full of meaning and significance and quite complete (ibid.).

Voloshinov argues that in order for those of us not present in the room to make sense of the word 'well', we need to know three key factors relating to its 'extraverbal context': '1) a *spatial purview* common to the speakers (the unity of what is visible – the room, the window and so on, 2) the couple's *common knowledge and understanding of the circumstances* and finally 3) their *common* evaluation of these circumstances' (p. 11). Only when this missing information is supplied can the 'mystery' of the word be resolved:

> At the moment of the exchange *both* invividuals *glanced* at the window and *saw* that it was snowing. *Both knew* that it was already May and long since time for spring, and finally, they were both sick of the protracted winter. *Both were waiting* for spring and *were annoyed* by the late snowfall. The utterance depends directly on all this – on what was '*visible to both*' (the snowflakes beyond the window), what was '*known to both*' (the date was May) and what was '*similarly evaluated*' (boredom with winter, longing for spring); and all this was grasped in the actual meaning of the utterance, all this soaked into it yet remained verbally unmarked, unuttered. The snowflakes stay beyond the window, the date on a page of a calendar, the evaluation in the mind of the speaker, but all this is implied in the word 'well' (ibid.).

Voloshinov goes on to argue that although in this particular example the extraverbal context is very narrowly defined in terms of space, time and participants, the 'unified purview' on which the utterance depends can broaden to include 'family, kinsmen, nation, class, days, years and whole epochs' (p. 12).

According to Voloshinov, *intonation* is the means by which 'an intimate connection' is forged between 'discourse and the non-verbal context' (p. 13). Returning to the previous example, Voloshinov argues that, semantically, the word 'well' is 'almost void' (p. 14). It may consequently be governed by 'any intonation – exultant, doleful, contemptuous and so on', and our register of that verbal mark, together with a knowledge of the context in which the utterance was made, is absolutely vital to our understanding of it:

> And it is above all in intonation that the speaker comes into contact with its [sic] listeners: intonation is social *par excellence*. It is particularly sensitive to all the variations in the social atmosphere which surrounds the speaker (ibid.).

Yet apart from being a crucial index of the relationship between speaker and interlocutor, intonation also bears an evaluated relationship to the topic of the discourse: what Voloshinov refers to as the 'object of utterance'. In the example cited earlier, the intonation with which the word 'well' is imbued will therefore be split between the human addressee and the object of the utterance: the weather. In this way, two distinct and often contradictory intonational inflections may be detected in a single word. Here, for example, the expression of mutual frustration and discontent which characterizes the exchange between speaker and addressee is combined with 'active indignation and reproach' directed at the weather itself.

These subtleties of verbal intonation will be demonstrated in my reading of John Clare's 'Child Harold' (1838–41) in Chapter 3, where I also focus on the fact the relationship between speaker, listener and 'object of utterance' is always inscribed by power. Voloshinov, too, implies this in his concluding remark: 'Thus all intonation is oriented *in two directions*: towards the listener as ally or witness, and towards the topic of the utterance, as if to a third, active participant. Intonation abuses, curses, humiliates or extols it' (p. 16).

In the latter part of the essay, Voloshinov considers how the tripartite relationship between speaker, listener and object of utterance which exists in 'living speech' may be translated into a 'work of art', and concludes that the relationship between author, reader and hero is a virtual equivalent (pp. 18–29). This discussion, which includes some interesting commentary on how the different literary genres position their readers as intimate or otherwise (see section IV with respect to *Dostoevsky's Poetics*) is one of the few places in the work of the Bakhtin school where the relationship between readers and 'real-life' interlocutors is directly addressed.

It will be seen, then, that the notes and essays produced by the Bakhtin group over a large number of years provide an important corollary to some of the key issues raised, but not developed, in the main texts. There are, as has been noted by many of the critics cited in the next chapter, many blind spots and lacunae in Bakhtin's own writings which these uncollected texts go some way to addressing, and the reader should not be too hasty in passing judgement on this or that 'limitation' without acquainting herself with the material being developed on the margins.

This chapter has aimed to provide the reader new to Bakhtin's work with a broad overview of what I consider to be his most interesting and suggestive concepts, theories and debates. Such a review is necessarily partial, and my inclusions and exclusions have been partly determined by the aspects of Bakhtin's writings that have proven most popular with literary critics, and partly by the interests of my own readings in Part Two. The discussion of all the texts has, moreover, been directed towards the discourse of dialogicality, and perhaps this is the point to remind the reader that this is not the *only* 'architectonic' theme to run through his work. There are readings of Bakhtin other than a dialogic one, and I trust that after the current vogue for dialogism has waned, they will be pursued. Aside from all that has not been represented here, however, it is my hope that every reader will find some concept, phrase or suggestion that they can carry into their own textual practice. Part Two reveals what has proven most useful for mine.

# 2

# DIALOGIC THEORY AND CONTEMPORARY CRITICISM

This chapter is a discussion of the way in which the discourse of dialogism has been taken up in recent years by critics working in the area of literary and cultural criticism. Some of these writers, as we shall see, have worked closely with Bakhtin's own texts; others have merely appropriated dialogism or one of its attendant concepts (polyphony, heteroglossia, carnival) for their own critical and theoretical purposes, sometimes in a context that bears little resemblance to Bakhtin's original usage. The theoretical and political issues surrounding this mass appropriation of Bakhtin's work were addressed in the Introduction, and surfaced again during some of the discussions of individual texts in Chapter 1. In this chapter my commentary is predicated on the assumption that dialogism, in its contemporary critical deployment, has become a category of philosophy, epistemology, pedagogy and politics, as well as textual analysis, which has a connotative significance far in excess of the original Bakhtin texts. This has inevitably led to problems of specifying exactly what dialogic criticism *is* (see again the discussion in the Introduction), but the broad range of texts and contexts to which it has been productively applied attests to its conceptual charisma. By referring to a broad sample of critics from diverse theoretical, political and disciplinary backgrounds, it is my hope that this chapter will offer a glimpse of the 'state of the art' of dialogic criticism in the 1980s and 1990s.

I have structured my discussion around three key points of engagement between contemporary cultural criticism and dialogic theory: dialogism and genre, dialogism and the subject, and dialogism and gender. It was my original intention to include a fourth category of 'dialogism and the reader', but research revealed that very few of Bakhtin's followers had *directly* addressed the relationship between dialogics and recent trends in reader theory.[1] Since the dialogue that occurs between text and reader is

---

[1] One significant exception to this is the chapter by David Shepherd, 'Bakhtin and the Reader' in *Bakhtin and Cultural Theory*, ed. K. Hirschkop and D. Shepherd (Manchester: Manchester University Press, 1989), pp. 91–108.

also one of the least well articulated areas in Bakhtin's own work while being of critical importance in so much of his analysis (see mention of this in Chapter 1), I have consequently chosen to reserve further comment until the Conclusion where this, and the other blind spots of dialogic criticism, will be revealed. In the meantime, readers should simply be aware that the Bakhtinian model of the dialogic utterance – the central relationship between speaker and interlocutor – is employed by literary and cultural critics to refer *both* to relations *within the text* and to that between text and reader.

## I
## Dialogism and Genre

As the last chapter will have revealed, Bakhtin's new dialogic model of 'text and world' was constructed in relation to one particular literary genre: the novel. Polyphony, heteroglossia, carnival, chronotope and double-voiced discourse are all exemplified, in his work, through reference to the novel or the novel's prehistory: dialogic thinking is seen to enter modern thought through the *vehicle* of the novel. One particular literary genre, then (and its key historical practitioners such as Rabelais and Dostoevsky), is made the agent of a latter-day Copernican revolution.

The single most striking feature, therefore, in the deployment of Bakhtin's analytic method by contemporary literary critics is that it is *not* genre specific. From the early 1980s, when Bakhtin's texts first started to find a wide academic audience in the West, his theoretical models were used to read (and reread) poetry and drama as well as the novel; to analyse film, music, and the visual and performing arts as well as literature. Almost immediately, therefore, the genre-specific focus of Bakhtin's own research was abandoned: these were analytic tools too valuable, a critical vocabulary too immediately useful and suggestive, to be monopolized by narratologists and other critics working specifically with fiction.

As we shall see in the following review of those critics who have plundered the Bakhtinian archive for their own diverse analytical purposes, many exponents of non-novelistic dialogic criticism do not even bother to mention the fact that they are utilizing concepts that were originally genre specific. Others have felt obliged at least to acknowledge the displacement, and some, like David Lodge or Robert Stam, have thought it a significantly serious matter to address at some length.[2]

Although David Lodge is one of those critics who has used Bakhtinian theory explicitly for the purposes of fictional analysis he, like Stam, considers the poetry–novel opposition in Bakhtin's writing to be an

---

[2]  See D. Lodge, 'After Bakhtin', in *After Bakhtin: Essays on Fiction and Criticism* (London and New York: Routledge, 1990), p. 90 ff. See also R. Stam, *Subversive Pleasures: Bakhtin, Cultural Criticism and Film* (Baltimore, MD, and London: Johns Hopkins University Press, 1989), p. 16.

unquestionable red-herring, and one directly related to the paradox (noted in Chapter 1) that if *all* language is 'innately dialogic', as Bakhtin would seem to be arguing in many instances, 'how can there be monologic discourse?' (Lodge, *After Bakhtin*, p. 90). By close scrutiny of the many contradictions in Bakhtin's own writings on this point, it is quite possible to argue that 'monologic discourse is a kind of fiction or illusion' (ibid., p. 95), and that what Bakhtin is really trying to say is that *certain types of writing* (e.g., the lyric, the epic) tend to suppress and conceal the inherent dialogicality of *spoken* discourse. There remains the problem, however, as Lodge also acknowledges, of whether even this sort of sliding scale of monologism–dialogism is tenable. Is the lyric poem *necessarily* any more repressive of dialogue than the novel? Can we really make these sorts of generalizations? Allowing for Bakhtin's own acknowledgement that much of the 'great poetry' of history has been subject to 'novelization' (i.e., the influence of the novel on its form), we would seem to be left with an extremely small sample of texts that are *typically* monologic. As Lodge concludes: 'But still the nagging doubts persist: what about Milton, Keats, Yeats, and many other ostensibly monologic poets? If they are all redeemable through the loophole of novelization, then the loophole would seem to be larger than the surrounding wall' (ibid., p. 97).

Robert Stam, meanwhile, who has effected one of the most radical and exciting appropriations of Bakhtin's dialogic theory for his readings in contemporary film, television and mass-media culture in general, perceives the genre limitation of Bakhtin's own work as one of several blind spots that should not inhibit our own critical practices. We have simply to accept that his 'occasional essentialist denigration of epic, drama, and poetry as necessarily "monological"' and his 'corollary idealization of the novel as intrinsically "dialogical"' (p. 16) is one of the occasions where Bakhtin was 'clearly and demonstrably wrong' (ibid.). This accepted, I feel that we should nevertheless acknowledge that Bakhtin, in his later writings, more or less admitted the erroneous genre-specificity of his dialogic theorizing. In 'The Problem of the Text' he writes:

> To what extent is a discourse purely single-voiced and without any objectal character, possible in literature? Isn't every writer (even the purest lyric poet) always a 'playwright' insofar as he distributes all the discourses among alien voices, including that of the 'image of the author' (as well as the author's other *personae*)?[3]

The way of explaining and excusing this red-herring at the heart of Bakhtin's thought, moreover, is to recognize that the mechanics of dialogism were revealed to him through what was, essentially, a *formalist* analysis of Dostoevsky's fiction. By focusing so intently on the infrastructure of these novels and then, latterly, having to tie their specificity of form and function to a social context, it is understandable that Bakhtin should have made an icon of the novel in this way.

I want to pass on now to a discussion of some of the critics who have employed Bakhtin's key concepts in readings of a range of texts,

---

[3]   M. Bakhtin, 'The Problem of the Text in Linguistics, Philosophy and Other Human Sciences' (1959–61), cited in Lodge, *After Bakhtin*, pp. 97–98.

fiction and non fiction, literary and nonliterary. I shall begin with those who, despite the attitude of the majority, have found it expedient to regard dialogism as a particular feature of the novel. Patricia Yaegar, for instance, locates one of the 'emancipatory strategies' of women's writing in its strategic deployment of the novel's dialogic/heteroglossic form.[4] Through a comparative analysis of Emily Brontë's textual presentation in a needlework sampler, a lyric poem ('The Philosopher') and *Wuthering Heights* (1847), Yaegar shows how the multivoicedness of the novel allows for an ideological perspectivism not possible in the other genres. The lyric poem may resist monologism through its stylized citation of other texts (Milton, Byron, Wordsworth), but it cannot effect the destabilizing *dialogue* between different voices that we find in *Wuthering Heights*:

> Thus in *Wuthering Heights*, Brontë's conversation with her culture is not conveyed in isolated fragments, as it is in the frame of her poem – but projected into the voices of characters who are at war with one another – or with the frame of the novel itself. As a piece of dialogism, parody, and laughter, the novel admits a new intersection of body and text, provides another way to rupture the authoritative, the normative, the social (p. 195).

Yaegar's particular point of focus here is therefore the way in which the dialogic features of a text like *Wuthering Heights* are commensurate with its moral and political indeterminacy. In this regard, she also lays emphasis on the novel as a genre of *process*, and explains the sequence of narrators in *Wuthering Heights* as the author's means of ensuring that the text's different ideological positions are repeatedly recontextualized.

The novelist whose work has attracted the most extensive dialogic treatment is Charles Dickens. Following Bakhtin's own lead in the essay 'Discourse in the Novel' (see pp. 64–65), critics like Kate Flint and Roger D. Sell have used the notion of polyphony and heteroglossia to 'rescue' Dickens's texts from criticisms of formlessness (in particular, their lack of authorial control) and political conservatism.[5] Although Flint's book on Dickens makes only one direct reference to Bakhtin, she uses the concept of the polyphonic text as bearer of 'a plurality of independent and unmerged voices and consciousnesses' (p. 48) to give positive new meaning to Dickens's complicated method of narration and to the clumsy, multiple plots that rarely add up to the required aesthetic whole. Both she and Sell relate this structural resistance to hierarchy and closure to Dickens's radical moral and political vision. Rather than seeing the novels as either hopelessly confused on political issues, or assimilatable to some presiding status quo (Sell writes of critics who have tried to 'wrench a *concordia discours*' from the polyphony of voices which comprise the texts), they prefer to celebrate Dickens as an author who, like Dostoevsky, left his 'ideological tensions . . . unresolved': 'Dickens, within the context of

[4] P. Yaegar, *Honeymad Women: Emancipatory Strategies in Women's Writing* (New York: Columbia University Press, 1988). Page references to this volume will be given after quotations in the text.

[5] K. Flint, *Dickens. Harvester New Readings* (Brighton: Harvester, 1986). Page references to this volume will be given after quotations in the text; R. D. Sell, 'Dickens and the New Historicism: The Polyvocal Audience and Discourse of *Dombey and Son*' in *The Nineteenth Century British Novel*, ed. J. Hawthorn (London: Edward Arnold, 1986), pp. 63–79.

his own culture, meant several things at once, discretely interpretable and self-contradictory' (Sell, 'Dickens', p. 68).

Kate Flint's reading of *Bleak House* (1853) is an especially good example of how a dialogic perspective can illuminate and rationalize a text recalcitrant to orthodox critical analysis. Having already drawn the reader's attention to some of Dicken's classic destabilizing devices such as the gap between narrator and focalizer (p. 50), and the interpolation of secondary tales into the main narrative (as in *Pickwick* and *Nicholas Nickleby*), Flint declares that:

> The most obviously dialogic of all the novels is *Bleak House*, with Esther's narrative being told in the first person and in the past tense, and the remainder being narrated in a multiplicity of registers and from a kaleidoscope of points of view, in the present tense, and in the third person (p. 52).

The effect of this is, according to Flint, to convey the disintegrating chaos of contemporary society lurking beneath the fragile veneer of order, respectablity and 'feminine' moral value represented by Esther Summerson:

> The assurance of order offered by Esther's narrative is, however, immediately denied by the more widely ranging chapters which show that the society of *Bleak House* is not one which can speak with a unified, communal, assured, voice. Although elements of a particular plot are tidied up at the end of the novel, the general sense of confusion, and of the elements which caused it, remain, as the use of the present tense indicates (p. 53).

Altogether, Flint's rereading of Dickens is an excellent example of how dialogism *as a principle* (without any detailed reference to Bakhtin's work) can offer a new perspective on texts which have fallen foul of traditional criticism. Eiichi Hari achieves something similar in his account of *Great Expectations* (1861) by arguing that the 'lack of closure' in this late novel should be regarded not as an aesthetic flaw but as the last great outburst of the 'carnivalesque' spirit which pervades Dickens's earlier fiction.[6] Although it may be argued that as Dickens matured he managed to repress the carnivalesque 'wildness' at the heart of his novels, *Great Expectations* should be seen as a late (and magnificent) exception in which the chaos of plot and confusion of narration (whose story is it?) complement Pip's own 'irrational passion' (p. 611). Behind all these readings of Dickens's work is the assumption that the polyphonic novel, as a genre, should be evaluated according to a different set of aesthetic and ideological criteria to those applied to typically monologic texts.

Apart from providing a model for rereading nineteenth-century novels, Bakhtin's categories of the polyphonic/dialogic have been profoundly useful in explaining the more self-conscious stylistic experiments of twentieth-century novelists. In her work on the contemporary Scottish writer George Mackay Brown, Rowena Murray employs an effective combination of Bakhtinian and reader-response theory to account for the

---

6   E. Hare, 'Stories Present and Absent in *Great Expectations*', *Journal of English Literary History* **53**, 1986, pp. 593–614.

multiperspectivism of Brown's prose writings.[7] Her analysis reveals both the way in which the reader has to recognize the polyphonic structuration of a novel such as *Greenvoe* (1972) (which is focused on the life of a remote island community) in order to appreciate its distinctive worldview, and the way in which the ability of the various characters to 'give voice' and 'dialogize' registers their control over their threatened community. On this last point she writes:

> In other words, when the inhabitants of Greenvoe lose control of their own village, they lose the opportunity to voice their own views. Stylistic variation [between voices/characters] in Chapter One of this novel was a means of conveying the diversity of human interaction within the small community; more than this, however, stylistic variation, the extent to which characters were able to voice their own views, was a marker of the extent to which they were agents in their own experience (p. 180).

While in the readings of Dickens and the Brontës cited above dialogism has been employed to disrupt and challenge received readings of 'classic' texts, Murray's explication of Brown's work suggests that a 'dialogic consciousness' is an a priori requirement to making sense of a text in which the strategic disappearance and reappearance of the 'omniscient narrative voice' is vitally linked to the text's political message:

> In Chapter Six, however, when the village is destroyed and its inhabitants are dispersed, an omniscient narrative voice takes over, allowing little stylistic variation; the effect is to suggest not simply the disintegration of the village, but also the characters' loss of control over their own lives, once the outside forces have taken over (p. 164).

Brown's work, Murray is implying, depends upon a readerly competence which recognizes the political significance of the interaction of voices within the text, and is also able to make the 'transitions' (recognizing where the characters are loquacious or silent; where they dialogize with one another and were they do not) when there is no narrator to supply them.

The critic who has worked most closely with Bakhtin's own 'stylistics' of fictional analysis – in particular, his model of double-voiced discourse – is David Lodge. In two essays from the early 1980s, 'James Joyce and Bakhtin' (1983) and 'Lawrence, Dostoevsky, Bakhtin' (1985), Lodge provided readers new to Bakhtin with a useful potted summary of his key ideas (see Chapter 1), and also showed how the new dialogic vocabulary could be put to particular use in the reading of modern fiction.[8] The faithfulness with which Lodge reproduces Bakhtin's own analytic method is attested by the fact that, in these essays on two different novelists, he performs very similar readings – focusing, in particular, on their deployment of the different modes of double-voiced discourse, namely, stylization, *skaz*, parody and hidden polemic. The reading of D. H. Lawrence includes a particularly good analysis of

---

[7]  R. Murray, 'Style as Voice: A Reappraisal of George Mackay Brown's Prose', unpublished Ph. D. thesis, Pennsylvania State University, 1986.
[8]  See Lodge, *After Bakhtin*.

stylization, with Lodge arguing that the 'more heightened and rhapsodic passages describing erotic experience' in texts like *Women in Love* (1920) read like a pastiche of popular romance texts – a device carried to even further (parodic) extremes in the 'Nausicaa' episode of James Joyce's *Ulysses* (1922) (p. 66). Bakhtinian *skaz*, meanwhile, is illustrated with reference to Lawrence's short story, 'Things', in which the third-person narration 'mimics' the speech patterns of the characters being described: 'Here Lawrence tells us how his two characters "felt", in the kind of language they would have used, perhaps actually did use, to explain and justify to themselves, to each other, and to an Other, their decision to leave France' (p. 68). In the course of his essay, Lodge acknowledges that after the dialogic experiments of *The Rainbow* (1915) and *Women in Love* (a text which, literally, begins and ends in dialogue), Lawrence lapsed into an increasingly 'totalitarian' monologism in which the despotism of the narratorial voice mirrored his own politics. It is Lodge's work on James Joyce, however, which offers the best illustrations of Bakhtin's more active categories of double-voiced discourse: readers looking for working examples of parody and hidden polemic are advised to turn to his readings of *Ulysses* in the essay 'Mimesis and Diegesis in Modern Fiction' (see note 2). In this reading, Lodge shows how the 'friendliness bordering on servility' of the central character, Harold Bloom, together with his 'fear of rejection', casts a strange, blustering self-consciousness over his (reported) speech which likens it to the polemic of Dostoevsky's 'underground man' (see Chapter 1). There will, of course, be further demonstrations of the different varieties of doubly voiced discourse in my own readings in Part Two of this book (see especially Chapter 3).

I want to move on now to discuss those critics who, self-consciously or otherwise, have used dialogic theory to read nonfictional fictional and, indeed, nonliterary works.

Since the 1980s, Don Bialostosky has been using Bakhtin in his readings of Wordsworth, his latest book in this area being but the impressive culmination of a decade of fruitful engagement.[9] In his earlier publication, *Making Tales*, he shows how, in Wordsworth's *Lyrical Ballads* (1799), the unificatory lyric voice is subsumed by various characters speaking 'the real languages of men'.[10] Thus, in one of the seminal texts of Romanticism where, if anywhere, we would expect to find an uncontaminated lyric mode, we find, instead, the most radical dialogism. It will be argued, of course, that some poetic texts (even those masquerading as lyrics) are more 'novelized' than others, but Bialostosky has shown that even the most apparently monologic of Wordsworth's texts (the 'Lucy' poems or certain sections of *The Prelude* (1799–1805), for instance) are subject to the same dynamic interplay of speaker, hero and listener.[11]

In more recent literary criticism, authors have stopped attempting to

---

9  D. Bialostosky, *Wordsworth, Dialogics, and the Practice of Criticism* (Cambridge and New York: Cambridge University Press, 1992).
10  D. Bialostosky, *Making Tales: The Poetics of Wordsworth's Narrative Experiments* (London: University of Chicago Press, 1984).
11  See. W. Wordsworth, *Poetical Works*, 5 vols. (Oxford: Clarendon, 1949–63) and *The Prelude: A Parallel Text* (Harmondsworth: Penguin, 1971).

justify their use of Bakhtinian theory on poetic texts. One particularly good example of just how commonplace the dialogic vocabulary has become is Calvin Bedient's book on T. S. Eliot's *The Waste Land* (1922): '*He do the police in different voices*'.[12] Bedient's use of the terms 'polyphony', 'heteroglossia' and 'chronotope' – all of which he draws upon extensively in his analysis of the text – is supremely nonchalant: they are merely part of a large poststructuralist arsenal of key concepts and theoretical frameworks to be deployed where and when appropriate. At no stage in his discussions does he attempt either to explicate the terms or comment upon their place in his theoretical schema. There is, however, an ironic twist to Bedient's thesis in as much as he is attempting to prove the existence of *a single protagonist* 'behind' all the multivocality and heteroglossia: the absent – present lyric 'I' who is merely 'ventriloquizing' the other voices (p. 12). Perhaps we should infer from this that it is at the level of criticism, rather than in the texts themselves, that the association of poetry with monologic unity still retains its nostalgic hold.

In the field of drama criticism, Bakhtinian theory has also proven especially popular – especially *vis-à-vis* the idea of carnival.[13] Students taking undergraduate courses on Shakespeare quickly learn to make 'carnivalized' readings of the comedies in which the world is regularly turned upside down, authority challenged and roles reversed, through the suppression of those laws that Bakhtin describes being broken down under the 'rule of carnival' (see Chapter 1). In *Practising Theory and Reading Literature*, Ray Selden utilizes Bakhtin in a just such a reading of *King Lear* and *Twelfth Night*.[14] Concerning *Lear*, he shows how Bakhtin's 'sociological perspective' is very different from that of orthodox Marxism, and better equipped to make sense of unstable (and, through carnival, 'inverted') hierarchies that we find in Shakespeare's plays. The appropriation of carnival by drama critics can hardly be seen as a transgression of Bakhtin's own 'rules of genre' since his own history of carnival includes reference to classical drama (see Chapter 1). More questionable, however, is whether Bakhtin's categories of stylistic analysis that have been used extensively in the reading of both fiction and poetry (e.g., polyphony and double-voiced discourse) can be applied to drama, since the latter is a genre in which many such dialogic features are *inherent*. In other words,

---

[12]   C. Bedient, '*He do the police in different voices': The Waste Land and its Protagonist* (Chicago and London: University of Chicago Press, 1986).

[13]   See M. D. Bristol, *Carnival and Theatre: Plebian Culture and the Structure of Renaissance England* (London: Methuen, 1985) which draws on the Bakhtinian model extensively but uncritically. More sceptical (in the sense that it does not have the same 'celebratory' emphasis on 'the people') is P. Stallybrass and A. White, *The Politics and Poetics of Transgression* (London: Methuen, 1987). See also R. Wilson's essay, 'Shakespeare's Roman Carnival' in *New Historicism and Renaissance Drama*, ed. R. Dutton and R. F. Wilson (London: Longman, 1992) and various (feminist) essays in *Gloriana's Face: Women, Public and Private in the English Renaissance*, ed. S. P. Cerasano and M. Wynne-Davies (Hemel Hempstead: Harvester Press, 1992). A further source of feminist/lesbian readings drawing on Bakhtin is V. Traub, *Desire and Anxiety: Circulations of Sexuality in Shakespearean Drama* (London: Routledge, 1992). (Many thanks to my colleagues Richard Dutton and Marion Wynne-Davies for supplying me with these references.)

[14]   R. Selden, *Practising Theory and Reading Literature* (Hemel Hempstead: Harvester Wheatsheaf, 1989), pp. 164–69.

is the idea of a polyphonic play a tautology? Bakhtin, himself, saw the matter quite differently inasmuch as he believed all dramatic work to be typically monologic. With respect to Shakespeare, for example, he wrote: 'In essence each play contains only one valid voice, the voice of the hero' (*Dostoevsky's Poetics*, p. 34). While many readers will and, indeed, have contested this view of the Shakespearean text as controlled by a single ideological representative, Bakhtin himself could not be persuaded that the dramatic production allowed for the 'plurality of fully valid voices' requisite for the polyphonic text (ibid.). His argument is, however, very strained and tenuous on this matter and constitutes, in my opinion, one of the grey areas in his work.

I would like to conclude this section by referring briefly to the deployment of dialogic theory in disciplines other than English Literature. As I observed in the Introduction, dialogism is a concept that has now infiltrated virtually every branch of the human and social sciences. Sociologists, lawyers, philosophers and historians, as well as linguists and literary critics, will be familiar with both the principle and its eminent usefulness in all manner of textual analysis. In film studies in particular Bakhtinian dialogics has achieved a recognition comparable to that in literary criticism, and one of the most impressive testaments to this particular engagement to date is Robert Stam's *Subversive Pleasures*.[15] Despite the fact that Bakhtin's is a pre-eminently *aural* theory of communication, and film is a predominantly *visual* medium, there is much in the dialogic model that has proven liberatory to an area of textual analysis still heavily dominated by structuralist theory.[16] In *Subversive Pleasures*, Stam draws on different aspects of Bakhtin's dialogic theory to renegotiate the text–spectator relationship, to investigate the significance of the 'extraverbal utterance', to explore the representation of ethnic voices and 'Third World' countries in world cinema, and to define some of the key strategies of postmodernist filmic technique. He also shows how Bakhtin's concept of the 'situated utterance' can be used to untangle some of the complex (and contradictory) politics of mass-media culture. To pick up on just one of these, Stam's discussion of postmodernist cinema makes it hard to imagine how analysis of the genre could exist without the concept of heteroglossia. His analysis of Yvonne Rainer's *The Man Who Envied Women* (1984) is a classic case in point:

> Rainer's *The Man Who Envied Women* goes even farther by horizontally juxtaposing or vertically super-imposing a variety of voices and discourses . . . These literal voices are then overlaid with any number of graphic and visual discourses: news photos, advertisements, citations and film clips . . . Such films practice what Bakhtin has called the 'mutual illumination of languages', languages that intersect, collide, rub off on and mutually relativize one another (pp. 51–52).

Heteroglossia, understood as 'the social diversity of speech types' takes on here an extended meaning that causes it to cross disciplines and

---

15   Stam, *Subversive Pleasures* (Baltimore, MD and London: Johns Hopkins University Press, 1989).
16   In his discussion of heteroglossia and the postmodernist film, Stam uses Bakhtin to criticize and supplement Christian Metz's structuralist analysis of filmic language. See *Subversive Pleasures*, p. 44 ff.

incorporate the visual with the verbal, the spoken with the textual. Although far removed from Bakhtin's original citation in medieval carnival and the history of novelistic discourse, it is so supremely 'at home' in this context that no one would dispute its applicability. We may, indeed, be tempted to argue that some dialogic categories appear to cross media (e.g., literature–film) more easily than they cross generic boundaries within their parent discipline (e.g., novel–poetry). What this brief overview will have shown, however, is that there are *no boundaries* left around Bakhtin's dialogic principles as far as the *practice* of criticism is concerned: the generic walls are down, and the scramble for the bit of theory that will match this or that bit of textual analysis seems likely to continue, for better or worse, until the novel is itself a dusty memory.

## II
## Dialogism and the Subject

As we saw in Chapter 1, Bakhtin's dialogic principle has offered the world a new model of the human subject as well as the language he or she uses and the literature he or she reads. In Voloshinov's two early texts, *Freudianism* (1927) and *Marxism and the Philosophy of Language* (1929), an attempt to 'socialize' early twentieth-century trends in human psychology is at the very heart of the theoretical agenda. In anticipation of more recent poststructuralist theory, the early Bakhtin group argued passionately for a human subject that is constituted by and through language, with the consequence that all their theories of language as being 'concretely' social, historical and (dialogically) *relational* were also theories of the subject (see Chapter 1). In Bakhtin's texts which deal specifically with literature, *Dostoevsky's Poetics* and *The Dialogic Imagination* (1934–41), these theories of the historical subject are extended to the textual subject. Bakhtin's novelistic hero is characterized by his 'unfinalizability': he [*sic*] is a subject not in a state of being but of becoming. This state of 'becoming' is, moreover, a profoundly ideological experience in which the subject wrestles with the *internally persuasive words* bidding for his attention (see the discussion in Chapter 1). As we observed in Chapter 1, however, Bakhtin's subject is a generally far less passive recipient of these contending linguistic-ideological forces than Althusser's; he [*sic*] is able to confront and challenge the alien voices through a process of 'objectification' and displacement. He becomes 'himself' through a dynamic exchange with another's discourse; that is, through the process of *dialogue*.

In contrast to psychoanalytic accounts of subject and gender acquisition, it may also be observed that Bakhtin does not associate subject development with distinct (and universally applicable) phases (e.g., preoedipal, oedipal; imaginary/symbolic). The Bakhtinian subject (and here I am referring to the formulations of Voloshinov as well as Bakhtin) is not 'programmed' through the psychosexual traumas of early childhood, but is formed and re-formed through a never-ending process of sociolinguistic interaction. This refusal to privilege childhood experience relates, too, to Voloshinov's trite (and undoubtedly problematic) dismissal of the unconscious/conscious opposition in *Freudianism* (see Chapter 1, section I). Since there is no consciousness 'outside' language (or, indeed, the social context in which the speech act is performed), it is impossible to conceive of an unconscious state except as a contradictory ideological formation (it will be remembered that Voloshinov presented Freud's 'unconscious' as the ideological 'displacement' of a disaffected bourgeoisie!). While I would wish to echo the doubts of many readers who will, at this point, question whether it is possible to theorize a notion of the subject without the acknowledgement of an unconscious, it is important to recognize that this *is* what the Bakhtin group were effectively attempting to argue.

As will be seen in the following discussion, the school of psychoanalysis that Bakhtin's theory has most in common with is object relations.[17] Laying aside the fact that this brand of psychoanalysis, like any other, seeks to understand the development of the subject through her psychosexual relationships with her parents, and that these relationships are conceived as universal, there is a clear similarity between the emphasis both sets of theorists place on the intersubjective ('dialogic') nature of subject acquisition, and on the social contextualization of any such exchange. Take, for example, the terms in which Nancy Chodorow describes the nature of 'separateness' in the following passage:

> The more secure the central self, or ego core, the less one has to define oneself through separateness from others. Separateness becomes, then, a more rigid, defensive, rather fragile, secondary criterion of the strength of the self and of the 'success' of individuation.
>
> This view suggests that no-one has a separateness consisting only of 'me'– 'not me' distinctions. Part of myself is always that which I have taken in; we are all to some degree incorporations and extensions of others. Separateness from the mother, defining oneself apart from her (and from other women),

[17]  Object-relations theory, which draws on the work of early twentieth-century post-Freudian psychoanalysts like Melanie Klein, and has been developed more recently in the writings of D. W. Winnicott and Dorothy Dinnerstein, 'stresses the construction of the self in social relationships rather than through instinctual drives' (see J. Kegan Gardiner, 'Mind Mother: Psychoanalysis and Feminism', in *Making a Difference*, ed. G. Greene and C. Kahn (London: Methuen, 1985, p. 130)). Gardiner writes that: 'According to the object-relations school, the child's primary task in its first years is achieving separation-individuation. This is a dual process by which the child becomes psychologically separate from its mother and simultaneously develops its own sense of self. The theory assumes that babies cannot at first distinguish themselves from their surrounding environments, including their mothers, and that they must establish ego and body boundaries and learn to perceive other people as truly other, not subject to their magical destructive control. They must also learn to perceive themselves as the agents of their actions, separate persons who can feel coherent while experiencing both positive and negative feelings about themselves and others' (pp. 130–31).

Nancy Chodorow (see note 18 below) is the theorist who has attended most closely to the implications of this theory in terms of gender. She has argued that since each child's (male or female) primary attachment is to the mother, boy children will find the process of individuation easier because it is based upon *difference*. Girl children, by contrast, cannot escape from their first relational bond with another female which is predicated upon *sameness*, and this 'relational self' becomes the basis for women's adult relationships and their own predisposition towards 'mothering' roles.

is not the only original goal for women's ego strength and autonomy, even if many women must also attain some sense of reliable separateness. In the process of differentiation, leading to a genuine autonomy, people maintain contact with those with whom they had their earliest relationships: indeed this contact is part of who we are. 'I am' is not definition through negation, it is not 'who I am not'. Developing a sense of confident separateness must be part of all children's development. But once this confident separateness is established, one's relational self can become more central to one's life. Differentiation is not distinctness and separateness, but a particular way of being connected to others. This connection to others, based on early incorporations, in turn enables us to feel that empathy and confidence that are basic to the recognition of the other as a self.[18]

Chodorow's argument that even our separateness from others should be seen as part of a larger relational identity – 'a particular way of being connected to others' – is fully consistent with Bakhtin's view of a subject that is at all times dependent upon the 'other' for his or her self-definition. For him, as well as for her, the 'me'–'not me' distinction is a false one: in any relationship, as in any utterance, who I am (and what I say) will be determined by the presence of my addressee. The *extent* to which distance or separateness is achieved in any particular relationship is, however, of concern to both Bakhtin and the object-relations theorists, with Bakhtin insisting that some sense of difference between parties is necessary to engender a fully dialogic relationship. In his early essay, 'Author and Hero', for example, he writes: 'What would I gain were another to fuse with me? He would see and know only what I already see and know, he would only repeat in himself the inescapable closed circle of my own life; let him rather remain outside me'.[19] Like Chodorow, Bakhtin is working with a model of the subject that at first sight seems paradoxical, but which is merely insisting that our separateness from others is the *dynamic* for our dialogic relation to them. Bakhtin's observations on 'identity' and 'merger' in the 'Speech Genres' essay are also interesting in this respect (see Chapter 1), formulating as they do a situation in which our *proximity* to our addressee will determine the manner of our linguistic exchange with them, and that in some instances this, in turn, gives rise to 'an apparent desire for speaker and addressee to merge completely' (*Speech Genres*, pp. 96–97).[20] The problems that the Bakhtinian model of the subject would perceive with such desire for merger (epitomized in some object-relations theory in the difficulty female children have in separating from the mother; see note 17) will be explored in my reading of Adrienne Rich in Chapter 4. It may be argued, of course, that Jacques

[18]  N. Chodorow, 'Gender, Relation and Difference in Psychoanalytic Perspective', *Socialist Review*, 1979. Reproduced in *Feminism and Psychoanalytic Theory* (Cambridge: Polity Press, 1989), p. 107. See also *The Reproduction of Mothering: Psychoanalysis and the Sociology of Gender* (Berkeley, CA: University of California Press, 1978).
[19]  M. Bakhtin, 'Author and Hero in Aesthetic Activity' (1919–24) in *Estetika Slovesnogo Tvorchestva*, ed. S. G. Bocharov (Moscow: Iskusstuo, 1979), p. 78. Reproduced and translated by G. S. Morson and C. Emerson in *Mikhail Bakhtin: Creation of a Prosaics* (Stanford, CA: Stanford University Press, 1990), pp. 53–54.
[20]  *Speech Genres and Other Late Essays*, ed. C. Emerson and M. Holquist, trans. V. McGee (Austin, TX: University of Texas Press, 1986).

Lacan also evolved a model of the human subject that was linguistically determined. Robert Stam observes how both he and Bakhtin 'converged' in their attempt to expose the 'linguistic dimension of Freud's thought' (p. 4), and how they both shared a 'preoccupation with the image of the mirror and the role of the other in [our] psychic life' (ibid.). There are major differences, however, in the way in which each theorist conceives the subject's relation to his or her linguistic inscription: where Lacan presents a doomed battle with the repressive and authoritarian forces of the Symbolic Order, Bakhtin prefers the vocabulary of reciprocity and exchange:

> Rather than the abstract otherness of Lacan's impersonal symbolic order, Bakhtin would presumably have meant the ongoing and reciprocally modifying interpersonal exchange of the historical subject. When Bakhtin reminds us that even our name is given us by another, he is calling attention not to a repressive 'nom du pere' but rather to evidence of the theoretical impossibility of solitude, since every word, even the solitary word, presupposes an interlocutor . . . For Bakhtin we do not 'fall' into language/the symbolic, but are enriched and fulfilled by it (Stam, *Subversive Pleasures*, p. 5).

Stam's own rhetoric in the last quotation, with its evocation of subject development as an angst-free process of happy reciprocity, is fairly typical of those critics who have turned to Bakhtin's dialogic model for an alternative vision of human subjectivity and the self–other relations upon which it is predicated. It could be said, indeed, that it is in its intersection with theories of the subject that dialogism is presented at its most utopian. The questions of power and authority that have entered other areas of dialogic criticism (see especially the discussion of gender below), are here significantly absent. Dialogism has been invoked specifically to heal wounds, to 'patch up' the Freudian/Lacanian 'family romance': for most critics, the vision of a subject in a state of perpetual intersubjective recreation (growing and shedding selves like the foliage of a tropical rainforest) is too consumately attractive to sully with worries about whether the exchange between two persons can ever be as equal or as supportive as their models would suggest. In almost every text cited in the review which follows, Bakhtinian 'dialogue' is called upon as an arbiter in the unhappy, angst-ridden discourses of Freud, Lacan, Kristeva or Sartre. The exception are those books and essays which perceive the dialogic model to be commensurate with the ethos of a particular theorist (e.g., Luce Irigaray), or those which focus on an unreconstructed postmodernist view of the subject as a site of fragmented anti-humanism.

In their recent book, *Mikhail Bakhtin: Creation of a Prosaics*, Gary Morson and Caryl Emerson set up the model of the dialogic subject as a 'self-in-relation' which is reproduced in only slightly variant form in the works of numerous other advocates.[21] Arguing that the Bakhtinian

---

21   G. S. Morson and C. Emerson, *Mikhail Bakhtin: Creation of a Prosaics* (Stanford, CA: Stanford University Press, 1990). See also B. Zylko, 'The Author-Hero Relation in Bakhtin's Dialogical Poetics', *Critical Studies*, **2**, 1–2, 1990, pp. 65–76. Zylko compares and contrasts Bakhtin's 'positive' (dialogic) model of the subject with that of Sartre and other existentialists in which the 'other' threatens our 'being' with the sense of 'alienation'.

subject 'exists only in dialogue', they quote from Bakhtin's comments on the 'Reworking of the Dostoevsky Book' to support their point:

> To be means to be for another, and through the other for oneself. A person has no sovereign internal territory, he is wholly and always on the boundary; looking inside himself, he looks *into the eyes of another* or *with the eyes of another* (*Dostoevsky's Poetics*, p. 287).

This is, indeed, an evocative statement of intersubjectivity which has many analogues in the writings of the Bakhtin group. To exist *only in relation* is also a concept that has manifest attractions for explaining the aberrant psychology and behaviour of some of the celebrated couples of literary history; for example, Cathy and Heathcliff in *Wuthering Heights*. Michael S. Macovski, in his analysis of this text, uses the Bakhtinian pronouncement 'to be means to communicate dialogically' to explain the enigma of Cathy's famous pronouncement, 'But Nelly, I *am* Heathcliff':

> Consciousness thus dissolves unless projected against the 'background' of the other. The limits of the 'I' emerge only amidst contrasts with the 'thou', much as the Freudian ego takes form only in relation to the superego . . . when she [i.e., Catherine] concludes that Heathcliff is, in her words 'always in my mind – not as a pleasure . . . but as my own being', she acknowledges that only in engaging the other does she 'become for the first time that which [she] is'.[22]

In the second part of his essay, Macovski proceeds to read *Wuthering Heights* as a story of thwarted dialogue which, as a hypothesis, bears some resemblance to Dale Bauer's notion of the 'failed community' in her construction of a 'feminist dialogics' (see below). Macovski argues that the text is structured upon a 'self-consciously flawed model of listening' (p. 367), and that the characters consistently fail one another as interlocutors through their metaphorical 'deafness'. Although this part of the argument is not tied very well to the speculation about Cathy and Heathcliff's intersubjectivity, the implication is clearly that the text's tragedy revolves around the characters' failure to recognize their dialogic need for one another.

A rather more sophisticated account of the 'self-in-relation' is provided by Mae Gwendolyn Henderson's ground-breaking essay on black women's writing: 'Speaking in Tongues'.[23] In this piece, Henderson uses Bakhtin's concepts of *dialogue* and *heteroglossia* to explain both the distinctiveness of black women's writing (to be discussed below in the section on gender) and the construction of a black, female subjectivity. *Vis-à-vis* the latter, Henderson supplements Bakhtin's theory of dialogue (which she sees as inherently 'conflictual') with Hans-Georg Gadamer's analysis of the 'I–thou' relation which she sees as 'consensual'.[24] This distinction between

---

22  M. S. Macovski, '*Wuthering Heights* and the Rhetoric of Interpretation', *Journal of English Literary History* **54**, 1987, pp. 363–84.
23  M. G. Henderson, 'Speaking in Tongues: Dialogics, Dialectics, and the Black Woman Writer's Literary Tradition', in *Changing Our Own Words: Essays and Criticism, Theory and Writing by Black Women*, ed. C. A. Wall (New Brunswick, NJ, and London: Rutgers University Press, 1989). Page references to this volume will be given after quotations in the text.
24  See H. G. Gadamer, *Truth and Method* (New York: Seabury Press, 1975).

the two theorists provides a useful corrective to the majority view of Bakhtinian dialogue which, as I have already observed, is manifestly blind to the power relations present in Bakhtin's own accounts of the dialogic relation. Henderson consequently combines Bakhtin with Gadamer to provide a full account of the inter- and intrasubjective relationships found in black women's texts: the way in which they layer and juxtapose *consensual dialogues* (black women speaking to black women, or black women speaking to black men) with *conflictual dialogues* which engage the discourses of 'the other': white women, white men and the discourses of colonialism and racism:

> It is this notion of discursive difference and identity underlying the simultaneity of discourse which typically characterizes black women's writing. Through the multiple voices that enunciate her complex subjectivity, the black woman writer not only speaks familiarly in the discourse of the other(s), but as Other she is in contestorial dialogue with the hegemonic dominant and sub-dominant or 'ambiguously non-hegemonic' discourses. These writers enter simultaneously into familial, or *testimonial* and public, or *competitive* discourses – discourses that both affirm and challenge the values and expectations of the reader (p. 20).

Through her readings of Sherley Anne Williams's *Dessa Rose* (1986) and Toni Morrison's *Sula* (1973), Henderson proceeds to demonstrate how these authors employ a plurality of voices to represent the complex structuration of black female subjectivity. The black woman experiences her 'being' and 'becoming' as a matrix of complex and ever-shifting racial and gender positionings:

> As gendered and racial subjects, black women speak/write in multiple voices – not all simultaneously or with equal weight, but with various and changing degrees of intensity, privileging one *parole* and then another. One discovers in these writers a kind of internal dialogue reflecting the *intra-subjective* engagement with the *intersubjective* aspects of a self, a dialectic neither repressing difference nor, for that matter, privileging identity, but rather expressing engagement with the social aspects of self ('the others in ourselves'). It is this subjective plurality (rather than the notion of a cohesive or fractured subject) that, finally, allows the black woman to become an expressive site for the dialectics/dialogics of identity and difference (pp. 36–37).

This emphasis on a 'plural' rather than a 'fractured' subject contrasts Henderson's deployment of the dialogic model with the postmodernist appropriations discussed below. However, as we have seen, this is far from being a 'liberal pluralism'. Henderson firmly grounds her accounts of dialogic relationships in a complex, historically specific power dynamic; and her view of the subject is, as a consequence, imbued with a volatility that so many of these readings lack.

Probably the most sophisticated account of the subject as a 'self-in-relation' is Anne Herrmann's *The Dialogic and Difference*.[25] In this book, which combines theoretical discussion with textual analysis of the writings

---

25   A. Herrmann, *The Dialogic and Difference: 'An/Other Woman' in Virginia Woolf and Christa Wolf* (New York: Columbia University Press, 1989). Page references to this volume will be given after quotations in the text.

of Virginia Woolf and Christa Wolf, Herrmann compares the Bakhtinian model of (gendered) subjectivity with the psychoanalytic theories of Lacan, Kristeva, Chodorow and Irigaray. Like Robert Stam (cited earlier), she sees Bakhtin's dialogism as a means of circumventing the tyranny with which Lacan invests the Symbolic Order:

> For Lacan the symbolic dissolves the mother-child dyad in order to insert a third-term in the figure of the father as language, the law, the Institution, a paradigm still largely indebted to the dialectic. Bakhtin begins with a synthesis, the inclusion of both speaker and addressee in any utterance, but the usurpation of one position by the other transforms the dialogic into a monologic voice, a discourse which is closed, authoritarian, and absolute (p. 18).

Although Bakhtin's model allows for the dominance of one subject over another (through the agency of patriarchy, for example) this authority need not be absolute or permanent: the monologic voice may, at any point, be challenged and interrupted. This is because while 'for Bakhtin we are all authors, participants in the reversed hierarchies, suspended privileges, and relativized norms of carnival . . . for Lacan we are always already authored' (ibid.). One might once again argue that Herrmann's is a rather utopian vision of how the dialogic subject can so easily side step Lacanian 'determinism', although – as we have seen in the earlier quotation – she does, at least, allow for a power dynamic in the intersubjective relationship.

After exploring the dialogic parameters of Kristeva's writing (in particular her focus on *intertextuality* which Herrmann sees as the problematic displacement of the Bakhtinian 'addressee' with the 'notion of discourse itself' – p. 17), Herrmann's chief point of focus is Luce Irigaray who she credits with 'reimagining the female Imaginary' (p. 22). According to Herrmann, Irigaray succeeds in rewriting Lacan's self-other relations in line with truly dialogic principles: 'Irigaray offers a mode of perceiving the feminine which is other to the masculine, not as the "other", not as another "one", but as the simultaneity of subject and object in a state of reciprocity' (p. 24). Within this rationale, Irigaray's celebrated vision of the feminine subject – 'she is indefinitely other in herself' – accrues new significance. In the context of Irigaray's metaphor of the 'specularized other', the notion of reciprocal otherness (an 'otherness' predicated upon 'dialogue' rather than 'difference') may be invoked to posit the feminine as (literally) self-reflexive. The feminine subject is defined *not* through her differential relationship to the masculine, but through her dialogic relationship to (another) feminine – she knows herself by her own reflection: 'Specularity allows for the possibility of female dialogue: it constructs the subject as gendered and in dialogue with itself as other' (p. 28).

Herrmann's presentation of the gendered subject is, as I said earlier, one of the most skilful attempts, to date, to graft dialogic theory on to psychoanalytic discourse. By adhering closely to Bakhtin's key principles of dialogue and reciprocity, she is able to elucidate Irigaray's texts in such a way as she side steps their essentialist tendencies, and produces a new relational model of the feminine subject that is eminently attractive to the feminist reader.[26] I will return to how this this model works in the analysis of fictional subjects in the next section, while my reading of Virginia Woolf's *The Waves* (1931) in Chapter 4 will explore its possibilities and limitations in practice.

All the critics I have considered so far in this section have been working with the assumption that Bakhtin's writings have presented us with just *one* version of dialogic subjectivity. This has been disputed by Nancy Glazener who argues that this is manifestly not the case.[27] In a literary history which encompasses classical and medieval prenovelistic discourse at one end of the spectrum, and twentieth-century fiction at the other, it is inevitable that Bakhtin should encounter many changes and developments in the representation of the subject. The most striking of these, according to Glazener, is felt in the transition from the public ('folk') body in pre-Renaissance and Renaissance literature to the individualized bourgeois body of the capitalist era. Indeed, it would be fair to say that in his work on Rabelais and Dostoevsky, Bakhtin identifies two very different models of subjectivity:

> For by the time of Dostoevsky, authoritarian asceticism had given way to an organic version of liberal individualism within dominant political, scientific and literary discourses . . . As a result of this ideological transformation, the embodiment of Bakhtin's characters mainly signifies their individualism, not their corporeal existence (pp. 116–17).

This historicization of Bakhtin's own encounter with different types of subjectivity offers, I feel, an important corrective to all those critics who have extrapolated from his writings a universal model of dialogic subjectivity. Failure to recognize that in, say, writing about the female characters of an Alice Walker novel one is dealing with a very different kind of subjectivity from the one represented by the actors of a medieval carnival could lead readers into a dangerous ahistoricism. Of the critics that I have covered in this review, for example, only Henderson (in her location of a black female subjectivity) indicates a *specific* historical/political context for her view of the subject. Black female subjectivity is seen as dialogically constructed, not because all subjectivity is necessarily so but because at this moment in their history, black women stand at the cross-roads of multiple and conflicting discourses of gender and ethnicity. The writings of the other critics surveyed here – Stam, Macovski and Herrmann – have seen dialogism as a means of revising existing psychoanalytic models of the subject in a way that preserves their universalism and ahistoricism intact.

---

26   Other feminist critics, such as Gail Schwab, have used Bakhtinian theory to argue that Irigaray's work is not essentialist because of its dialogic textuality. In 'Irigarayan Dialogism: Power and Powerplay', Schwab argues that Irigaray is a profoundly dialogic author whose texts represent many different voices and positionings (p. 57). She is also an author who is acutely aware of the dialogic context in which she writes (i.e., she attends to her audience) (pp. 58–59). Schwab's essay appears in *Feminism, Bakhtin, and the Dialogic*, ed. D. Bauer and S. J. McKinstry (Albany, NY: State University of New York Press, 1991), pp. 57–72.

27   N. Glazener, 'Dialogic Subversion: Bakhtin, the Novel and Gertrude Stein', in *Bakhtin and Cultural Theory*, ed. K. Hirschkop and D. Shepherd (Manchester: Manchester University Press, 1989), pp. 109–29.

As I will, it is hoped, demonstrate in my own readings of Woolf and Rich in Chapter 4, this is not, in my opinion, in accord with a Bakhtinian model of the dialogic subject which is plural rather than singular (i.e., there are many possible subject positions, not just one).

The critics who have annexed dialogism to a postmodernist view of the subject should be aware, at least implicityly, of a historical context. Their concern is with the subject of the here and now: the decentred, fragmented and 'inauthentic' subject of late-capitalist culture whose 'essence' has dissolved into a baggage of quotations. In the Introduction I discussed some of the ways in which a dialogic epistemology could be seen both to compare with and yet differ from this popular view of postmodernism, but *vis-à-vis* the literary cultural representation of the subject the conjunction of the two has proven rather unproblematically attractive.

In his essay on James Joyce's *Portrait of the Artist as a Young Man* (1914–15), for example, R. B. Kershner uses Bakhtinian notions of dialogue, heteroglossia and intonational quotation to propose that Stephen Daedalus's character is formed by, and through, a bricolage of multiple voices and texts – none of them his own.[28] This view obviously upsets the popular conception of the novel as a *Bildungsroman*, with Stephen as 'the model of a creative, generative consciousness, increasingly master of language' (p. 881): instead he is a subject that is living proof of Voloshinov's theory that 'consciousness itself is all but identified with language, and both consciousness and language develop through interactive processes' (p. 888). In this essay, Kershner explores the processes through which Stephen becomes a sophisticated 'collage of texts', emphasizing that, from the beginning, this was a journey of alienation: 'Stephen, like the modern novel itself, is a product of heteroglossia. There is no language in which he is at home' (p. 882). Central to Kershner's argument is the hypothesis that it was the 'incremental repetition' of these borrowed words and phrases that (paradoxically) confronted Stephen when he was most in crisis over his identity. He quotes the passage: 'I am Stephen Daedalus. I am walking beside my father whose name is Simon Daedalus. We are in Cork, in Ireland. Cork is a city. Our room is in the Victoria Hotel. Victoria and Stephen and Simon. Names.' (p. 863). Later, in his adolescent 'self-consciously esthetic phase' (p. 884), Stephen's 'repetitions' become more complex. His mind becomes a saturated tissue of liturgical and classical languages, to the extent that a large majority of his sentences contain phrases which ought, as Kershner argues, to be included in 'intonational quotation marks' (the species of 'double-voicedness' that Bakhtin classifies as stylization and *skaz*: see Chapter 1). Kershner sees Stephen using the repetition of these borrowed words as a way of displacing their 'menacing quality' (p. 884), but in terms of his subjectivity, this 'ventriloquism' renders Stephen an exemplary postmodern 'pastiche':

For all his objectifying analysis of the social and literary languages surrounding

28  R. B. Kershner, 'The Artist as Text: Dialogism and Incremental Repetition in Joyce's *Portrait*', *Journal of English Literary History* **53**, 1986, pp. 881–94.

him, all his attempts to eschew the language of the market place, Stephen eventually must become aware that his own private language is a hybrid, that he is *spoken through* even in his private thoughts, in a sort of mental ventriloquy (p. 892).

This postmodernist deployment of polyglossia and heteroglossia in the presentation of a decentered anti-humanist subject is, of course, far removed from Bakhtin's 'celebratory' espousal of the terms in his history of the novel. Instead of the multiplication of voices and dialects being associated with the representation of different social groups, they are cast as signifiers of subjective disintegration. What Kershner has effectively done is removed the concept of heteroglossia from its original 'dialogic' context so that it is stripped of its connotations of *relationship*. Within the postmodernist economy, voices proliferate but they do not communicate, and it remains a matter of opinion whether this adulterated version of a Bakhtinian concept can be considered properly dialogic.

In *Subversive Pleasures* Robert Stam offers a description of a postmodernist textual subject similar to Kershner's. His candidate is Woody Allen's Zelig (from the film of the same name) whom he presents as an exemplary instance of how one becomes a subject through a process of linguistic hybridization:

> Zelig exemplifies the contemporary condition of what Lawrence Grossberg calls 'nomadic subjectivity'. The self, in this sense, forms a kind of shifting hybrid sum of its discursive practices. Internally persuasive discourse is affirmed, for Bakhtin, through 'assimilation', through a tight interweaving of the words of others 'with one's own word'. Zelig, in his constant metamorphoses, represents the person who has lost all capacity to distinguish between his own and the alien word (p. 214).

Like Kershner's, this is a plausible but 'adialogic' application of the principle of heteroglossia to describe the 'nomadic subjectivity' of the postmodern subject. Stam's distance from his Bakhtinian source is instanced by the hegemony he affords the 'internally persuasive word'. It will be remembered that in Bakhtin's own account (see Chapter 1) the subject's 'ideological becoming' depends upon an active negotiation of the other's words through a process of 'objectification'. Allen's Zelig, on the other hand, appears to be completely in their thrall. What Kershner and Stam's readings would seem to suggest is that while certain items in the Bakhtinian vocabulary can easily be transported to a postmodernist critical context, their inherent dialogicality is left behind.

There is evidence in the work of other critics, moreover, that, *vis-à-vis* the notion of the subject, dialogics and postmodernism are fundamentally incompatible epistemologies. In a ground-breaking discussion of the relation of postmodernism to feminism in her book *Feminine Fictions*, Patricia Waugh has argued how the popular view of the postmodern subject (espoused by writers like Kershner and Stam) may be applicable to the representation of the subject in the work of male authors, but is by no means common in women's writing.[29] The reason for this, she

---

[29]   P. Waugh, *Feminine Fictions: Revisiting the Postmodern* (London and New York: Routledge, 1989). Page references to this volume are given after quotations in the text.

argues, is that 'for many women there can be no prior subject or self whose fragmentation becomes a political necessity':

> Postmodernism expresses nostalgia for but loss of belief in the concept of the human subject as an agent effectively intervening in history, through its fragmentation of discourses, language games, and decentering of subjectivity. Feminism seeks a subjective identity, a sense of effective agency and history for women which has hitherto been denied them by the dominant culture. Postmodernist writers express the disintergration of the potency of the 'individual vision' mediated through the 'unique' style of modernism and stress the inability of the contemporary subject to locate 'himself' historically . . . Feminist writers, in the meantime, appear to be pursuing the sort of definition of identity and relationship to history which postmodernists have rejected (p. 10).

Waugh's reasoning here is that women writers' representation of female subjectivity rejects the postmodernist vision of a fragmented, decentred self simply because it is predicated upon a myth of wholeness and autonomy that women – as marginalized *political subjects* – have never enjoyed in the first place. She goes on to argue, moreover – both in *Feminine Fictions* and the more recent *Practising Postmodernism/Reading Modernism* – that women writers have espoused, instead, a *relational* model of subjectivity that she presents in terms of object-relations theory, but which may equally be thought of as dialogic.[30] She writes:

> The exclusion of gender from postmodern discussions has left its theorists largely blind to the possibilities of challenging autonomy through a relational concept of identity. If women's identity has tended, broadly, and allowing for differences across this, to be experienced in terms which do not necessarily see separation gained only at the expense of connection, one would expect some sense of this to be expressed in discourses other than the theoretical and psychoanalytic. Women's sense of identity is more likely, for psychological and cultural reasons, to consist of a more diffuse sense of the boundaries of self and their notion of identity understood in relational and intersubjective terms (*Practising Postmodernism*, p. 135).[31]

This 'alternative' reading of a *female* postmodernist subject, would seem, to me, to have a more convincing claim on Bakhtinian dialogics than some of the postmodernist appropriations cited earlier.

In conclusion it may be said that dialogism has provided literary and cultural critics with a model of self-other relations that can be usefully employed to challenge and/or refine existing psychoanalytic formations. The limitations of this engagement depend, first, on the tendency to divest the dialogic model of a power dynamic: the notion of a 'dialogic subject' has been somewhat naïvely pitted against the psychosexual struggles featured in the writings of Freud and Lacan. Secondly, there has been a blindness to the problems of grafting a notion of the dialogic on to universalist models of subjectivity. In this last respect, as in the postmodernist readings cited

---

[30] P. Waugh, *Practising Postmodernism/Reading Modernism. Interrogating Texts Series* (London: Edward Arnold, 1992).

[31] For those requiring an introduction to postmodernist theories and theorists I would recommend P. Waugh, *Postmoderism: A Reader* (London and New York: Edward Arnold, 1992).

above, a *partial* appropriation of the dialogic principle has impeded a truly radical revisioning of subjectivity. The next step is for readers and critics to go beyond an interpretation of the dialogic as a model of amicable exchange and reciprocity, and to explore subjectivity in relation to the political/social/historical constraints and expectations present in Bakhtin's accounts of spoken and written dialogue. I shall attempt to pursue this path myself in the readings of Virginia Woolf and Adrienne Rich in Chapter 4.

# III
## Dialogism and Gender

Reviewing the extensive feminist appropriation of Bakhtin in the past ten years, the first question that needs to be asked is 'why?' Why should a writer whose work is so markedly silent on questions of gender prove so attractive to so many different areas of feminist theory and criticism? Why has Wayne Booth's attempt to discredit Bakhtin's *Rabelais* book (1965) on the grounds of its blatant misogyny had so little effect?[32] Why use *another* male theorist to account for the qualitative difference of women's writing when we now have a large body of feminist theory to engage with instead? The short answer to all these questions is 'dialogism' itself. As will be seen in the review which follows, 'dialogue' has proven a term infinitely applicable to so many of the critical/epistemological/political debates in which feminists have been involved as we passed from the 'strident'(!) seventies to the more self-reflective nineties. Like 'difference' and 'ambiguity', 'dialogue' has become an indispensable item of vocabulary for negotiating the complexities (and apparent contradictions) of a de-essentialized feminism. In the introduction to the collection of essays, *Conflicts in Feminism*, for example, Marianne Hirsch and Evelyn Fox Keller write about the need of 'new ways for feminists to confront divergent positions with one another, and to enact the dynamic of their disagreement'.[33] Dialogue is a concept which touches the heart of what it means to be a feminist: a concept evocative of sisterhood, of the perpetual negotiation of sameness and difference, of our dealings with men and patriarchal institutions, of our relationship to a language which simultaneously is, and is not, our own.

In terms of theoretical and methodological specifics, Nancy Glazener has identified two major attractions of Bakhtin's dialogic theory for feminists:

> First, his assertion that literature represents a struggle among socio-ideological languages unsettles the patriarchal myth that there could be a language of truth transcending relations of power and desire. Second, Bakhtin's insistence

---

32   W. Booth, 'Freedom and Interpretation: Bakhtin and the Challenge of Feminist Criticism', *Critical Inquiry*, **9**, 1, 1982, pp. 45–76.
33   *Conflicts in Feminism*, ed. M. Hirsch and E. Fox Keller (London and New York: Routledge, 1990), p. 377.

that words and discourses have socially differential significance implies that linguistic and literary forms are necessarily shaped by the gender relations that structure society . . . The concept of subjectively defined utterance ensures that for as long as gender has a share in the social construction of subjectivity, part of every utterance's intelligibility will derive from its orientation toward gender.[34]

According to Glazener, then, it is the *social situatedness* of Bakhtin's theories of discourse and utterance that signal their fundamental relevance for feminist criticism. Although Bakhtin himself fails to recognize the crucial role of gender in his conceptualization of social language (in the specification of the addressee, in the 'rules' of extraverbal context, in 'dual-tone speech', in heteroglossia, in 'speech genres'), its relevance is implicit in everything he writes. If it matters so acutely that we identify the class, ethnicity and social status of a speaker, 'his' hierachical relationship to his addressee, and the context in which his utterance is made (written or spoken) (see the discussion of the 'Speech Genres' essay in Chapter 2), then it follows that it matters what sex he or she is. As Glazener and other critics like Clive Thomson have observed, gender can simply be added to Bakhtin's contextualizing schema: it is an oversight that (for the theoretically pragmatic) is easily corrected.[35] In a shrewd aside, however, Thomson advises us that it is only a *power-inscribed* version of the dialogic that is truly useful for feminists:

Bakhtin also plays a constructive theoretical role for the feminist project. His work points in the direction of a feminist dialogic theory, and there is a general agreement that the addition of the category of gender to the theory of the dialogic is possible. But the addition of this category entails adjustments in the utopian tendency in Bakhtin's dialogic. The dialogic interplay of female voices ought to be seen as a struggle – not as freeplay – because the relation between voices always takes place in a political arena where powerful interests seek to oppress the less privileged ones. Although such a corrective to the liberal and humanist appropriateness of Bakhtin's dialogic theory have been suggested by other critics, the feminist voices I have been dealing with have made it more systematic and insistent in keeping this issue to the forefront in their work (p. 158).

This call to preserve the element of power and struggle present in Bakhtin's own dialogic discourse is one that I have had repeated personal recourse to in this chapter, and Thomson's comment leads us to a consideration of those feminist critics who have, indeed, kept it in mind. The one that has most self-consciously rejected an anodyne, conciliatory version of the dialogic is Dale Bauer who, in the first chapter of *Feminist Dialogics*, writes:

My first reaction to Bakhtin was to become seduced by his theory of dialogism since it seemed to offer a utopian ground for all voices to flourish; at least all voices could aspire to internal polemic or dialogism. Yet Bakhtin's blind spot is the battle. He does not work out the contradiction between the

---

[34]   Glazener, 'Dialogic Subversions', pp. 109–10.
[35]   C. Thomson, 'Mikhail Bakhtin and Contemporary Anglo-American Feminist Theory', *Critical Studies*, **1**, 2, 1989, pp. 141–61.

promises of utopia or community and the battle which is always waged for control.[36]

My presentation of Bakhtin's work in Chapter 1, and further discussions in this chapter, will, it is hoped, have proven that this blind spot does not extend to all of Bakhtin's work – although there are, admittedly, enough of the conciliatory discourses for critics to make this liberal/democratizing reading of dialogism if they will. Bauer's call for a 'dialogics of battle' is well made, however. As feminists we can never forget that our dialogues rarely exist between equal parties, although a modified version of that possibility is, as I shall explain below, perhaps one way of redefining what we mean by 'women's writing' (i.e., women writing *for* other women perceived to be their 'equals').

I want to move on first, however, to another aspect of Bauer's work: her identification of 'feminist dialogics' as a new *school* of feminist criticism. In *Feminist Dialogics: A Theory of Failed Community*, 'feminist dialogics' is invoked in a specific critical context to refer to the way in which women resist inclusion and assimilation by patriarchal communities: 'Resistance to exclusive, androcentric communities requires a "language of defiance" (Elizabeth Meese) which is implicit in Bakhtinian notions of "multi-vocality" and "dialogue"' (p. xi). This notion of dialogue as a power-inscribed activity in which two parties struggle for supremacy and/or the right to independence from one another relates to Bauer's strong feelings (quoted above) on how feminists must redefine the Bakhtinian term: 'Bakhtin's model relies on a positive space, a community he celebrates because of its activity, its engagement of others. By adding a feminist turn to it, the dialogic community Bakhtin theorizes becomes a much more ambivalent territory (p. xiv). Bauer explores what form such dialogic resistance may take in her readings of the novels of Henry James, Nathaniel Hawthorne, Edith Wharton and Kate Chopin. Wharton and Chopin, for example, demonstrate the failure of the 'interpretive community' to offer women a proper dialogic space, as a consequence of which they search for alternative (and sadly self-destructive) ways of 'talking back'.[37] Of Edna Pontellier in *The Awakening* (1899) she writes:

> Edna Pontellier's awakening is really a search to avoid definition by her community, a deadening definition of 'women' that would reduce her to a peculiar truth of her culture . . . Her suicide, then, is a sign of her failure to continue the subversive dialogue she would wage with the creole ideologies and, at the same time, a failure of the community (p. xv).

Bauer's, then, is a complex – one might even say perverse – appropriation of the dialogic principle for feminist purposes. Instead of seizing upon its connotations of negotiation and 'sisterhood' (i.e., dialogue *between* women), she comandeers it as a model for the fraught and volatile relationship women (both actual and textual) have with patriarchal communities which 'fail'

---

[36]   D. Bauer, *Feminist Dialogics: A Theory of Failed Community* (Albany, NY: State University of New York Press, 1989). Page references to this volume will be given after quotations in the text.

[37]   Bauer's notion of an 'interpretive community' derives from Stanley Fish's 'reader-response' theories of how we make sense of texts. See S. Fish, *Is There a Text in this Class?: The Authority of Interpretive Communities* (Cambridge, MA, and London: Harvard University Press, 1980).

them. Certainly this is a very specific understanding of 'feminist dialogics', and one that could hardly be employed to describe a whole school of critical practice. It is not surprising, then, to discover that in her more recent (edited) collection of essays, *Feminism, Bakhtin, and the Dialogic*, Bauer has expanded the definition to include all manner of theoretical and critical engagement.[38] Indeed, the problem now is to discover what 'feminist dialogics' *is not*, as much as what *it is*. In their introduction to the volume, Bauer and McKinstry avoid a direct attempt at definition, evidently preferring that multiple meanings should accrue around the term as they use it in different contexts. Feminist dialogics is a way of thinking that 'challenges the assumption in contemporary culture of a monolithic or universal feminism' (p. 1); it is a way of living that 'overcomes the public-private split' (ibid.); it is an epistemology which, like 'standpoint theory', believes that 'context' and 'positionality' are all (p. 2); it is a new model of pedagogy which shows 'genders, classes and races in dialogue rather than in opposition' (p. 3); and, most importantly, it is the latest (and, the editors believe, the most radical) form of feminist political resistance:[39]

> A feminist dialogics is, above all, an example of the cultural resistance that Teresa de Lauretis argues is a necessary strategy for feminist political practice. For the object is not, ultimately, to produce a feminist monologic voice, a dominant voice that is the reversal of the patriarchal voice (even were such a project conceivable), but to create a feminist dialogics that recognizes power and discourse as indivisible, monologism as a model of ideological dominance, and narrative as inherently multivocal, as a form of cultural resistance that celebrates the dialogic voice that speaks with many tongues, which incorporates multiple voices of the cultural web (p. 4).

Feminist dialogics is, then, according to this oblique listing, an epistemology, a pedagogy, a politics and a lifestyle *as well* as being a school of literary and cultural criticism. Indeed, the latter is not cited as the *objective* of a feminist dialogics at all; it is simply (by inference) one of the arenas in which it is practised and made visible. In the allusion to a 'politics of resistance' (see the quotation above) we see the residue of Bauer's earlier definition of feminist dialogic practice, but the concept has now been broadened out to include the more conciliatory negotiating strategies that feminists may be involved with, both in their textual practices and in their lives.

Leaving behind the problems of global definitions, I want to move on now to the ways in which dialogic theory has been annexed by feminist critics in specific instances, starting with the extensive contribution it has made to gynocriticism.[40] Readers will be aware that the project of specifying the *difference* of women's writing has not abated, despite the large body

[38] Bauer and McKinstry, *Feminism, Bakhtin, and the Dialogic*.
[39] 'Standpoint theory', as represented by the work of feminist scholars like Dorothy Smith, Nancy Hartstock and Sandra Harding, argues for a 'strategic essentialism' which will enable women to analyse their oppression from within the context of their own experience.
[40] Elaine Showalter coined the term 'gynocriticism' to describe the study of the history, styles, themes, genres and structures of writing by women. See E. Showalter, 'Towards a Feminist Poetics', in *The New Feminist Criticism*, ed. E. Showalter (London: Virago, 1986).

of theory which suggests that all attempts at linking textual practice to authorial gender are doomed to failure. Dialogism has, however, enabled feminists to approach the old problems from a number of new perspectives (e.g., how do we claim specificity for women's writing/black women's writing/lesbian writing without falling foul of essentialism?). First, there are those critics like Dale Bauer (see above), Patricia Yaegar and Mary O'Connor who have located the revolutionariness of women's writing *not* in the creation of some new language but in a dialogizing with existing patriarchal discourse.

In her book, *Honeymad Women*, Patricia Yaegar sets out to develop a new theory of women's writing based on Levi-Strauss's metaphor of the 'honeymad woman' who 'eats honey in bizarre amounts, who feeds on it wildly and to excess'.[41] It is a metaphor which allows her to suggest notions of supreme playfulness. Rather than accept the view that women are forever exiled from a patriarchal language which is not their own, the writing of women in the past is a rich testimony to all manner of 'emancipatory strategies'.[42] Yaegar argues that we do not have to await the 'new women's language' advocated by the French feminists since women have been making language their own for hundreds of years. Women's language, according to Yaegar, is characterized by its dialogic relationship to 'dominant (masculine) discourse'. In a pilot essay for the book, she demonstrates this strategy with reference to Eudora Welty's *The Golden Apples*: (1949), a text which revolves around a self-conscious incorporation ('plagiarism') of W. B. Yeats.[43] In *Honeymad Women* she focuses on how the novel, as a genre, has supported this sort of dialogic play:

> We need . . . to pay less attention to women's silences and more attention to the ways women address men's silences and get them to speak. We need especially to attend to the ways in which women writers have ended these silences, have persuaded male writers to speak in women's direction by a peculiar subterfuge: women writers have incorporated men's texts in their own and entered into dialogues with these texts that these male writers have refused to initiate . . . the novel is a form women choose because its multivoicedness allows the interruption and interrogation of the dominant culture. The novel's polyvocality gives the writer an opportunity to interrupt the speech practices, the ordinary patriarchal assumptions of everyday life (pp. 30–31).

Yaegar's reading of Charlotte Brontë's *Villette* (1853), in the chapter 'The Bilingual Heroine', is an intriguing and persuasive account of how

---

41   P. Yaegar, *Honeymad Women*. Page references will be given after quotations in the text.
42   Myriam Díaz-Diocaretz argues something similar in her essay, 'Bakhtin, Discourse, and Feminist Theories', *Critical Studies*, 1, 2, 1989, pp. 121–39: 'The writing subject may be marginalized or constrained by patriarchy's ways of legitimizing itself, but this confinement or exclusion is not necessarily textualized . . . A feminist critical vision has to work precisely at the site where the speaking or writing subject – in its dialogic nature – is grounded, or from which it is interacting, whether embedded within patriarchal notions or not. Viewed from this Bakhtinian perspective, texts are no longer seen as the static dichotomy between *non-dominant* (the social realm of women) and *dominant* (patriarchy) material forces, but in a new, fully dynamic field in which *all situations of the word* become equally contested and challenged' (p.134–35).
43   P. S. Yaegar, '"Because a Fire Was in My Head": Eudora Welty and the Dialogic Imagination', *PMLA*, **99**, 1984, pp. 955–73.

'multivoicedness' gives rise to a distinctive feminine/feminist discourse. Her thesis is that the second language of the novel (French) 'serves an emancipatory function . . . enacting a moment in which the novel's primary language is put into process, a moment of possible transformation when the writer forces her speech to break out of the old representations of the feminine and posit something new' (p. 36). *Villette*'s incorporation of this 'abnormal discourse' serves to relativize the dominant discourse, making it into simply 'one of many possible modes of speech' (p. 41). In this Yaegar is not arguing that French, in itself, is a subversive 'feminine' language; merely that it functions as a 'counterpoint' and thus creates a dialogic space in which the female character can renegotiate her own positioning.

Like Bauer, Yaegar conceives dialogue as a category of struggle and resistance, evocative of women's constant efforts to claim a space in androcentric language and culture. Similar in conception is Mary O'Connor's thesis on contemporary black American women's writing.[44] O'Connor argues that writers like Alice Walker, Gloria Naylor and Ntozake Shange produce texts in which a dialogic interaction with dominant and ruling discourses (discourses of gender and ethnicity) is the source of power and herald of change:

> The more voices that are ferreted out, the more discourses that a woman can find herself an intersection of, the freer she is from the dominating voice, from one stereotypical and sexist position. The male voices are heard, but not contested, in these books (p. 202).

This emphasis on the black women's text being the site of multiple and competing discourses is reminiscent, too, of Mae Gwendolyn Henderson's argument in 'Speaking in Tongues' (discussed in the section on subjectivity above). Henderson, it will be remembered, characterized the black woman's subjectivity in terms of dialogic inscription by these multiple voices, and she understands the distinctiveness of black women's writing (including its *popularity*) in similar terms:

> It is this quality of speaking in tongues, that is, multivocality . . . that accounts in part for the current popularity and critical success of black women's writing. The engagement of multiple others broadens the audience for black women's writing, for like the disciples of Pentecost who spoke in diverse tongues, black women, speaking out of the specificity of their racial and gender experiences, are able to communicate in a diversity of discourses (p. 36).

Other critics have, however, put dialogism to quite a different use in their attempt to account for the specificity of women's writing. Rather than focus on women writers' polyphonic proliferation of, and dialogic engagement with, the cultural/textual discourses with which they are surrounded, writers like Anne Herrmann, Jane Marcus and myself have preferred to look at the way their texts dialogize with a female or feminist addressee.

[44] M. O'Connor, 'Subject, Voice and Women in Some Contemporary Black American Women's Writing', in *Feminism, Bakhtin, and the Dialogic*, ed. Bauer and McKinstry, pp. 199–212.

In my essay 'Dialogic Theory and Women's Writing' I propose that rather than search for the elusive 'difference' of women's writing in either the sex of the author (i.e., who a text is by) or in its content (i.e., what it is about) we concentrate, instead, on *who a text is for*.[45] Women's writing is best understood not as writing *by* women but as writing for them: what genders a text is not its authorship but its *potential readership* – the way in which interlocutors *within* the text (i.e., the textual addressees) and its actual readers are positioned as female or, indeed, feminist.

Contrary to Bauer's formulation of a 'dialogics of antagonism', my own engagement with contemporary feminist fiction led me to focus on the special intimacies of address – manifested in a range of textual and contextual codes – associated with one woman speaking or writing to another. Although not all female-authored texts address a female audience, many of those that we would wish to designate 'feminist' do.[46] This, I suggest, is why many of us choose to read women-authored texts for our pleasure: it is not simply that they focus on themes and issues that relate to our 'experience' as women but that they address themsleves *to us* (either literally or analogously, through the surrogate presence of a female interlocutor in the text). As Teresa de Lauretis has argued in her attempt to define 'feminist cinema', it is political sense that many feminists now feel an urgent need for dealing with texts that speak to them directly: we have simply spent too many years legitimating our foothold in texts that position the reader as male.[47]

My investigations into how the gendering of a text's reader/interlocutor is translated into specific textual strategies has been supported by the work of the American feminist critics, Anne Herrmann and Jane Marcus. In *The Dialogic and Difference* (discussed above in the section on subjectivity), Herrmann illustrates the way in which a feminist text can either address itself to an adversarial male or to a sympathetic female 'ally', through a comparison of the writings of Virginia Woolf and Christa Wolf:

> The rhetorical difference [i.e., the difference between Woolf and Wolf] lies in the difference of addressee; Woolf constructs her addressee as *antagonist*, whose otherness is attributed to difference in gender and class. Wolf constructs her interlocutor as ally, as someone who mirrors her own point of view . . . for [Christa Wolf] any construction of the subject implies the inclusion of another subjectivity as a way of guarding against objectification (p. 43).

Despite my repeated claims elsewhere that we must recognize *all* dialogic activity as a power dynamic (there is always, at least, the potential for one party to dominate the other in some aspect of their social relations), there nevertheless do exist texts (such as Wolf's *The Quest for Christa T*) (1968), in which 'the listener is normally found *next to* the author as his ally' (*Bakhtin School Papers*, p. 24: see Further Reading). Similarly, although

[45]   'Dialogic Theory and Women's Writing' in *Working Out: New Directions for Women's Studies*, ed. H. Hinds, A. Phoenix and J. Stacey (Brighton: Falmer Press, 1992), pp. 184–93.
[46]   There are, of course, texts like Virginia Woolf's essay' Three Guineas' whose feminism depends upon an antagonistic relationship with a male addressee (see the discussion of Anne Herrmann's volume following, and the reference in note 25 above).
[47]   T. de Lauretis, 'Guerrilla in the Midst: Women's Cinema in the 80s', *Screen*, **31**, 1, Spring, pp. 6–25.

all writing by women most certainly does not position the reader as an ally (either for strategic rhetorical purposes like Woolf's essays or because it claims no special gender-specific solidarity), much contemporary feminist writing brings that sense of equality and community to metatextual consciousness.[48] In her analysis of *Christa T*, Herrmann shows how a special 'comradeship' is forged between subject (Christa T), narrator and reader through the strategic deployment of the pronouns 'we' and 'us':

> The 'us' refers to the narrator and the narrated in the novel, to the questioner and respondent of the interview, and to the participants in a socialist society. It represents the political ideal of a socialist collectivity as well as the discursive reality of a divided subjectivity (p. 77).

In other texts, however, the reader/interlocutor may be positioned as female/feminist/lesbian by more subtle means. Here, Jane Marcus's reading of Virginia Woolf's *A Room of One's Own* (1929) is especially fascinating, suggesting as it does that this is a text which covertly positions its reader as lesbian through a coded use of 'ellipsis' and other rhetorical devices.[49] This artful means by which a 'woman writer seduces a woman reader' constitutes a special category of dialogic activity which Marcus calls 'sapphistory': 'The question marks and ellipses, to which we supply the silent assent and fill in the blanks, seal the pact of our conspiracy' (p. 167). This, is, indeed, a quite different reading of Woolf to Herrmann's cited earlier (though Herrmann was referring specifically to *Three Guineas* (1938) and not *A Room of One's Own*), and serves to draw our attention to the many different levels of positioning that may coexist within a text. While the overt addressee of a text may be positioned as male/heterosexual/white/middle class, the covert addressee may be female/lesbian/black/working class – or some combination of those specifiers. It is this volatility that makes text-reader positioning so complex and politically charged.[50]

To conclude, the work of Herrmann, Marcus and myself has employed the notion of dialogicality to posit a model of women's writing which defines its specificity in terms of the positioning of its addressee. Although

---

[48] In 'Dialogic Theory and Women's Writing', I cite the example of Marge Piercy's novel, *Small Changes*, (1973), which opens with the dedication: 'For me. For you. For us. Even for them'. This statement clearly registers a bond between the self and the female 'other', and positions it *against* the (implicitly) masculine third person plural.

[49] J. Marcus, 'Sapphistory: The Woolf and the Well', In *Lesbian Texts and Contexts*, ed. K. Jay and J. Glasgow (New York: New York University Press, 1990), pp. 164–79.

[50] I discuss the question of simultaneous/multiple reader-positioning in my essay '"I the Reader": Text, Context and the Balance of Power' in *Feminist Subjects, Multi-Media* ed. P. Florence and D. Reynolds (Manchester: Manchester University Press, forthcoming). My argument here draws on the work of Stuart Hall whose 'Encoding/Decoding [in TV discourse]' (1973) suggests that texts identify and position complex 'hierarchies' of readers/viewers (see S. Hall, *Culture, Media*, Language (London: Hutchinson, 1980), pp. 128–38, and Martin Montgomery's essay, 'D-J Talk' in *Media, Culture and Society*, 8, 4, 1986, pp. 421–40, which shows how certain groups within an audience/readership can be alternatively included and excluded by a particular discourse. See also Sara Mills's essay, 'Reading as/like a feminist' in *Gendering the Reader*, ed. S. Mills (Hemel Hempstead: Harvester Wheatsheaf, 1994), and my own 'Pre-Raphaelite Painting and the Female Spectator: Sexual/Textual Positioning in D. G. Rossetti's *The Beloved*' in the same volume.

most of my discussion here has focused on the addressee as the reader or spectator of the text, I have also been concerned with the way in which texts enact or describe dialogic relationships between women: the letters, poems and novels which address a second-person interlocutor *within* the text.[51] In this respect, my reading of Adrienne Rich's Twenty-One Love Poems (1978) in Chapter 4 has a special significance as the only one of my chosen texts that takes the form of an actual dialogue between speaker and interlocutor.

I want to move on, in the final part of this section, to look at the way in which the Bakhtinian categories of carnival and chronotope have been 'gendered' by feminist readers, and also to consider how we should deal with the significant absence of women writers in Bakhtin's history of the novel.

To take the last point first, there is, indeed, an element of scandal in the fact that women authors – seen by even the orthodox literary establishment as instrumental in the genesis and development of the novel form – should be so entirely absent from Bakhtin's account. In her essay, 'The Dilemmas of a Feminist Dialogic', Diane Price Herndl indicates how difficult it is to excuse Bakhtin's gender blindness in this particular respect:

> If the novel is, indeed, a feminine genre, then Bakhtin's overlooking women writers is not as easily glossed over as Wayne Booth claims. If multivoicedness is a feminine characteristic, if dialogism is largely a gender-, rather than a genre-marked trait, then Bakhtin was not merely culturally backwards, but was ignorant of the very nature of the genre. On the other hand, if feminine language is novelistic, has been novelized, then novelization is much more monologic than Bakhtin claims. If it has the power to control women's language, and therefore women's thinking, then it is authoritarian – Bakhtin just did not see this because it was *he*, as a man, who wielded the authority.[52]

To this criticism on a point of principle may be added the fact that a comparative study of female-authored (or, indeed, female-addressed) texts may have supported and/or challenged many details in Bakhtin's history and analysis of the novel. The preceding discussion, for example, suggests that women writers have evolved a distinctive form of 'hidden dialogue' and 'hidden polemic' (see Chapter 1) replete with a special consciousness of gender. It now remains for feminist critics to do Bakhtin's work for him, and to review every aspect of his dialogic superstructure with an awareness of gender.

One of the aspects of Bakhtin's work that has been most extensively scrutinized by feminist critics has been his presentation of *carnival*. In Chapter 1 I brought forward some of the accusations that have been made about the supposed misogyny of *Rabelais and his World*, together with the attempts of critics like Robert Stam to defend Bakhtin against such imputations. For critics like Nancy Glazener and Clair Wills, however,

---

51   See 'Dialogic Theory and Women's Writing', pp. 187–89. In this section I discuss A. Walker, *The Color Purple* (London: Women's Press, 1983) and J. Rule, *This is Not For You* (London: Pandora, 1982).
52   D. Price Herndl, 'The Dilemmas of a Feminine Dialogic' in *Feminism, Bakhtin, and the Dialogic*, ed. Bauer and McKinstry, pp. 7–24.

Bakhtin's own 'political correctness' is of less concern than the ultimate 'usefulness' of the concept.[53] The appropriation of carnival as a metaphor for profeminist disruption/subversion is, according to Glazener, much too naïve and simplistic:

> The concept of the anarchically disruptive, diffusely subversive other, which parts of Bakhtin's work and certain strains of feminist theory have endorsed, is more mystifying than enlightening, and . . . tends to overshadow the analysis of particular strategies for ideological contention and subversion (p. 111).

One of the particular problems she identifies with such an uncritical appropriation is that it is historically and politically untenable to draw comparisons between Bakhtin's 'folk' and 'women' when the latter simply do not represent the space 'outside' high/dominant culture in the same sense (p. 114). Glazener is further critical of Bakhtin's own depiction of the lower classes as a 'monolithically subversive force', since this obscures the subtle and complex movement of alliegances *across* classes. Wills echoes this concern by claiming that Bakhtin's carnival has too often been read as a simple opposition of 'high' and 'low' cultures, with women too easily assimilatable into the latter category: 'Celebratory claims for the power of the carnivalesque to undo hierarchies are merely a fetishizing of the repressed' (p. 137). Wills compares this with the unhelpful fetishization of a space 'outside' the symbolic order by certain French feminists, and argues that the only way in which either carnival or the semiotic can be seen as potentially subversive is through their active *engagement* with the forces of opposition.[54] Linking this necessary dialogue between public and private, between 'high' and 'low' discourse with the challenges facing women's writing, she concludes:

> The transgressive potential of women's writing hinges on the relationship between the excluded and the low. I have argued that for Bakhtin carnival must be brought into dialogue with official forms through the medium of literature, in order to be politically effective; analogously, the 'lawlessness' of the witch, the hysteric, the proletarian woman, must be brought within the public sphere, conforming to some extent with its norms, if it is to become a language which can engage politically with the 'official' language (p. 140).

In short, both carnival and 'hysteria' (the particular manifestation of extra-Symbolic behaviour that Wills focuses on in this essay) are subversive only to the extent that they *make visible* their dialogue with the forces of opposition. Bakhtinian carnival *can* be gendered in a way that is useful for feminist criticism, but its mechanics have to be overhauled *as well* as its categories extended.

Compared with carnival there has been little attention paid by feminist

[53] See Glazener, 'Dialogic Subversion', and C. Wills, 'Upsetting the Public: Carnival, Hysteria and Women's Texts', in *Bakhtin and Cultural Theory*, ed. Hirschkop and Shepherd, pp. 130–51.
[54] Wills is referring to the feminist 'misappropriation' of Julia Kristeva's 'semiotic' (the phase of ego development prior to the child's entry into language) as an inherently 'feminine' space, when in Kristeva's original formulation it is explicitly 'nongendered'. See R. Felski, *Beyond Feminist Aesthetics* (London: Hutchinson Radius, 1989) for a full discussion of this misreading (pp. 33–35).

critics to Bakhtin's category of the *chronotope*. One exception is Mary O'Connor's eminently interesting essay, 'Chronotopes for Women under Capital' which shows – through readings of two texts by contemporary women authors – how the chronotope may be gendered.[55] (In Bakhtin's own writings – see the discussion in Chapter 1 – it is very clearly 'gender-neutral'.) O'Connor's argument is that the emphasis on *presentness*, which Bakhtin associates with the novel as a genre (i.e., its material conjunction of time and space), finds a particular defamiliarizing expression in the domestic interiors of women writers:

> The world of domestic acquisition provided women with both power and entrapment: control over the objects and some social relations in the home, but ultimately controlled and constituted by the patriarchal and capitalist systems that pretended to stay outdoors (p. 140).

In the two texts that O'Connor chooses to write about, Alice Munro's short story 'Fits' (from *The Progress of Love*, 1986) and Bharati Mukerjee's novel *Wife* (1975), the 'presentness' of the domestic worlds in which the female protagonists are trapped is turned to frightening and macabre effect: the chronotope of the domestic idyll (see Chapter 1) suffers a carnivalesque inversion and becomes a chronotope of domestic horror. Inasmuch as space and time are always socially and historically inscribed, it is clear that all the chronotopes Bakhtin discusses in 'Forms of Chronotope in the Novel' can be reread with a gendered awareness, and this is one of the things I shall be attempting to do in my own readings of Toni Morrison and Jeanette Winterson in Chapter 5.

Despite the spectacular absence of gender-consciousness in Bakhtin's own writings, then, the past ten years have proved dialogism and its attendant concepts eminently attractive to feminist critics. It could be argued, indeed, that – as an epistemological category – 'dialogue' has vied with 'difference' as one of the key (re)structuring principles of feminist thought. Unlike its role within literary and cultural studies in general, moreover, dialogism in feminism is always tied to a visible political project. Although the focus of that project shifts from critic to critic ('dialogue' as a focus of gender antagonism or a symbol of 'sisterhood', for example), feminist dialogics can never escape the question of power. It has no investment in the political fudge the democratic connotations of the term have offered certain liberalists.

In its overview of three key areas of contemporary literary and cultural criticism in which dialogic theory has been centrally involved, this chapter will, it is hoped, have provided readers with some sense of how far Bakhtin's original categories have been stretched, appended and, indeed, have mutated. As Paul de Man wrote as long ago as 1983, 'Dialogism can mean, and indeed has meant many things to many critics, sometimes without reference to Bakhtin'.[56] Such a 'free' appropriation is not entirely without problems, however. As we have seen, some of the blind spots

55   M. O'Connor, 'Chronotopes for Women under Capital: An Investigation into the Relation of Women to Objects', *Critical Studies*, **2**, 1–2, 1990, pp. 137–51.
56   P. de Man, 'Dialogue and Dialogism', *Poetics Today*, **4**, 1, 1983, pp. 99–107.

in Bakhtin's own writings – such as the total absence of women writers from his literary history of the novel – appear so enormous that we are forced to doubt (if only fleetingly) the legitimacy of his account and its consequent usefulness. Similarly, the feminist writings on carnival warn us against a naïve and ahistoric appropriation of the term – a question that leads back directly to the anxiety expressed by Ken Hirschkop of whether, by reading and 'applying' Bakhtin out of context, we risk an especially dangerous form of political anachronism (see Chapter 1).

Whatever the dangers, however, there can be no doubt that Bakhtin's dialogism has proven one of the most 'transportable' theories of the twentieth century. It is a category especially in tune in with the discourses of the contemporary world (post-1945): discourses of democracy, negotiation, compromise and – above all – *difference*. Dialogism, indeed, may possibly be regarded as the theoretical balm we needed to heal a world split open by the contemporary obsession with difference. In textual criticism dealing with constructions of subjectivity, in particular, dialogism has offered an apparent way out of the binarisms of psychoanalysis though, as we saw in my earlier discussion, this is an area of appropriation in which the principle of dialogicality has been most depoliticized.

While the consensus, then, must be that dialogic theory has played a vital role in the development (and refinement) of many areas of textual criticism, there is a lingering question mark over whether its overall contribution has been radical and (re)visionary or conservative and reactionary. I think what this chapter has suggested is that the politics of dialogic criticism depend entirely on the project of the individual reader and critic, with the corollory that feminist criticism (as a mode of analysis that is inherently political) would appear to be the field within which dialogism has been most vigorously interrogated and radically engaged. In every area of textual criticism, however, from the stylistic analysis of the novel to a new understanding of subjectivity, politics and text-reader relations, it is fair to say that dialogism has achieved for us, as readers and critics, what Bakhtin saw it achieving for Dostoevsky. Referring specifically to the latter's 'extraordinary artistic capacity for seeing everything in terms of coexistence and interaction', Bakhtin concludes:

> It made him deaf and dumb to a great many essential things; many aspects of reality could not enter his field of vision. But on the other hand this capacity sharpened, to an extreme degree, his perception in the cross-section of a given moment and permitted him to see many and varied things where others saw one and the same thing. (*Dostoevsky's Poetics*, p. 30).

This is a tribute to, and a warning of, the powers of a 'dialogic mindset' that we, as followers of Bakhtin's own writings, would do well to heed.

# Part Two

---

# READINGS

---

# Preface

The three chapters which comprise Part Two of this book take the form of paired readings of literary texts. Each pair of readings focuses on a particular aspect, or aspects, of the dialogic theory discussed in Part One and the presiding interest of each chapter – genre (Chapter 3), Subject (Chapter 4) and Gender (Chapter 5) – replicates the three foci of discussion in Chapter 2. It should be emphasized, however, that this is not a watertight separation of criteria: as will become obvious, Chapter 4 ('Self-In-Relation') probably has as much to say about gender as Chapter 5 ('Gendering the Chronotope'), and all the chapters, not only Chapter 3 ('The Polyphonic Text'), are both implicitly and explicitly concerned with questions of genre.

The purpose of the readings, as I explained in the Introduction, is both to demonstrate the usefulness of certain aspects of dialogic theory in the reading of literary texts and to suggest ways in which Bakhtin's own key concepts and definitions need to be expanded and revised in the light of textual engagement. The theoretical implications of these revisions will then be taken up and discussed in greater detail in the Conclusion which follows.

Some explanation is needed for my choice of texts. It is a selection which is partly personal (texts that I am interested in, familiar with and which I have had experience teaching) and partly a response to the rationale of the series. When setting down guidelines for our authors in the *Interrogating Texts* series, Pat Waugh and myself (as series editors) advised a careful balance of 'classic' and less well-known literature, suggesting that we would especially welcome authors belonging to 'alternative' but recognizable canons (e.g., contemporary feminist literature). In this way, the readings would be of texts that a large number of our readers would be familiar with (and would have access to in high-street bookshops) without them necessarily having reached school and university syllabuses. Since three of my own texts (Adrienne Rich's *The Dream of a Common Language* (1978), Jeanette Winterson's *Sexing the Cherry* (1989) and Toni Morrison's *Beloved* (1989) fall into the category of popular feminist literature, I hope our reasoning proves correct! I should also mention, on this point, that I make no apology for five of my selected texts being by female authors: this can be explained partly by my particular wish to write gender into the dialogic equation (and all the texts in Chapters 4 and 5 deal with this quite self-consciously), and partly because they reflect the direction of my own most recent reading and research interests.[1] Another criterion we recommended to our authors regarding the range of texts represented in these readings was that they come from a variety of historical periods or movements (e.g., the nineteenth century, Modernism, Postmodernism) and represent, where possible, more than one mode or genre (i.e., fiction, poetry, film or drama). In my own case, I have selected two nineteenth-century texts (John Clare's 'Child Harold' (1841) and Emily Brontë's *Wuthering Heights* (1847)) one modernist (Virginia Woolf's *The Waves*, (1931)), and the three contemporary feminist texts cited earlier. Our final recommendation on the choice of texts was that at least one them should be *resistant* to the theory (or a particular aspect of the theory) in question. My official candidate for this role is John Clare's 'Child Harold' which, as a long *poem*, should be resistant to a theory associated with the novel. In practice, however, most of the texts prove resistant to some aspect of the theory through which they are read, thus pointing to the problems and limitations of Bakhtin's key concepts and categories.

I now offer a short summary of the theses developed in each of the following chapters, and relate this to the particular aspect(s) of dialogic theory under consideration.

Chapter 3 ('The Polyphonic Text') offers readings of two very different nineteenth-century texts: Emily Brontë's classic novel *Wuthering Heights* and the peasant-poet John Clare's long poem 'Child Harold'. As the title suggests, the latter was intended as a continuation of Lord Byron's famous poem of the same name (1812–18), and was begun while Clare was 'incarcerated' in Matthew Allen's lunatic asylum at High Beech, Essex.[2] It was during my work with John Clare's 'asylum manuscripts' that I first engaged with Bakhtinian theory, and this reading (which derives from my doctoral research on the subject) shows how the concept of 'polyphony' (see Chapter 1) enabled me to legitimate a text previously dismissed by Clare's critics. The story of how I had to persuade my supervisor that it was possible to use a theory conceived in relation to the novel to read a poetic text makes a significant point about dialogism and genre, namely, how far things have moved on since 1984! At that time the only critic I could find to support me in my enterprise was Don Bialostosky

---

[1] For an account of my changing literary interests see the chapter '"I the Reader": Text, Context, and the Balance of Power' in *Feminist Subjects, Multi-Media*, ed. P. Florence and D. Reynolds (Manchester: Manchester University Press, forthcoming). See also my chapter 'Dialogic Theory and Women's Writing' in *Working Out: New Directions for Women's Studies* (Brighton: Falmer Press, 1992), pp. 184–93.

[2] For an account of Clare's tragic life, including the remarkable conditions under which he wrote 'Child Harold', see the introduction to *The Later Poems of John Clare*, ed. E. Robinson and G. Summerfield (Manchester: Manchester University Press, 1964) or J. W. Tibble and A. Tibble, *John Clare: his Life and Poetry* (London: Heinemann, 1956).

in his readings of Wordsworth[3] Ten years on, as my discussion in Chapter 2 testifies, 'polyphony' is invoked to read all manner of texts.

The particular aspects of Bakhtin's theory that I utilize in the reading are his model of the polyphonic text as a collection of multiple and discrete voices/consciousnesses free of authorial control, and his theory of *intonation* (see Chapter 1) which I employ as a means of distinguishing *between* the voices in terms of a speaker-listener power dynamic. On a more microcosmic level, I also attend to the way in which the text is *doubly voiced* (see Chapter 1): in particular, its deployment of what Bakhtin referred to as *stylization*.

This reading of 'Child Harold', which attests to the fact that Bakhtin's model of the polyphonic text can, indeed, be transported *across* genre, compares, somewhat provocatively, with the reading of *Wuthering Heights*. Here we have a situation in which what is obtensibly a prototypically polyphonic novel (comparable, say, with Dickens's *Bleak House* (1853) discussed in Chapter 2) resists and challenges many of the Bakhtinian concepts and definitions that *ought* to apply. First, and most striking, is the fact that although this is a text comprising many (apparently) independent voices, the *hostility* which exists between virtually all the characters means that few of the voices are ever 'in dialogue' with one another. This is a text whose verbal intercourse is primarily antagonistic and conflictual, thus dispelling many of the 'conciliatory' notions of dialogic exchange present in the work of Bakhtin and, more significantly, his followers (see Introduction). Like Clare's poem, *Wuthering Heights* is a text which reminds us most effectively that all dialogues are inscribed by power and that (to cite Dale Bauer, Chapter 2, pp. 101–102) dialogic communication frequently takes the form of 'a battle'. The reading also offers a very direct challenge to Bakhtin's own definition of *carnival*. Although as prototypically carnivalesque as it is polyphonic, *Wuthering Heights* can only be assigned that label if we are able to rewrite the good-humoured provisionality of Bakhtin's own model of anarchy and usurpation. While Heathcliff's challenge to the hegemony of the Linton dynasty may appear, at first sight, to have the quality of a 'folk' uprising, the seriousness of his intent is quite outside the bounds of Bakhtin's 'holiday' frolics. The final challenge to Bakhtinian theory comes in the form of Nelly Dean whose third-party presence at most of the conversations between the other characters led me to query whether 'dialogue' necessarily is a 'two-sided act' (between speaker and addressee)? Are not dialogues *often* made in the presence of more than two persons? This would appear to be another undeveloped area of Bakhtinian theory that I will return to in the Conclusion.

Together, then, the readings of *Wuthering Heights* and 'Child Harold' work to undermine the genre specificity of Bakhtin's original work on the polyphonic text, at the same time as showing how eminently useful

---

[3] See D. Bialostosky, *Making Tales: The Poetics of Wordsworth's Narrative Experiments* (London: University of Chicago Press, 1984). (For a discussion of this text, see Chapter 2, p. 86.)

his theories are in revealing aspects of texts that have previously gone unseen.

Chapter 4 explores the way in which a dialogic model of subjectivity, as profiled in Chapter 2, may be used to read the 'self-other' relationships represented in two twentieth-century texts: Virginia Woolf's *The Waves* and Adrienne Rich's *The Dream of a Common Language*. My choice of texts here was determined by the fact that I wanted the readings to be an interrogation not only of subjectivity but also of gendered subjectivity: an opportunity to explore what Bakhtin's model might offer the feminist reader in terms of a new understanding of the feminine and/or lesbian subject. In this last respect, *The Waves* and *The Dream of a Common Language*, both constitute highly self-conscious texts, focusing on the processes by which the subject is gendered and sexualized.

While, in the past, the characters in *The Waves* have sometimes been read as six facets of a single (androgynous) subject, I have preferred to explore the *differences* between them and show how their dialogic interaction impacts differently on male and female characters. I should acknowledge, too, that having determined that one of the texts considered in this study should be modernist, and realizing that the author I knew best was Woolf, my first choice of novel was *To the Lighthouse* (1927): an exemplary dialogic text in every respect. I later decided against this choice simply because I felt it was a text that had been done to death, both in my own teaching and writing and in other people's criticism. *The Waves*, by contrast, has the reputation for being Woolf's most difficult and least popular novel, and I felt that here a dialogic reading might offer a new way through its sometimes turgid psychological analyses.

Rich's collection of poetry, by contrast, quickly presented itself to me when I began my mental search for a text that was (1) contemporary, (2) concerned explicitly with representations of the lesbian subject, and (3) addressed a *second-person interlocutor* (as does the 'Twenty-One Love Poems' on which I focus). This last criterion was a very important one for me when making my selection, since the deployment of the second-person pronoun – 'thou'/'you' – is the most explicit form of dialogic inscription available to us, and yet its impact (even in the study of letters and epistolary fiction) has been consistently overlooked. Rich's sonnets, therefore, addressed as they are to a feminine 'other' who is positioned both 'next to' and 'against' the speaker, involve us in a special kind of writerly/ readerly relationship. In this context, it would also have been appropriate to look at some actual letters or the rare example of a fictional text like Jane Rule's *This is Not For You* (1970) which is written entirely in the second person.[4]

Together, then, Woolf's novel and Rich's poetry provide the reader with a range of interesting perspectives from which to view/review the representation of the sexual/textual subject as a 'self-in-relation'. Both readings discuss the ways in which a dialogic analysis of the subject both compares with, and differs from, a psychoanalytic approach; be this Freudian, Lacanian or from the object-relations school (see Chapter 2). Although, as I noted in Chapter 2, Lacanian psychoanalysis also allows

[4]  J. Rule, *This is Not For You* (1970) (London: Pandora, 1987).

for the *linguistic* construction of the subject, there is not the same sense of verbal *process and exchange* that distinguishes the dialogic model developed by Voloshinov and Bakhtin; and although, as one of my readers pointed out to me, Freudian and Lacanian theories are also concerned with the ongoing processing of relationships outside the immediate family circle, it is a feature of dialogic subject analysis that it at no time attempts to interpret the intersubjective relations between nonfamily members in terms of the primary oedipal relationships.

My reading of *The Waves* opens with a section which suggests some of the obvious points of contrast with a post-Freudian reading of the text, and then proceeds to analyse the dialogicality of each of the characters through their relations with each other and their relationship to language. My thesis is that the text presents us with a spectrum of character types ranging from the profoundly dialogic (Bernard) to the monologic (Rhoda), with the proviso that none of these positions is permanently fixed. I am also concerned with the way in which gender and sexuality are intrinsic to these self-other relations and, in particular, the way in which Rhoda's precarious subjecthood may be related to her lack of a reciprocating female 'other'.

The question mark hanging over Rhoda's subjectivity/sexuality is then taken up and pursued in my readings of Rich's poems in which subjecthood is related very specifically to the female subject's dialogic relationship with 'an/other woman', be she mother/lover/friend or some other role model. What is important to understand about Rich's work in this respect (and what, I feel, has been frequently misconstrued in other readers' attempts to 'essentialize' her position) is that she is challenging/criticizing the primary significance of the mother/daughter bond, as well as apparently celebrating it in such poems as 'Sibling Mysteries'. What I discovered in my readings of *The Dream of a Common Language* is the great complexity with which Rich approaches the way in which the female subject is formed/re-formed through her (sexualized) relationships with other women. In 'Twenty-One Love Poems', for example, the relationship being honoured depends upon the play of difference rather than the drive to pseudo-maternal intimacy and merger. Dialogue is, of course, the means that we can negotiate this difference and I read Rich's poems as a call for this: 'it is the [dialogic] reciprocity of the other that we need, not her sameness' (see p. 172).

Chapter 5 was also conceived as an attempt to write gender into the dialogic vocabulary, this time with special reference to Bakhtin's concept of the chronotope. As I observed in Chapters 1 and 2, the textual time-space that Bakhtin identifies/classifies in 'Chronotope in the Novel' (*The Dialogic Imagination* (1934–41)) is gender neutral, and it was clear that if chronotope were to become a useful principle of fictional analysis then this would have to be revised. The two texts I have chosen to precipitate this revision are Jeanette Winterson's *Sexing the Cherry* and Toni Morrison's *Beloved*. These two contemporary feminist novels both make the movement *between* chronotopes central not only to their narrative technique but also to their central thematic preoccupations. In *Sexing the Cherry* this is a preoccupation with the extent to which an individual is bound to the social/psychological order into which he or she is born. (Is it possible, through an effort of the imagination, to inhabit other historical spaces and identities?) *Beloved*, too, is a manifestly *polychronotopic* text (my term; see p. 175), in which the central characters are shown re-entering the chronotopes of their collective history through the process Sethe calls 'rememory' (see p. 186). For both Winterson and Morrison, moreover, the different time-space continuums occupied by their characters are very distinctively gendered: Jordan's travels take him on sea journeys (gendered masculine) to cities in which he is submerged in the 'language of women'.[5] The women of 124 Bluestone Road, meanwhile, move in and out of a series of chronotopes strung together by the mother–daughter bond. There are masculine chronotopes to be visited in this novel, too (such as Paul D.'s imprisonment in Albert), but the predominant interest is in the psychic time-space shared by the slave mothers and their female children.

My central thesis *vis-à-vis* these two texts concerns the ease with which the characters in Winterson's novel travel between the different chronotopes, in contrast to Morrison's novel in which we witness an acutely painful unidirectional passage into the blood-stained past of slavery. This reveals that although both authors self-consciously gender their chronotopes, Morrison's have a *materiality* (implicit in Bakhtin's own imagery of time 'thickening' and 'taking on flesh': see below) that Winterson's lack.

This foreword to Part Two will, it is hoped, have provided readers with both a 'methodology' of why these particular texts were chosen for analysis, how they are related to one another and what the central dialogic engagement will be in each chapter. As I mentioned earlier, I will return to the wider theoretical issues raised by the readings in the Conclusion.

5   J. Winterson, *Sexing the Cherry* (London: Bloomsbury, 1989), p. 29.

# 3

# DIALOGISM AND GENRE

*The Polyphonic Text:*
*Readings of Emily Brontë's* Wuthering Heights *and*
*John Clare's 'Child Harold'*

## I
### *Wuthering Heights*
*Emily Brontë*

**H**e entered, vociferating oaths dreadful to hear': thus opens Chapter Nine of Emily Brontë's *Wuthering Heights*.[1] The speaker of the 'bad language' (p. 91) on this occasion is Hindley Earnshaw, but it might as easily have been his son, Hareton, or, indeed, Heathcliff: all three men (past, present and future 'masters' of Wuthering Heights) share the same propensity for violent and profane expletives; all *resist dialogue* (as a mode of communication associated with reciprocal exchange and negotiation) with a torrent of threat and abuse.

In terms of the *popular* representation of dialogism discussed in Part One, *Wuthering Heights* might appear, on first impressions, to be a somewhat maverick choice of text. On the level of its 'represented discourse' (the second category in Bakhtin's classification of discourse in the novel, see Chapter 1) it eschews dialogue for polemic: the protagonists rarely talk *to* one another or even pause to listen to what the other has to say. They prefer, instead, to rant and rave, to dismiss or ridicule their interlocutor's reply before it is even uttered. At the same time, each statement is made *in anticipation* of a hostile response. Witness, for example, the following extract from Chapter Two. In a brutal parody of the bourgeois tea-party

---

[1]  E. Brontë, *Wuthering Heights* (Harmondsworth: Penguin, 1965), p. 114. Page references to this volume will be given after quotations in the text.

(where polite conversation is 'tactfully' exchanged) Lockwood is offered his first glimpse of how the 'inmates' of the Heights communicate with one another:

> 'Perhaps I [Lockwood] can get a guide among your lads, and he might stay at the Grange till morning – could you spare me one?'
> 'No, I [Heathcliff] could not.'
> 'Oh, indeed! Well, then, I must trust to my own sagacity.'
> 'Umph!'
> 'Are you going to mak' the tea?' demanded he [Hareton] of the shabby coat, shifting his ferocious gaze from me to the young lady [Catherine II].
> 'Is *he* to have any?' she asked, appealing to Heathcliff.
> 'Get it ready, will you?' was the answer, uttered so savagely that I started. The tone in which the words were said, revealed a genuine bad nature. I no longer felt inclined to call Heathcliff a capital fellow (p. 54).[2]

It will be seen that even with a stranger in their midst the three characters – Heathcliff, Hareton and Catherine – make no pretence of civility. Not a single word of goodwill is ever given or received between them, and all the utterances are issued in a spirit of defensive animosity. The *tone* in which the utterances are made is a further barometer of their extreme aggressiveness.[3] Here, Lockwood notes the 'savageness' of Heathcliff's command as the sign of a 'genuine bad nature', and throughout the text we are treated to a vocabulary ('growled', 'snarled', 'snapped') which represent the characters as more dog-like than human ('My caress provoked a long, guttural snarl. "You'd better let the dog alone," growled Mr Heathcliff, in unison . . .' (p. 48)).[4] The extract also illustrates the tendency of certain characters (in particular, Heatchliff and Hareton) to stifle dialogue by either their refusal to speak (Heathcliff's 'umph!'), or by their refusal to be spoken to (Heathcliff: 'What *can* you mean by talking in this way to me?' (p. 69)). All these verbal characteristics, meanwhile, are illustrative of the way in which each character attempts to assert his or her *power* over that of his interlocutor. If we wish to follow up Dale Bauer's assertion that in every dialogic encounter a 'battle . . . is always

---

2   The tea-party, as the linguistic site of polite, bourgeois small-talk is parodied throughout the text. The other occasion on which its conventions are rendered most absurd is during Heathcliff's first visit to the Grange after his 'return'. Here we see Linton struggling to preserve propriety through the exchange of 'polite' conversation while Catherine and Heathcliff declare their passionate feelings for one another: "'[Heathcliff] I've fought through a bitter life since I last heard your voice, and you must forgive me, for I struggled only for you! . . ." "[Linton] Catherine, unless we are to have cold tea, please come to the table", interrupted Linton, striving to preserve his ordinary tone, and a due measure of politeness. "Mr Heathcliff will have along walk, wherever he may lodge tonight; and I'm thirsty"' (p. 136).

It may also be observed that Catherine and Heathcliff are flagrantly abusing the rules of 'speech tact' that Bakhtin/Medvedev saw as the key to successful linguistic interaction in social groups (see the discussion of *The Formal Method* in Chapter 1, section II).

3   A full discussion of the significance of *intonation* in verbal exchange will appear in the reading of John Clare's 'Child Harold' which follows. See also my review of Voloshinov's essay 'Discourse in Life and Discourse in Poetry' in Chapter 1, section VII).

4   Examples of other verbs and adjectives used in the text to suggest the 'nonhuman' quality of the speech include: (Catherine) 'snapped' (p. 53); (Linton) 'whining' (p. 138); (Isabella) 'wheedling' (p. 187); (Heathcliff) 'howled' (p. 204).

waged for control', then we need look no further than *Wuthering Heights*.[5] Here is a text where virtually every dialogic exchange takes the form of a battle, where speakers are monolithically 'powerful' or 'powerless' in their relations with one another.[6] While this gives rise, it must be said, to a rather unsubtle demonstration of how power relations are inscribed in spoken dialogue (to be compared with the more delicate 'manipulations' illustrated by John Clare's poem in the reading which follows), it does emphatically remind us that dialogue is not always friendly. *Wuthering Heights* is a text in which the ill-mannered ('tactless') dialogue of characters does, indeed, expose the 'blind spot' (Bauer, *Feminist Dialogics*) in Bakhtin's theory.

Aside from its representation of dialogue at this most literal level, however, *Wuthering Heights* has many claims to classic dialogic status. It is, in the first place, a *polyphonic novel* in the manner of Dostoevsky, Dickens and the other nineteenth-century novelists whom Bakhtin cites: a novel in which the author allows her characters their full independence and refrains from imposing her own moral and ideological control over their destinies. It is a novel of a 'plurality' of 'unmerged voices and consciousnesses' (*Dostoevsky's Poetics* (1929), p. 6); of characters whose voices and viewpoints are held distinct from one another, and whose discursive community, although less extensive than Dickens's, is equally *heteroglossic* – incorporating representatives of many different social classes and linguistic registers. It is, moreover, a text which readily demonstrates the novel's origins in earlier *carnivalized literature*. In line with Bakhtin's own descriptions of the novel's development in the eighteenth and nineteenth centuries, it signals its generic hybridity through the use of *inserted genres* ('letters, found manuscripts, retold dialogues, parodies on the high genres, parodically re-interpreted citations' (ibid., p. 108; see Chapter 1, section IV), and through its attendant *intertextuality* – in particular, its self-conscious allusions to the traditions of romance literature and its *stylization* of Byronic rhetoric.[7] *Carnival* may also be seen as a structuring principle on a thematic level, since *Wuthering Heights* is

---

[5]  D. Bauer, *Feminist Dialogics: A Theory of Failed Community* (New York: State University of New York Press, 1989). See the discussion in Chapter 2.

[6]  By this I mean that in virtually every dialogic exchange one character asserts his or her power over the other, though Cathy and Heathcliff and Catherine and Hareton are involved in relationships in which the balance of power shifts from one to the other – both in the course of particular dialogues (see especially Cathy's 'death-bed' scene), and as the dynamic of their relationship changes.

[7]  Examples of 'inserted genres' in *Wuthering Heights* include Catherine's childhood diary (pp. 62–64); Heathcliff's account (to Nelly) of his and Cathy's first visit to the Grange (pp. 88–92); Nelly's Scottish ballad, 'The Ghaist's Warning' (p. 117); Cathy's relation of Heathcliff's story of his first visit to Wuthering Heights following his return from abroad (p. 138); Isabella's letter to Nelly (pp. 173–82); Isabella's account (to Nelly) of her life at Wuthering Heights (pp. 208–18); the housekeeper's account (to Nelly) of life at the Heights (pp. 245–46); Catherine (II)'s account to Nelly of her visits to the Heights (pp. 279–86); Zillah's account (to Nelly) of events at the Heights (pp. 323–28).

Although there is now a fairly wide recognition of the intertextuality of the Brontë texts (especially their point of reference in Romantic literature), Brontë readers and scholars have generally been slow to acknowledge the clear connection between certain Byronic heroes like Manfred and Heathcliff at the level of linguistic register. Compare, for example, Heathcliff's *contemptus mundi* following Cathy's death with this last speech by Manfred:

ostensibly a text in which the forces of law and order are temporarily suspended, hierarchies reversed and rulers dethroned, in the process of which, *laughter* and *billingsgate* (see Chapter 1, section V) may be seen to play an actively subversive role.

The extent to which the novel really does uphold these claims to dialogic status is the subject of the discussion which follows, together with further scrutiny of the representation of spoken dialogue in the text, in particular the role of Nelly Dean as interlocutor. My thesis is that although *Wuthering Heights* would appear to be a model polyphonic text in terms of its superstructure, its articulation of the categories of heteroglossia, carnival and double-voiced discourse is frequently at odds with their representation in Bakhtin's own writings.

Bakhtin's first, and non-negotiable, criterion for a text to be considered polyphonic is the 'freedom' and 'independence' of the characters from authorial control. Although, as I discussed in Chapter 1, this led him into some difficult water over what the role of the author actually was, the principle that a character should be positioned 'alongside' the author as 'an equal consciousness' – and not as a mouthpiece of his or her ideological position – was maintained (see Chapter 1). The question of whether *Wuthering Heights* allows its characters this degree of freedom is a difficult one. Although, on first impression, it might appear to be a text similar to Dickens's *Bleak House* (1853) in its articulation of multiple and contesting centres of consciousness (see the discussion of Kate Flint's reading of Dickens in Chapter 2, pp. 83–84), there is the well rehearsed problem of the narration.[8] How 'reliable' a narrator is Nelly? How accurately does she represent the behaviour (and, indeed, the languages) of her characters? To what extent are they, and their actions, brought under her monologic control?

What gives us the impression that the characters are 'free' is partly, I would suggest, the representation of the individual speech types. This, in turn, relates to the important point that the bulk of the narration takes

---

Spirit: But thy many crimes
Have made thee –
Manfred: What are they to such as thee?
Must crimes be punish'd but by other crimes,
And greater criminals? – Back to thy hell!
Thou hast no power upon me, *that* I feel;
Thou never shalt possess me, *that* I know:
What I have done is done; I bear within
A torture which nothing could gain from thine.

See *Byron: Poetical Works*, ed. J. Jump (Oxford: Oxford University Press, 1970), p. 406.

*Manfred's* theme, the incestuous love of brother and sister, is also an obvious textual precursor to the love between Cathy and Heathcliff in *Wuthering Heights*, as is the passion it arouses in the breast of its guilty lover who, Heathcliff-like, mediates his rage and loss in expressions of physical violence: 'I have gnash'd my teeth in darkness till returning morn,/Then cursed myself till sunset' (ibid., p. 397; cf., *Wuthering Heights*, pp. 204–205).

[8]   See, for example, N. M. Jacobs's 'Gendered and Layered Narrative in *Wuthering Heights* and *The Tenant of Wildfell Hall*', *Journal of Narrative Technique*, **16**, 1986, pp. 204–19. See also Lyn Pylett's chapter on Nelly Dean in *Emily Brontë*. Macmillan Woman Writers (London: Macmillan Education, 1989) and J. Kavanagh, *Emily Brontë* (Oxford: Basil Blackwell, 1985).

the form of 'reported dialogue' – once, twice or even three times removed from the actual event. No two characters in the text speak with exactly the same linguistic register: specificities of age, class background, education and gender draw small or large distinctions between each of them – with the corollory that many of the characters experience changes in their speech in the course of the text as they are socially 'upgraded' or 'degraded', and depending on their intercourse with the other characters. These varieties of speech type I will return to in the next part of the discussion, but *vis-à-vis* the illusion of 'character independence' I believe they perform a vital function. It is an illusion endorsed, partly, by the fact that their speech is reported in a consistent manner no matter who is doing the narration. Heathcliff's language is very characteristically his own, for example, whether it is Lockwood, Nelly or one of the intradiegetic characters (e.g., Isabella, Zillah) who is reporting it.[9] Even Joseph's dialect – which one would imagine Lockwood or Isabella having difficulty understanding, let alone quoting – is faithfully and consistently reproduced. Because of this, and because so much of the narration does consist of this sort of reported dialogue, we are often (as readers) inclined to forget who is telling us what, when, and instead respond to the characters as though we were being directly addressed by them *in medias res*. Recognition of this 'willing suspension of disbelief' reminds us, too, of the dangers of being too sophisticated about the system of narration employed in *Wuthering Heights*. Although Emily Brontë takes some measures to alert us to, and then prove, the credibility of the story-telling (the explanation of Nelly's unusual eloquence, for example, p. 103), the fact that there is so little change in the representation of the characters' dialogue no matter who is reporting suggests that we should not put too much emphasis on the monologizing control of the narrator. What we may conclude, indeed, is that it is the extensive use of reported dialogue as an *inserted genre* within the text, rather than the complicated system of narration *per se*, that both distinguishes it and confirms its polyphonic status. The characters are received by us as independent, autonomous centres of consciousness no matter who is representing (or, indeed, misrepresenting) them. Because we are given 'their own words' (through one of the classic conventions of the realist novel) we believe that we are being given their authentic selves.

The moment we stop accepting the way in which the text positions us, as readers, however, and begin critically to examine the manner of its narration, it becomes increasingly hard to argue that *Wuthering Heights* does allow the characters the freedom requisite of a fully polyphonic text. Although Nelly, Lockwood and the intradiegetic narrators do not appear to tamper with the reported dialogue of the characters, they *do* pass extensive moral judgement on their behaviour – an ideological

---

[9]  According to Gérard Genette's typology, an *intradiegetic narrator* is one who is also a character in the narrative told by the *extradiegetic narrator*. The latter is one who is 'above' or 'superior' to the story he or she narrates. In *Wuthering Heights* it is debatable whether there are any fully extradiegetic narrators since even Lockwood is tangentially involved in the action. See S. Rimmon-Kenan, *Narrative Fiction. New Accents* (London and New York: Routledge, 1989), pp. 94–96.

filtering which is repeatedly brought to metatextual consciousness in the asides of the characters themselves. In Chapter Seventeen, for example, Nelly observes: 'But you'll not want to hear my moralizing, Mr Lockwood: you'll judge as well as I can, all these things; at least you'll think you will, and that's the same' (p. 220). It can equally well be argued, however, that it is Nelly's ironizing self-consciousness in statements such as these which suggests why her and Lockwood's opinions do not produce the monological control they ought to. By making us aware of her views and prejudices and, indeed, of her partiality in the reporting of events, Nelly relinquishes her narratorial authority.[10] The extent of her failure in enforcing this control is manifest in the history of the novel's consumption as romantic fiction: despite Nelly's repeated attempts to convince us of the moral depravity of her hero and heroine, generations of readers have sought to excuse and reclaim them by every means possible. If Nelly's narration does attempt to impose a monologizing frame on the novel, then never was monologism less successful.

Nelly's authority is also undermined, as Patricia Yaegar and other critics have noted, by the fact that she shares the narration with Lockwood and the intradiegetic narrators.[11] All her reported dialogues come courtesy of Lockwood (despite his dissembling aside in Chapter 10 that he will allow the story to continue in Nelly's 'own words', p. 130), and the constant 'reframing' of events by different narrators ensures that her bid for control is being repeatedly challenged. On several counts, then, I would argue that *Wuthering Heights* does create at least the *illusion* of 'freedom' *vis-à-vis* its characters. The preponderance of reported dialogue, together with the fact that there is no single authority doing the reporting, incline the reader to override the text's punctuation and establish direct contact with the voices that appear within the multiple sets of quotation marks.

Having established *Wuthering Heights* as a text that allows its characters sufficient 'freedom and independence' to be regarded 'polyphonic' in Bakhtinian terms, I want to move on now to explore more fully the different voices which comprise it.

*Wuthering Heights* is a novel which should, perhaps, be considered *polyglossic* as well as polyphonic. At several points in the text, when the inhabitants of the Grange visit those at the Heights and vice versa, there is the indication that these are characters who not only speak with different accents and social registers (i.e., *heteroglossia*) but also with different *languages*. The difficulty the modern reader experiences with

10   The fact that Nelly is far from being a neutral participant/observer in the events she relates is shown most explicitly in what she does and does not tell Edgar regarding Catherine II's visits to the Heights. Having told Catherine that she will spend some time thinking over whether or not she will 'tell' on her, we are told that: 'I thought it over aloud, in my master's presence; walking straight from her room to his, and relating the whole story, with the exception of her conversations with her cousins, and any mention of Hareton' (p. 286).
11   Patricia Yaegar discusses this in her chapter on *Wuthering Heights* in *Honeymad Women* (New York: Columbia University Press, 1988). She argues that the sequence of narrators in the text acts as the author's means of ensuring that the action (and ideology) is repeatedly recontextualized: 'Once again the text is operating on itself as primary material and putting into process what the earlier machinations of plot have uncovered' (p. 200).

the faithful transcription of Joseph's dialect (now extensively glossed in most editions) is matched by Lockwood, Isabella and Catherine II. The latter also finds it difficult to make much sense of Hareton who, raised at the Heights without any outside education, has evolved a strange 'pidgin' which combines Joseph's dialect with the blasphemous rhetoric of his two 'devil daddies' (Hindley and Heathcliff). When first presented with one of Hareton's curses ('I'll see thee damned before I be *thy* servant' p. 230), Catherine's surprise is caused not so much by affront but by incomprehension. Hareton's thick accent, combined with his use of the archaic second-person personal pronoun, makes his words as foreign to her as if he had spoken in Norwegian. On a subsequent visit she blames her own inability to make sense of his words on his possible retardment: '"Is he all as he should be?" asked Miss Cathy seriously, "or is he simple . . . not right? I've questioned him twice now, and each time he looked so stupid, I think he does not understand me; I can hardly understand *him*, I'm sure!"' (p. 254). The cultural and educational differences represented by life at the Heights and life at the Grange are manifested in the second generation by the evolution of separate languages, and the union of Hareton and Catherine II at the end of the novel can only be achieved when each, in effect, becomes bilingual.

Aside from this most extreme polarization of linguistic expression, *Wuthering Heights* is a text in which every character's speech is very carefully graded in terms of class and education – and these factors are commensurate (though not in any simple way) with power. There is, of course, a crude split between educated and noneducated characters (Lockwood, Edgar, Isabella, Hindley and the two Catherines on the one hand; Nelly, Heathcliff, Hareton, Joseph, Zillah and the other servants on the other). But all these are educated or not educated to different degrees, with Nelly (as has already been mentioned) being exceptionally well read for a housekeeper, and Heathcliff and Hareton being launched, belatedly, on programmes of self-improvement. It is significant, however, that the fundamental *class* differences distinguishing the characters cannot be altogether eroded through education, and this is evidenced most obviously in their spoken language. Despite their 'book learning', Heathcliff and Hareton will retain a vestige of their regional accent and gruff elocution, and Nelly her 'provincialisms' (p. 103). Yet what is especially interesting within the social microcosm represented by this text is that the power is not all on the side of those with the 'cultural capital' of genteel pronounciation.[12] Although the female characters, in particular the two Catherines, depend heavily upon their spoken articulacy (including their

---

[12] 'Cultural' or 'symbolic' capital is one of a group of related concepts that French sociologist, Pierre Bourdieu, espoused to explain the more covert ways in which society's ruling groups maintain their authority. Children born into 'educated', middle-class households acquire standards of social behaviour and 'taste' that will facilitate their progress through life and ensure their power over those without these skills. It is important to recognize that 'cultural capital' cannot necessarily be 'bought' with money and education gained later in life: the person of working-class origins who attempts self-improvement in these areas will never be able to feel as 'at home' in them as those with inherited cultural 'wealth'. See P. Bourdieu, *In Other Words: Essays Toward a Reflexive Sociology*, trans. M. Adamson (Stanford, CA: Stanford University Press, 1990).

superior class register and more extensive vocabularies) to challenge the social, economic and physical domination of the men, the less articulate male characters (principally Heathcliff and Hareton) attempt to win back power by making refined and polite speech appear ridiculous. This is especially noticeable in the tea-taking ceremonies which, as I observed earlier, become parodic inversions of bourgeois gentility. Returning to the occasion of Lockwood's first visit to the Heights, it is worth reminding ourselves how ridiculous the narrator's pleasantries and euphemisms are made to appear:

> 'It is strange', I began in the interval of swallowing one cup of tea and receiving another, 'it is strange how custom can mould our tastes and ideas; many could not imagine the existence of happiness in a life of such complete exile from the world as you spend, Mr Heathcliff; yet, I'll venture to say, that, surrounded by your family, and with your amiable lady as the presiding genius over your home and heart –,' (pp. 54–55).

His allusions to Catherine II as an 'amiable lady' and, later, a 'benificent fairy' (p. 55) are absurdly juxtaposed to Joseph's description of her as a 'witch' and a 'nowt' (p. 57) and, indeed, all such attempts at 'sociable conversation' (p. 58) are rendered facetious and misplaced. The fact that Lockwood's sentiments appear most ridiculous when directed to, or about, the female present is, moreover, far from gratuitous. Here, and throughout the text, a 'refined' use of language is associated with the feminine principle, to the extent that the men who share in its use (Lockwood, Edgar and Linton) are branded 'effeminate'. By making the Heights into a separate machochismic kingdom, with its own 'alternative' language and culture, Heathcliff, Hareton and Joseph succeed in temporarily undermining the authority of the educated English middle class, and install a new philistinism in its stead. This accounts for why, at the end of the novel, Joseph is so appalled to find Hareton reading books with Catherine. Not only is he compromising their composite gender identity ('This hoile's nother mensful, nor seemly fur us . . .' p. 347), but also inviting back the authority of the educated classes, temporarily suspended under the 'carnival' of Heathcliff's reign.

Apart from making 'educated speech' appear affected and effeminate, Heathcliff and Hareton also compensate for their exclusion from its *parole* through the alternative authority of 'bad language'. The 'curse' becomes their most habitual form of expression, a manner of utterance which, as I indicated at the beginning of this reading, is aggressively adialogic. Such pronouncements may be seen to establish power over the addressee in three ways: first, as we have seen, by forbidding a response; secondly, by the curse's cultural transgressiveness (the fact that it *is* bad language); and, thirdly, by its evocation of supernatural agency: to curse someone is to intimate that simply by 'giving voice', a punishment will be visited on the recipient. For subjects lacking more orthodox kinds of linguistic capital, therefore, cursing is incribed with important power. Heathcliff and Hareton may not be able to challenge their adversaries through the sophistications of language use, but they can invest their limited vocabularies with the alternative authority of 'damnation'. In this respect, it is also significant that Catherine II, once transferred to the linguistic economy of the Heights, drops her orthodox verbal skills (she has shown, by this time, how the skilful manipulations of her tongue can upset even Heathcliff) for the more primitive power of the curse.[13] Readily adopting the guise of 'witch' which the male members of the household foist upon her, she exults in the possibility of matching their curses with her own. In response to criticism from Joseph she declares:

> 'You scandalous old hypocrite! . . . Are you not afraid of being carried away bodily, whenever you mention the devil's name? I warn you to refrain from provoking me, or I'll ask your abduction as a special favour. Stop, look here, Joseph', she continued, taking a long, dark book from a shelf. 'I'll show you how far I've progressed in the Black Art – I shall soon be competent to make a clear house of it. The red cow didn't die by chance; and your rheumatism can hardly be reckoned among providential visitations!' (p. 57).

Abiding by the rule that when in Rome one should do as the Romans, Catherine effectively concedes the success of Hindley, Heathcliff and Hareton in routing the language of middle-class gentility from their kingdom.[14] A superior accent has no purchase here: linguistic superiority is established and sustained through a constant barrage of oath and invective.

I would argue in conclusion, then, that *Wuthering Heights* is a text which is profoundly polyglossic and heteroglossic. Although the social canvass may be less broad than Dickens's, competition between the different linguistic registers which *are* represented is extremely highly charged. For while it might at first appear that the power of the characters resides in their shifting economic capital, and the front line of the battle is emphatically linguistic. Neither Heathcliff nor Hareton can assume stewardship of the Heights until they have 'bought into' the *parole* of the existing ruling group (which they both do through their belated educations), and (in the case of Heathcliff) made their own 'barbaric' tongue the 'official language' of the kingdom.

Heathcliff's establishment of an alternative code of cultural and linguistic practice at the Heights is also one of the principal ways in which *Wuthering Heights* may be read as a 'carnival' text. I would suggest, however, that in this respect as in its subversion of existing hierarchies generally, the novel does not conform to the 'spirit' of carnival implicit in Bakhtin's writings. While life at Wuthering Heights may be seen to represent a grotesque, carnivalized inversion of the law, order and 'hierarchical rank' (*Rabelais* (1965) p. 10) represented by the domestic superstructure of Thrushcross Grange, the means by which the status quo is challenged is not good

[13]   See Catherine II's audacious attempt to provoke Heathcliff's repressed emotions: 'I don't hate you. I'm not angry that you struck me. Have you never loved *anybody*, in all your life, uncle/*never*? Ah! you must look once – I'm so wretched – you can't help being sorry and pitying me' (p. 307).

[14]   Throughout this chapter, my allusions to Wuthering Heights as a 'kingdom' is in part acknowledgement of the feudal and patriarchal systems of government that operate within its walls – characteristics of rulership shared by the kingdoms featured in Brontë's 'Gondal' poems. See E. Brontë, *The Complete Poems*, ed. J. Gezari (with introduction) (Harmondsworth: Penguin, 1992).

humoured and innocent enough to correspond with Bakhtin's analysis. Heathcliff is, in short, too maliciously motivated to be regarded as one of the 'folk'. While he, like they, may be seen to represent the 'forces from below' which set out to remove existing 'barriers of caste, property, and profession' (ibid.), his mission is carried out not in the spirit of humour but of revenge.

In this last respect, it is significant that although there are several references to *laughter* in the novel (the majority of them associated with Catherine I), it is most certainly not the carnivalesque laughter that Bakhtin describes in *Rabelais*. Carnival laughter, it will be remembered, is characterized by an 'ambivalence which renders it simultaneously gay and triumphant' and 'mocking and deriding' (ibid., p. 12) (See Chapter One, p. 56). It is also purportedly 'universal', being 'directed at all and everyone, including the carnival's participants' (ibid.). The laughter of Catherine and Heathcliff, on the other hand, is 'mocking and deriding' without ever being 'gay', and is targeted exclusively at the weaknesses of others. Catherine's tendency to use laughter as an expression of contempt can be traced back to her early childhood, where the chastisements of her parents merely had the effect of 'hardening' her further and 'she laughed if I [Nelly] told her to say she was sorry for her faults' (p. 84). Perhaps the most graphic illustration of the malicious nature of her humour in adult life is the laughter she directs at Isabella for her infatuation with Heathcliff. Although it could, of course, be argued that the viciousness of this ridicule is partly defensive, Catherine's laughter is clearly meant to signify that she regards the situation as too absurd to be taken seriously:

> She did laugh as she saw Heathcliff pass the window . . . 'Come in, that's right!' exclaimed the mistress, gaily, pulling a chair to the fire. 'Here are two people sadly in need of a third to thaw the ice between them; and you are the very one we should both of us choose. Heathcliff, I'm proud to show you, at last, somebody that dotes upon you more than myself. I expect you to feel flattered – nay, it's not Nelly; don't look at her! My poor little sister-in-law is, breaking her heart by mere contemplation of your physical and moral beauty (pp. 143–44).

This use of laughter to humiliate Isabella in the presence of Heathcliff and Nelly has no vestige of Bakhtinian carnival in it. In carnival, the 'degradation' of individuals and institutions is practised with the purpose of regeneration and catharsis (see Chapter 1). The motive here, by contrast, is irredeemably cynical: Catherine brings Isabella 'down' with the intention of keeping her there. This is laughter as the flagrant assertion of power. Reading between the lines, one could once again argue that Catherine's laughter is a disguise for her own insecurities; or that laughter, itself, is a poor substitute for more material power.[15] However, along with her sharp tongue, laughter remains Catherine's primary weapon throughout the text – so much so, that when she takes to her death-bed one of the things she is first to mourn is the loss of her 'laughing self': 'Oh, I'm

---

[15] I discuss the implications of Catherine I's lack of material power in my chapter on 'Sexual Politics' in *Feminist Readings/Feminists Reading* (Hemel Hempstead: Harvester Wheatsheaf, 1989), pp. 38–39.

burning! I wish I were out of doors – I wish I were a girl again, half savage and hardy, and free . . . and laughing at injuries, not maddening under them' (p. 163).

Catherine I's laughter sets the tone for all the laughter in *Wuthering Heights*. On the rare occasions when Heathcliff laughs and grins it is with the same vindictive savagery, and all those removed to the Heights end up catching its hollowness (see Isabella, p. 217, and Catherine II, p. 341). While the anarchic manner in which certain characters set about 'dethroning' others might, at first, seem commensurate with Bakhtinian carnival, therefore, the nature of the laughter with which that activity is accompanied is an index of their dark, 'nonregenerative' intentions. In the case of Heathcliff, moreover, we have to recognize that his desire to topple the existing hierarchies (the inheritances of the Earnshaws and the Lintons) is not carried out in order to achieve a new democratization of power but to install himself at the head of a new oligarchy. It is simply a coup to replace one totalitarian and patriarchal regime with another. Out of line with Bakhtinian carnival, too, is the fact that the reversals of fortune which occur within the narrative are carefully engineered rather than spontaneous. This is not a situation in which a gratuitous cessation of law and order allows the 'low' characters to usurp temporarily the 'high' but a lengthy and premeditated takeover. There is also the matter that the revolt was *meant* to be permanent; the fact that the text does conform to the carnivalesque model by closing with a restitution of the former hierarchies (through the union of Catherine II and Hareton both the Lintons and the Earnshaws are back on the throne) cannot altogether erase the spirit in which Heathcliff's campaign was carried out. This is quite unlike the Bakhtinian reading of carnival as an event in which all the participants (the 'folk' as well as the hierarchies they displace) *know* that the inversion of power is only temporary: that, come nightfall, all will revert to their former roles.

Rather than use these last qualifiers to argue that *Wuthering Heights* cannot properly be read as a carnivalesque text, however, I would prefer – like Nancy Glazener and Clair Wills – to regard them as a salient critique of Bakhtin's own political conservatism.[16] As was argued in Chapter 2, Bakhtin's model of carnival lacks proper cogniscance of the seriousness of the power struggle by reducing the event to a species of sophisticated 'play'. None of the inversions of linguistic and economic power presented in *Wuthering Heights* are presented in this spirit, but this could be more a case for redefining the category of carnival than denying the carnivalized status of the text.

Having reviewed some of the ways in which the novel both conforms to and stretches Bakhtin's categories of polyphony, heteroglossia and the carnival, I want to return now to its representation of dialogue. As I intimated in my opening remarks, *Wuthering Heights* is a rather recalcitrant text as far as the analysis of spoken dialogue is concerned, partly because

---

16   See N. Glazener, 'Dialogic Subversion: Bakhtin, the Novel and Gertrude Stein' and C. Wills, 'Upsetting the Public: Carnival, Hysteria and Women's Texts', both in *Bakhtin and Cultural Theory*, ed. K. Hirschkop and D. Shepherd (Manchester: Manchester University Press, 1989). Both texts are discussed in Chapter 2, pp. 108–109.

so much of the conversation consists of attempts by characters to *silence* their interlocutors rather than engage in dialogue with them. In addition to this, there is the problem of Nelly Dean. Her presence at all the dialogues she 'reports' means that they take place between *three* people, while most of Bakhtin's writings focus on dialogue as a quintessentially binaristic relationship.

I begin this part of the discussion, however, with some thoughts on Nelly's interlocutory role in the novel generally. If we look first at her function *vis-à-vis* the other characters, it would seem clear that she represents an 'authority' to which they all repeatedly appeal. This is not to say that her opinion is regarded as some 'objective' moral standard but rather that she is called upon to sanction the characters' own principles and actions. The most obvious instance of this is, of course, Catherine I's attempts to justify her reasons for marrying Edgar. The fact that Nelly disputes and challenges every one of these 'excuses' does not affect the vital role she performs in enabling Catherine to articulate her situation. In the absence of the rightful interlocutor (in this case Heathcliff, hidden, with dramatic irony, behind the screen), Nelly becomes the 'sounding board' that Bakhtin would argue is necessary for the realization of all thought and utterance. Indeed, on this occasion, and in a number of interviews with Heathcliff, Nelly becomes an *interlocutory substitute* for the lover whom the speaker is unable to talk to (Catherine I and Heathcliff are forbidden to talk to one another for large sections of the narrative, first by Hindley and then by Edgar). The interviews which Heathcliff has with Nelly after Catherine's death are especially important in this respect, since through them we learn more about the nature of his feeling than we do in any of his actual conversations with Catherine herself – excepting the last. Apart from being an interlocutory substitute for characters within the text, Nelly may also be seen as a *surrogate reader* (i.e., we enter the text vicariously, through her). It is via her presence that we, as readers, are given access to the dialogues of the characters, and in such a way that they often appear to appeal to us directly. It is through this means, I would suggest, that the reader becomes far more involved in the text than she should by rights of the system of double narration.

It is when we look more closely at how Nelly's presence affects the *dynamics* of the dialogues between the other characters, however, that we realize the extent to which she raises questions never discussed in Bakhtin's own literary analysis. First, it is a presence which causes many of the dialogues – even the most purportedly 'intimate' – to be split between two addressees. In the same way that they appeal to Nelly in the *absence* of the beloved, so are Catherine and Heathcliff likely to appeal to her in the midst of their address. Thus Catherine, on her death-bed, turns from Heathcliff (who has temporarily turned his back on *her*) to Nelly to exclaim: 'Oh, you see, Nelly! He would not relent a moment to keep me out of the grave! *That* is how I'm loved!' (p. 196). On this, as on numerous other occasions, Nelly's presence is exploited by the speaker as a means of gaining additional power over the primary interlocutor. Referring to a third person in their presence is a classic means of humiliation, and Catherine has frequent recourse to it, not only in her attempts to gain interlocutory power over Heathcliff as here but also in her degradation of Isabella. Concerning the latter, there are a number of occasions upon which Catherine and Heathcliff conspire in the humiliation of the third party by this means. Having been informed of her infatuation with him by Catherine, Heathcliff observes of Isabella: 'I think you belie her . . . She wishes to be out of my company now, at any rate!' (p. 144). In this way, Isabella becomes a mere totem through which Catherine and Heathcliff negotiate the price of their affection for one another, and is denied an interlocutory subject status of her own. Edgar, too, is humiliated in similar fashion a few pages later. Following his attempts to intevene in the argument between Catherine and Heathcliff, the latter exclaims (in his presence): 'and that is the slavering, shivering *thing* [my italics] you preferred to me' (p. 154).

The question of how the presence of a third person or term may affect the dynamics of dialogic exchange is rarely addressed in the writings of the Bakhtin group, the notable exception being Bakhtin's postulation of a 'superaddressee' in the late essay 'The Problem of the Text' (see Chapter 1, section VII). The superaddressee, it will be remembered, is the speaker's 'ideal' interlocutor: one who will understand what she is saying, even if the immediate addressee does not. In literary texts, the superaddressee thus performs a similar function to the interlocutor of 'hidden dialogue' and 'hidden polemic': he or she is the presence *outside the text* to which the speaker appeals.[17] What is different about Bakhtin's analysis of this phenomenon in the late essay, however, is the way in which he acknowledges that, in any given utterance, the speaker may direct her address to *both* the textual addressee and the unnamed 'other'; that is to say, the dialogue is tripartite rather than binary.

In *Wuthering Heights*, I would suggest, Nelly is positioned as a notional superaddressee *within* the text, although she herself is uncomprehending of many of the thoughts and confessions she is made a recipient of. At the same time, then, that she performs the role of 'sounding board', Nelly may also be perceived as the *vehicle* through which the leading characters – principally Catherine and Heathcliff – make manifest their dialogues with a number of key moral and spiritual debates *outside the text*. Indeed, Nelly acknowledges the surrogacy of her role on these occasions with rejoinders like 'she [Catherine I] went on to herself' (p. 197) and 'he [Heathcliff] only half addressed me' (p. 322).

The extratextual discourse that Catherine and Heathcliff most frequently engage with is whether or not there is an afterlife, and the fact that most of their speculations are 'above Nelly's head' suggests that their proper interlocutory destination is the Victorian philosophers, theologians and poets whom Emily Brontë was herself familiar with. Take, for example, the following extract in which Catherine I adopts a blatantly Byronic rhetoric:

---

17   There is a clear similarity of function between the 'superaddressee' of Bakhtin's late essay and the 'unnamed', extratextual addressee of 'hidden polemic' (see the discussion in section IV of Chapter 1, *The Problems of Dostoevsky's Poetics*). What is different in his analysis in the later piece, however, is the way he acknowledges that, in *any given utterance*, the speaker may address her speech to *both* the textual addressee and the superaddressee.

'And', she added, musingly, 'the thing that irks me most is this shattered prison, after all. I'm tired, tired of being enclosed here. I'm wearying to escape into that glorious world, and to be always there; not seeing it dimly through tears, and yearning for it through the walls of an aching heart; but really with it, and in it' . . . She went on to herself (p. 197).

Nelly is quite correct to infer that Catherine is not addressing her on this particular occasion: despite her notional invocation, 'Nelly, you think you are better and more fortunate than I . . . '(ibid.), Catherine's 'polemic' is directed to the discourse of Romanticism.

In its representation of dialogue, then, as in its deployment of the carnivalesque, *Wuthering Heights* is a text which responds well to a dialogic analysis, but at the same time exposes several blind spots and limitations in Bakhtin's own theory. This reading has revealed, in particular, how any model of spoken dialogue (actual or reported) needs to go beyond its characterization as an amicable exchange between two bodies mutually dependent on the anticipated response of the other ('The word is a bridge between myself and another . . .' – *Marxism and the Philosophy of Language* (1929), p. 86). Many of the utterances which appear in *Wuthering Heights* will, as we have seen, appear profoundly *adialogic* according to this definition, but what they really teach is that dialogue is often as much about resistance and noncooperation as it is about engagement and reciprocity. Along with Dale Bauer, I therefore propose that Bakhtin's notion of the dialogic be extended to encompass the 'battle' as well as the more gentle modes of communication. The reading has shown us, too, how power relations need to be rethought with respect to Bakhtin's theory of carnival. *Wuthering Heights* can be regarded as a carnivalesque text only if we are working with a less playful, less good-humoured and altogether less utopian definition than the one Bakhtin represents in *Rabelais*. The reversals of fortune which occur in Brontë's text do not represent a 'holiday' from oppression but rather constitute a critique of power relations that extend way beyond the novel's closure. A further lacuna in Bakhtinian theory is revealed by the tripartite dialogues featured in the text. Nelly's presence at all the dialogues she reports gives rise to a special set of interlocutory circumstances not allowed for in Bakhtin's theory. Once again, these are intimately related to questions of power, with the presence of a third party often being manipulated by the speaker to impress or humiliate his or her 'primary' interlocutor. Nelly's interlocutory presence also raises the complex questions about 'address' *vis-à-vis* Bakhtin's categories of 'hidden dialogue' and the 'superaddressee' by presenting the possibility that an interlocutor *in the text* (i.e., 'not hidden') may be the foil for a dialogue with a person or discourse who remains unnamed. Had Bakhtin chosen Brontë rather than Dickens as the British novelist on whom to perform his close textual analysis in *The Dialogic Imagination* (1934–41) then some of these questions may possibly have been answered. As it is, I would like to hope that this rereading will incline future readers to pursue some of the issues I have raised.

## II
## 'Child Harold'
### *John Clare*

---

Then he the tennant of the hall & Cot
The princely palace too hath been his home
& Gipsey's camp where friends would know him not
In midst of wealth a beggar still to roam
Parted from one whose heart was once his home[18]

John Clare's 'Child Harold' is a poem of many voices. One of the original manuscript versions (Northampton MS 6) is formally divided into a series of discrete stanza-song units by a system of line divisions, and the above quotation indicates just some of the identities that the personal pronoun assumes in its picaresque wanderings after 'the one whose heart was once his home'.[19] In this essay I explore these 'novelizations' of the lyric genre by reading the poem against Bakhtin's notion of the polyphonic text as presented in *Problems of Dostoevsky's Poetics* (1929).[20] This will include reference to the following features of the text: (1) as a site of interaction between a number of independent voices and its subsequent resistance to closure; (2) its tendency towards simultaneity and coexistence rather than sequence and development; (3) its use of double-voiced speech (in particular, *stylization*) (see Chapter 1 for a discussion of these terms). The reading also depends substantially on Bakhtinian theories of *intonation* as interpreted by various commentators and, as in the discussion of *Wuthering Heights*, I shall be especially concerned with the class registers represented by the different voices.

The reader unfamiliar with Clare criticism will doubtless find it hard to believe that such a modest programme of analysis represents a radical challenge to previous 'interpretations' of John Clare's asylum poem. Largely on account of repeated efforts to establish his name as a respected Romantic poet, few scholars have appeared willing

---

18 J. Clare, 'Child Harold', *Later Poems*, Vol. 1, ed. E. Robinson and D. Powell (Oxford: Oxford University Press, 1984), p. 62. Further page references to this volume will be given after quotations in the text.
19 Throughout his manuscripts Clare uses a system of line divisions to indicate breaks in the text. A single underline is used to separate individual stanzas and the verses of songs, while the double underline always indicates *the end of a piece of writing*, be it song, stanza sequence or biblical paraphrase. In Northampton MS 6 these line divisions are of the utmost consequence since they effectively divide the poem into a series of discrete stanza-song units. The length of these stanza sequences varies considerably – from one to eight stanzas – but all units end with a song. No previous editors or commentators have noted the existence of these line divisions or their potential consequences for the reading of the poem. A full description of the Northampton MSS is to be found in Chapter 4 of my Ph.D. thesis, 'John Clare and Mikhail Bakhtin – The Dialogic Principle: Readings from John Clare's Manuscripts 1832–1845', University of Birmingham, 1987.
20 M. Bakhtin, *Problems of Dostoevsky's Poetics*, ed. and trans. C. Emerson (Manchester: Manchester University Press, 1984). Page references will be given after quotations in the text. For explanation and discussion of these terms, see Chapter 1.

to submit Clare's writings to the same theoretical speculations as his more illustrious contemporaries. To 'deconstruct' his work actively or, as in this case, to question the existence of an authentic authorial voice that can be identified as the 'essential' John Clare, would be deemed suicidal. Yet it is almost certainly this anxious inhibition, more than anything else, that has maintained Clare's status as a 'minor poet'.

'Child Harold' is, indeed, a text that has suffered badly at the hands of traditional literary criticism. Most existing readings have deemed the poem a failure on account of the fact that it shows neither 'development' nor 'resolution': the two major prerequisites for a long poem.[21] The very profundity of its indeterminacy has invited readers to conclude that, while showing 'potential', it was nevertheless a victim of its author's mental instability, his inability to finish what he had begun. Admittedly the temptations to read the poem in biographical terms are great: the MS 8 version of the poem, for example, is textually interwoven with Clare's autobiographical account of his 'Journey out of Essex'.[22] It seems curious, nevertheless, that bearing in mind the obvious instability of Clare's identity at this time (most commentators remark on the existence of his 'delusions'), no one has thought that the 'I' of the poem might be similarly unstable. I would suggest that for the twentieth-century reader there are several reasons why it should seem preferable to read 'Child Harold' as a text of not one, but many voices. First there is the fact that Clare's writing shows a long history of poetic surrogacy; Clare was a prodigious imitator from his earliest years, and a great deal of his work bears very obvious intertextual traces of other authors.[23] Secondly, there is the whole weight of structuralist and poststructuralist critical theory which, since Barthes's 'Death of the Author', has resisted the easy association of author and personal pronoun (see note 23 to Chapter 1). Meanwhile, if we turn specifically to Bakhtin, we are reminded that his conception of the polyphonic text depended absolutely on the rejection of any *transcendent ego*: true dialogue between voices is characterized by the fact that the author's voice is in no way superior to that of his or her

[21]   The dialectical model of the imagination as a 'journey through evil and suffering . . . to a greater good' as proposed by M. H. Abrams in *Natural Supernaturalism: Tradition and Revolution in Romantic Literature* (New York: Norton, 1971), p. 193, has been especially influential in determining an appropriate schema for the long poem.

[22]   'Child Harold' has two principal manuscript sources: Northampton MS 6 and Northampton MS 8 (related material is also to be found in Northampton MSS 7, 49, 57 and Bodleian MSS Don. a. 8 and Don. c. 64). Of these sources, MS 8 is the earliest, being a small pocketbook Clare first used at the High Beech asylum, and then during his 'escape'. As I have shown in my thesis, MS 8 is an extraordinary document in which poems, letters, biblical paraphrases, accounts and quotations are bizarrely juxtaposed. 'Child Harold' and 'Don Juan' are the two principal poems contained in the manuscript, while entries to the journal 'Journey Out of Essex' frequently occur at the foot of the pages containing the poems.

[23]   Earlier commentators have shown that Clare effectively learnt to write poetry by imitation, and kept up the practice throughout his career. During one period, he also executed a number of successful forgeries, passing off imitations of various sixteenth- and seventeenth-century poets as 'lost manuscripts'.

characters.[24] Likewise, the free interplay between the different voices in 'Child Harold' depends upon the fact that none may be thought identifiable with the author *per se*; none represents an 'essential' John Clare. This brings us to the final reason for recognizing a number of different personal pronouns within the poem, and that is its formal organization into a number of discrete sections (see note 19). The following reading therefore demonstrates how the more substantial 'units' of stanzas and songs correspond, on an intonational level, with a number of different narrative personae or voices. This is not to propose that every stanza-song unit is commensurate with a single voice: on the contrary, a number of units establish an internal dialogue between two or more voices. Indeed, it is the extension of this dialogic activity from the macrocosmic organization of the text, through to the interaction between voices, and extending even to the level of the sentence and the individual word, that constitutes the text's claim to full polyphonic status (see Chapter 1). The following discussion focuses on six of the most readily characterized voices (or narratorial subject positions) that constitute 'Child Harold'. Three of these are analysed with respect to single stanza-song units, but it should be noted that the section on the *two voices* represented by the text's use of the traditional ballad genre is necessarily wider ranging, as is the section on biblical discourse. The reading ends with an assessment of to what extent the interaction of these voices may be seen to profile Bakhtin's characterization of the 'polyphonic text' as outlined above.

By far the most readily identifiable of the voices to be found in 'Child Harold' is the 'Byronic'.[25] It is also the most pervasive, recurring in a number of individual songs and stanzas as well as in the longer sequences. There are, in addition, several single lines in the poem which directly, or indirectly, echo Byron's texts.[26] Its most sustained presentation, however, is in the stanza-song unit beginning 'My Life hath been one love – no blot it out' (p. 45) which consists of a sequence of eight stanzas and one song. Here the narrator presents himself as a bold lover or rake, a man who has had many loves, yet remained faithful to none:

> I have had many loves – & seek no more –
> These solitudes my last delights shall be
> The leaf-hid forest – & the lonely shore

[24] 'Thus the new artistic position of the author with regard to the hero in Dostoevsky's polyphonic novel is a *fully realized and fully consistent dialogic position*, one that affirms the independence, internal freedom, unfinalizability, and indeterminacy of the hero. For the author the hero is not "he" and not "I" but a fully valid "thou", that is, another and autonomous "I" ("thou art")' (Bakhtin, *Dostoevsky's Poetics*, p. 63).

[25] In an 'advertisement' which appears in MS 8 (p. 38) Clare refers to the poem as a 'new canto' of 'Child Harold', suggesting that he regarded his poem as an addition to Byron's work.

[26] See R. Protherough, 'A Study of John Clare's Poetry, with Particular Reference to the Influence of Books and Writers on his Development in the Years 1820–25', unpublished B.Litt., Oxford University, 1955. Protherough notes how the first lines of Byron's poems often acted as a stimulus for Clare, and cites several examples of this, including the first line of 'Child Harold' ('Many are poets though they use no pen').

> Seem to my mind like beings that are free
> Yet would I had some eye to smile on me
> Some heart where I could have a happy home in
> Sweet Susan that was wont my love to be
> & Bessy of the glen – for I've been roaming
> With both at morn & noon & dusky gloaming
>                                     (p. 47)

The key to the tone of this whole sequence is one of contempt and defiance: contempt for life, religion and death; defiance against authority, exile and pain. In a tirade against 'Madhouses Prisons Whore shops' and other corrupt institutions, the speaker assumes an arrogant superiority over both his listener and what Voloshinov has identified as 'the object of the utterance' (see Chapter 1, p. 78).[27] As we saw in the preceding reading of *Wuthering Heights* it is, indeed, the power relationship between the speaker and his or her interlocutors that establishes the tone of an address, and here he asserts an unqualified domination over them. The authority is, moreover, a register of class. This is not a humble peasant-poet who speaks, but an aristocratic libertine who has the wealth and status that enable him to renounce the world – its deceits and hypocrisies – with contempt. Syntactically, as well as in their intonational stance, these stanzas bear an obvious debt to Byron, reproducing *Don Juan*'s use of half and hanging lines, together with its ironic rhymes. In terms of Bakhtin's categories of *double-voiced speech*, this is very obviously *stylization*, with the text retaining 'the general intention of the original' while, at the same time, 'casting a slight shadow of objectification over it' (*Dostoevsky's Poetics*, pp. 189–90; see Chapter 1). And if, syntactically, these stanzas are a stylization of *Don Juan*, the intonation itself can be seen to be imported directly from *Childe Harold*, whose narrator frequently assumes a voice of proud contempt towards a corrupt and fickle world.[28] A specific analogy can be drawn between Childe Harold's response to a thunderstorm and that annexed by Clare's speaker in the song that ends the unit. As will be seen from the following extracts, both protagonists seek divine supremacy over their 'object of utterance', the mortal world, through their communion *with* it:

> Could I embody and embosom now
> That which is most within me, – could I wreak
> My thoughts upon expression, and thus throw
> Soul, heart, mind, passions, feelings, strong or weak . . .
> And that one word were Lightning
>                     (*Childe Harold*, Canto III, stanza xcvii)

[27]   Working with Voloshinov's concept of intonation, Don Bialostosky has identified the active agents in any given utterance thus: 'Every instance of intonation is oriented *in two directions*: with respect to the listener as ally or witness and with respect to the object of the utterance as the third, living participant whom the intonation scolds or caresses, denigrates or magnifies. *The whole social orientation is what determines all aspects of intonation and makes it intelligible*'. D. Bialostosky, *'Making Tales': The Poetics of Wordsworth's Narrative Experiments* (London: University of Chicago Press, 1984), pp. 42–3.
[28]   See Byron's *Childe Harold*, Canto III, stanza cxiv, *Poetical Works*, p. 225. Further page to this volume (referenced in note 7 above) are given after quotations in the text.

Roll on ye wrath of thunders – peal on peal
Till worlds are ruins & myself alone
Melt heart & soul cased in obdurate steel
Till I can feel that nature is my throne

(p. 48)

The persona of this defiant and ironic lover reappears throughout the poem on occasions too numerous to mention here.[29] The 'Byronic' voice is always immediately and obviously apparent because it repeats a specific power relationship *vis-à-vis* its interlocutors, and because it is a blatant stylization of Byron's own texts. It is important to realize, however, that while the Byronic voices represent a dominant discourse type (aristocratic, educated, ruling class), they are not themselves dominant within the text's overall polyphonic structure. For although these particular speakers assert the confidence of power, it is a power that can be swiftly undermined when heard in dialogue with a discourse of *powerlessness*. The cavalier defiance of a stanza like 'Cares gather round' (ibid.) which ends the sequence we have just been looking at, or a song like 'The sun has gone down' (ibid., p. 43), is effectively sobered when read in juxtaposition to the pathetic 'I've wandered many a weary mile' (p. 49): and it is to such songs, representing the most powerless of the voices in the poem, that I now turn.

It is, of course, no coincidence that the most vulnerable subject positions are found in the songs. The Spenserian stanza is part of an elevated literary tradition, and its mastery indicates access to the education of the ruling classes. The song and ballad, by contrast, were the property of 'the people' and their inclusion in Clare's *œuvre* has always been regarded as appropriate for a peasant-poet. Raymond Williams, for example, laments the fact that Clare, although well placed to contribute to the oral tradition he had inherited, was turned away from what should have been his 'natural' idiom by a literary market moving in the opposite direction.[30] Whatever one feels about this (and it is part of the purpose of this reading to challenge the necessity of finding for Clare an authentic voice), 'Child Harold' offers plenty of evidence that Clare never did forsake the popular genres. The example I have chosen to illustrate the way in which the stylistic simplicity and naïvety of such songs has been used to reinforce the pathos of the speaker is 'I think of thee at early day' (p. 72). Here the vulnerability of the speaker's position may be seen to owe partly to his interrogative stance. Whereas the Byronic hero achieves his authority by *stating* his feelings and opinions (even if they are, in themselves, negative), here the speaker reveals his uncertainty by phrasing his concerns as rhetorical questions:

[29] See, for example, the opening stanza: 'Many are poets – though they use no pen' (*Later Poems*, 1, p. 40); the song, 'The sun has gone down' (ibid., p. 43); the unit beginning 'Tis pleasant now days hours begin to pass' (ibid., p. 55); and the stanza, 'This life is made of lying and grimace' (ibid., p. 59).

[30] *John Clare: Selected Poetry and Prose*, ed. M. Williams and R. Williams (London: Methuen, 1987).

I think of thee at early day
& wonder where my love can be
& when the evening shadows grey
O how I think of thee

. . .

I think of thee at dewy morn
& at the sunny noon
& walks with thee – now left forlorn
Beneath the silent moon

I think of thee I think of all
How blest we both hath been
The sun looks pale upon the wall
& autumn shuts the scene

I can't expect to meet thee now
The winter floods begin
The winter sighs through the open bough
Sad as my heart within

(ibid.)

The extreme simplicity of the verse form here (the song is written in regular abab quatrains) combines with the impotence of the statement (he is able to do no more than 'think' of her), to conjure up a speaker whose experience and expectations are likewise severely limited. In intonational terms, the speaker debases himself both before his subject of address and his object of utterance (in this case the very *question* of whether he will ever see her again). For although he addresses himself directly to 'Mary', his veneration is tentative and half-hearted. It is the voice of one who knows his laments will go unheeded and unheard; it begs for sympathy, but at the same time acknowledges that it will receive none. It is an expression of admiration, mixed with an admission of helplessness and shame. It is a voice that is, in short, in 'hidden polemic' with a potential rebuff (see Chapter 1). Meanwhile, as one of the most pathetic voices in 'Child Harold', the wider dialogic effect of 'I think of thee at early day' is made specific by its formal combination with another of the 'Byronic' stanzas, 'Abscence [sic] is worse than any fate' (p. 71). Thematically united (both deal with the problem of absence), the pathos of the song is bizarrely juxtaposed to the cynical conclusions of the stanza. While the latter views its 'object of utterance' with contempt and disgust, the song, as we have seen, admits a helpless despair in the face of something it cannot even name. Whereas the power of the speaker in the stanza allows him to be critical of 'Abscence' as an abstract concept, the powerlessness of the speaker in the song makes him a victim of its actuality.

Yet despite the generic suitability of the ballad form to the articulation of a victimized and socially inferior subject position, it does not follow that it should always be put to this purpose. There are, indeed, in 'Child Harold' a number of other songs and ballads which engage with the oral folk tradition to produce relatively powerful registers of voice: these constitute the third of the voice types to be discussed here, to which I now proceed.

In Bakhtinian terms, the ballads which come closest to an 'unconditional imitation' of the folk genre are those whose speakers and addresses are anonymous and unspecified. One example of this is 'Her cheeks are like roses' (p. 68) which is built on clichés ('I will love her as long/As the brooks they shall flow'), giving its vows the authority of an ancient tradition. Whereas the previous song bespoke the fear and insecurity of the alienated ego, this, as a representative of a 'timeless' oral tradition, is supremely confident:

> Ere the flowers of the spring
> Deck the meadow & plain
> If theres truth in her bosom
> I shall see her again
>
> I will love her as long
> As the brooks they shall flow
> For Mary is mine
> Whereso ever I go
>
> (ibid.)

For although the song includes a last verse which identifies the subject of the avowal as 'Mary', she remains, like the speaker, essentially archetypal: a simple vehicle of sentiment on which to hang a conventional declaration of love.

The dialogic significance of these songs in 'Child Harold' is considerable, both within their individual units and within the poem as a whole. 'Here's a health unto thee', for example, comes at the end of a six stanza unit whose internal homogeneity it severely disrupts (see pp. 65–67). This sequence (to be discussed below), which begins with the stanza 'Sweet come the misty mornings in september', develops a particularly elegant 'meditative' tone of address that does not appear elsewhere in the poem, but which is rudely interrupted by the song. The generic shift makes it impossible to entertain a common identity for the speaker of both stanzas and song. Instead, the two set up an incongruous dialogue with one another, with the cheerful lightness of the song effectively undermining the bourgeois obsession of the stanzas. Here again we see the popular tradition challenging the seriousness of high literary discourse, proving that, in intonational terms, power can never be simplistically reduced to class.

So far we have considered voices whose social dialects and their attendant power relations represent extremes within the intonational spectrum: a polarization comparable to that which occurs in *Wuthering Heights* (see the discussion above). Not surprisingly, the poem yields others whose register is far more complex, with the speaker's tone revealing significant contradictions and paradoxes. This is certainly the case with the long stanza sequence beginning 'This twilight seems a veil of gauze & mist' (p. 49–52). On account of its Petrarchan imagery and certain archaism of expression, I have posited the model for this discourse among the sixteenth- and seventeenth-century poets Clare read and imitated throughout his career. One of the most suggestive crossreferences would seem to be with Sir Philip Sidney's *Astrophil and*

*Stella*, which echoes not only the imagery but also many of the sentiments expressed in these sections of 'Child Harold'. Stella, like Mary, is addressed as an object of enduring devotion, a love that is literally as immortal as the stars. Comparable, too, is a pervasive use of paradox and oxymoron, tropes endemic to the sixteenth-century court tradition. Finally, as with the Byronic influence, there are lines in 'Child Harold' which would seem to plagiarize directly those found in Sidney's poem.[31] With such obvious sympathies in sentiment, imagery and phrasing, further similarity at an intonational level is only to be expected, and the eight stanzas comprising the sequence are united by the same 'courtly' deference to both listener and 'object of address' that we find in Sidney. I quote the second and third stanzas:

> Remind me not of other years or tell
> My broken heart of joys they are to meet
> While thy own falsehood rings the loudest knell
> To one false heart that aches too cold to beat
> Mary how oft with fondness I repeat
> That name alone to give my troubles rest
> The very sound though bitter seemeth sweet
> In my love's home & thy own faithless breast
> Truths bonds are broke & every nerve distrest
>
> Life is to me a dream that never wakes
> Night finds me on this lengthening road alone
> Love is to me a thought that ever aches
> A frost bound thought that freezes life to stone
> Mary in truth & nature still my own
> That warms the winter of my aching breast
> Thy name is joy nor will I life bemoan
> Midnight when sleep takes charge of nature's rest
> Finds me awake and friendless – not distrest

(p. 49)

Placed within the context of the sequence as a whole, moreover, it will be seen that the shifting subjects of address to be found in these two stanzas (from an unspecified interlocutor to Mary and back again) extend to Nature in the first, 'Sleep' in the fourth, and 'England' in the fifth *without any significant change in intonation*. The same relationship between speaker, listener and object of address is sustained throughout. This position of dignified subservience, which is in stark contrast to the bravura of the Byronic sequence (discussed above), is further evidence of the complex dance of intonation and social register that make up the poem. For although the Petrarchan voice, like the Byronic one, is privileged in class terms, it affects a position of powerlessness *vis-à-vis* its various interlocutors. And while, in the final two stanzas of the sequence, the speaker becomes newly

---

31    See especially the MS 8 stanzas (presented at the end of the MS 6 text in *Later Poems*): 'O she was more than fair – divinely fair' and 'Her looks was like the spring her very voice' (p. 87), which adopt forms of eulogy very similar to Sonnet 77 of Sir Philip Sidney's *Astrophil and Stella*. See Sidney, *Selected Poems*, ed. K. Duncan-Jones (Oxford: Oxford University Press, 1973), p. 157.

assertive, defying both addressee and circumstance with an aggressive declamation of his love: 'For her for one whose very name is yet/My hell or heaven – & will ever be' (p. 50), he remains, unlike his Byronic counterpart, subservient before his 'object of utterance': 'To make my soul new bonds which God made free'. Supported by its distinctive sixteenth-century vocabulary and diction, this unit therefore constitutes another identifiable narratorial persona within the poem. It is also interesting to observe that, in this instance, the particular intonational quality of the stanzas is carried through into the song, 'O Mary sing thy songs to me'.[32]

Yet Bakhtin's polyphonic text is characterized not simply by the articulation of independent voices but also by their relation to one another, and the final significance of the unit we have just considered lies in its positioning immediately after the 'Byronic' sequence discussed earlier. This is one of the most distinctive breaks in the poem in intonational terms, comparable, as the critic William Howard has rightly observed, to the transition from a loud, fast movement in musical symphony to a slow, soft one.[33] Between the 'Thunderstorm' poem discussed above and 'This twilight seems a veil of gause & mist', there is a significant shift of power. As we have seen, a proud, disdainful lover is replaced by a humble, reverential one, and the intertextual referent is no longer Byron but Sidney. In a sequential reading of the MS 6 version of the poem, this transition will be heard as one of its key junctures: an interface at which not only the voices but also other polarized features in the poem (such as the imagery) are brought together in dialogic confrontation.

The next group of voices to be considered are those associated with biblical rhetoric. The first rather surprising factor to note here is that, despite the fact that 'Child Harold is embedded in biblical material in its original manuscript sources, the incidence of explicitly biblical discourse in the poem itself is relatively small. While it is true that in MS 8 the formal intertextualization of material makes a reading of 'Child Harold' unavoidably implicated in the biblical quotations and paraphrases that surround it, the MS 6 version bears few direct allegiances. The most significant exceptions are the two stanzas, 'The lightenings vivid flashes' and 'A shock, a moment in the wrath of God' (p. 69). Here the rhetoric of prophecy combines with the imagery of apocalypse in an obvious crossreference to the paraphrase from Revelations 21 and 22 to which the stanzas are juxtaposed in

---

[32] Note also the thematic continuity provided by the thematic references to 'rest' in both stanza and song.

[33] See W. Howard, *John Clare* (Boston: Twayne, 1981). Howard divides the poem into nine 'movements' comparable to those of a musical symphony. The places he chooses for the breaks between movements are, however, rather odd. With respect to the section of the poem in question, he proposes that the first movement ends after the 'Byronic' stanza, 'I have had many loves and seek no more'. This means that his second movement begins with 'Cares gather round I snap their chains in two' and goes on to include the whole of the 'Petrarchan' stanza sequence and the songs which follow. How he can have failed to observe a break between the 'Thunderstorm' poem and 'This twilight seems a veil of gause & mist' is hard to imagine.

MS 6.[34] Their significance in intonational terms lies in the fact that they contribute another 'powerful' voice to the repertoire of the poem as a whole: a speaker whose relation to both his addressees and his 'object of utterance' invokes a divine authority, more uncompromising even than the Byronic hero:

> A shock, a moment, in the wrath of God
> Is long as hell's eternity to all
> His thunderbolts leave life but as the clod
> Cold & inna[ni]mate – their temples fall
> Beneath his frown to ashes – the eternal pall
> Of wrath sleeps oer the ruins where they fell
> & nought of memory can their creeds recall
> The sin of Sodom was a moments yell
> Fires death bed theirs their first grave the last hell
>
> (p. 69)

In Bakhtinian terms, the relation here between the speaker and the discourse is particularly interesting since the former, while anonymous, assumes the diction and intonation of the God he describes. It will be observed that each statement, made in the present tense, is ennunciated as an incontrovertible fact: a simple repetition of His 'Truth'. This may thus be seen as a stylization of biblical rhetoric, comparable to the previous stylizations of Byron, Sidney and the ballad tradition. A similar transference of biblical authority is to be heard in the voice of the speaker in the stanza '& he who studies nature's volume through' (p. 43). While not prophetic in the manner of the apocalyptic stanzas, this stanza likewise describes God's omnipotence in the voice of biblical sermonizing. 'Thus saith the great & high & lofty one' (p. 53), meanwhile, is an actual paraphrase of Isaiah 57. Incorporated into the sequence beginning 'Now melancholly [sic] autumn comes anew', the source for this stanza has apparently gone unnoticed by any of Clare's previous editors and critics. Robinson and Powell note an earlier version in MS D20, but fail to cite the paraphrase which occurs on the last page of MS 8 from which it evidently derives: 'Thus saith the great & high & lofty one that inhabits eternity whose name is HOLY "I dwell in the high & holy place, with him also that is of contrite & humble Spirit that trembles at my word"'. Unlike the other biblical stanzas, this one does not merely stylize the rhetoric of an omnipotent God but incorporates direct quotation. In intonational terms it therefore represents an interesting swing between the humility of the speaker ('Thou high & lofty one – O give to me/Truths low estate') to the absolute authority of the Father himself. Most significant, however, is the way in which this stanza, based as it is on an external source, reads as in no way incongruous to the sequence into which it is inserted. The preceding and succeeding stanzas, addressed respectively to 'Nature' and 'Mary', share a comparable intonational humility; clear evidence that homogeneity of tone is frequently more important than content in determining the

---

34   In MS 6 these stanzas occur in opening 18 (pp. 34–35) directly opposite the Revelations paraphrase (see *Later Poems*, 1, p. 150) which includes the lines: 'From me into hell everlasting & fire/With the devil's own tortures & never expire'.

aesthetic coherence of the written word. In conclusion it may thus be seen that the contribution of the scriptural voice to 'Child Harold's overall polyphonic structure, while undoubtedly significant, is less wide ranging than earlier commentators such as Mark Minor have implied.[35] The stanzas cited here are the only ones which are specifically identifiable as scriptural in origin, to which may be added the 'Thunderstorm' poem discussed above. Together they constitute the deep bass of the poem's intonational spectrum: the discourse of absolute (because divine) power and authority, the polarized opposite of the powerless peasant exile.

The final voice I wish to deal with in this reading of 'Child Harold's polyphonic composition cannot be ascribed to a single textual source. It belongs to the unit beginning 'Sweet come the misty mornings in september' and ends with the song 'Heres a health unto thee bonny lassie O' (pp. 65–67), discussed above. Consisting of six stanzas, this is one of the most unified sequences in the whole poem, both in terms of its intonational continuity and its imagery, which focuses on the cumulative metaphor of the 'village bells'. The mood of the passage is reflective, and the nearest it comes to a specific literary referent is probably the eighteenth-century meditation poem and its Romantic variant in texts like Wordworth's 'Tintern Abbey':

> Sweet comes the misty mornings in september
> Among the dewy paths how sweet to stray
> Greensward or stubbles as I well remember
> I once have done – the mist curls thick & grey
> As cottage smoke – like net work on the sprey [*sic*]
> Of seeded grass the cobweb draperies run
> Beaded with pearls of dew at early day
> & oer the pleachy stubbles peeps the sun
> the lamp of day when that of night is done
>
> What mellowness these harvest days unfold
> In the strong glance of the midday sun
> The homesteads very grass seems changed to gold
> The light in golden shadows seems to run
> & tinges every spray it rests upon
> With that rich harvest hue of sunny joy
> Natures lifes sweet companions cheers alone –
> The hare starts up before the shepherd boy
> & partridge coveys wir on russet wings of joy
>
> (p. 65)

It will be seen from the first two stanzas that the position of the speaker *vis-à-vis* his interlocutors is one of equanimity. This speaker venerates Nature, not from a position of subservience but as an intimate equal. In terms of a power relationship, this means that the voice in this unit exhibits neither the authority of the Byronic or biblical discourses, nor the (relative) humility of the Petrarchan passages. In its first five stanzas,

---

[35] See M. Minor, 'Clare, Byron, and the Bible: Additional Evidence from the Asylum Manuscripts', *Bulletin of Research in the Humanities*, **85**, spring, 1982, pp. 104–26. In this important article, Minor discusses the thematic similarity between the paraphrases and the poems by grouping the former into categories such as 'Promises or Reminders of Divine Deliverance for Israel' and 'Statements of Personal Affliction'.

the sequence registers a dialogue of equality between speaker, listener and 'object of utterance'. It is a voice which is in consensus with its 'future answer word', where the speaker is in *harmony* with the world he decribes. Here is the fifth stanza:

> Sweet solitude thou partner of my life
> Thou balm of hope & every pressing care
> Thou soothing silence oer the noise of strife
> These meadow flats & trees – the Autumn air
> Mellows my heart to harmony – I bear
> Lifes burthen happily – these fenny dells
> Seem Eden in this sabbath rest from care
> My heart with loves first early memory swells
> To hear the music of those village bells
>
> (p. 66)

This illusion of a dialogic relationship based on equality (what so many of Bakhtin's followers have presented as its abiding characteristic) is, however, temporary. Although the reader may perceive in these first five stanzas a final escape from the power struggle inherent in the other voices, and although she may read the absence of any recognizable stylization as commensurate with an independent voice (be it Clare's own or that of the narrator), the final stanza delivers a sting that reveals the earlier equanimity to be a foil to a hidden obsession:

> For in that hamlet lives my rising sun
> Whose beams hath cheered me all my lorn life long
> My heart to nature there was early won
> For she was nature's self – & still my song
> Is hers through sun & shade through right & wrong
> On her my memory forever dwells
> The flower of Eden – evergreen of song
> Truth in my heart the same love story tells
> – I love the music of those village bells
>
> (p. 67)

It will now be seen that the autumn landscape and 'village bells' addressed with such apparent innocence in the preceding stanzas are, in fact, *metaphors* for the beloved: 'For *she* was nature's self' [my italics]. This information causes the reader to redouble and reassess both the semantic and intonational impact of the sequence. Since we now know that nature and bells are not simply objects to which the speaker relates in democratic dialogue but, instead, symbols for an object of reverence (Mary), our whole register of the power relationship necessarily changes. The speaker is no longer equal with his object of utterance, but once again its subject and devotee. Despite the pride and triumph evident in the assertion of the final stanza, this speaker, like that of the Petrarchan sequence, is characterized by his reverential relationship to his interlocutor. What appeared as a passage of intonational harmony in the poem proves, at last, but another variant in the power struggle between speaker and addressee.

The six voices surveyed here are merely a representation of the total which constitute 'Child Harold'. They were selected because they represent the most pervasive voices in the poem and, inevitably, the largest of the stanza-song units. Many of the remainder, including those occuring in the units comprising just one stanza/one song, are admittedly more difficult to characterize in terms of literary models, although all may be analysed intonationally on the basis of the relationship between speaker, listener and 'object of utterance' used in this reading. For intonation, to quote Clark and Holquist, is 'the sound that value makes', and all the voices which contribute to the polyphony of 'Child Harold' can be registered at a particular point on a scale that mixes literary models with class dialect in a complex dialectic of power.[36] Dialogue here, as in the text's ambivalent approach to the Romantic imagination, is essentially a dialogue between polarized opposites.[37] The 'powerful' voices of the Byronic aristocrat, the biblical prophet and the ballad singer are continually challenged by that of the 'powerless': the peasant exile, the languishing courtly lover. Yet while these power relations are inscribed in class distinctions, they also cut across them. The ballad singer uses the authority of the oral tradition to proclaim his love as proudly as the Byronic hero, while the Petrarchan lover, for all his literary sophistication, is representative of a discourse that is humble and ingratiating. Thus although the various voices which comprise the text are far from neutral politically, the power positions they represent intonationally are not necessarily commensurate with class. Neither do the voices which represent a dominant ideology and/or a dominant ideological position *dominate* the text's overall polyphonic structure. This brings us back to the first of Bakhtin's criteria for the polyphonic text: the text as '*a plurality of independent and unmerged voices and consciousnesses*' (*Dostoevsky's Poetics*, p. 6).

The Bakhtinian definition of the polyphonic text, as we saw in the reading of *Wuthering Heights*, demands absolute equality among its voices, even as it necessitates the absence of a transcendent authorial presence. 'Child Harold' satisfies both these conditions. Powerful and powerless voices are engaged in a dialogue which is without a final victor. The authority of the Byronic aristocrat always stands to be undermined by the doubt and pathos of the peasant exile. As in a reading of the formal composition of the manuscripts, it is in the *juxtaposition* of these positions that the text's essential dialogism is to be found. Sometimes the transition is *between* individual units (such as the juxtaposition of the Byronic and Petrarchan sequences at the beginning of the poem); sometimes it is *within* them. Everywhere in the text it will be seen that one voice knocks against its neighbour, challenging, supporting or undermining it. Some of these voices recur frequently throughout the text or may, as in the case of

---

[36] K. Clark and M. Holquist, *Mikhail Bakhtin* (Harvard: Harvard University Press, 1984). See the discussions of intonation in Chapter 1.
[37] In a later section of my thesis I use the dialogic model as a means of exploring the ambivalence towards the discourse of the 'Romantic imagination' in Clare's writing through a close examination of its imagery and syntax. Whereas here I have considered dialogic activity between 'relatively whole utterances', there I use it as a means for explaining the oscillations which are present within individual stanzas and songs.

the Byronic and biblical discourses, exist in intimate dialogue with one another.

One of the key features of 'Child Harold' as a whole, moreover, is its intertextual bias which locates many of the voices as imitations or stylizations of other genres. None of these voices, as a consequence, can be said to be that of the essential 'John Clare'. The personal pronoun of this poem, as was noted at the beginning of the reading, is a picaresque adventurer, a chameleon who adopts many personae but who resides permanently in none.

This plurality of voices and the absence of any authorial unifying consciousness is inevitably realized as a structural feature. The polyphonic text is distinguished both by its tendency to *simultaneity* and its resistance to closure: 'The fundamental category of Dostoevsky's mode of artistic visualizing was not evolution, but *co-existence* and *interaction*' (*Dostoevsky's Poetics*, p. 28). Formally divided into a number of stanza-song units, 'Child Harold' invites a synchronic rather than a diachronic reading.[38] While there may be consecutive development *within* the individual groups, in the poem as a whole the voices must be thought of as being simultaneous with one another. The text, as Tim Chilcott has acknowledged with respect to Clare's asylum poetry in general, does not 'evolve' as much as 'revolve'.[39] Meanwhile, because none of these voices is finally dominant and because, semantically, they come to no final 'conclusions', 'Child Harold' fulfils the final criterion of the polyphonic text in being *without closure*. No synthesizing voice marks its beginning or its end. The symphonic finalé that William Howard has proposed, presenting the last song of the MS 6 text as the poem's natural and inevitable conclusion, is better replaced by the metaphor of the musical 'round' in which all the voices are located at various points on an ever-revolving cycle.[40] At some points these voices will harmonize; at others, counterpoint. At all times, however, they will maintain a *polyphony* that depends on the essential plurality of 'unmerged consciousnesses'.

---

[38] 'Diachronic' and 'synchronic' are the linguistic terms deployed by Ferdinand de Saussaure to distinguish between ongoing, chronological time and the individual 'moment in time'. See T. Hawkes, *Structuralism and Semiotics* (London: Methuen, 1978), pp. 19–20.

[39] See T. Chilcott, '*A Real World and Doubting Mind': A Critical Study of the Poetry of John Clare* (Hull: Hull University Press, 1985), p. 228.

[40] Howard's reading of 'Child Harold' is based on the assumption, by no means incontrovertible, that Clare's 'Winter Canto' is the 'official ending' of the poem (i.e., he ignores the fact that the MS 8 stanzas – printed by Robinson and Powell immediately following the end of the MS 6 text – might have been written later). Even the fact that what he designates the 'Winter Canto' consists of just one stanza and one song does not deter him. He concludes: 'Clare could not have added anything to "Child Harold" without running the risk (already apparent in several stanzas and songs of the autumn canto) of being too repetitive. Contrary to the view that "Child Harold" is an incomplete poem, the song "In this cold world without a home/ Disconsolate I go" brings the poem to a logical end' (*John Clare*, p. 298).

# 4

---

# DIALOGISM AND THE SUBJECT

*Self-in-Relation:*
*Readings of Virginia Woolf's* The Waves
*and Adrienne Rich's* The Dream of a Common Language

---

## I

### *The Waves*

*Virginia Woolf*

---

I t is possible to read *The Waves* as a profoundly monologic text.[1] Despite the fact that it contains six speaking characters, their utterances are usually described as 'monologues' – and these virtually indistinguishable from one another in terms of style and register. Critics like Makiko Minow-Pinkney have also failed to see any dialogue between the voices.[2] She writes: 'Though described by its author as a "play-poem", the novel has no dramatic impetus. The monologues are not addressed to each other, they achieve no dramatic interaction' (p. 172). This apparent structural and linguistic monlogism has also contributed to the supposition that all six principal characters may be reduced to one presiding consciousness: Bernard. His statement at the end of the novel, 'I am many people: I do not altogether know who I am – Jinny, Susan, Neville, Rhoda, or Louis' (p. 212) is taken as an unequivocal testament to this fact, and Virginia Woolf (who has herself been identified with Bernard) is thus seen to be

---

[1] V. Woolf, *The Waves* (Harmondsworth: Penguin, 1992). Page references to this volume will be given after quotations in the text.
[2] M. Minow-Pinkney, *Virginia Woolf and the Problem of the Subject* (Brighton: Harvester Press, 1987).

the author of the prototypical 'cubist' text in which supposedly different characters are merely the many facets of a single human subject.

What I am going to argue here, however, is that this monologization of the text is not necessarily the best way to make sense of it: certainly in terms of its investigation of subjectivity, a premature conflation of differences into Bernard's 'expansive ego' is most unproductive.[3] Even if this *is* a text which begins and ends with images of merger and dissolution, its analytic focus is an attempt to compare and contrast, to explore how (to invoke Bernard's metaphor) 'the virginal wax that coats the spine melted in different patches for both of us' (p. 185). In my own reading, therefore, I have chosen to keep voices and characters sufficiently separate to sustain their sense of difference from one another, and to hear the dialogues between them. As Bakhtin wrote in his early essay, 'Author and Hero':

> What would I gain were another to fuse with me? He would see and know only what I already see and know, he would only repeat in himself the inescapable closed circle of my own life; let him rather remain outside me (*Estetika Slovesnogo Tvorchestva*, p. 78).

Dialogue depends on differences (even if it has been read by too many of Bakhtin's followers as a quick means of resolving them), and by re-presenting *The Waves* as a polyphonic novel composed of a plurality of 'unmerged . . . consciousnesses' (*Dostoevsky's Poetics* (1929), p. 6), the reader can gain a liberatory new perspective both on its formal composition and on its representation of the subject.

Before I outline how I intend to deal with the question of subjectivity, however, I would like first to propose how a dialogic reading of the text might be expected to differ from a Freudian and, to a lesser extent, a Lacanian one. Referring back to the discussion in Chapter 1, the reader will recall that the Bakhtinian subject is at all times 'socially defined': he or she is constituted by and through language, and by the political and ideological context in which she offers forth her utterances. She is a subject without an 'unconscious' (since Voloshinov in his critique of Freudianism refused to entertain a space outside of language), and a subject who exists in a permanent state of 'unfinalizedness'. In terms of a reading of *The Waves*, this view of subjectivity as an open-ended process of 'becoming' would differ substantially from a Freudian (or, indeed, a Lacanian) reading with its emphasis on the distinct phases of development associated with the oedipal complex. Although it is a text that lends itself extremely well to such interpretation, it can equally be argued that *The Waves* deals in subjects who are perpetually forming and re-forming themselves (there is, for example, the classic image of Bernard as a snake shedding one of his 'life-skins'). While as children each character is, indeed, forced to renegotiate his or her relationship with their parents, this is only one of many subsequent relationships, and is by no means the dominant one for all the characters. Thus, while for a

---

3  See Minow-Pinkney, *Virginia Woolf*: 'Bernard seems to experience a megalomaniac inflation of the ego rather than its dissolution, as in Rhoda's case' (p. 168).

psychoanalytic critic the passage in the first section which describes the characters' relationships with their 'fathers' is heavily loaded (the fact, for example, that Rhoda has 'no father'), in a dialogic reading this is divested of its overwhelming determinism.[4] By the same token, a dialogic reading shifts attention away from familial to nonfamilial relationships altogether. While a Freudian reading would side step this issue by reading the relationships which *are* presented through an oedipal grid, I would argue that *The Waves* is a fascinating case study in subjectivity precisely because it explores the growth and development of six characters *in relation to one another* and not to their parents. In the first section of the book, indeed, the reader has the disturbing sense of these children of wealthy parents as already cast off and abandoned: among the lawns and bushes of the kindergarten, it is not only Rhoda who is without a father. And in the absence of parents, the children begin to define their subject and gender difference through intersubjective exchange with one another: Bernard discovers he is 'Bernard' not through some complex refraction of the oedipal mirror but by recognizing his difference from Neville. As he recalls at the end of his life: 'It was Susan who cried, that day when I was in the tool-house with Neville; and I felt my indifference melt. Neville did not melt. "Therefore", I said, "I am myself, not Neville", a wonderful discovery' (p. 185).

Another way in which we might expect a dialogic reading of the text's representation of subjectivity to differ from a Freudian/Lacanian one is in its presentation of the character's relationship to language and ideology. As was mentioned in Chapter 1, the Bakhtin school produced a much more active view of the subject in this respect – allowing him or her to contest and 'objectify' the 'internally persuasive word' of another's discourse, to challenge and/or negotiate his or her appropriation by another's ideological position. In a reading of *The Waves* this would mean that Louis *need not* be permanently fixed in his unhappy relationship to the Symbolic Order simply because he lacked the 'cultural capital' to secure his place within it, nor Rhoda (a woman without a father) situated for ever outside its 'loop'.[5] The fact that neither of these characters does appear to achieve full intergration would not, in a dialogic reading, blind us to the fact that subtle changes do take place. Louis's success as a lawyer gives him institutional access to the phallocentric hegemony, while the authority of the written word – the signature (p. 127), the typewriter (ibid.) – enable him to reverse the ostracization caused by his Australian accent.

The last area, I would suggest, in which a dialogic reading of the text would differ from a Freudian one is in many ways the most important: the fact that the individual is to be defined and understood in terms of

---

4 Minow-Pinkney (ibid.) uses Julia Kristeva's *About Chinese Women* to draw a significant connection between Rhoda's inability to 'take up her place' in Lacan's Symbolic Order with her 'lack' of a father: 'her uneasy relationship with language and exclusion from time mutually imply each other. Kristeva argues that 'there is no time without speech. Therefore, no time without the father. That's what the father means: sign and time'. Rhoda 'has no father', and is accordingly excluded from and rejects genealogical continuity, temporal order, the clock of objective time' (p. 161).
5 'Cultural capital'; see note 12, Chapter 3.

*fully intersubjective relations*, and not as the passive subject of projected and introjected drives which, according to the predetermined schema of the oedipal process, he or she has no power to resist or control. While it is true that other models of psychoanalysis (in particular, those associated with Nancy Chodorow and the object-relations school) go some way to recognizing a more dynamic parent–child relationship, the parent (simply because she or he *is* the parent) is given the greater agency.[6] In a dialogic universe, on the other hand, the relative power of interlocutors is never fixed, even if it is always present. The subject 'becomes' through a process of fully interactive exchange, in the course of which the roles of initiator and recipient (speaker and addressee) may move back and forth several times.

Implicit in this brief review of how a dialogic reading of *The Waves* might differ from a Freudian one is the crucial point that, for the Bakhtinian, subjectivity is *plural*. We are interested not in the construction of a universal model of the subject but of *many subjects*: in the differences *between* subjectivities, and in the difference *within* a single subjectivity. And the means, I would suggest, through which we best explore the nature of these differences as they are represented in *The Waves* is through dialogism itself; the way in which each subject constructs and conducts his or her relationship with others (what I shall refer to subsequently as 'self-other relations'), and with language (both written and spoken). In both these categories, moreover, we find variable relations between the six characters. While Bernard and Susan may be similar in one particular, for example, they may be different in another. This frustrates the possibility of seeing any of the characters as equivalents for, or opposites of, any of the others: the crossgender pairing of Bernard and Susan, Neville and Jinny, Louis and Rhoda, for instance.[7] In the course of my own reading I hope to show that the group lines up differently *vis-à-vis* the different expressions of dialogic relations, although it is true that when we add up the evidence, a sliding scale of dialogism – monologism does present itself, with Bernard as the most fully 'dialogized' character, and Rhoda as the least.

I begin my investigations, then, with a consideration of how the different characters in Woolf's novel construct and conduct their self-other relations; how they posit their interlocutor (singular or plural), and how they respond to his or her presence. This includes a complex interrogation of the role gender both does and does not play in the articulation of such relations: while a male and female character may appear similar in the way in which they relate to others, for example, their gender difference may effect an important qualitative difference.

The last point most certainly applies to the first connection I wish to explore, which is that between Bernard and Jinny. Both Bernard and Jinny are characters whose subjectivities are ostensibly dialogic; their identities have been formed through their relationship with multiple others, upon

---

[6]   See N. Chodorow, *The Reproduction of Mothering: Psychoanalysis and the Sociology of Gender* (Berkeley, CA: University of California Press, 1978). See Chapter 2, pp. 90–91, for a discussion of Chodorow's work.

[7]   This is Louis's own grouping. See *The Waves*, p. 176.

whom they are entirely dependent for the realization of 'the self'. Hence Bernard's statement, 'To be myself . . . I need the illumination of other people's eyes' (p. 87), and Jinny's life-long dependency on a male admirer who (like the train window) will give her back an appropriate vision of herself. Both are subjects who are perpetually looking outwards for new and varied points of contact (as Bernard says, 'Anybody will do. I am not fastidious. The crossing-sweeper will do; the postman; the waiter in this French restaurant' (ibid.). Yet the fact that Bernard's interlocutors are sought to confirm his identity at the centre of a multilayered, heteroglot society, as a 'man speaking to men' (in the course of *The Waves* he singles out only two female interlocutors apart from the other characters), while Jinny's are given a narrowly sexual function, draws an important point of contrast between them. The insatiable appetite for dialogic exchange which makes Bernard a humanist makes Jinny merely a permissive woman.

A similar contrast along gender lines may be found in the pairing of Rhoda and Louis. While this is the relationship between characters that the text is itself most explicit about (Louis himself refers to them as 'conspirators' p. 107), there is an important qualitative difference in their approach to self-other relations which is the difference of gender and sexuality. Although both resist dialogic exchange and feel their identities as threatened by it as Bernard and Jinny feel themselves 'realized', Louis's alternative point of relation – what I shall refer to as 'the Institution' – is very different from Rhoda's unpeopled space: the distant grove with marble columns evocative of Keats's 'cold pastoral' (p. 78).[8] Louis's inability to communicate is predicated simply upon his lack of cultural capital, as is demonstrated by his paranoid 'hidden polemic' with the 'average men' of the London eating shop (pp. 68–70).[9] It is consequently compensated fairly straightforwardly (as I have already indicated) by the alternative relationship he develops with a succession of institutions (in particular, education and the law). Rhoda, however, finds nothing upon which to construct even a semblance of self-other relations except a succession of dreams. While Jinny and Bernard ask the question 'Who comes?', Rhoda is represented by the faltering 'To whom?' (p. 41). Referring back to the discussion of Dale Bauer's work in Chapter 2, one can see Rhoda as the archetypal victim of a 'failed community': among the heteroglossic crowds of potential interlocutors who she simultaneously fears, despises

---

[8]   See John Keats's 'Ode to a Grecian Urn':

> O Attic shape! Fair attitude! with brede
> Of marble men and maidens overwrought,
> With forest branches and the trodden weed;
> Thou, silent form! dost tease us out of thought
> As doth eternity: Cold Pastoral!

J. Keats, *Poetical Works*, ed. H. W. Garrod (Oxford: Oxford University Press, 1956), p. 260–62.

[9]   In his paranoid 'hidden polemic' with hostile forces, Louis may be compared with Dostoevsky's 'Underground Man'. See Mikhail Bakhtin's discussion of this text in *Problems of Dostoevsky's Poetics* (Manchester: Manchester University Press, 1984): 'He [the Underground Man] *fears* that the other might think he *fears* that other's opinion' (p. 227).

and desires, she finds no suitable addressee.[10] Although Percival's death provides her with a temporary vocation – gathering violets for his grave – she comments ironically 'Look now at what Percival has given me' (p. 120) – such a commitment to mutual annihilation is premature. Eager as she is to cast in her lot with Percival ('we will gallop together over desert hills where the swallow dips her wings in dark pools . . .' p. 124), the next section finds her still alive and without an interlocutor. Her words fly through the air and are caught by no one.

Invoking Anne Herrmann's Bakhtinian reworking of Irigaray (see Chapter 2, pp. 94–96), I believe a strong case can be made for explaining Rhoda's existence 'outside the loop of the world' (pp. 14–15) in terms of her sexuality and failure to identify a suitable feminine addressee.[11] Locked in a phallocentric, heterosexual economy of desire she is absurdly 'mated-off' with Louis whose 'embraces' she 'fears' (p. 157), while her own identity founders through her lack of a reciprocating feminine subject who will enable her to be 'indefinitely other in herself' rather than the feminine complement to a masculine principle.[12] That Rhoda *is* searching for such an addressee is suggested by a few incidental textual clues: the fact that the swallow who flies over her pool is female, for instance; or her fixation on a series of female alter-egos – Jinny, Susan, Miss Lambert and the girls at school whose luggage labels she used to read. Therefore, although their common fear of dialogic exchange does much to bind Louis and Rhoda together – they are both characters who effect to be destroyed and 'effaced' through contact – their differences of gender and sexuality invites us to read their adialogicality (commensurate in Rhoda with an asexuality) in very different ways.

In terms of their self-other relations, the other two characters – Neville and Susan – do not form a 'natural' pair. Susan, I would suggest, is the one character in Woolf's text whose subjectivity may be easily described in terms of a traditional Freudian model. Her identity pivots on her relationship to her parents (in particular, her father who appears repeatedly in the text as an object of passionate desire ('And there is my father, with his back turned, talking to a farmer. I tremble. I cry. There is my father in gaiters. There is my father' (p. 46)), and to her own children. For although she, like the other characters, is dialogically defined by a host of nonfamilial relationships – the opposition of her maternal body to Jinny's sexualized one, for example – her main subject development follows a classic Freudian trajectory in which desire for the father is finally resolved in the production of male children. In this respect, it is significant that it is her son ('His eyes will see when mine are shut . . . I shall go mixed with them beyond my body and see India' p. 131) and not her husband who becomes her principal interlocutor in later life; indeed, her husband is rarely mentioned.

---

10    D. Bauer, *Feminist Dialogics: A Theory of Failed Community* (New York: State University of New York Press, 1989). See the discussion in Chapter 2, pp. 101–103.
11    A. Herrmann, *The Dialogic and Difference: 'An/Other Woman' in Virginia Woolf and Christa Wolf* (New York: Columbia University Press, 1989). See discussion in Chapter 2, pp. 94–96.
12    L. Irigaray, 'This Sex Which Is Not One', in *New French Feminisms*, ed. E. Marks and I. de Courtivron (Brighton: Harvester Press, 1981), pp. 99–106.

There is a coda that may be added to Susan's self-other relations, however, that unsettles their more obvious Freudianism. First, the fact that she forms interlocutory relationships with nonhuman subjects by identifying herself 'not as a woman' but as part of Nature: 'At this hour, this still early hour, I think I am the field, I am the barn, I am the trees; mine are the flocks of birds, and this young hare who leaps . . .' (p. 72). Secondly, the fact that at the high tide of her life, at the moment her subjecthood would appear to be most full and (to use Bernard's word) 'robust', she challenges the 'internally persuasive words' that have constructed her persona of 'natural happiness' (p. 146) and cries: 'I am sick of the body, I am sick of my own craft, industry and cunning, of the unscrupulous ways of the mother who protects, and collects under her jealous eyes at one long table her own children, *always her own*' (p. 147, my italics). This questioning of Freudian determinism through the process that Bakhtin identified as the objectification of the 'internally persuasive word' (see Chapter 2) unsettles any easy cataloguing of Susan's subjectivity. While the family may dominate her self-other relations, she nevertheless acquires a dialogic purchase on her positioning within the phallocentric machine.

Neville's subjectivity is characterized by his need for exclusive relationships: for his dialogue with 'one other only'. For the first half of the novel, his self is defined purely in relation to Percival. And Percival is a true Bakhtinian other: an other whose difference from Neville promotes the electric spark of dialogue by eschewing the possibility of 'fusion' (see the quotation from Bakhtin at the beginning of this reading). While Percival is the sportsman, the soldier, the hero, Neville knows that he will be 'a clinger to the outsides of words all my life' (p. 35). And when, through death, Percival is taken from him, Neville seeks another who will provide him with the same dialogizing code of difference: a certain 'carelessness' of movement, a 'dexterity' with the hands (p. 137). Inasmuch as his self is defined and developed through a consecutive series of (homo)sexual relationships, Neville's life may, perhaps, be compared with Jinny's. There remains the crucial difference, however, that whereas Jinny positions herself as the *addressee* of her dialogues (she is an object of admiration), Neville retains the position of the desiring *subject*; and where Jinny's passivity is commensurate with her power (she is always the desired, never the desiring), Neville's hero-worship betokens his powerlessness.

Having explored some of their more obvious differences through this review of the characters' self-other relations, I want to move on now to a consideration of how their contrasting attitudes to language – the medium of dialogue – draws further distinctions. The role of language in structuring the subject is given two symbolic inscriptions in *The Waves*: first, the attitude of the different characters to spoken language (the *voice*); and, secondly, the contrasting perspective on written language represented by Bernard's generic association with the novel, and Neville's with poetry. Voice and text exist in the novel as further indices of how dialogized each character is: where he or she stands on the scale of a dialogic–monologic subjectivity.

The human voice is certainly one of the most emotionally charged images in Woolf's novel, inspiring, as it does, delight and reassurance in some characters, and fear and repulsion in others. The character most in love with the human voice is, not surprisingly, Bernard. His habit of pushing out into the 'heterogeneous crowd' (p. 134) means that that he is perpetually surrounded by a cacophony of voices; and speech, even the most ordinary, everyday speech – is regarded by him (as by Bakhtin) as a thing of glory. As he observes at Percival's farewell dinner, 'To speak about wine even to the waiter, is to bring about an explosion' (p. 88); and it is significant that while he waits for his friends he is speculating not upon what they will look like but what conversation they will have: 'I think of people to whom I could say things: Louis, Neville, Susan, Jinny and Rhoda. With them I am many-sided. They retrieve me from darkness' (p. 87). But the most evocative expression of Bernard's life-long romance with the spoken word comes in the final section when, approaching death, it is temporarily taken from him. Loosing his hold on the life of the body, he levitates to a spirit world and gains the distant, silent perspective of the ghost:

> Now tonight, my body rises tier upon tier like some cool temple whose floor is strewn with carpets and murmurs rise and the altars stand smoking; but up above, here in my serene head, come only fine gusts of melody, waves of incense . . . When I look down from this transcendency, how beautiful are even the crumbled relics of bread! (p. 223).

From this distance, the voices of his fellow men and women are faint – reduced to a murmur – and all possibility of dialogue is lost. Bernard is out of earshot. By the same token, his return to earth is signalled not by a change of focus but by a sudden influx of noise: 'Listen: a whistle sounds, wheels rush, the door creaks on its hinges' (p. 226) – brought about by the presence of an interlocutor under whose gaze 'I begin to perceive this, that and the other' (ibid.).[13] To be alive, for Bernard, as for Bakhtin, means to hear, to speak, to 'dialogize'.

For Louis and Rhoda, meanwhile, the fear of dialogue that we saw expressed in their dislike of self-other relations is corroborated by their terror of the human voice. The silent ghost's eye perspective of the world that, for Bernard, is commensurate with death is, for them, an object of desire. As Rhoda says to Louis, 'If only we could mount together, if we could perceive from a sufficient height' (p. 176). Both crave a distant, voiceless space beyond the noise of the world: the silent, frozen chronotope of a Poussin painting or Keats's 'Ode to a Grecian Urn'. As they await the return of their friends at the Hampton Court reunion dinner, Rhoda is terrorized by the prospect of impending dialogue: a terror encapsulated in her observation, 'They have only to speak' (p. 178). Yet the fact that Louis's distaste for the spoken word has a specific sociocultural dimension associated with the stigma of his Australian accent should remind us, once

---

13  Bernard's final interlocutor, whom he characterizes as 'a person . . . I scarcely know save that I think we met once on the gangway of a ship bound for Africa' (p. 225) is clearly his 'reaper'. She is also glimpsed by Rhoda before her death: 'The good woman with a face like a white horse at the end of the bed makes a valedictory movement and turns to go' (p. 158).

again, that his subject identity is not so close to Rhoda's as it would at first appear. The voice is an object of terror for him not merely because it demands response but because it is a palpable expression of his class inferiority.

This brings me to the symbolic function of *heteroglossia* in *The Waves* ('heteroglossia', it will be remembered, is understood most simply as 'the social diversity of speech types'; see Chapter 1, pp. 62–63) – the way in which the human voice is used as a register for how the different characters negotiate class difference.

It is as well to remind ourselves at this point that all the characters in this novel belong to an élite socioeconomic group, with Louis's family background in banking merely frustrating his pretensions to landed-gentleman status. Educated at the same kindergarten, schools and (for the men), university, both male and female characters would have shared the same social dialect; if we listened to them at one of their dinner-parties they would, with the exception of Louis, sound (painfully!) the same. This superficial intergration into Lacan's Symbolic Order conceals, however, considerable differences between the characters – whose subjectivities are marked not only by their inscription in the language of the ruling group but also by their own dialogic relationship to 'the social diversity of speech types'. This is to say that, in a Bakhtinian economy, their subjectivity is defined not only by the language they *use* but also by their relation to the languages of others. Thus, while Bernard's own language would be indistinguishable from that of his peers – he is, it will be remembered, a millionaire – his novelist's passion for the 'heterogeneous crowd', with its carnivalesque mixture of voices, corroborates the essential dialogicality of his subjectivity. Unlike Neville who cannot tolerate the coarse accents of 'horse-dealers and plumbers', or Rhoda, whose dislike of the crowd ('You smelt so unpleasant, too, lining up outside doors to buy tickets' p. 156) is commensurate with her dislike of the noisy materiality of the working classes, Bernard embraces the diversity of speech types that accompany his passage through the world.

Turning from the spoken to the written word, a very particular distinction is drawn between Bernard, the novelist, and Neville, the poet. Throughout Woolf's text, the two genres are used to symbolize the difference between the two characters, with the inherent dialogicality of the novel befitting Bernard's subjectivity, and the monologism of poetry typifying Neville's. In her characterization of the genres, Woolf, indeed, draws close to Bakhtin's comparison in 'Epic and Novel' (see Chapter 1). Where poetry is the literature of tradition and the past, with its focus on a single hero, the novel is the literature of the present and of multiple centres of consciousness. Where poetry complements its focus on the single life with a single (lyric or epic) voice, the novel reproduces the heterogeneous voices of the crowd. Where poetry is concerned only with the lives of great men, the novel champions the weak, the human, the ordinary. Thus in the extended dialogue between Bernard and Neville in Section III, we see Neville linking his single-minded, 'heroic' passion for Percival with a 'natural' predisposition to poetry ('I am a poet, yes. Surely I am a great poet. Boats and youth passing and distant trees, "the falling fountains of the pendant trees"' (p. 61)), while Bernard learns to treasure action, stories and all the incidental details of daily life that Neville 'never reaches' (p. 68). Looking down the street he sees an old woman pause against a lit window and observes that this is: 'A contrast that I see and Neville does not see; that I feel and Neville does not feel. Hence he will reach perfection, and I shall fail and shall leave nothing behind me but imperfect phrases littered with sand' (ibid.). For the novelist's art has nothing to do with the quest for perfection or truth; it is, to recall Bakhtin's own comments in *Dostoevsky's Poetics*, a genre which records 'simultaneity' rather than 'sequence' (see Chapter 1), which celebrates the individual moment without caring how it may or may not develop in the next. As Bernard observes at Percival's farewell party: 'I shall never succeed, even in talk, in making a perfect phrase. But I shall have contributed more to the passing moment than any of you: I shall go into more rooms, more different rooms' (p. 101).

After establishing this fundamental difference between the two characters and their respective genres, however, the text begins to question whether the categories are quite as watertight as they might at first appear. In the same way that Bakhtin modified his original statment that all poetry is monologic with a recognition of new generic hybrids like the 'novelized poem' (see Chapter 1), so Woolf's characters break into one another's territories. By the end of the novel, we find Neville instructing us that to 'make poetry' we must listen to others talk 'and bring to the surface what he said and she said' (p. 152), and Bernard casting aside the 'arbitrary design' of the classic-realist text and reaching, instead, for the 'little language' of children, lovers and, it must be said, poets: 'broken words, inarticulate words, like the shuffling of feet on the pavement' (p. 183). Both characters, it would seem, have been converted to the hybrid form of the prose poem: a textuality like Woolf's own.

In symbolic terms, then, the prose/poetry distinction in *The Waves* serves to illustrate not only the difference *between subjects* (the difference, here, between dialogic and monologic types) but also the fact that their subjectivities are not necessarily fixed and immutable. Here we may, once again, invoke Bakhtin's category of 'unfinalizability', a condition he saw as endemic to the novel hero (see Chapter 1). For although much of the preceding discussion has served crudely to classify the characters into monologic and dialogic types, with Bernard, Jinny and Susan at one end of the spectrum and Louis, Rhoda and Neville at the other – we are frequently reminded that they all exist in a state not of 'being', but of 'becoming'. Throughout the text this volatility is expressed in the tendency of all the characters to exchange positions temporarily with one another, and for some of the characters (in particular Bernard and Rhoda) to assume the chameleon identities of others (for Bernard this is Byron, for Jinny the other girls at school). Such role play suggests that none of the characters is permanently fixed in his or her identity, that with effort and imagination, change may be possible. Having said this, the characters that appear to be most capable of change and growth are those which are the most dialogically oriented in the first instance. Bernard, Jinny and Susan all develop strategies to accommodate their life changes – to adjust their behaviour, expectations or style of dress to a manner appropriate to their advancing years; Neville, too, as we have seen, modifies his blinkered high-mindedness and adopts a more prosaic and dialogic relationship to the world. Rhoda and Louis, however, never become 'robust' in the manner Bernard describes. They fail to grow because they fail to inter-relate. Neither one acquires a person or an idea with whom they can creatively dialogize (although Louis, as we have seen, forms a defensive relationship with the forces of social authority), and this renders them incapable of exploring alternative subject positions.

To conclude, I propose that *The Waves* is a text whose representation of the subject is productively read through a dialogic lens. A dialogic conception of subjectivity as plural, historically specific and 'unfinalizable' (that is to say, *ever*-changing) unsettles many of the neat conclusions that a post-Freudian or a post-Lacanian reading of the text could so quickly achieve. Abandoning the hypothesis that Woolf's text adds up to a universal statement on the acquisition of subject and gendered identity, we can begin to explore – through the dance of characters – the complex mixture of drives and circumstances that make one person similar to another in one respect, and different in another.

The grid I invoked to map out these differences was dialogism itself. Through my focus, first, on how the characters constructed and conducted their self-other relations I was able to explore both major and subtle differences between them. The model of the subject as a 'self-in-relation' is, as we may recall, founded upon the Bakhtin school's model of the utterance as an act of communication dependent upon both speaker and addressee. This reading showed that the subject is crucially defined both by her choice of addressee (whether the addressee is singular or plural, more or less powerful than herself), and by her relationship with them. Thus while Bernard's expansive ego is constructed upon his happy dialogue with multiple interlocutors all of whom he regards as his 'equals', Rhoda's 'facelessness' is attributable to her failure to find the mirror of a reciprocating 'other'.

In the second part of the reading, I turned from analysing the characters through a model of the subject based on Bakhtin's theory of language to an investigation of how they responded to language itself. My conclusion here was that although those characters who were most dialogically oriented in their self-other relations were also the most 'at home' in written and/or spoken language, language may itself be seen as the space through which changes in subject position can be negotiated. In this respect, Woolf's text would appear to corroborate fully the Bakhtinian view that language is both the template upon which the human subject is constructed and the medium through which it is changed.

## II

### *The Dream of a Common Language*

*Adrienne Rich*

---

This reading of Adrienne Rich's representation of the subject in *The Dream of a Common Language* begins at the point where the story of Rhoda, in *The*

*Waves*, breaks off.[14]

Rhoda's failure to secure a suitable subject position for herself may be explained, as we have seen, by her lack of a reciprocating feminine 'other': neither the oedipal models of subject and gender acquisition, nor the heterosexual economy in which she is expected to develop her adult self, provide her with 'an/other' with whom she can dialogize. Using Anne Herrmann's Bakhtinian reading of Irigaray, we can posit her as a character classically in need of an alternative model of subject development, one in which:

> The specular subject constitutes itself as a split subject not in the Lacanian mirror but through 'an/other woman', as historical, fictional and self-reflexive female subject. The specular subject which neither assimilates nor annihilates the other ensures the possibility of a female subjectivity and makes possible a differently constructed subject position (p. 147).

This 'differently constructed subject position' is, I propose, to be found in the work of a great many contemporary women writers, including Adrienne Rich.[15] While it may not be desirable to always read the difference in Irigarayan terms (Rich's own preferred psychoanalytic model in the early 1980s was Nancy Chodorow), the notion of women realizing their subject and gendered identity through and/or against a female other (whether mother, lover, friend, or 'unknown' role model) as opposed to an abstract masculine principle (the 'Phallus') is an attractive one. In terms of literary and cultural representation this alternative has been made the self-conscious focus of many contemporary texts ranging from Alice Walker's *The Color Purple* (1983) to Susan Suleiman's film, *Desperately Seeking Susan* (1984).[16] A feature of such texts, moreover, is the emphasis they give to the dialogic process in the construction of identity: as in *The Waves*, language (both spoken and written) is given huge symbolic significance in the heroine's *Bildungsroman*. In *The Color Purple*, for instance, Celie discovers an alternative subject position for herself through her spoken dialogues with Shug, and her written ones with Nettie, while Roberta, in *Desperately Seeking Susan*, 'fetishizes' her need for a reciprocating other with a newspaper advertisement. In this way, the positing of a 'differently constructed subject position' is inextricably linked to a notion of dialogic exchange: language ('the utterance') is the medium through which the self 'becomes'.

Before proceeding with a reading of how such alternative subject positions are represented in Rich's poetry, however, there are a number of theoretical issues implicit in the preceding discussion that need to be confronted directly. Perhaps the most serious of these is the conflation of

14   A. Rich, *The Dream of a Common Language: Poems 1974–1977* (New York and London: W. W. Norton & Co., 1978). Page references to this volume will be given after quotations in the text.
15   See my 'Dialogic Theory and Women's Writing', *Working Out: New Directions for Women's Studies*, ed. H. Hinds, A. Phoenix and J. Stacey (London and Washington: Falmer Press, 1992), pp. 184–93. This essay is discussed in Chapter 2, pp. 105–107.
16   See Jackie Stacey's discussion of this film in her essay 'Desperately Seeking Difference', in *The Female Gaze: Women as Viewers of Popular Culture*, ed. L. Gamman and M. Marshment (London: Women's Press, 1988), pp. 112–29.

subjectivity with sexuality in the Irigarayan model. Although Herrmann, in her readings of Virginia Woolf and Christa Wolf, skirts round the question of whether the 'other woman' represented in these texts is (actually or potentially) lesbian, it is obvious that she exists as an object (subject) of desire; that her ability to form/transform the subject depends upon her *desirability*.[17] In the same way that the Freudian and Lacanian models of subject acquisition, based on a masculine–feminine dynamic, are resolved in (adult) heterosexuality, so it follows that a model predicated upon an exclusively feminine dynamic should be implicated with lesbian sexuality. Irigaray's writings have certainly been used by lesbian critics in this way, as has Nancy Chodorow's focus on mother–daughter relationships.[18]

While Chodorow herself discusses the mother–daughter bond within a strictly orthodox heterosexual economy (she is specifically concerned with explaining why women have more difficulty than men in separating from the mother and forming relationships with the opposite sex), Adrienne Rich rereads Chodorow's analysis as evidence for why many women are potentially lesbian: 'If women are the earliest sources of emotional caring and psychological nurturance . . . why in fact . . . [do women] ever re-direct that search?'[19] This is a provocatively (and self-consciously) disingenuous construction of lesbian desire that has been much criticized by lesbian critics since its publication in 1980.[20] For many lesbians, meanwhile, the problem lies not only in its universalism (the fact that Rich is failing to discriminate between women in different social and historical contexts) but also the fact that it reduces all lesbian relationships to an expression of the maternal bond.

This last point of criticism returns us to the problem with all psychoanalytic accounts of subject acquisition that I raised in my reading of *The Waves*: that is, their focus on set phases of ego development within the narrow confines of the nuclear family (whether literal or symbolic). Although French feminist critics like Irigaray and Kristeva provide models of subject acquisition which allow for long-term development via nonfamilial relationships, these are still seen as reworkings of the subject's early oedipal and preoedipal relationships with the mother. Two key difficulties may therefore be seen to arise from any attempt to formulate a 'differently constructed (female) subject position' on the back

17   See Herrmann, *Dialogic and Difference*. With reference to the presence of literary precursors in the work of both Virginia Woolf and Christa Wolf, Herrmann writes: 'Ultimately the relations between women become more and more eroticized as they begin to acquire an affiliation based on their art, although the 'other' woman never openly exists as a lesbian' (p. 4).

18   See Adrienne Rich's deployment of Chodorow in her famous essay 'Compulsory Heterosexuality and Lesbian Existence', in *Blood, Bread and Poetry: Selected Prose 1979–1985* (London: Virago, 1987), pp. 23–68.

For a discussion of Irigaray and lesbianism, see M. Whitford, *Luce Irigaray: Philosophy in the Feminine* (London and New York: Routledge, 1991), p. 154 and E. Grosz, 'The Hetero and the Homo: The Sexual Ethics of Luce Irigaray', *Gay Information*, **17–18**, 1988, pp. 37–44.

19   Rich, 'Compulsory Heterosexuality', p. 35.

20   See dialogue between Rich and her critics which prefaces the essay in *Blood, Bread and Poetry*, pp. 68–75.

of existing psychoanalytic models like Herrmann and Rich have done in some instances: first, an unproblematized conflation of subjectivity with (lesbian) sexuality; and, secondly, the implication that the feminine 'other' through which the subject 'realizes' herself and/or her sexuality is always reducible, in the last instance, to the mother.

A dialogic model of the subject can, I propose, avoid these conditions while retaining the significance of a reciprocating feminine other in the construction of *certain* female subjectivities. As we observed in the reading of *The Waves*, dialogism is hostile to *any* universalizing theories of the subject, and a dialogic critic would therefore find it unproductive to speculate that *all* female subjectivities were defined through such relationships. The Bakhtinian subject, as we have also seen, is not tied, even 'in the last instance', to her parental relationships: relationships with nonfamily members, both in early childhood and in later life, can be as – if not more important – in constructing and reconstructing a subjectivity which is perceived as 'unfinalizable'. Nor will all these relationships be sexualized. A dialogic view of the subject sees the nature of the relationships informing the subject to be as various as they are multiple: therefore, while it is the case that many women will construct alternative subject positions for themselves through a sexualized relationship with a feminine other (e.g., Celie's relationship with Shug in *The Color Purple*), the dialogue may equally manifest itself as an (ostensibly) nonsexualized (yet equally highly charged) 'fascination' (e.g., Roberta's obsession with Susan in *Desperately Seeking Susan*).[21] This notion of female subjectivity as open ended and revisionary (in the course of our lives we are able to explore and adopt new subject positions) would seem to me a better way of understanding the vital role played by the feminine other than by narrowly identifying it with the mother and/or a phase in early childhood development. For many of the women represented in literary and other texts, the feminine other through which a character is at last able to realize/negotiate her subjectivity (through a process of interactive dialogization) may not appear until much later in life (or, as in Rhoda's case, not at all). She may also be an/other who bears no relation to a mother-figure, with the dialogue between the two women being far removed from a mother–daughter relationship. Allowing for the widest possible variety of self-other relations in this way, dialogic theory can, perhaps, hold on to all that is most useful in Irigaray's model of feminine alterity without subscribing to its psychoanalytic foundations. Women are constantly negotiating and renegotiating their subjectivities through their (multiple) relationships with one another as daughters, lovers, friends and admirers. It would be wrong to perceive the feminine other as narrowly sexual and/or maternal in her influence.

---

21  See Stacey, 'Desperately Seeking Difference': 'What interests me about these films is the question of the pleasures of the female spectator, who is invited to look or gaze with one female character at another, in an interchange of feminine fascinations. This fascination is neither purely identification with the other woman, nor desire for her in the strictly erotic sense of the word. It is a desire to see, to know, to become more like an idealised feminine other, in a context where the difference between the two women is repeatedly re-established' (p. 115).

The poems which comprise *The Dream of a Common Language* illustrate the many and varied forms dialogic relationships between women can take: relationships between mother and daughter, between sisters, between lovers, between groups of women, and between friends. While my focus here will be on the intersubjective relationship between the lovers in the sonnet sequence 'Twenty-One Love Poems', I want to open the discussion of Rich's work by looking at some of the other relationships represented in the collection and what these have to say – either explicitly or implicitly – about the dialogic function of the feminine other in the construction of the subject.

Although the dialogic model of the subject I have been promoting in this and the previous reading offers us an escape from the puppet strings of the mother, Rich herself is reluctant to let go of them. In 'Sibling Mysteries' the speaker explores the claustrophobic but *necessary* burden of her relationship with both mother and sister – how the relationship with the sister leads them both back to the mother, through the primary identification of each in the other:

> Tell me again because I need to hear
> how we bore our mother-secrets
> straight to the end . . .
> how sister gazed at sister
> reaching through mirrored pupils
> back to the mother
>
> (p. 50)

Here, and throughout the poem, particular emphasis is placed on the role of the sister as a dialogic addressee – 'I know my heart, and still/I need to have you tell me' (p. 48). While within a Lacanian model of analysis this would be translated into a specifically *specular* reflex (the imagery in the above quotation confirms the sister as a 'mirror'), a dialogic reading will want to take the reference to interlocution as literally as possible: the sister 'leads' the subject via the mother to her 'self' through a *rearticulation* of their shared pasts: 'we are translations into different dialects/of a text still being written/in the original' (p. 51). Throughout the poem, shared linguistic intimacy is represented as being as important as shared physical intimacy: the two images, the bodily and the oral, are placed side by side:

> I need to have you tell me
> hold me, remind me
>
> (p. 48)

> Let me hold you and tell you
>
> (p. 52)

This degree of intimacy between two subjects takes us to one of the extreme poles of dialogicality that I described in Chapter 1: the 'degree-zero' that Bakhtin describes in the 'Speech Acts' essay as the place where speaker and addressee exist in a state of 'maximal internal proximity' (*Speech Acts and Other Essays* (1986), pp. 96–97) (see Chapter 1). It is the place, moroever, where power differentials are erased or, at least, temporarily suspended. The reciprocity that the sister offers the speaker in Rich's poem is absolute and unqualified; and it depends on the sisters being positioned side by side each other, as equals. Despite a period of several years in which they were estranged (represented, symbolically, in the text as years of *silence* in which 'you and I/hardly spoke to each other' (p. 50)), they now offer each other a 'responsive understanding' (*Speech Acts and Other Essays*, pp. 96–97) that is marked by its *exclusivity of others*:

> how we told
> among ourselves our secrets, wept and laughed
> passed bark and root and berry
> from hand to hand
> whispering each one's power
>
> (p. 52)

Such exclusivity of address, as I have argued in my earlier work on dialogic theory and women's writing, is one of the most potent symbols of female bonding to be found in contemporary feminist writing, with innumerable texts celebrating the 'private language' women share – either in familial or sexual relationships, as here, or in groups. The subjectivity of the speaker in this poem, then, is predicated upon a dialogue of extreme intimacy that nevertheless escapes a slippage into the 'merger' that Bakhtin considered inimical to the conditions necessary for 'true' dialogue (see the discussion in Chapter 2).

In several of the other poems in this collection, however, the extreme intimacy between interlocutors does give rise to images of merger – both in terms of symbiotic subjectivities and the notion of a 'common language'. To take the latter first, we find that Rich's 'dream' depends largely upon the factor of exclusivity introduced in relation to the earlier poem: that is to say, the possibility of women creating and sharing a language that is in some way marked off from that of their male contemporaries. On one level, indeed, Rich's text may be seen to share in the radical feminist utopianism of the 1970s which posited this as a 'real' possibility. In line with the textual experimentations of the French feminists, and the imaginings of fantasy writers like Marge Piercy in *Woman on the Edge of Time* (1976) or Sally Miller Gearheart in *The Wanderground* (1985), Rich, too, imagines women escaping to a 'country that has no language, no laws' ('Twenty-One Love Poems', XIII) and making for themselves a new one:[22]

> the music on the radio becomes clear –
> neither *Rosenkavalier* nor *Götterdämmerung*
> but a woman's voice singing old songs
> with new words, with a quiet bass, a flute
> plucked and fingered by women outside the law
>
> (p. 51)

It is a vision expressed, perhaps, most idealistically in the poem 'Phantasia for Elvira Shatayev', in which the women climbers, symbolically removed from the world of masculine discourse, develop a single 'voice' which

---

[22]   M. Piercy, *Woman on the Edge of Time* (London: Women's Press, 1976) and S. Miller Gearheart, *The Wanderground: Stories of the Hill Women* (London : Women's Press, 1985).

is so perfectly shared that it is, in effect, no voice at all but, instead, a *dialogic silence*:

> If in this sleep I speak
> it's with a voice no longer personal
> (I want to say *with voices*)
> When the wind tore our breath from us last
> we had no need of words

(p. 4)

In terms of a dialogic model of the subject, this returns us once again to Bakhtin's description of a form of address so intimate that there is 'an apparent desire for speaker and addressee to merge completely' (*Speech Acts and Other Essays*, p. 103). As we noted above, Bakhtin saw this degree of intimacy as in many ways inimicable to the conditions necessary for effective dialogue which, to be fully interactive, has to be predicated upon *difference*. In this poem of (extrafamilial) 'sisterhood', however, empathetic silence takes the place of dialogue as the difference and distance between subjects is collapsed. Within a psychoanlaytic discourse, such representations would be seen as Rich's attempt to draw an overt connection between the special bonding experienced by adult women (either in couples or in larger groups) and the daughter's preoedipal relationship with the mother – as, for instance, the sisters in 'Sibling Mysteries' are united through their shared (preconscious) memory of the mother's body:

> Remind me how we loved our mother's body
> our mouths drawing the first
> thin sweetness from her nipples
>
> our faces dreaming hour on hour
> in the salt smell of her lap Remind me
> how her touch melted child grief
>
> how she floated great and tender in our dark
> or stood guard over us
> against our willing

(p. 48)

In 'Phantasia for Elvira Shatayev', this preconscious (and therefore unspoken) bond is represented through the image of the (umbilical) 'cable of blue fire' (p. 6) that ropes the women's bodies together. The subjectivity represented in such a poem, predicated as it is upon a preoedipal mother–daughter bonding, is therefore effectively *adialogic*: the women concerned may be defined in terms of a 'feminine other', but there is not sufficient distance between them for this to take the form of a reciprocating or fully interactive relationship. This is the silent communion of preconsciousness and, indeed, of death.

Yet there is, I would suggest, a way in which this preoedipally oriented subjectivity *is* dialogized, and that is in the way in which the women thus bonded exist in (antagonistic) relationship to a masculine 'other'. I have already noted, for example, the way in which the 'exclusive' relationship between the sisters in 'Sibling Mysteries' is defined, in part, through the secrets they shared about the 'strange male bodies' of their lovers (p. 49). Positioned too close to one another to effect a dialogue between themselves, they practise a *coauthored dialogue* with the masculine other. This means that although their immediate identification may be with a feminine other (prefigured in the body of the mother), their subjectivities are still *ultimately* defined by their relationship to the masculine principle.

This is the dilemma that Rich would also seem to be addressing in 'Origins and History of Consciousness' in which the speaker shows that women cannot live forever in exclusive relationship to one another but must, at some point, engage in dialogue with 'the outside world'. While merger with a feminine other may be easily achieved:

> It was simple to meet you, simple to take your eyes
> into mine, saying: these are eyes I have known
> from the first
>
> (p. 8)

sooner or later it is necessary to 'move/beyond this secret circle of fire' (p. 9) and speak, once again, with the father, the brother, the rapist and the 'man-who-would-understand' (see the poem 'Natural Resources' p. 60). In conclusion, it could thus be said that while Rich is evidently drawn to the idea(l) of a female subjectivity defined, like Irigaray's, exclusively in terms of a feminine 'm/other', her texts expose the utopianism of this vision. Women may draw together in relationships of such intimacy that they appear to 'merge completely' and reproduce what Kristeva has referred to as the 'chora' of the mother–child relationship.[23] Because, however, no subject can ever exist independently of her social context, all women are simultaneously defined through and against their relationship to the masculine principle (Lacan's Symbolic Order); indeed, the exclusivity of their relationship to one another (its 'private languages' and 'dialogic silences') ultimately *depends* upon the existence of the 'other'.[24] The subject is still, therefore, a dialogic subject – even if the dialogue is now between plural rather than singular subjects. The shift may be represented diagramatically as follows. Instead of a model in which female subjectivity is defined through a dialogue between gendered *individuals*,

---

[23]   See Kristeva's interview with Susan Sellers reproduced in *Literary Theory: A Reader*, ed. P. Rice and P. Waugh (London : Edward Arnold, 1989), pp. 128–34. Kristeva describes the 'chora' as follows: 'The word chora means receptacle in Greek, which refers us to Winnicott's idea of 'holding': mother and child are in a permanent stricture in which one holds the other, there's a double entrance, the child is held but so is the mother' (pp. 130–31).
[24]   For a discussion of the 'private languages of women' see my 'Dialogic Theory and Women's Writing', pp. 187–89.

$$♀ \longleftrightarrow ♂$$

or

$$♀ \longleftrightarrow ♀$$

Rich's vision is of a subject which is defined in relation to a feminine other in the first instance, and a masculine other in the second:

$$♀ \longleftrightarrow ♀ \quad = \quad ♀♀ \longleftrightarrow ♂$$
$$(1) \qquad\qquad (2)$$

Several of the sonnets which comprise 'Twenty-One Love Poems' present the female subject in these terms, although this is a text which also permits a much more dynamic relationship *between* subjects. The speaker of the poem exists in a fully dialogic relationship to her lover and interlocutor, in which the desire for merger is balanced against the acknowledgement of difference. These are women who have left the preoedipal, predialogic Garden of Eden for the dangerous city streets. Their subjectivities, like their love, are explained by and through language. Silence is no longer the sign of secret conspiracy, but of estrangement and death. To become ourselves, we need another who will hear us and talk back to us: who will build a bridge between our differences. I begin, however, with a consideration of those sonnets which describe the $♀♀ \longleftrightarrow ♂$ relation: in particular, numbers I and IV.

In both these sonnets, the dialogic relation (or perhaps we should say 'anti-relation') between the female subject and the masculine other is expressed in terms of spatial imagery. Indeed, I shall be arguing that *geography* and *sound/silence* are the two sets of images primarily responsible for structuring the sequence as a whole – if not, indeed, the collection as a whole (as, perhaps, is signalled in the title of the poem 'Cartographies of Silence'). Sonnet I uses the image of the street – the thoroughfare of sex, prostitution, rape and other expressions of violence against women – to chart the (metaphorical) distance between a 'lesbian existence' which 'no one has imagined' (the tender, cultured lives of educated women living in elegant, music-filled apartments on opposite sides of the city) and 'compulsory heterosexuality'. It is a distance that is conceived, paradoxically, as both short and long. From the red begonia on the apartment window to the street below is but a short distance; the 'blurt of metal' is forever within earshot, just a few threatening feet away. Yet for a woman to walk from her apartment to that of her lover is a correspondingly *long* distance. The anonymous male – the pimp, the drunk, the rapist – lurks as a possibility behind every street corner, and the female subject is forced to orient herself in relation to that fact: 'We need to grasp our lives inseparable/from those rancid dreams' (p. 25). The lesbian must learn to accept that her identity is dialogically conceived in these terms.

The dangerous and threatening (hetero)sexual distance that lesbians have daily to traverse is given a specifically dialogic expression in Sonnet IV. Here we are shown the gauntlet the speaker has to run as she travels from the haven of her lover's apartment to her own ('I come home from you through the early light of spring/flashing off ordinary walls . . . p. 26) in terms of a hostile verbal exchange between herself and a man in the elevator:

> I'm lugging my sack
> of groceries, I dash for the elevator
> where a man, taut, elderly, carefully composed
> lets the door almost close on me. *For god's sake hold it!*
> I croak at him – *Hysterical,* – he breathes my way.

This flash of angry words between the two parties exposes the raw inequality of power in gendered relations: if a woman is forced to speak out for her rights, for her presence to be acknowledged (for her body to be allowed into an elevator), she is accused of 'hysteria'. This is because in the unwritten law of the street, women are not expected to speak except when spoken to; and then they *must* respond, even when that address takes the form of abuse. This returns us, with some force, to the point I have continued to make throughout this book about the 'dark' underside of dialogic relations. Always an expression of power, not all dialogues are friendly. We are dealing with a model of language, text and subject in which motives of fear, hostility and revenge frequently inform the relationship between the speaker and his or her addressee.

Sonnet IV also effects a dialogue with the male 'other' at a more complex level, however, by incorporating the text of a male torture victim:

> *My genitals have been the object of such a sadistic display*
> *they keep me constantly awake with the pain . . .*
> *Do whatever you can to survive.*
> *You know, I think that men love wars . . .*

(p. 27)

Back in the security of her apartment, her female-defined space filled with the comforts of coffee, music and warmth, the speaker is once again verbally assaulted, though this time with the written as opposed to the spoken word. This time, too, the violence is conveyed not in the address, since the man in the letter is positioning her as his 'ally' (see discussion of Anne Herrmann's reading of Christa Wolf in Chapter 2, pp. 106–107), but in the details of his own assault. This representation of a male subject as victim of the patriarchal machine inevitably challenges the essentialism implicit in much of Rich's work which posits 'men' as a monolithic enemy (see the unforgiving 'Natural Resources', for example, which refuses to indulge even the 'nice ones'). Here the female subject is forced to acknowledge that in certain circumstances, on particular issues, a man may be positioned next to her *vis-à-vis* a mutual antagonist: while 'masculinity' or 'patriarchy' may thus be conceived as the 'other', masculine gender, *per se*, may not.

The sonnet ends with a sequence of images which replicates the movement of the speaker between this complex negotiation of self and other, between interior feminine spaces and exterior masculine ones. Consumed with 'incurable anger' at what she has read, she cries: 'I am crying helplessly, and they still control the world, and you are not in my arms'. In this sequence the phrase, 'and they still control the world' compares with the geographical distance separating the lovers: the streets of 'rainsoaked garbage' and 'tabloid cruelties' (Sonnet I) through which they 'also have to walk' to reach one another. Both the final sequence of images and the poem as a whole are given a tripartite structure in which masculine violence stands between a woman and her feminine lover/other. In terms of the thesis of subjectivity that we are pursuing in this chapter, this forces yet another constraint upon Herrmann's vision of a 'differently constructed' subjectivity. Not only are female subjects still partially defined through their dialogic relation to the masculine other but this other may also *interrupt* the dialogue between the subject and her feminine interlocutor. What Rich's poems in *The Dream of a Common Language* repeatedly show is that however great the *desire* of the female subject to define herself, her life and her language in self-reflexive 'feminine' terms, the mirror of masculine alterity cannot altogether be escaped.

The division that the material reality of living in a patriarchal world forces upon female subjects only partly accounts, however, for the complex nature of the difference between them. In 'Twenty-One Love Poems' more than any of the other poems in this particular collection, Rich is candid about the extent of the differences that may exist between women; and between women who are lovers, just as between mothers and daughters, sisters and friends. In relationships that at first appear to be predicated upon similarity and likeness ('Your small hands, precisely equal to my own – /only the thumb is larger, longer' Sonnet VI, p. 27), the signs of difference are felt, repeatedly, as both painful and surprising. Unlike relationships with men, where difference is the determining attraction throughout, women frequently find it hard to realize and accept their differences from one another: cannot easily negotiate the complicated mixture of self-and-other defining qualities.[25] Yet it is an acknowledgement of such difference that makes Rich's treatment of self-other relations in 'Twenty-One Love Poems' more fully dialogic than in many of her other texts. Positioning her lover as an interlocutor who is a stranger as well as a friend, an adviser as well as a conspirator, she comes closer to Bakhtin's model than in her poems which strive (however unsuccessfully) for a condition of absolute intimacy and merger. Here is an image of feminine intersubjectivity which is not reducible to the *chora* of mother and child (see note 23 above); a vision in which the subjects have to adjust constantly the sense of their relationship to one another through spoken dialogue; a vision in which merger and 'dialogic silence' are tantamount to death.

The sonnet which is, perhaps, most eloquent on the disturbing intrusion of difference in relations between the self and a feminine other is number XII. Here Rich uses a description of the two lovers asleep in bed to express the bewildering paradox of intimacy and distance, dialogue and silence. After an opening testament to the dissolution of bodily and psychic

---

25  A great deal of popular psychology has focused on this subject. See, for example, S. Orbach and L. Eichenbaum, *Bittersweet: Love, Envy and Competition in Women's Friendships* (London: Arrow Books, 1987).

boundaries that the sign of two women sleeping together might be thought to represent ('a touch is enough to let us know/we're not alone in the universe, even in sleep' p. 30), she acknowledges that the speaker and her addressee nevertheless inhabit different 'ghost towns' from which they 'almost address each other' – but not quite. The second octet opens with the blunt and painful acknowledgement that:

> we have different voices, even in sleep
> and our bodies, so alike, are yet so different
> and the past echoing through our blood streams
> is freighted with different language, different meanings
> (pp. 30–31)

In a volume whose vision is presented as 'the dream of a common language' these are brutal admissions, indeed; the moment when Rich would appear to recognize most fully the extent of the cultural and historic specificity separating one individual from another, despite the global factors – age, nationality, gender – that appear to unite them:

> though in any chronicle of the world we share
> it could be written with new meaning
> that we were two lovers of one gender,
> we were two women of one generation
> (p. 31)

In accordance with the Marxist stance of the early Bakhtin group, Rich appears to be refuting any universal model of the gendered subject and/or the language through which she is inscribed.

In Sonnet IX Rich explores one of the local differences separating the two lovers: their past histories ('your face at another age' p. 29). The past life of the other/lover is experienced by the speaker as 'silence': 'Your silence today is a pond where drowned things live/I want to see raised dripping and brought into the sun' (ibid.). It is a geographical space which exists outside the dialogue of their own lives: a dark and fearful uncharted territory which the speaker needs to 'fathom' if she is to achieve a fully intersubjective relationship with her lover: 'whatever's lost there is needed by both of us – /a watch of old gold, a water-blurred fever chart, a key . . .' (ibid.). Here we see the imagery of silence and geography combined to evoke the *distance* separating subjects, and language presented both as the cause of the separation (subjects with different histories speak different languages), and the means of reconciliation:

> I'm waiting
> for a wind that will gently open this sheeted water
> for once, and show me what I can do
> for you, who have often made the unnameable
> nameable for others, even for me
> (ibid.)

The implication here is clearly that our pasts may be recovered through our present dialogues, and hence incorporated into our self-other relations.

In 'Twenty-One Love Poems', then, it would seem that Rich is relinquishing her dream of women sharing a common language and/or subjecthood, and envisaging instead a sisterhood predicated upon both difference and dialogue. The more visible the differences become, indeed, the more urgent the need for dialogue becomes also. The strength of women, according to this model, lies not in their commonality (the 'likeness' of their bodies, their psychology, or even a 'common language'), but in the connections drawn between them through their acts of communication. It matters less that they speak *the same* language than that they are engaged in dialogue.

In this dialogic model of sisterhood/subjecthood it is silence and not difference that is the great enemy. The devastating consequence of silence between women is given several powerful expressions in the collection as a whole, though I wish to concentrate in particular on Sonnet XX in conjunction with 'A Woman Dead in her Forties'. In both these texts, the consequence of 'not having spoken' is represented as a gross betrayal of sisterhood, not only for the addressee concerned but also for the subject herself. Both poems may, indeed, be read as suggestive statements on the crucial role of the other in the realization of the self. If we deny the other – by refusing to enter into dialogue with her – we also deny our own self: a fact that Rich acknowledges in the final line of Sonnet XX in which she recognizes her 'mute' subject as a manifestation of her own soul: 'a woman/I loved, drowning in secrets, fear wound round her throat/and choking her like hair' (p. 35).

In 'A Woman Dead in her Forties', meanwhile, the treachery of not having spoken once (of not having declared her love while there was still time) is visited upon the speaker as the loss of her own poetic voice. To deny an addressee is tantamount to literary suicide, since without that addressee the writer is herself deprived of a voice. With her interlocutor now permanently lost to her the speaker is 'half-afraid to write poetry' (p. 57): confronted with the irreversible silence of death, her words bounce back at her.

This reading of Rich's poetry will have shown that Rhoda's crisis of identity would not have been solved as easily at it first appeared it might be. The idea that her inability to acquire an authentic and sustainable subject position might have been mitigated by her finding a feminine reciprocating other is, according to Rich's testament, only partly true. What these poems would seem to say is that while a 'differently constructed subject position' – one in which the subject is defined in relation to a feminine rather than a masculine other – may offer a better description of women's *primary* identifications, their subjectivities cannot escape a secondary definition by the masculine principle. In dialogic terms, this is seen in the fact that the exclusivity of the relationships women form with one another (in terms of coded language and intimate forms of address, for example) is paradoxically dependent on the (antagonistic) presence of the male; and, further, that masculine discourse always threatens to interrupt and silence the closed circle of women-only dialogue.

With these conditions in place, one could speculate that Rhoda's subjecthood would have been better served by her discovery of a feminine other, but that she was still unlikely to have had an easy time of it. Despite a utopian longing in that direction, Rich's poems disabuse us of the possibility of a female subjectivity conceived entirely in terms of intimacy and merger. The factors of history, class, race, nationality and gendered identity that mark women's differences from one another in the material world also resound in their intersubjective relations. As we saw in the reading of Sonnet IX, there can never be total intimacy between a subject and her female mother/lover/other: the deep pool of one's personal and political history is present as the silent underside of any relationship. And while it is a pool that dialogue can fathom (fragments of the past can be newly shared between both parties), it can never be fully dredged.

Even had Rhoda found her missing female other, then, she would not have secured a permanent and stable ego identity; rather, like Rich's protagonists, she would have been forced to acknowledge the differences as well as the similarities between herself and that other: to negotiate and renegotiate the differences in a continual process of active (and interactive) dialogue. There would be even less room for silence in Rhoda's new world than in the old.

For having acknowledged that claiming an authentic and satisfactory female subjectivity cannot be achieved through a simple merger with mother, sister, lover or friend, Rich's poems expose the raw and ever-bleeding wounds of our difference, and present dialogue as the only means of healing them. Without a common language, such communication will never be easy: there will be times when when even a lover will not know the archaeology of our carefully 'freighted' words (Sonnet XII). But it is the reciprocity of the other that we need, not her sameness. It is through the dialogue of difference that we become who we are; not once, but over and over again.

# 5

# DIALOGISM AND GENDER

*Gendering the Chronotope:*
*Readings of Jeanette Winterson's*
Sexing the Cherry *and*
*Toni Morrison's* Beloved

## I

### *Sexing the Cherry*

*Jeanette Winterson*

Since the publication of her most recent novel, *Written on the Body* (1992), Jeanette Winterson has elicited much criticism from feminist readers over her representation of gender.[1] After *Oranges are not the only fruit* (1985), a 'classifiable' lesbian *Bildungsroman* with a cast of almost exclusively female characters (the key exceptions being Pastor Spratt and Jeanette's father), her novels have featured heroes of both sexes, heroes who move between the sexes, and heroes whose sexual preferences are similarly unfixed.[2] In *The Passion* (1987), for example, the indeterminacy of Villanelle's gendered identity is signalled both by her cross-dressing and by her history of love affairs with both men and women, while *Written on the Body* is the panegyric of a supposedly 'genderless narrator' whose androgynous costume (he/she always wears shorts) and lovers of both sexes have left the feminist literary establishment feeling cheated, confused and, occasionally outraged.[3] Lesbian readers, in particular, have experienced

1   J. Winterson, *Written on the Body* (London: Jonathan Cape, 1992).
2   J. Winterson, *Oranges are not the only fruit* (London: Pandora, 1985).
3   J. Winterson, *The Passion* (Harmondsworth: Penguin, 1987). Further page references will be given after quotations in the text. For criticism of Winterson's recent work see, for example, Laura Cumming's review in the *Guardian*, 3 September 1992.

this 'sliding' of gendered and sexual identity – this refusal to 'name' –
as a serious political betrayal. What texts like *The Passion* and *Written on
the Body* would seem to say is that love is love is love: that gender, age,
class, ethnicity, nationality and sexual orientation are all accommodated
within the great universals; that desire is an emotion which transcends
all specificities, and which we all recognize and experience as 'the same
thing'.[4] In *Sexing the Cherry* (1989), as in *The Passion*, this universalism
is ensured by the inclusion of a broad spectrum of characters of
different gender and sexual preference.[5] The stories of the Twelve
Dancing Princesses in *Sexing the Cherry*, for example, place accounts
of heterosexual and homosexual desire side by side, hence 'normalizing'
the latter and giving the impression that one's sexual preference is
a matter of chance, not choice. Similarly, in *The Passion*, Villanelle's
love affair with another woman is made part of the same romantic
continuum as Henri's unrequited love for her, his hero-worship for
Napoleon, or Patrick's fantasies about the mermaids (p.24). Despite her
protestation that her desire for another woman was 'not the usual thing'
(p. 94), Villanelle's love affair cannot be said to be lesbian in any real
political sense.

It could also be argued that it is by removing her characters to the realms
of fantasy and history that Winterson has left behind the question of what
it is to be a woman and/or a lesbian in any more material sense. Although
*Oranges* is no more 'realist' than the other novels in textual terms, its
protagonists have to bear the historical and political consequences of
their generation, gender and sexual preferences. In *The Passion*, *Sexing
the Cherry*, and *Written on the Body*, these constraints are apparently
discarded as the characters free themselves from the shackles of 'the
single life':

> Thinking about time is like turning the globe round and round, recognizing that
> all journeys exist simultaneously, that to be in one place is not to deny the
> existence of another, even though that place cannot be felt or seen, our usual
> criteria for belief.
>   Thinking about time is to acknowledge two contradictory certainties: that our
> outward lives are governed by the seasons and the clock; that our inward
> lives are governed by something much less regular – an imaginative impulse
> cutting through the dictates of daily time, and leaving us free to ignore the
> boundaries of here and now and pass like lightning along the coil of pure
> time, that is, the circle of the universe and whatever it does or does not
> contain . . . (*Sexing the Cherry*, p. 100)

In Bakhtinian terms, what the narrator is describing in the above quotation
is that, owing to the subjective nature of time, it is possible for all
individuals *to move between chronotopes*. *Chronotope*, it will be remembered,
is Bakhtin's term for the time-space correlative as it is represented in literary
fiction, and in these readings of Winterson and Morrison I will primarily be

---

[4]   See my essay on Winterson and romantic love: '"Written on Tablets of Stone?": Roland
Barthes, Jeanette Winterson and the Discourse of Romantic Love', in *Volcanoes and Pearl
Divers: Essays in Lesbian Feminist Studies*, ed. S. Raitt (London: Onlywomen Press, forthcoming).
[5]   J. Winterson, *Sexing the Cherry* (London: Bloomsbury, 1989). Page references to this
volume will be given after quotations in the text.

concerned with the way in which their texts both conform to, and deviate from, Bakhtin's formulation, especially *vis-à-vis* questions of gender (see Chapters 1 and 2). Bakhtin's own representation of chronotope is, it will be remembered, blindly gender neutral, while these two texts (contrary, perhaps, to the wishes of their authors) reveal that all time and space is gendered; that every chronotope, like every house, city or nation is characterized by the sex of its ruling class. Even if, as in the writings of these authors, the gendered identity of subject and chronotope are transformed and/or reversed by the encounter, the rules are never suspended. Wherever we travel in this world, its past, or in 'the cities of the mind', gender travels with us: we cannot escape its influence.

It is not until the end of his essay on the chronotope (in the 'concluding remarks' written in 1973) (see Chapter 1, p. 71) that Bakhtin acknowledges the possibility of there being literary texts in which *multiple chronotopes* exist side by side. The bulk of his analysis, as we saw in Chapter 2, is concerned with identifying the chronotopes associated with the different historical *genres* of literature (e.g., the chronotope of chivalric romance, the chronotope of the idyll, etc.), and only latterly does it appear to have occurred to him that, in more recent literature especially, it is common for chronotopes to coexist and for there to be 'complex interactions among them' (*Dialogic Imagination* (1934–41), p. 252). This crucial reassessment also helps us, as readers, to situate the chronotope within Bakhtin's more general dialogic theory, since the notion of a text being comprised of multiple independent (yet also *interdependent*) chronotopes bears a strong structural similarity to his earlier conceptualization of the polyphonic novel. Indeed, much of the vocabulary used to describe the latter reappears in the description of the *polychronotopic text* (my term) quoted in Chapter 1 (see pp. 71–72). Within a single text, individual chronotopes, like individual voices, are distinguished by their autonomy and independence: they are both, as it were, 'independent centres of consciousness'. Without ever merging, however, the chronotopes enter into a complex dialogue with one another which is, at all times, a dialogue inscribed by power: 'Chronotopes are mutually inclusive, they co-exist, they may be interwoven with, replace or oppose one another, contradict one another or find themselves in ever more complex interrelationships' (ibid.). In the same way that the different voices represented within a text may be constantly seeking to dominate one another, so do the chronotopes, though the mark of the fully polychronotopic text, like its polyphonic equivalent, is that the contending forces are held in equilibrium. One chronotope may seek to dominate – it may, indeed, hold temporary sway – but it is not allowed to swallow up the others with which it is juxtaposed.

Both *Sexing the Cherry* and *Beloved* (1988) are, as we shall see, self-consciously polychronotopic texts. Indeed, the coexistence of chronotopes not only structures the form of these novels but is also central to their philosophical theses, which are predicated on the assumption that their characters have access to chronotopes beyond their immediate present. In this last respect it is important to realize, however, that Winterson and

Morrison have moved into territory significantly beyond Bakhtin's own, since Bakhtin believed that although it was the privilege of author and reader to move between the different chronotopes, the characters themselves could not: 'The relationships themselves that exist *among* chronotopes cannot enter into any of the relationships contained *within* chronotopes' (p. 252). For Bakhtin, the relationship between chronotopes as between the charactes who inhabited them was a dialogue based on the existence of clear spatiotemporal boundaries: I may look across the fence into this other life, but I may not actually enter it. This restriction is not surprising when we remind ourselves of the Marxist origins of the Bakhtin school. Throughout their work there is simply too much emphasis on the 'concrete' specificity of the historical moment for such transport/transcendence to be easily conceivable.

Before I proceed to an analysis of some of the different chronotopes represented in *Sexing the Cherry*, and the movement of certain characters across them, it is first necessary to mention some of the problems I had in identifying and classifying the different chronotopes in the first place.

One of the obfuscations of Bakhtin's analysis of the literary chronotope is that the term is used to cover both the dominant *generic* spatiotemporal form of a text (i.e., 'adventure' or 'idyll') *and* the subset of more 'local' chronotopes that might occur within it (e.g., the chronotope of the road, the chronotope of encounter, the chronotope of the threshold). These secondary chronotopes may, themselves, be associated with a particular genre (e.g., the chronotope of the road is often found within the adventure chronotope), but they may also appear in less congruous contexts and form an oppositional and contrapuntal relationship with the main chronotope. In a text like George Eliot's *Middlemarch*, for example, which may be generically associated with Bakhtin's 'provinical life chronotope', the secondary 'chronotope of encounter' (the highly charged meetings of Dorothea with Ladislaw, Lydgate and Rosamund) creates a significant spatiotemporal counterweight.[6] Time which moves so slowly and routinely in the chronotope of Middlemarch's bourgeois society ('day in, day out the same round of activities is repeated', *Dialogic Imagination*, p. 248) is suddenly speeded up, and space and place take on a new super-real quality in the lives of the protagonists. How we finally classify these secondary chronotopes is, however, a problem since they can represent such a wide range of things in the 'work' of the novel. The 'encounter chronotope' may have a purely narratological function, for example (being instrumental in acceleration/deceleration of time, or in the moving forward of the plot), or it may have special symbolic or ideological purpose within the 'theme' of the novel). The 'castle chronotope' which Bakhtin identifies in connection with Gothic fiction is the classic instance of a tempospatial site which may perform *all* of these duties, with the special set of chronotopic circumstances which prevail within the walls of the castle being symbolically associated with the psychology of its occupants, and this, in turn, relating to various ideological conventions (e.g., romantic love, female sexual desire). A chronotope may therefore

6   G. Eliot, *Middlemarch* (1871–72) (Oxford: Clarendon Press, 1986).

be labelled differently *according to the textual function under discussion at any one time*.

These problems of classification presented themselves to me as soon as I attempted to carve up the spatiotemporal continuum of *Sexing the Cherry*. While I identified four, clear chronotopic horizons (the two 'historical presents', 1630–66 and 1990; the 'enchanted cities' inhabited by Fortunata and her sisters and 'visited' by Jordan; and the sea voyages undertaken by Jordan and Nicholas Jordan), there was the complication that the protagonists from each of these time zones also belonged to the ideological chronotope of 'romantic love': a continuum which would appear to hang suspended above the historical life of the world and in which time becomes, in Bahktin's words, 'empty time' (see Chapter 1, p. 68).

> I gave chase in a ship, but others make the journey without moving at all. Whenever someone's eyes glaze over, you have lost them. They are as far from you as if their body were carried at the speed of light beyond the compass of the world.
> Time has no meaning, space and place have no meaning, on this journey. All times can be inhabited, all places visited (*Sexing the Cherry*, p. 87).

This then led me to question whether it were better to identify the 'enchanted cities' as chronotopes in their own right or as expressions of the 'romantic love' chronotope. There was also the possibility of subsuming the city chronotopes within Bakhtin's own category of the 'adventure chronotope', since all of Jordan's narrative can be accommodated within this particular generic classification. This, in turn, led to the further possibility of presenting the subjective temporal experience of the individual narrators as a chronotopic continuity (i.e., we would talk about 'Jordan's chronotope', 'Dogwoman's chronotope', etc.). This last formulation would, however, inevitably undermine the key theoretical premises of the text: that individual characters can inhabit/move between different chronotopes, and that chronotopes are *intersubjective* and not commensurate with individual consciousnesses. Another difficulty was the way in which one chronotope slides into another. Since Jordan's sea journeys are the means by which he arrives at his 'enchanted cities', should they not be regarded as part of the same continuum rather than a discrete chronotope? Alternatively, perhaps they should be classified as simply part of the time-space belonging to the historical present of seventeenth-century England. My decision to retain a separate category for the voyage was, in the end, determined by the issue of gender since, as I shall explain below, it seems to constitute an archetypally 'masculine' chronotope.

The first of the chronotopes I want to consider is that relating to the historical present 1630–66. This is the chronotope shared by Jordan and Dogwoman, although represented mostly through the narration of the latter, alerting us immediately to the problem (noted above) of whether a chronotope can ever be the property of more than one character. This is to say, is Dogwoman's spatiotemporal experience of seventeenth-century

England ever the same as Jordan's? Are they really 'living in the same world'?

Dogwoman's presentation of the chronotope 1630–66 is, in terms of Bakhtin's own schema, typically Rabelaisian (see Chapter 1). Rabelais, it will be remembered, was credited by Bakhtin with inventing a chronotope of the 'here and now' and of purging the spatial and temporal world of a 'transcendent world view' (*Dialogic Imagination*, p. 168). Dogwoman shares Rabelais's dislike of metaphysics. In response to Tradescant's pronouncement that 'every mapped-out journey contains another journey hidden in its lines' (p. 18) she responds: 'I pooh-poohed this, for the earth is surely a manageable place made of blood and stone and entirely flat' (p. 19). Her first-person narration and personal preference for 'living in the present' conspire to give her representation of the Civil War the quality that Gerard Manley Hopkins referred to as 'haeccetas' ('thisness').[7] In contrast to Jordan's journeys through the two-dimensional fairy landscapes of the 'enchanted cities', suspended somewhere between past, present and future, Dogwoman inhabits a world of causality and corporeality: of action, reaction and change; of birth, growth, ageing and death. This anti-transcendentalism is also associated, as in Rabelais's own writings, with a focus on the body and its functions: both Dogwoman's *own* body which eats, excretes, nurtures and murders, and those of her fellows.

Indeed, all the great historical moments of the chronotope Dogwoman inhabits are represented in terms of bodies. While the constitutional and ecclesiastical reforms threatened by the revolution remain remote possibilities ('At first the civil war hardly touched us' p. 65), Dogwoman offers a vivid account of the king's beheading, the flesh-corrupting pestilence of the plague and the flesh-consuming purge of the Fire of London. Her observation on the plague, that 'city is thick with the dead. There are bodies in every house and in a street south of here the only bodies are dead ones' (p. 159) sums up her relationships to a chronotope 'thick' with the materiality of the bodily present.

This metaphoric association between history and the body inevitably brings us to the question of how that body is gendered. Refracted through the parodic femaleness of Dogwoman's own body (pp. 19–21) there is a strong inclination to read the chronotope 1630–66 as a continuum in which the feminine ('procreative') principle holds sway ('a time measured by creative acts, by growth and not destruction', *Dialogic Imagination*, p. 200); in which the 'degradation' of the body is concomitant with its regeneration and renewal (this is, after all, the spirit in which Dogwoman begins the fire). Such a reading is, indeed, very much in line with Bakhtin's own gendering of the Middle Ages through the symbol of the 'grotesque body' (see Chapter 1). There is the complication, however, that in *Sexing the Cherry* the (female) body does not effect its degradation in the spirit of carnivalesque revolution; instead of the overthrow of law and order, it is associated with the preservation of the constitutional status quo. Dogwoman, it will be remembered, is on the side of the Royalists,

---

[7] Hopkins's use of the term derives from the medieval philosopher Duns Scotus and refers to the way in which things/people/places express their 'essential being'.

and her body (together with her nurturance/destruction of other bodies) is inscribed not with the sign of revolution but of counter-revolution. Contrary to Bakhtin's own meditations on the body in the context of the medieval carnival or the writings of Rabelais, Dogwoman's body may be seen to represent a deeply conservative force. The procreative and destructive powers of her body are unleashed not as a catalyst for change but for the preservation of the kingdom. While she avenges herself on *some* men, moreover (see the vivid account of her murder of Preacher Scroggs and Neighbour Firebrace pp. 96–98), it is with the purpose of protecting others (Jordan, Tradescant, the King). And just as Dogwoman herself is no protofeminist, so we should not make the mistake of reading the chronotope that her body so massively fills as unproblematically 'feminine'. While it is true that her narration of the years 1630–66 causes them to be 'coloured' female, it is a reactionary femaleness which draws clear parallels between women's traditional procreative role and the preservation of existing patriarchal institutions (monarchy, church and State). Despite Dogwoman's own 'phallic' power, it is a chronotope in which relations between the sexes, as between rich and poor, king and commoner, will remain unchanged: which is why Jordan has to journey elsewhere.

From his early infancy, Dogwoman knows that she will not be able to keep Jordan in 'her world':

> And when Tradescant left Jordan and I went home, he skipping ahead and carrying his ship and I a few steps behind. I watched his thin body and black hair and wondered how long it would be before he made his ships too big to carry, and then one of them would carry him and leave me behind forever (p. 19).

The chronotope of seventeenth-century England is not Jordan's 'natural' home, and very little of his 'textual' time is spent there, although the retrospective story of his life is supposedly narrated from its shores (the time-space between his return to England in 1666 and his final departure). Why Jordan is unhappy to remain in the chronotope into which he was born is, I would suggest, profoundly implicated not only in his search for an 'alternative identity' ('the missing part of himself' pp. 86–87) but also for an alternatively defined gender. Like many of Winterson's characters, he is uncomfortable with the binaristic sex-stereotyping of masculine/feminine and his quest for Fortunata is clearly a quest not only for love but also for his own feminine 'supplement'. Seventeenth-century England, as we have seen in the discussion of Dogwoman's narration, is a chronotope in which masculine and feminine roles are held firmly in place and in which Jordan's heroic ideals are constrained by traditional patriarchal expectations. His journeys across the world, like those of his alter-ego, Nicholas Jordan, in the twentieth century, may thus be seen as a quest for a new order of heroism: a heroism defined in terms other than conventional masculinity. What this 'new heroism' might look like is embodied in the ecological campaigning of the young woman chemist at the end of the novel, of whom Nicholas Jordan observes: 'Surely this woman was a hero? Heroes give up what's comfortable in order to protect what they believe in or to live dangerously for the common good. She was doing that, so why was she being persecuted?' (p. 159).

But before both Jordan and his twentieth-century namesake arrive at a time-space in which they may redefine their gendered identities, they have first to make the 'voyage out'; and the voyage is a chronotope that is gendered masculine. For the two men, setting sail from England means entering a time-space continuum in which the female principle (their mothers, lovers and the feminine parts of their selves) is temporarily suspended. Being aboard ship is to be in the exclusive company of men, and to take one's bearings (emotional and otherwise) from that fact. This gendered situatedness is conveyed, incidentally, in the opening of one of Jordan's sentences: 'At sea, and away from home in a creaking boat, with Tradescant sleeping beside me . . .' (p. 43). Being 'at sea' has removed Jordan from the influence of his mother who was his first heroic role model ('I want to be like my rip-roaring mother who cares nothing for how she looks, only for what she does' p. 114), and placed him in the sole company of his surrogate father, Tradescant. It is a belated oedipalization, with the complication that Jordan resists the pressures of the super-ego that would fashion him as a hero in Tradescant's own mould. While Tradescant sleeps, Jordan dreams about the city of the Dancing Princesses. Even at their furthest geographical remove, women are still on Jordan's mind, and for this reason he will never achieve the 'uncontaminated' masculinity of his mentor. Lacking both the necessary family background (Tradecant's own father was a 'hero' p. 114) and the capitalistic single-mindedness, Jordan's attraction to the 'alternative route' becomes a metaphor for his unfixed gender/identity – despite conventional yearnings in that direction:

> I want to be brave and admired and have a beautiful wife and a fine house. I want to be a hero and wave goodbye to my wife and children at the docks, and be sorry to see them go but more excited about what is to come. I want to be like other men, one of the boys, a back-slapper and a man who knows a joke or two . . .
>
> For Tradescant, being a hero comes naturally. His father was a hero before him. The journeys he makes can be traced on any map and he knows what he's looking for. He wants to bring back rarities and he does . . . (pp. 113–15).

In the chronotopic present of the twentieth century, Nicholas Jordan embarks upon his first sea voyage bearing the same burden of gendered stereotyping as his precursor. He, too, is torn between the glamour of traditional masculine heroism (symbolized by the lives of the soldiers and sailors in *The Boy's Book of Heroes*), and a burgeoning consciousness of its limitations, epitmomized by the sexually stereotyped behaviour of his father ('My father watches war films . . . My father watches submarine films . . . My father watches ocean-going films' p. 133). For Nicholas, as for Jordan, the sea voyage will represent his first full initiation into the world of orthodox masculinity ('There was a lot about camraderie and mates. It's not homosexual, of course' p. 134) but, once again, the purpose of the journey is to find his missing feminine complement. Indeed, for Nicholas Jordan, this end is achieved before he ever sets sail: his 'missing part' is waiting for him on the banks of the Thames:

She had a rowing boat tied to a tree, and we took it out and floated on the eery water, the orange of the campfire burning in the distance. I wanted to thank her for trying to save us, for trying to save me, because it felt that personal, though I don't know why (p. 164).

If the voyage, then, is a masculine chronotope, a spatiotemporal rite of passage that the two heroes of the text have to pass through before they can renegotiate their gendered identities, what is it they discover in the alternative chronotope of their destination that enables them to effect that change? How are time and space gendered in Jordan's enchanted cities? Is it simply the (empty) time and space of romantic love, or are they 'alternative worlds' in their own right?

In all the enchanted places to which Jordan travels (the 'city of words' where the Dancing Princesses used to live; the 'city of movable buildings' where they now do; and the 'city of love'), the conventional laws of time and space are suspended: past, present and future no longer form a diachronic sequence, space cannot be charted ('Fold up the maps and put away the globe' p. 88), and gravity can no longer be guaranteed to hold one to the ground:[8] 'The family who lived in the house were dedicated to a strange custom. Not one of them would allow their feet to touch the floor. Open the doors off the hall and you will see, not floors, but bottomless pits' (pp. 14–15). Such a chronotope exists in sharp contrast to that represented by the sea voyage, in which the passage of time is marked by the projected *end* of the journey (i.e., the quest causes time to stretch itself into a teleological sequence), and space is charted in terms of conquest and possession.

At first sight, the chronotopes of the enchanted cities may appear to conform to the adventure chronotope described by Bakhtin in his essay. In the adventure chronotope, it will be remembered, time effectively 'stands still' between the start and end of the action represented by the 'meeting' of two lovers and their marriage (see Chapter 1). The 'empty time' in between is effectively immune from the effects of the passing years, and the characters consequently do not age. This fairy-tale convention applies, in particular, to Fortunata whom, we are told, should have been an 'old woman' by the time Jordan discovers her. Instead, she is magically unchanged: 'When I came to I was in a much smaller room, propped in a chair on one side of the fire. Opposite me, attentive and smiling, was the woman I had first seen at dinner, what seemed like light years ago and might have been days' (p. 104).

The apparent arbitrariness of time is, in this context, linked explicitly to the wayward clock of the human heart. Romance, as I indicated earlier, claims its own chronotope: operates according to a time-keeping which (in Winterson's texts at least), is willfully ahistorical and universal. Throughout the centuries, lovers have fallen in and out of the black hole of love, and in their falling entered a world cut off from the rules of time and space governing their everyday, 'historical' existences. This image of all the lovers of past and future centuries sharing, albeit temporarily, the same time/space vacuum (the chronotope of 'being in love') is

[8] For a definition of 'diachronic' and 'synchronic' see note 38 to Chapter 3.

captured by Jordan's subsequent reflection on Fortunata's extratemporal manifestation.[9] Represented in the text as 'Memory I' it reads:

> The scene I have just described to you may be in the future or in the past. Either I have found Fortunata or I will find her. I cannot be sure. Either I am remembering her, or I am still imagining her. But she is somewhere in the grid of time, a co-ordinate, as I am (p. 104).

Yet it would be wrong, I feel, simply to conflate the chronotopes of the cities Jordan visits with the chronotope of romance. While his journeys to and through the former are all *prompted* by his quest for Fortunata (the quest for love/the quest for 'the missing part of himself'), the cities themselves represent an alternative vision of time and space which is *in excess of* the romance chronotope. While romance is most typically about the temporary suspension of time, the hiatus between 'meeting' and 'marriage', what Jordan learns in his journeys through the enchanted cities is the *synchronicity of time*: the simultaneity of past, present and future:

> The future lies ahead like a glittering city, but like the cities of the desert disappears when aproached. In certain lights it is easy to see the towers and the domes, even the people going to and fro. We speak of it with longing and with love. *The future*. But the city is a fake. The future and the present and the past exist only in our minds, and from a distance the borders of each shrink and fade like the borders of hostile cities seen from the floating city in the sky. The river runs from one country to another without stopping (p. 167).

In this passage, which echoes many others earlier in the text, Jordan allows the synchronic chronotope to consume the diachronic chronotope of the quest/journey, thus renouncing a belief in all salvational destinies ('love', 'the future'). The world he is about to sail into is not to be charted by his destination (a point/place in the future), but by 'empty space and points of light' (ibid.). Through his encounter with Fortunata, he has learnt that 'the answer' is not to exist outside of time, but to be *coexistent* with all its temporal mutations. Wherever he journeys in the world, it will not be to the future and it will not be in straight lines.

This returns us, again, to the question of gender. Assuming, as I have done, that the chronotope of the voyage is gendered male, it is clear that any time-space in which Jordan is to renegotiate his gendered identity must offer reconnection with the feminine principle. In the chronotope of heterosexual romance, this is provided, quite simply, through contact with the sexual 'other', and in *Sexing the Cherry* the hero becomes classically 'whole' through his union with Fortunata. But the chronotopes of the enchanted cities offer Jordan more ways of exploring his gender than simply through romantic and sexual encounter. In *Sexing the Cherry*, as in Woolf's *Orlando*, the characters' ability to move between chronotopes also offers them the opportunity to move between genders.[10] In his quest

---

9  A good visual illustration of this romantic 'time-space' is Dante Gabriel Rossetti's painting *The Blessed Damozel* (1879), the background to which is filled with clone-like representations of kissing lovers! See C. Wood, *The Pre-Raphaelites* (London: Weidenfeld & Nicolson, 1981), p. 103.

10  V. Woolf, *Orlando: A Biography* (1928) (London: Hogarth Press, 1990).

for Fortunata, Jordan is forced to adopt female disguise (p. 26) and through the experience learns much about what it means to be 'gendered female': 'I have met a number of people who, anxious to be free of the burdens of their gender, have dressed themselves men as women and women as men' (p. 28). Freeing himself of the 'burden' of his own (conspicuous) masculinity does not, however, free him from its shame, and it is during his time 'as a woman' that Jordan becomes aware of the 'crimes' of his sex, and what women think of men as a consequence:

> After my experience in the pen of prostitutes I decided to continue as a woman for a time and took a job on a fish stall.
>
> I noticed that women have a private language. A language not dependent on the constructions of men but structured by signs and expressions, and that uses ordinary words as sign words meaning something other.
>
> In my petticoats I was a traveller in a foreign country. I did not speak the language. I was regarded with suspicion.
>
> I watched the women flirting with men, pleasing men, doing business with men, and then I watched them collapsing into laughter, sharing the joke, while the men, all unknowing, felt themselves master of the situation and went off to brag in bar-rooms and to preach from pulpits the folly of the weaker sex.
>
> This conspiracy of women shocked me. I like women; I am shy of them but I regard them highly. I never guessed how much they hate us or how deeply they pity us (p. 29).

It is significant that, in this passage, men and women are presented as occupying linguistic and cultural spheres so different from one another that they may be accounted separate chronotopes ('I was a traveller in a foreign country' ibid.). Although the 'city of words', in which Jordan first sets eyes on Fortunata, is not an exclusively 'female' time/space, his experience of it is 'gendered' feminine. The above passage also draws attention to the important correlation between chronotope and language. One of the key demarcations between chronotopes may be their deployment of different languages. Persons in different times, different places, speak in different tongues, and although Jordan can disguise his sex he cannot disguise his feminine 'illiteracy'. Women, he discovers, have a 'private language' which, in Bakhtinian terms, is predicated upon each speaker knowing, or being able to anticipate, 'the future answer word' (see Chapter 1, p. 64) of her interlocutor so exactly that the 'common language' becomes a coded one.[11]

Jordan's experience of a female time/space continues in his journey to the 'city of movable buildings' where the Twelve Dancing Princesses now live. Each of the stories he is told involves the escape of the princess from the patriarchally defined chronotopes of their respective marriages to their present home together. It is significant that only one of the princesses has been allowed to retain the lover of her choice, and she is female: a mermaid. These stories, like his experience of working on the fish stall, reveal to Jordan the abuse of masculine privilege that is concomitant with patriarchy, and we can assume that this 'education' is one of the reasons why Jordan chooses not to stay in seventeenth-century London at the end

---

[11] See my discussion of the 'common languages of women' in 'Dialogic Theory and Women's Writing', pp. 187–90.

of the novel. For Jordan is a 'new man' whose travels through the various chronotopes have taught him not only how to reconceive time and space but also how to regender it. But is it really that simple?

In conclusion, I want to question the *ease* with which Winterson's characters are allowed to move between/through/across chronotopes, and the implications of this in terms of gender and other materially inscribed factors such as social class and ethnicity which, in our common experience, cannot easily be transcended.

*Sexing the Cherry* is a text which (in the tradition of mystical writers like William Blake) tells us that we should not be trapped in the time/space in which we 'chance' to be living. Through our 'inward lives' (p. 99) we have access to a different 'clock' and through our imaginations we can travel to different lands; adopt the skins, personae, sexes of different people. Indeed, the 'rules of daily time' (ibid.) as we are taught them are compounded of lies:

> LIES I: There is only the present and nothing to remember.
> LIES 2: Time is a straight line.
> LIES 3: The difference between the past and the future is that the one has happened while the other has not.
> LIES 4: We can only be at one place at a time.

The fact that these popular dictates *are* lies is demonstrated by the contrary experience of the text's four main protagonists, who effect an intersubjective 'dance' with one another across time and space. In the same way that Jordan's 'inward life' enables him to make journeys beyond his immediate present, so do we find Nicholas stumbling involuntarily into his namesake's world (see pp. 89 and 137), and the young woman chemist into the time, space and *body* of Dogwoman (see pp. 89–90 and p. 149).

What some readers, myself included, may find problematic about this reincarnating time travel is that it is conceived as a wholly positive, 'painless' experience. Neither Nicholas Jordan nor the young woman experience any fear in their transportation to another chronotope, and throughout the text the fact that we may simultaneously inhabit different times/different lives is seen as unequivocally liberatory: 'I [Young Woman] don't know if other worlds exist in space or time. Perhaps this is the only one and the rest is rich imaginings. Either way it doesn't matter. We have to protect both possibilities. They seem to be interdependent' (p. 145). The young woman's use of the phrase 'rich imaginings', here, captures the spirit in which all time travel is deemed to be undertaken, and implies that what the 'other world' will offer us is some form of desirable or educative experience. In Winterson's writing this is undoubtedly linked to the fact that the primary experience, for all characters, in all ages, is romantic love. The *purpose* of slipping through the 'black hole' (p. 137) of time is to (re)discover our 'missing part' (heart). It is not, as in Toni Morrison's novel, to come face to face with the bloody spectre of our ancestors' oppression; to find ourselves reliving a story that has been considered too horrific to 'pass on'.[12]

---

12   T. Morrison, *Beloved* (London: Picador, 1988), p. 275. Further references to this volume will be given after quotations in the text.

The ease with which the characters in *Sexing the Cherry* appear to pass from one world to the next also calls into question the apparent amaterialism of the text. In the same way that readers and critics have regretted the absence of a more 'concrete' social context for the characters in *Written on the Body* (issues of gender, social class and sexuality all have a crucial bearing in matters of health care), so may one dispute the way in which an orphan child (Jordan) is allowed to escape the 'burden' (p. 28) not only of his gender but also of his socioeconomic privations, through what appears to be sheer effort of mind. One could also argue, of course, that this sort of realist 'causality' is not the responsibility of the fantasy text (especially one whose primary intertextual referent is the fairy-story). This is a fair point, but it will still fail to satisfy all those who regard gender, sexuality and social class as nontranscendable categories.

In Winterson's defence, however, I would argue that the characters in *Sexing the Cherry* never *do* 'transcend' their genders even though they may challenge their definition. Jordan, it will be remembered, is made most aware of his interpellation as a male subject when he is dressed as a woman, and even in the midst of his re-education knows that he cannot easily discard the legacy of his socialization: 'I was much upset when I read this first page, but observing my own heart and the behaviour of those around me I conceded it to be true' (p. 30). While his exploration of other chronotopes helps him to renegotiate his gendered identity, to redefine it in the same way that he redefines time and space, he never ceases – even temporarily – to be a man. Dogwoman, similarly, is as firmly grounded in her gender as in her chronotope. The fact that her vast bodily size enables her to exert physical force over men does not improve her status as a female subject in seventeeth-century England. When she wishes to attend the King's trial she has to wheedle her way through the gates by pleading the *weakness* of her (female) body. Against the State, the largest women in the world – even the woman the size of an elephant (pp. 19–20) – has no *effective* power.

While allowing, however, that the characters in the novel are not as free from the constraints of their material existence as it might at first appear, there is still the sense that the *travel* between chronotopes is remarkably easy. Most of us would expect to experience *some* stress, anxiety and discomfort on a journey from London to Paris, together with a period of cultural readjustment when we arrive at our destination and when we return. How, then, can Jordan cross oceans and centuries so effortlessly?

The literary chronotope, according to Bakhtin's definition is the textual space in which 'time . . . thickens, takes on flesh, becomes artistically visible' (*Dialogic Imagination*, p. 84). The chronotopes in *Sexing the Cherry*, with the significant exception of Dogwoman's, are two-dimensionally *thin*; they are the chronotopes of fairy-story and the characters can pass in and out of them as insentiently as ghosts.

This is manifestly *not* the case in Morrison's novel, to which I now turn, in which the chronotopes are thick with the flesh and blood of slavery.

## II

### *Beloved*

#### *Toni Morrison*

---

In a conversation with Denver at the beginning of *Beloved*, Sethe makes clear just how 'thick' the chronotopes of the 'rememoried' past can be:

> 'Some things go. Pass on. Some things just stay. I used to think it was my rememory. You know. Some things you forget. Other things you never do. But it's not. Places, places are still there. If a house burns down, it's gone, but the place – the picture of it – stays, and not just in my rememory, but out there in the world. What I remember is a picture floating around out there outside my head. I mean, even if I don't think it, even if I die, the picture of what I did, or knew, or saw is still out there. Right in the place where it happened.'
>
> 'Can other people see it?' asked Denver.
>
> 'Oh, yes, yes, yes. Someday you will be walking down that road and you hear something or see something going on. So clear. And you think it's you thinking it up. A thought picture. But no. It's when you bump into a rememory that belongs to somebody else. Where I was before I came here, that place is real. It's never going away. Even if the whole farm – every tree and blade of grass of it dies. The picture is still there and what's more, if you go there – you who never was there – if you go there and stand in the place where it was, it will happen again; it will be there for you, waiting for you. So, Denver, you can't never go there. Never. Because even though it's all over – over and done with – it's going to be there always waiting for you. That's how come I had to get all my children out. No matter what.'
>
> Denver picked at her finger nails. 'If it's still there, waiting, that must mean that nothing ever dies'.
>
> Sethe looked right in Denver's face. 'Nothing ever does,' she said (pp. 35–36).

The palpability of time past, the way it can, at any moment, reach out and grab you – seize hold of you with the tenacity of a baby's clutch – is presented by Sethe not as a wonder to be embraced but as a hazard to be avoided. It is, in particular, the inextricability of time and space that make the chronotopes of the past so potentially dangerous; the way in which time *converts* to space ('Places, places are still there'), the way it 'takes on flesh' and 'thickens'. For the chronotopes that Sethe moves in and out of are not, as for Jordan, the 'rich imaginings' of romance and fairy-tale, but the dark, blood-stained annals of her own personal past and of her race. The multiple chronotopes that comprise this past are, moreover, for the most part 'unspeakable' (p. 58), and much of her recent life has been spent in protecting Denver from their influence ('As for Denver, the job Sethe had of keeping her from the past that was still waiting for her was all that mattered' p. 42). For the protagonists of *Beloved*, the fact that past, present and future may be seen to coexist is not a liberatory delight but a threat.

The desire to shut a permanent door on the chronotopes of the past is something shared by both Sethe and Paul D. In the very first pages of the novel, Sethe recalls a conversation with Baby Suggs in which she explains the latter's inability to remember her eight children with the statement: 'that's all you let yourself remember' (p. 5). Paul D., similarly, has managed to contain the dark memories of his own past in the 'tobacco tin' lodged in his chest: 'By the time he got to 124 nothing in this world would pry it open' (p. 113). But 'prying open' the lid to the past and re-entering its chronotopes is what Morrison's novel is all about, and especially fascinating, in Bakhtinian terms, is the fact that it is a past reconstituted *through dialogue*. Things that have been 'unspeakable' for eighteen years are exposed and rematerialized through Sethe's dialogic encounters with Paul D. and Beloved. Both, in turn, though in significantly different (and differently gendered) ways, perform the role of the Bakhtinian interlocutor: they become the 'listening other' whose presence is necessary for 'the word' to be spoken, for the past to be narrativized and hence *realized*.

At first Sethe and Paul D. are frightened by the prospect of what unknown horrors their conversation might bring to light. The encounter serves not only to reactivate the 'rememory' of their personal pasts but also to lead them into previously hidden corners of their shared chronotope; to make visible events (such as Halle with 'butter all over his face' p. 8) which one or the other had not actually witnessed. After their first, involuntary 'rememory' the interlocutors are guilty and apologetic with one another ('I didn't plan on telling you that'/'I didn't plan on hearing it' (p. 71)), and Sethe is desperate to return to a present in which she can continue the 'serious work of beating back the past' (p. 73).

All the work Sethe puts into 'keeping the lid on' the Pandora's Box of the past is, however, undone by the appearance of Beloved who, from the start, compels her to speak the 'unspeakable':

> 'Tell me,' said Beloved, smiling a wide happy smile. 'Tell me your diamonds'.
>
> It became a way to feed her. Just as Denver discovered and relied on the delightful effect sweet things had on Beloved, Sethe learned the profound satisfaction Beloved got from storytelling. It amazed Sethe (as much as it pleased Beloved) because every mention of her past life hurt. Everything in it was painful or lost. She and Baby Suggs had agreed without saying so that it was unspeakable; to Denver's enquiries Sethe gave short replies or rambling, incomplete reveries. Even with Paul D., who had shared some of it and to whom she could talk with at least a measure of calm, the hurt was always there – like a tender place in the corner of the mouth that the bit left.
>
> But as she began telling about the earrings, she found herself wanting to, liking it. Perhaps it was Beloved's distance from the events itself; or her thirst for hearing it – in any case, it was an unexpected pleasure (p. 58).

At this stage, Sethe has no idea at all why Beloved's interlocutory presence should elicit this rememory, and attempts to explain it (ironically) by the latter's 'distance from the events' (ibid.). The story of the diamonds is, however, just one of several discrete chronotopes that are revisited in the course of the novel, with Beloved's clamour for stories of the past ('Denver noticed how greedy she was to hear Sethe talk' p. 63) opening up the floodgates of dialogue.[13] For although, as I shall discuss below, the dialogue between Sethe and Beloved is the most psychologically complex of all the interlocutory relationships represented in the text, her arrival is the catalyst for change between *all* the protagonists. Number 124, for years a silent house, becomes suddenly noisy, as Sethe and Beloved, Denver and Beloved, and Sethe and Paul D. reconstruct the 'unspeakable' past in the dialogic space between them.

The dialogue between Beloved and Denver (pp. 78–85) is a testament to Sethe's pronouncement (quoted at the beginning of this reading) that the chronotopes of the past can be 'accessed' even by those who have no original part in them. The chronotope, for Morrison as for Winterson, is not the property of the individual – her memory or her imagination – but is profoundly *intersubjective*, which would also seem to account for why it is most effectively reconstructed through dialogic exchange. Through an act of intense interlocutory concentration, Beloved and Denver access and enter the chronotope of Denver's birth. Although the reader has already had glimpses into this particular time/space through Denver's own rememory of it, it is significant that the climax of this story is realized only through the dialogic interconnection of the two girls, with Denver the speaker and Beloved the 'active' listener:

> Denver was seeing it now and feeling it – through Beloved. Feeling how it must have felt to her mother. Seeing how it must have looked. And the more fine points she made, the more detail she provided, the more Beloved liked it. So she anticipated the questions by giving blood to the scraps her mother and grandmother had told her – and a heartbeat. The monologue became, in fact, a duet as they lay down together, Denver nursing Beloved's interest like a lover whose pleasure was to overfeed the loved . . . Denver spoke, Beloved listened, and the two did the best they could to create what really happened, how it really was, something only Sethe knew because she alone had the mind for it and the time afterward to shape it: the quality of Amy's voice, her breath like burning wood (p. 78).

But between them, Denver and Beloved *do* succeed in raising the spirit of that past (reproduced verbatim in the text which follows, pp. 78–85) in all its multisentient palpability. Correspondent with Bakhtin's theory of the dynamics of spoken dialogue (and, indeed, of 'hidden dialogue' and 'hidden polemic'; see Chapter 1), it is the pressure exerted by the 'future answer word' of the interlocutor (in this case, Beloved's 'questions') that prompts and shapes the discourse of the speaker, forcing her (Denver) to supply the 'detail' that was lacking in the earlier 'rememories' of the story. Chronotope here is thus made a causal expression of dialogicality,

---

13   Although, as with *Sexing the Cherry*, the number of chronotopes to be found in *Beloved* will be dependent upon the different classificatory frameworks that may be imposed on the text, the following would seem to constitute discrete tempospatial horizons: (1) the narratological present (beginning with Paul D.'s arrival at 124 Bluestone Road); (2) early life at Sweet Home; (3) escape from Sweet Home (including Denver's birth); (4) the baby's death; (5) Sethe's trial and imprisonment; (6) Baby Suggs's life at 124 *before* the arrival of Sethe and the baby; (7) Paul D.'s imprisonment in Albert and his escape; (8) Denver's childhood; (9) Sethe, Denver and Beloved's life at 124 after Paul D.'s departure; and (10) Beloved's 'time before'.

giving rise to a significant configuration between two discrete strands of dialogic theory.[14]

The interlocutory power that *Beloved* exerts over Denver and Sethe in order to make them feed her stories is very different from that of Paul D., and the difference is partly a difference of gender. Where Beloved elicits the rememories of her 'mother' and 'sister' through the affected intimacy of the 'beloved' child, Paul D. claims his patriarchal right to 'the truth' (p. 163). The conversation between them, in which Sethe circles 'dizzingly' around the room and confesses, obliquely, to the murder of her child, is a 'court-room' dialogue in which Sethe is the guilty defendant and Paul D. the silent judge. The story of the horror gets told – but stammeringly, defensively. Explanation and self-justification subsume and veil the details of the act. These are not the words of a woman speaking to her lover but to the patriarchal authorities that would judge child murder, under any circumstances, a crime. Although she appeals to him as a friend ('You know what I mean?' p. 162) her voice is at all times thick with fear and shame. She has told her story, but she has not revisited its chronotope. The time-space which she re-enters in her confession to Paul D. is not the context of the baby's death but of her trial and imprisonment. These are not the dialogic conditions necessary to take her back to where she needs to be.

It is Beloved, alone, who can provide Sethe with the interlocutory support necessary for her to open the door on the this, the most repressed of all her rememories. The strained and objectified account of her escape from Sweet Home as it is told to Paul D. is transformed, in Beloved's hearing, into a minute-by-minute reconstruction. It is a narration that is not only subjective but also intersubjective; as with Denver's experience, cited above, it is Beloved's interlocutory presence that allows Sethe to re-enter the time-space buried for the past eighteen years – and this, precisely because Beloved *shares* the chronotope, knows what she is about to say:

> Thank God I don't have to rememory or say a thing because you know it. All. You know I would never a left you. Never. It was all I could think of to do (p. 191).

> This is the first time I'm telling it and I'm telling it to you because it might help explain something to you although I know you don't need me to do it. To tell it or even to think over it. You don't have to listen either, if you don't want to (p. 193).

Having 'clicked' (p. 175) that Beloved is the reincarnation of her murdered baby, Sethe has at least found the interlocutory presence she needs to

---

[14] It is significant that Bakhtin himself never drew any specific parallels between chronotopes and his model of the dialogic/polyphonic text despite the fact (as was noted in the reading of *Sexing the Cherry* above) they belong to the same conceptual grid. What we are witnessing in this chapter are two texts whose multivocality is commensurate with their polychronotopic status; and, in the case of *Beloved*, a text whose chronotopes are (re)activated/made visible through dialogic exchange.

rememory and 'exorcise' her action: the only person close enough to the event to understand her motive and *not* pass judgement.[15]

The fact that Beloved later does become the most tyrannical of adjudicators, converting Sethe's candid vindication into a cringing, self-flagellating plea for forgiveness, does not lessen the initial catharsis her presence affords the female occupants of Number 124. Although within the ideological denouement of the text, the 'incestuous' dialogic circuit Beloved forges between herself, Sethe and Denver has, at last, to be broken by the reinsertion insertion of the masculine principle (Paul D.), the woman-only auditorium she creates is a temporary necessity.[16] Sethe and Denver can only gain access to the buried chronotopes of the past through her presence, and the total exclusion of men.

After Paul D.'s departure, 124 becomes a 'safe' all-female environment in which the three women give voice to the most 'unspeakable' thoughts and resurrect, through their dark dialogues, the most distressing of past chronotopes. For Sethe, 'locking the door' (p. 199) means that she is able to wander even further into the dark spatiotemporal corridors of her time at Sweet Home, and of her escape, and of the few precious days at 124 before the baby's death; a catalogue of sweet and painful rememories, given 'flesh' through Beloved's own introjected memory of them. It is significant that in the monologue beginning 'Beloved, she my daughter' (p. 200), Sethe slides back and forth, unselfconsciously, between the second- and third-person pronoun. Sometimes she is speaking about Beloved; sometimes she is speaking to her. But were it not for Beloved's presence we know that she would not be speaking at all.

For Denver, isolation at 124 with her mother and Beloved enables her finally to confront the extent of her fear of the one and her love of the other, and then her love of both, and her fear of both. The chronotopes she 're-enters' are the repressed rememories of her childhood: her time at Lady Jones's school, her days with Grandma Suggs, and – even more importantly – the time she never spent with the 'angel daddy' she never knew. None of Denver's monologue is actually addressed to Beloved, but she is its facilitation all the same: 'She played with me and always came to be with me when I needed her. She's mine, Beloved, she's mine' (p. 209).

For Beloved herself, meanwhile, Sethe is the vital interlocutory presence that enables her to put into sequence the dark, fragmented chronotopes of her own past: her own history and her own prehistory. The space/place that Beloved returns to is the ambiguous 'black hole' that Denver has identified earlier in the text as 'the time before' (p. 75). Whether this place

15  The fact that Sethe is dependent on this intimacy ('knowing') to speak out would seem to make her earlier observation that she could tell Beloved things because of 'her distance from the events themselves' (p. 58) deeply ironic.

16  This is a text whose sexual politics may be read as an appeal for the integration of male and female through a 're-education' of relations between the sexes. Certainly the separatist all-female family at 124 is not designed to survive permanently, but exists as a temporary chronotopic necessity. In *Sisters and Strangers* (Oxford: Basil Blackwell, 1992), Patricia Dunker observes that, throughout her work, Morrison has subscribed to 'the balance of women and men in "nurturing relationships"' (p. 254).

is womb, tomb, limbo – or, putting aside metaphysical explanations – the 'brothel' of Paul D.'s suggestion (p. 52) is never clear. Nor is a proper temporal distinction drawn between the nasty place inhabited by the men 'without skin' (pp. 210–11), and the dark and pleasant waters ('the space under the bridge') where she is 'reunited' with her mother and effectively reborn (see pp. 210–13). The sequence in which these rememories are given suggests that the early happy union with mother simply dissolves into the period of masculine possession ('storms rock us and mix the men into the women and the women into the men that is when I begin to be on the back of the man' p. 210). But equally indistinct is the moment when Beloved flows back into the body of the mother and herself.

If the boundaries between the chronotopes are themselves indistinct, however, the dialogic conditions which activate this remembering are not. It is by addressing Sethe in the present that Beloved is able to realize the nature of the relationship between their two 'faces' in the past. By speaking the first person plural ('we') she glimpses the 'chora' of the mother–child dyad that she and Sethe have formed.[17]

Through Beloved's presence at 124, and through the temporary exclusion of the masculine principle (Paul D./Lacan's 'law of the father') Sethe's family are able to explore – through dialogue with one another – the preoedipal space (Kristeva's 'semiotic') that had previously been denied them. They are able to experiment with relationships that 'free' people take for granted: what it is to be a mother, a child, a sister. But once this exploration has been achieved, once the repressed 'infant babble' (the noises Stamp Paid hears emitting from the house, p. 172) is given voice, the incestuous female bond has once again to be broken; and this is effected, predictably, through Paul D.'s return.[18]

What is significant about Paul D.'s return in dialogic terms is that his displacement of Beloved's 'ghost' is complete only when he has finally replaced her as Sethe's interlocutor. His 'manly presence' which, at the start of the novel, seems enough to 'whoosh away' (p. 37) all the ghosts, is clearly not enough. His permanent union with Sethe, dependent upon their joint commitment to 'rememorying' the past together, is also dependent upon dialogic trust. Sethe has to accept that Paul D. can be an intimate interlocutory presence in the same way (though never, of course,

[17] See note 23 to Chapter 4.

[18] Morrison's text is one in which the invitation to a psychoanalytic (specifically Lacanian) reading is explicit throughout, especially as Lorraine Liscio has pointed out, in its focus on the female characters' problems of 'crossing over' the 'threshold of language' and taking up their place in the Symbolic Order. Liscio also notes how this association between femaleness/speechlessness may be seen as problematic: 'Her use of this trope . . . risks reinstating essentialist beliefs about maternal discourse: association with the mother means to be denied the status of a speaking subject and therefore to be always objectified in others' narratives' (p. 35). See L. Liscio, '*Beloved*'s Narrative: Writing Mother's Milk', *Tulsa Studies in Women's Literature*, 11, 1, 1992, pp. 31–46. Similarly problematic, it seems to me, is the way in which a Lacanian reading will posit Paul D. as the masculine agent necessary to restore Sethe and Denver to a (nonpsychotic) subject position within the symbolic realm. The advantage of my own dialogic reading of the text is that it makes the relationship between male and female characters (and masculine and feminine principles) much less unidirectional. Even at the end of the novel, Sethe and Paul D. are actively negotiating their gendered identities via their interaction with one another.

in *quite* the same way) as Beloved was: she needs to and, indeed, does, trust her 'future answer word to him':

> She looks at him. The peachstone skin, the crease between his ready, waiting eyes and sees it – the thing in him, the blessedness, that has made him the kind of man that can walk into a house and make women cry. Because with him, in his presence, they could. Cry and tell him things they only told each other (p. 272).

In the latter part of this reading I want to move on from the dialogic conditions which facilitate the rememorying of the chronotopes in *Beloved* and focus, in some more detail, on how they are gendered.

In the last section we saw how 124, after Paul D.'s departure, becomes a woman-only space. This period of time, I would suggest (the time from his departure to when Denver breaks rank by seeking employment in the outside world), forms a discrete chronotope within the temporal management of the text, but is only one among several others which are also 'gendered female'. The eighteen years between the baby's death and Paul D.'s arrival, for example, are what first establish 124 as a 'separatist' zone, with the death marking a chronotopic watershed between the time when 124 was 'a cheerful, buzzing house' (p. 86) full of 'laughing children, dancing men, crying women' (i.e., a place of mixed gender) and when the men left and the neighbours no longer visited. The gendered identity of the house is so intense during this period (Denver observes that it is 'a person rather than a structure. A person [female?] that wept, sighed, trembled and fell into fits' p. 29) that the intrusion of Paul D. is registered by its bricks and mortar as an outrageous violation (see p. 18). Although Sethe and Denver interpret the quaking as the protest of the ghost rather than the house itself, it is clear from what follows that 124 has a gendered will of its own above and beyond any supernatural forces that might inhabit it. Thus when Paul D. exorcises the 'baby's venom' (p. 3) (or believes he does so), he fails to account to the chronotopic hold of eighteen years of woman-only occupation, and the house, in the end (and with the assistance of the rematerialized Beloved) expels him from its time-space.

Paul D.'s retreat from 124 may, indeed, be seen as a fascinating enactment of Bakhtin's 'chronotope of the threshold' (see Chapter 1). Although Bakhtin fails to describe how such chronotopes have been represented in literature in any detail, Paul D.'s movement from bedroom, to kitchen, to Baby Suggs's room, to storeroom, to coldhouse and, finally, to the shed may be read as a discrete chronotopic event within the textual time of the novel. Within a matter of days, Paul D. is sucked through an increasingly dark, increasingly cold, spatiotemporal corridor into a new chronotopic limbo. Because of the 'unfinished business' between Sethe and Beloved, 124 can no longer contain him.

Paul D.'s return to 124 demands that he pass through the same series of thresholds in the opposite direction: 'His coming is the reverse of his going. First the cold house, the store room, then the kitchen before he reaches the beds' (p. 263). Although Beloved has now left the house, Paul D. is still aware of it as a gendered space which he must enter with caution and respect. And it is only possible for him to stay, as I observed earlier, when Sethe decides to make him her partner in dialogue.

The various thresholds, then, that Paul D. must pass through before he arrives at the chronotopic core of 124 may be seen to represent the cultural and linguistic barriers separating women from men in the historical period covered by the novel. Men and women, in this nineteenth-century slave community, cannot easily pass into one another's worlds.[19] Indeed, the text makes it clear that in the same way that Paul D. will never fully understand the 'thickness' of the mother love that caused Sethe to murder her baby, nor will *she* ever properly understand his humiliation – his emasculation – during his last days at Sweet Home and his imprisonment in Albert. The ideological 'hope' of the text rests, however, in the possibility of negotiating a new time-space which the men and women freed from slavery will eventually come to share, while the 'thresholds' of 124 Bluestone Road may be seen as emblematic of the transitional period that must precede such integration.

Although the majority of the chronotopes which comprise the fragmented temporal continuum of the text are gendered female, Paul D.'s rememories allow us glimpses into others which are emphatically masculine. These include life at Sweet Home after Mr Garner's death and following the arrival of 'Schoolteacher'. In the early days, Sweet Home, like 124 before the baby's death, was a place in which the sexes were equally represented; a time in which they were, in Sethe's words, 'all together' (p. 14). After Garner's death, however, the question of who really has power – men or women, masters or slaves – becomes newly visible. What had been hidden beneath Garner's paternalistic benevolence is now out in the open ('without his life each of theirs fell to pieces' p. 221). Suddenly all the men, including Paul D., are made aware both of the extent of their physical power as men, and the curbs upon it. In retrospect, Paul D. begins to perceive how his masculinity has been defined within the walls of slavery (symbolized, of course, by the walls of Sweet Home itself). He sees how it differs from the masculinity of 'free men' like Garner and the schoolteacher; how it is, in effect, a pseudo-masculinity because it has no purchase outside the chronotopic economy of Sweet Home itself. In terms of the gendering of the Sweet Home chronotope, Schoolteacher's arrival may be likened to the 'sin' of Adam and Eve in the Garden of Eden. Before he came, the male and female slaves appear to have lived together *relatively* unconscious of either their gender or their slavery. After Garner's death, and with Schoolteacher's teachings, they become painfully aware of both things and have to run away – both from their slavery and from one another. Paul D. attempts to escape for the sake of his self-respect (his 'manhood'), Sethe for the sake of her children.

After his attempted escape from Sweet Home, however, Paul D.'s punishment is to be plunged into a chronotope even more barbarously masculine. In Albert, Georgia, Paul D. enters a time-space stripped

[19]  This 'separate spheres' existence of men and women in the community is illustrated by Paul D.'s reference to 'house fits': 'the glassy anger men sometimes feel when a woman's house begins to bind them, when they want to yell and break something or at least run off' (p. 115).

bare of all 'feminine' love and tenderness: 'Listening to the doves in Alfred, Georgia, and having neither the right nor the permission to enjoy it because in that place mist, doves, sunlight, copper dirt, moon – everything belonged to the men who had the guns' (p. 162). It is in this world, far removed from the 'thick', maternal love that causes Sethe to twist a knife into her own daughter, that Paul D. comes face to face with the forces inscribing and denying his masculinity (brute strength; the gun) and perceives, in retrospect, how its ideology has ostracized him from the world of women. Thus when Sethe confesses her crime of love to him, he is unable to make the leap back into the space/time where people 'love big': 'Meanwhile the forest was locking the distance between them, giving it shape and heft' (p. 165).

In comparison to *Sexing the Cherry*, then, movement between chronotopes in Morrison's novel is a fraught, dangerous and frequently painful affair which finds symbolic parallel in the 'escape narratives' of Seth and Paul D. There is the difference, too, that chronotopic travel in *Beloved* is unidirectional: from present to past. Although the structure of the text is, like *Sexing the Cherry*, suggestive of a world in which past, present and future time are, in some manner, coextensive, most of the characters are even more wary of the future than they are of the past, and would never trust that a leap into the unknown would bring them happiness. It is a contrast that can be explained most pointedly by suggesting that where *Beloved* rewrites nineteenth-century American history from the perspective of the slave, Winterson writes seventeenth-century British history from the perspective of the colonizer. Although the latter designates its male characters 'explorers' whose sole quest is the discovery of exotic fruits, we know that the most rapidly expanding trade at that time was not in pineapples or bananas but in slavery. Viewed in this way, one can begin to recognize that it is only when chronotopes are seen in the full (social, ethnic, national *and* gendered) materiality that the 'thickness' which Bakhtin assigns them can be properly understood.

Morrison's text contrasts with Winterson's, too, in that we rarely see characters exploring a time-space outside their own, past subjective experience. Their travel across time is nearly always a rememorying of a chronotope they once occupied, although, as we saw in the dialogue between Beloved and Denver, the 'palpability' of time past (the way in which, in Sethe's words, 'places are still there', pp. 35–36) indicates that, for Morrison as for Winterson, we do have access to 'worlds' outside our own.

In *Beloved*, gender, like the ethnic consciousness with which it is so profoundly implicated, is presented as a significant obstacle to chronotopic migration. While Denver and Beloved have access to the chronotope of Sethe's escape and Denver's birth, for example, Sethe and Paul D. are unable to travel the distance between their gender-specific sufferings. Paul D. never visits the emotional time/space in which Sethe murdered her baby, and she is similarly oblivious of his time in Albert.

The fact, however, that this is a text in which the female chronotope dominates means that the narrative is more focused on the 'exclusions' of women-only worlds than vice versa. Along with Paul D., we see Stamp

Paid unable to cross the threshold of 124. Burdened with the guilt of telling Paul D. 'the truth' about Sethe, he stands outside her door and is confronted with a nonsensical 'babble': the 'undecipherable language' of women (pp. 198–99). It is, moreover, the women and not the men of Bluestone who take it upon themselves to 'exorcize' Beloved's ghost (p. 257) since they, alone, have the 'thickness' of love necessary to enter the chronotope of a child's murder.

In the years which follow, in which it is disputed whether there really *was* a ghost at 124, it is significant that – apart from Paul D., Edward Bodwin and the 'little boy' (p. 267) – it is only the women of the town who claim to have seen 'it' (p. 265). And this is clearly because 'Beloved' came from a time/space that, deep in their 'unspoken' hearts (p. 199), all slave mothers have visited.

# Part Three

## CONCLUSION

# 6

# CONCLUSION

*Reader*: Don't you think it's rather clichéd to end a book on dialogics with a dialogue?
*Author*: Yes, of course.
*Reader*: So why do it?
*Author*: Because I thought it would be the best way to tackle the questions that have been raised in the course of the book head on. And because I see it as an opportunity for giving the reader a voice.
*Reader*: You mean me?
*Author*: Yes, I mean you.
*Reader*: So what kind of issues are we going to talk about here?
*Author*: The issues behind the headlines, I hope! The theoretical and political implications of particularly problematic areas of Bakhtinian theory, taking into account the questions raised by the readings in Part Two. And I'd like, if possible, to cover the three main themes running through the book: gender, genre and subjectivity.
*Reader*: What if you don't know how to answer the questions?
*Author*: What if you don't know how to ask them?! Go on. You start.
*Reader*: OK. Here's an easy one to begin with. Do you think Bakhtin was wrong to identify dialogism as a feature of the novel at the expense of other literary modes and genres?
*Author*: Yes. As I explained in Chapter 2, the subsequent appropriation of Bakhtinian theory by literary critics has paid little attention to this discrimination. Since the early 1980s, readers have employed Bakhtin's categories of polyphony, carnival, heteroglossia and the various species of doubly voiced discourse (i.e., stylization, parody, *skaz*, hidden polemic, etc. (see Chapter 1), to read all manner of texts: poetry, drama, film . . . there is no apparent restriction. And, of course, this was something that Bakhtin slowly came to recognize in his own writings as he moved from attributing the 'invention' of the polyphonic novel to a single author (Dostoevsky) through to the category of *novelized discourse* which, as we saw, could include certain types of poems.
*Reader*: How, then, would you define 'novelized discourse'?

*Author*: Any text which represents more than one voice, opinion or centre of consciousness; and one that, following Bakhtin's prescription for the polyphonic text in *Dostoevsky's Poetics* (1929), allows each of these voices a certain autonomy and independence from authorial or narratorial control.

*Reader*: So this would exclude a lyric poem like . . . um . . . Thomas Hardy's 'The Darkling Thrush' which is concerned solely with the thoughts and feelings of the poet-speaker?[1]

*Author*: (*Aside*: Where on earth did you dredge that example up from!) Well, not necessarily, because at the stylistic level of double-voiced discourse it may be possible to show that the speaker's words are in dialogue with a whole range of 'future answer words': be these the opinions of unidentified individuals outside the text (possibly, a 'superaddressee'; see Chapter 1), or, as is particularly apposite in the case of the Hardy poem, a whole range of contemporary *discourses* (e.g., early twentieth-century views on religion).[2]

*Reader*: OK. But if we acknowledge the 'inherent' dialogicality of all words and utterances in this way (see Chapter 2), can there *be* such a thing as a monologic text?

*Author*: Good question! As I indicated in Chapter 2, many critics now see the distinction between the dialogic and the monologic text as something of a red-herring, but rather than dispense with it altogether I suggest we think of dialogicality as a *relative value*. Texts can be more or less dialogic than one another according to a sliding scale, with the absolute (and, perhaps, hypothetical) values of monologism and dialogism at either end. According to this scheme, Hardy's poem would be inclined to the monologic end of the scale and James Joyce's *Ulysses* to the dialogic end, but we could also argue for elements of monology and dialogy in each.

*Reader*: Does what you have just said about texts also apply to the Bakhtin group's representation of subjectivity? Are some *subjects* more monologic/dialogic than others?

*Author*: A difficult issue! I presume you're alluding to my reading of Woolf's *The Waves* in Chapter 4?

*Reader*: Yes.

*Author*: Well, this is just one of many instances in which my own readings hypothesized a scenario not present in Bakhtin's own writings.

The 'dialogic subject', you'll remember, is a configuration that came into being largely through the work of Bakhtin's followers (see Chapter 2). What the original texts state (i.e., *Freudianism* (1927) and *Marxism and the Philosophy of Language* (1929)) is merely that the subject is (1) social and (2) constituted through its intersubjective relations with others. What recent theorists have done is imbue this simple construction with some of the other popular connotations of dialogism (i.e., 'reciprocity', 'simultaneity', 'process', 'democracy') and formulated a model of the subject predicated upon a somewhat idealized model of verbal utterance.

1   T. Hardy, 'The Darkling Thrush', *Thomas Hardy: The Complete Poems* (London: Macmillan, 1976), p. 150.
2   '"Future answer words": Mikhail Bakhtin', *The Dialogic Imagination* (Austin, TX: University of Texas Press, 1981), p. 280.

To come back to your original question, my own analysis of subjectivity in *The Waves* did, indeed, present some characters as being more dialogic than others and, rather like my formulation of monologic-dialogic texts (see above), I proposed a sliding scale with Rhoda at one end and Bernard at the other. What I would hesitate to do, however, is use this reading of subject representation *in a fictional text* to make pronouncements about subjectivity in general. Even as the characters in Woolf's novel have been seen as the artful/'artificial' separation out of a single subject into a six constituent parts, so would I be unwilling to suggest that any one of us could/should be 'fixed' in Rhoda's position. The 'extreme' subject positions Woolf represents in her novel do not conform to our common 'lived experience' where we may be more or less monologic/dialogic at different periods of our lives, and in our relations to different people/circumstances. I suppose I basically endorse Voloshinov's thesis in *Marxism and the Philosophy of Language* that *all* subjects are intrinsically social and dialogic. It's rather like the example of the lyric poem: there's always some 'other' that we're in dialogue with.

*Reader*: But they might not be the one we want/need, as in Rhoda's case?

*Author*: Ah, yes. A subtle point! That introduces another set of values entirely. We need to remember that not all dialogues are necessarily *productive* . . . and *vis-à-vis* the dialogic construction of the subject, this is certainly an area where more work could be done.

*Reader*: This presumably relates, too, to your strong feelings about the lack of attention to *power* in the way critics have utilized dialogics in their theorization of subjectivity?

*Author*: Yes. Well, the way power has been left out of the dialogic equation altogether really.

*Reader*: Can you say something about power and subjectivity first?

*Author*: Well, as I argue in Chapter 2, many readers and critics appear to have seized upon dialogics as a way out of the fraught, power-laden relationships between children and parents in the psychoanalytic models of subject development. While I acknowledge that one of the problems with the oedipal models (including, incidentally, that of Chodorow and the object-relations school) is that power is largely unidirectional (i.e., the child is always reacting to the authority of the parent(s)), to posit a model of intersubjective relations that is always amicable and democratic seems to me utopian.[3] As in spoken utterance, all dialogue presupposes a balance of power between the two parties, even if it is dynamic: shifting from subject to subject. And one of the reasons the dialogic model of subjectivity has been divested of power is clearly because it has been read as falsely universal. Despite the fact that in the work of Bakhtin and Voloshinov, subjects, like utterances, are always socially and historically situated, many of the critics cited in Chapter 2 have overlooked these constraints and conceived a subject predicated upon a universalized model of fair and equal dialogic exchange.

*Reader*: So, do you think you were successful in correcting this 'utopian' model of intersubjectivity in your own readings?

---

[3]   N. Chodorow and 'object-relations' psychoanalysis; see note 17 to Chapter 2.

*Author*: (*Aside*: What a mean question!) To an extent. In my reading of *The Waves* I pay particular attention to the way in which each character is constantly evaluating his or her social/sexual status in relation to others. Similarly, in my reading of Adrienne Rich's 'Twenty-One Love Poems', I show that, for all the emphasis traditionally placed on similarity/equality in the construction of the lesbian subject, difference and power are still instrumental: both in the dialogic exchange between women, and in their (composite) dialogue with the male/heterosexual world.

*Reader*: Your mention of Adrienne Rich reminds me of something else I remember thinking when reading that chapter.

*Author*: Oh?

*Reader*: Something about whether *difference* was a necessary condition of dialogue. Or, to put it another way, is it possible for dialogue to exist between intimates?

*Author*: Hmm. This is a fascinating point, and one around which there is some ambiguity in Bakhtin's own writings. While, when writing about the subject, he famously declared: 'What would I gain were I to fuse with another?' (see Chapter 2), his later writings (e.g., *Rabelais* (1965) and the 'Speech Genres' essay (1986); see Further Reading) are especially interested in forms of intimate dialogue in which there is 'a maximum internal proximity of the speaker and addressee' (Chapter 1).[4]

*Reader*: But isn't this to confuse theories of the subject and theories of the utterance in Bakhtin's work?

*Author*: Yes (*hesitantly*) . . . but, as we have seen, the former *is* predicated upon the latter and the same theoretical issue would seem to apply *vis-à-vis* the function of difference.

*Reader*: (*Sensing authorial evasion*) So *does* dialogue depend upon difference?

*Author*: Well, going back to what I've just said about Adrienne Rich's poem I think this could be more false logic inasmuch as there is always *some* degree of difference between subjects whether we are thinking about them as speakers–addressees in a verbal exchange or as existential subjects in relation to one another. Once again, I would want to replace the either/or equation with the sliding scale or cline. Some dialogic exchanges clearly presuppose more difference than others (e.g., Anne Herrmann's analysis of an antagonistic relationship between narrator and reader in Virginia Woolf's 'Three Guineas'), but even the most intimate will involve some degree of difference.[5]

*Reader*: So you're admitting that difference *is* a condition of dialogue?

*Author*: Yes. It's both a condition *and* a consequence.

*Reader*: While still on the *dynamics* of the dialogic contract, I'd like to

---

4  'What would I gain were I to fuse with another?', Mikhail Bakhtin, 'Author and Hero in Aesthetic Activity' (1919–24) in *Estetika Slovesnogo Tvorchestva*, ed. S. G. Bocharov (Moscow: Iskusstuo, 1979), p. 78. Reproduced and translated by G. S. Morson and C. Emerson in *Mikhail Bakhtin: Creation of a Prosaics* (Stanford, CA: Stanford University Press, 1990), pp. 53–4. See also *Speech Genres and Other Late Essays*, ed. C. Emerson and M. Holquist, trans. V. McGee (Austin, TX: University of Texas Press, 1986), p. 96–7.

5  See A. Herrmann, *The Dialogic and Difference: 'An/Other Woman' in Virginia Woolf and Christa Wolf* (New York: Columbia University Press, 1989). For a full discussion of readers as allies/adversaries, see Chapter 2.

pick up on your suggestion that dialogues can be between more than two persons.

*Author*: You mean what I conclude in my reading of *Wuthering Heights* after considering Nelly's 'third-person presence' in the novel?

*Reader*: Yes.

*Author*: Well, what her role alerted me to was the *frequent* presence of third parties in both everyday and textual dialogue, and how this configuration gives rise to a special set of (power-inscribed) interlocutory circumstances not allowed for in Bakhtin's theories. How often, for example, do we manipulate our utterances to one person via the mediating presence of another? (Just as Cathy provokes Heathcliff's anger and jealousy by addressing her complaints to Nelly, for example.)[6] How often do we quote/invoke another's words to support or privilege our own? At a more existential (and certainly more speculative!) level, I might also use this tripartite interlocutory model to suggest that our personal relations are rarely between two people only: there is nearly always someone else's ghost or shadow fracturing our address . . .

*Reader*: Back to the theme of sexual triangles, I see! [cf. Introduction, pp. 1–5]. What exactly are you saying about dialogic theory here?

*Author*: That the dialogic contract (spoken/textual) is frequently between more than two persons, and that several aspects of dialogic theory need to be rethought in the light of this possibility.

*Reader*: I think it's probably time for us to turn our attention to questions of gender. This book is clearly intent on writing gender into Bakhtin's theory, but – having done it – do you really think it's worth the effort?

*Author*: Yes, I do, though I perceive there to be different ways of justifying the undertaking.

First of all, as a teacher of literary theory who gives lectures and seminars on Bakhtin, I think it's vitally important that we reveal where an awareness of gender is lacking in such work.

*How* we 'write it in' is, as you rightly imply, another matter. As Clive Thomson suggests (see Chapter 2), it's not possible simply to 'add' gender to the key dialogic concepts like polyphony, carnival and chronotope. Despite the fact that Bakhtinian theory is centrally concerned with the 'social situatedness' of all utterance, this does not allow for the peculiar dynamics of power/politics implicit in the gendered positioning of interlocutors. Once we start gendering the multiple voices present in a polyphonic text, for example, we quickly perceive Bakhtin's notions of 'equality' and 'free interaction' to be spurious: even if male or female voices are given equal *representation* in a text, complex social/political forces are likely to impact upon their 'total' authority.

*Reader*: You don't mention this in your readings of *Wuthering Heights* and 'Child Harold' in Chapter 3, both of which you present as 'prototypically polyphonic texts'.

*Author*: You're right! I could have said a good deal more about gender in

---

6  See *Wuthering Heights* (1847) (Harmondsworth: Penguin, 1985): "'Oh, you see, Nelly! He would not relent a moment to keep me out of the grave! *That* is how I am loved! Well, never mind! That is not *my* Heathcliff. I shall love mine yet and take him with me – he's in my soul'" (p. 196).

both these readings, but with respect to Clare, at least, I have redressed the balance in an essay which is a feminist reappraisal of this 'generic' reading.[7]

The feminist issue being raised *vis-à-vis* polyphony in both these texts is, how 'equal' is 'equal'? And how do other related terms and concepts in the Bakhtinian vocabularly bear up once we've gendered them? The notion of 'reciprocity', for example (upon which the dialogic contract turns), means something different if we are talking about an exchange between a male/female speaker/addressee, or an exchange between two females. While a power dynamic will be operating in both sets of relationships, this will be attended by a complex (and perhaps contradictory) working out of sexual politics in the male–female exchange.

*Reader*: So what does this mean for a feminist 'appropriation' of Bakhtin: that it's a foolish undertaking?

*Author*: No. Simply that many of the key terms (polyphony, carnival, chronotope) will have to be completely reconceptualized if they are to be useful.

*Reader*: There have already been several attempts to rewrite carnival from a feminist perspective, haven't there?

*Author*: Yes. And not surprisingly since Bakhtin's own reading of Rabelais's carnivalesque text is, at first sight, hideously patriarchal and misogynistic! (See Chapter 1.) Whether you lay the blame for this on Rabelais or Bakhtin (see Stam's argument, Chapter 1, pp. 56–57) hardly matters; carnival is a 'boy's game', and the temporary overthrow of hierarchy it is supposed to represent not only ignores the issue of women's oppression but also through the image of the 'grotesque body' is instrumental on its promulgation (Chapter 1). What this means for feminist criticism is that, to be useful, carnival needs not so much to be revised as to be rewritten. As Clair Wills suggests (Chapter 2), for carnival to be an effective category of feminist analysis the 'forces of oppression' need to be identified (i.e., gendered) and effectively engaged with. This rewrites the script of Bakhtin's marketplace festivities to such an extent, however, that critics must question whether or not it is useful preserving the term.

*Reader*: Do you think you proved something similar in your 'gendering of the chronotope' in Chapter 5, or is this a concept that bears up to feminist appropriation rather better?

*Author*: It's certainly less difficult to 'recruit' than carnival, since in Bakhtin's original essay (in *The Dialogic Imagination*, 1981) it is expressly 'gender neutral' whereas the carnivalesque idiom, as we've seen, is incontrovertibly patriarchal. No, on the whole I thought my attempts to illustrate the gendering of time-space in two 'polychronotopic' texts (Chapter 5), worked well, though this is not to say that the tempospatial horizons of *all* works of fiction would yield to a masculine/feminine carve-up so easily!

---

7  See my chapter, 'John Clare's "Child Harold": The Road Not Taken', *Feminist Criticism: Theory and Practice*, ed. S. Sellers (Hemel Hempstead: Harvester Wheatsheaf, 1991), pp. 143–56.

*Reader*: Don't you think the 'carve-up' you made of both these texts was problematic anyway? In the reading of *Sexing the Cherry* you're quite candid about the difficulty you had establishing a taxonomy for the different chronotopes represented by the book.

*Author*: This is true. As I suggest, the classification will depend upon the criteria of your investigation in the first place. Because my own objective was the analysis of gender, I looked for chronotopic horizons that would maximize the differences within the text.

*Reader*: And this is quite different from Bakhtin's own classification of chronotopes which is largely generic (Chapter 1)?

*Author*: Yes, it is. It was only in his 1973 coda to the chronotope essay that Bakhtin explored the possibility of 'subgeneric' chronotopes (e.g., the chronotope of 'meeting', the chronotope of the 'threshold', etc.), and I think some interesting work could be done exploring the (gendered) tension between the generic chronotope (e.g., the inherent masculinity of the 'adventure chronotope') and its subgroups (e.g., the existence of an expressly 'feminine' time-space within this).

*Reader*: Your reading of *Beloved* suggests that you want us to take Bakhtin's description of the 'materiality' of chronotopes very seriously?

*Author*: Yes. I found the phrase 'Time . . . thickens, takes on flesh' immensely suggestive, especially when exploring the differences between Winterson and Morrison. There was, of course, a big political point here: that Morrison's focus on the 'unspeakable' horrors of black slavery meant that 'past' and 'future' were not spaces/places the characters explored for fun but out of grim necessity. These were quite different journeys 'across time' from those undertaken by Jordan (a seventeenth-century colonialist!) in *his* questioning of gender identity.

*Reader*: And it's 'time' for us to move on again, I think!

*Author*: Indeed.

*Reader*: Throughout this book you've been hinting at the surprising lack of attention that has been paid to the text-reader relationship in dialogic theory. Would you like to take this (final!) opportunity to expand?

*Author*: Yes, this has emerged as a peculiar blind spot – not only in Bakhtin's own writings but also in those of his followers. As I explained at the beginning of Chapter 2, I was fully expecting to include a whole subsection on the interface between dialogic and reader-response theory, but found only a handful of writers that had tackled this.[8]

*Reader*: Tell me first how you account for this silence in the work of the Bakhtin group itself?

*Author*: Well, the first thing to say is that it's not a *complete* silence or invisibility. Bakhtin's theories of authorship in *Dostoevsky's Poetics* and of 'speech-tact' in *The Formal Method* (1927) (see Chapter 1) identify the 'text-reader' as the dialogic construct under consideration, but it is true to say that the group's own analysis is far more concerned with speakers and addressees *within the text*. The problem seems to be essentially one of

---

8   See D. Shepherd, 'Bakhtin and the Reader', in *Bakhtin and Cultural Theory*, ed. K. Hirschkop and D. Shepherd (Manchester: Manchester University Press, 1989). See also the work of Rowena Murray and Dale Bauer cited in Chapter 2 and notes 7 and 36 to that chapter.

a failure to discriminate between the two types of dialogic relationship, and there is a particular disregard for the power of the reader in the construction of a text's meaning.

*Reader*: Can you give an example of this?

*Author*: Yes, the example of Bakhtin himself (which I alluded to in Chapter 1)! For all that he modified his view of Dostoevsky as the 'inventor' of the polyphonic text, Bakhtin never seems to have grasped that the real invention – the theory that enabled the stylistic feature to be seen for the first time – was his own. This is despite the fact that in the essay on 'Discourse in the Novel' in *The Dialogic Imagination* (1981) he accepts the need for a 'sensitive reader' to perceive the heteroglossic complexity of the literary text! (Chapter 1.)

*Reader*: So where does this place Bakhtin in the debates over where we 'locate' a text's 'meaning', that's to say, in the author, the text or the reader?

*Author*: Firmly on the side of the text, it would seem: and it reminds us that, at one level, the focus of the Bakhtin group is very strictly formalist. At the same time, I think we have to accept that there is a significant discrepancy between what Bakhtin and his group *consciously thought* (or didn't think!) about the text-reader relationship, and what their actual writings betray. If we infer an analogy between the model of the speaker-addressee within the text, and that of the text-reader, then we *must* concede more power to the reader. If we look at the limited data provided by the Bakhtin group itself, then the text clearly wins out.

*Reader*: You say that you've also been surprised by how few critics have explored the connection between dialogics and reader-response theories?

*Author*: Yes. I've found only one published essay which tackles the connection head on, and that's David Shepherd's 'Bakhtin and the Reader' which explores, in particular, the similarities and differences between Bakhtin's work and Stanley Fish's theory of the 'interpretive community'.[9]

I've also been interested in the text-reader relationship in my own work on women writers, of course (Chapter 2), arguing that the gendered specificity of address in certain texts might be used to define them as 'women's writing' (i.e., writing *for* women).

*Reader*: Does this imply that you see the relationship between text and reader as equivalent to that between speakers and addressees in everyday conversation?

*Author*: Well, it's the same dynamic, and Voloshinov's metaphor of 'word as bridge' (see quote at beginning of Introduction) still holds true: to whatever *extent* (and this varies considerably from theorist to theorist) the reader (like the verbal addressee) is necessary to the production of a text's meaning.

One significant difference, however, lies in the fact that whereas in dialogues between identifiable speaker-addressees (either in everyday conversations or as represented in texts) the interlocutor is usually singular, a textual audience is always *plural* and any analysis must at

9  S. Fish, 'interpretive communities'; see note 37 to Chapter 2.

least allow for the possibility of multiple subject positionings. This is to say (as I suggested in the Introduction), the text-speaker might be privileging different reader-addressees at different times.

*Reader*: Does this, perhaps, relate to what you were saying earlier about dialogues not necessarily being between two persons only?

*Author*: I suppose it does! The classic models of reader reception allow for at least three readers ('real', 'ideal' and 'implied'), and what my own work has suggested is that even within an apparently homogeneous readership (e.g., 'feminist'), there is potentially a wide range of reader positions contending for the text's 'meaning'.[10] This is another occasion on which the model of dialogue as a site of battle rather than conciliation seems appropriate. As I argue in '"I the Reader"', texts can sometimes arouse great jealousies among their different readerships. Certainly, there is no simple two-way traffic between a text and a (single) reader.

*Reader*: Several of your answers have, like this one, suggested that – for all it's evident attraction – you believe the basic building brick of dialogic thought – the notion of the word/utterance as 'a two-sided act' – needs to be rethought.[11]

*Author*: Yes. You could well be right. Realizing that dialogues were not necessarily between two persons only was a great breakthrough for me. I think I would like to preserve the notion of 'meaning' depending on reciprocity, while acknowledging that the interlocutors on which the 'bridge' depends (Voloshinov) may be multiple, changing and (to reintroduce the notion of power), *in competition with one another*.

*Reader*: And you're suggesting that we should look for this 'fractured address' in dialogues *within the text* (and presumably in spoken conversation) as well as in the text-reader relationship?

*Author*: Yes. Definitely.

*Reader*: And if you had to offer a single word which would sum up what's been lacking in the dialogic theory to date it would be . . .

*Author*: Power. All dialogues (however public/intimate; however many persons or positions are involved) are inscribed by power.

*Reader*: You set that question up!

*Author*: Of course!

*Reader*: Proving your authority?

*Author*: No. Proving yours!

*Reader*: On what grounds?

*Author*: (*With irony*) Well, I *needed you* to ask it.

*Reader*: (*Irritated*) This is getting trivial. And it's hardly an appropriate way to end a book aspiring to scholarly status.

*Author*: Agreed. But one final question.

*Reader*: What now?

---

10 'Real'/'ideal'/'implied' reader; see W. Booth, *The Rhetoric of Fiction* (Chicago, IL: University of Chicago Press, 1961). For further details see note 42 to Chapter 1. See also my chapter '"I the Reader": Text, Context and the Balance of Power' in *Feminist Subjects, Multi-Media*, ed. P. Florence and D. Reynolds (Manchester: Manchester University Press, forthcoming)

11 'The word is a two-sided act': V. N. Voloshinov, *Marxism and the Philosophy of Language*, trans. L. Matejka and I. R. Titunik (New York: Seminar Press, 1973), pp. 85–86.

*Author*: Who are you?
*Reader*: (*With sarcasm*) Very amusing! You're the one who's been telling everyone 'there's no such thing as an abstract addressee'![12]

---

12   'Abstract addressee', Voloshinov, *Marxism*, p. 85.

# FURTHER READING

## Works by the Bakhtin Group

Listed alphabetically by author and chronologically according to the date of first publication (given in brackets). See Chapter 1 for a discussion of the disputed authorship of some of these texts.

BAKHTIN, M. (1924) 1990: *Art and Answerability: Early Philosophical Works by M. M. Bakhtin*, ed. M. Holquist and V. Liapunov. Austin, TX: University of Texas Press.

BAKHTIN, M. (1929, 2nd ed. 1963) 1984: *Problems of Dostoevsky's Poetics*, ed. and trans. C. Emerson. Minneapolis, MN: University of Minnesota Press.

BAKHTIN, M, (1934–41) 1981: *The Dialogic Imagination: Four Essays by M. M. Bakhtin*, ed. M. Holquist, trans. C. Emerson and M. Holquist. Austin, TX: University of Texas Press.

BAKHTIN, M. *et al.* (1952–3) 1986: *Speech Genres and Other Late Essays*, ed. C. Emerson and M. Holquist, trans. V McGee. Austin, TX: University of Texas Press.

BAKHTIN, M. (1965) 1984: *Rabelais and His World*, trans. H. Iswolsky. Bloomington, MN: Indiana University Press.

MEDVEDEV, P. N. (1928) 1978: *The Formal Method in Literary Scholarship: A Critical Introduction to Sociological Poetics*, trans. A. G. Wehrle. Baltimore, MD, and London: Johns Hopkins University Press.

VOLOSHINOV, V. N. (1927) 1976: *Freudianism: A Critical Sketch*, trans. I. R. Titunik and ed. in collaboration with N. H. Bruss. Bloomington, MN, and Indianapolis, IN: Indiana University Press.

VOLOSHINOV, V. N. *et al.* (1924–8): *Bakhtin School Papers.* ed., A. Shukman, Russian Poetics in Translation No. 10. Oxford: RTP Publications.

VOLOSHINOV, V. N. (1929) 1986: *Marxism and the Philosophy of Language*, trans. L. Matejka and I. R. Titunik. Cambridge, MA: Harvard University Press.

## Books on Bakhtin and Dialogic Theory

BAUER, D. (1989): *Feminist Dialogics: A Theory of Failed Community*. Albany, NY: State University of New York Press.

BAUER, D. and S. J. MCKINSTRY, eds. (1991): *Feminism, Bakhtin and the Dialogic*: Albany, NY: State University of New York Press.

BIALOSTOSKY, D. (1992): *Wordsworth, Dialogics and the Practice of Criticism*. Cambridge and New York: Cambridge University Press.

CLARK, K. and M. HOLQUIST (1984): *Mikhail Bakhtin*. Cambridge, MA: Harvard University Press.

DANOW, D. K. (1991): *The Thought of Mikhail Bakhtin*. London: Macmillan.

HERRMANN, A. (1989): *The Dialogic and Difference: 'An/Other Woman' in Virginia Woolf and Christa Wolf*. New York: Columbia University Press.

HIRSCHKOP, K. and D. SHEPHERD (1989): *Bakhtin and Cultural Theory*. Manchester and New York: Manchester University Press.

HOLQUIST, M. (1990): *Dialogism: Bakhtin and His World*. London and New York: Routledge.

LODGE, D. (1990): *After Bakhtin: Essays on Fiction and Criticism*. London and New York: Routledge.

MORSON, G. S., ed (1986): *Bakhtin, Essays and Dialogues on His Work*. Chicago: University of Chicago Press.

MORSON, G. S. and C. EMERSON, eds. (1989) *Rethinking Bakhtin: Extensions and Challenges*. Evanston, IL: Northwestern University Press.

MORSON, G. S. and C. EMERSON (1990): *Mikhail Bakhtin: Creation of a Prosaics*. Stanford, CA: Stanford University Press.

STAM, R. (1989): *Subversive Pleasures: Bakhtin, Cultural Criticism and Film*. Baltimore, MD, and London: Johns Hopkins University Press.

TODOROV, T. (1984): *Mikhail Bakhtin: The Dialogical Principle*. trans. W. Godzich. Minneapolis, MN: University of Minnesota Press.

## Chapters and Articles on Bakhtin and Dialogic Theory

This selection does not include chapters included in the edited collections listed above. Details of individual items are given in the footnotes.

BIALOSTOSKY, D. (1986): 'Dialogics as an art of discourse in literary criticism', *Publications of the Modern Languages Association*,' **101**, 5, pp. 788–97.

BOOTH, W. (1982): 'Freedom and Interpretation: Bakhtin and the Challenge of Feminist Criticism', *Critical Inquiry* (special double issue on Bakhtin), **9**, 1, pp. 45–76.

DE MAN, P. 'Dialogue and Dialogism', *Poetics Today*, **4**, 1, pp. 99–107.

DÍAZ-DIOCARETZ, M. (1989): 'Bakhtin, Discourse, and Feminist Theories', *Critical Studies* (special double issue on Bakhtin), **1**, 2, pp. 121–39.

HENDERSON, M. G. (1989): 'Speaking in Tongues: Dialogics, Dialectics, and the Black Woman Writer's Literary Tradition', in *Changing Our Own Words: Essays and Criticism, Theory and Criticism by Black Women*, ed. C.

A. Wall. New Brunswick, NJ, and London: Rutgers University Press.

HIRSCHKOP, K. (1992): 'Is Dialogism for Real?', *Social Text*, **30**, pp. 102–13.

KERSHNER, B. (1986): 'The Artist as Text: Dialogism and Incremental Repetition in Joyce's *Portrait*, *Journal of English Literary History*, **53**, pp. 881–94.

KRISTEVA, J. (1980): 'Word, Dialogue and Novel', in *Desire in Language: A Semiotic Approach to Literature and Art*. trans. L. S. Roudiez. New York: Columbia University Press.

O'CONNOR, M. 'Chronotopes for Women Under Capital: An Investigation into the Relation of Women to Objects', *Critical Studies*, **2**, 1–2, pp. 137–51.

PEARCE, L. (1992): 'Dialogic Theory and Women's Writing' in *Working Out: New Directions for Women's Studies*, ed. H. Hinds, A. Phoenix and J. Stacey. Brighton: Falmer Press, pp. 184–93.

PEARCE, L. (1994 forthcoming): '"I the Reader": Text, Context and the Balance of Power' in *Feminine Subjects: Multi-Media: New Approaches to Criticism and Creativity*, ed. P. Florence and D. Reynolds. Manchester: Manchester University Press.

RUTLAND, B. (1990): 'Mikhail Bakhtin and Categories of the Discourse of Postmodernism', *Critical Studies* (special double issue on Bakhtin), **2**, 1–2, pp. 123–36.

SELL, R. D. (1986): 'Dickens and the New Historicism: The Polyvocal Audience and Discourse and *Dombey and Son*', in *The Nineteenth-Century British Novel*, ed. J. Hawthorn. London: Edward Arnold, 1986.

THOMSON, C. (1989): 'Mikhail Bakhtin and Contemporary Anglo-American Feminist Theory', *Critical Studies*, **1**, 2, pp. 141–61.

THOMSON, C. (1990): 'Mikhail Bakhtin and Shifting Paradigms', *Critical Studies* (special double issue on Bakhtin), **2**, 1–2, pp. 1–12.

# INDEX